J. Johnson   12-10-88.

Que.
Cunningsburgh.

The Care of House Plants

Each entry in this book contains full details of how to care for one particular plant. The practical text describes its history, care requirements and needs; the illustrations show how and when to carry out operations such as repotting, propagating, pruning and training. There's no need to worry whether a general instruction applies to your plant: the pictures show the right one every time.

The Care of House Plants

by David Longman

illustrated step by step

Peter Lowe

Hibiscus rosa-sinensis

Platycerium alcicorne

Contents

Line illustrations by Sandra Pond and Will Giles.

Copyright © 1979 by Eurobook Limited

ISBN 0 85654 6216

Photographs by Jeremy Finlay, A-Z Botanical Collection
Plants by courtesy of Longmans Ltd

Printed in Italy by Sagdos SpA
4.87-19-12-7500

Azalea indica

Ficus radicans variegata and *Pilea cadierii*

Cyclamen persicum

Introduction

The principles of growing plants indoors

On the shelves in a bookshop or library under gardening there are always a number of books on house plants. So why another one? A brief explanation of what this book sets out to achieve will give you the answer. Its main aim is to provide clear and detailed information that applies directly to each particular plant. Each one is dealt with as an individual. We show you what it looks like, give its history and explain how to choose a good specimen in the shop or garden centre. We tell you how big and how quickly it grows, if and when it flowers, how much light, heat, water, humidity and food it needs. We explain when to repot and prune it, how to propagate it, how long it will live, what plants it grows best among and how easy it is to grow. Simple step-by-step drawings illustrate important aspects of its day-to-day care and maintenance and there is a colour section for each plant showing exactly what can go wrong. Of course we give advice on how to put it right! All instructions are given in everyday language and are always as precise and detailed as possible.

The majority of the plants mentioned are easily obtainable either from florists or from the growing number of specialist plant shops. Those that are more difficult to obtain we feel are worth mentioning for they are plants that any collector would like to own and as you achieve success with more demanding plants you will certainly be on the look out for new and interesting varieties.

Plants in the home

Indoor plants are everywhere these days, not only in the big formal displays of hotels, banks and offices, but odd little plants nurtured tenderly on filing cabinets in offices, on window-sills in kitchens, on bathroom shelves and in doctors' waiting rooms. They add something to our quality of life, and for this we must be grateful.

Why are they so popular? There are probably many reasons. Urban people live in a world of hustle and bustle, of plastics, disposable containers and instant entertainment on television. Plants represent stability: they go on living and growing in their own time, and there is not very much we can do to hurry them along, except to provide them with their basic needs. They are a kind of living furniture, a decoration that helps to make a room more comfortable, more friendly and less formally rigid. There is a sense of achievement when new leaves appear, or a plant flowers for the first time. They are very precious possessions to many people—often with pleasant associations, of a friend, a place, or of a cutting given and successfully rooted.

Growing plants indoors or in pots close to the house is by no means a new pastime. For the first evidence of indoor plants we must go back some five thousand years to the Chinese who grew plants in ornamental pots in their palaces. There is evidence

Canes are for supporting tall plants, the paintbrush for cleaning velvety leaves. A small trowel and fork are useful but old kitchen spoons and forks are good substitutes.

cane

paintbrush

fork

cover pot

trowel

seed tray

plant ties

raffia

mist sprayer

plant ring

secateurs

sharp knife

razor blade

scissors

brocken crockery for drainage

Large or climbing plants need support. The stems can be fixed to canes or trellises by ties, rings or raffia, but must never be strangled by tight knots.

Pruning tools. Knives, scissors and secateurs must always be kept sharp as a ragged cut will damage the plant. Use a razor blade for delicate cuttings, secateurs or a knife for woody stems. Scissors are useful for removing dead flowers and damaged leaves.

in the form of bas relief images dated to 1400 BC that the Egyptians collected plants. The hanging gardens of Babylon were made up of plants grown in pots on terraces and there is evidence that plants were grown indoors throughout the Roman and Greek civilizations, and indeed into the Dark and Middle Ages. Monasteries did much to further the practice, although it must be admitted that most of their indoor cultivation was of rare herbs and plants used in medicines rather than for decoration.

The nineteenth century was the real hey-day of plant collectors and breeders. By then the art of building heated greenhouses and conservatories was

Different plants need different types of compost to grow well.

sharp sand

compost

Moss sticks support large plants and allow aerial roots to absorb extra moisture.

The watering can's long spout reaches through the foliage to the soil and also makes it easier to water hanging baskets and plants on high shelves.

watering can

insecticide

plant food

rooting powder

plant pots

leaf shine

saucers

Some plants are susceptible to pests or diseases and need treating with commercial sprays. Nearly all benefit from plant food in the growing season. Rooting powder contains hormones which stimulate root growth in cuttings. Keep all sprays in a secure place.

Leaves should be kept clean so that the plant can absorb light. Leaf shine helps to repel dust but check that it is suitable for your particular plant before you use it. It can be harmful to some leaves.

sponge

charcoal

moss stick

Containers. Seeds and cuttings start in seed trays before being planted into the smallest pot. They will need larger containers as they grow. Cover pots provide decoration and humidity. Saucers protect the furniture and can be used for watering from below.

Use pieces of broken brick or china for drainage in the bottom of pots and troughs. Pieces of charcoal stop water from becoming stagnant and smelling. Use them in hanging baskets, bowls with no drainage holes and when rooting cuttings in water.

well developed. The aristocratic and the wealthy vied with each other to have the most exotic and rare plants which they would bring into their houses to impress their guests. Nurserymen such as Veitch and Sanders sent collectors all over the world to find new species and varieties. The invention of the Wardian travelling case in 1834 by Nathaniel Ward helped very much with the importation of rare material. It was essentially a small portable greenhouse which provided a protected atmosphere for specimens during their shipment.

With the changing world of the twentieth century large private collections were dispersed or destroyed. Fashions and customs changed, and between the wars in the 1920s and '30s many plants disappeared. However, not all were lost for the art of indoor plant growing was already popular in all sections of society. In the late 1950s and early '60s the pendulum of fashion swung again, and plants began to appear in ever increasing numbers in our homes and later spread into offices, banks, restaurants and hotels. Today they have become an accepted and expected part of our life.

What is an indoor plant?
How do we, today, define an indoor plant? They are plants grown indoors either for their ornamental foliage or flowers or both. They must be able not only

to survive but also to grow in the conditions in which we live and work, bearing in mind that these conditions change daily and are not designed primarily for the plant's benefit.

What do plants need to survive and grow? A plant basically requires a high intensity of daylight (which can be produced or added to artificially by the introduction of special light bulbs and fluorescent tubes). Most plants however resent direct sunlight in the middle of the day in summer for this can burn their leaves. The more green they are the more likely they are to succeed indoors away from the light. Variegated and brightly coloured species need to be in as light a position as possible. They like a circulation of air, without being in a draught so do not leave plants shut in a closed room that is never used. They do not like too much fluctuation of temperature, although this is inevitable today when central heating is turned off at night. Some plants tolerate central heating better than others but humidity is something they all miss more than anything indoors. Humidifiers on radiators help. Where possible stand pots on wet pebbles or pack the pots around with wet peat or moss in an outer container.

Whether they are grown inside or out, all plants need water from time to time. It is important to know your particular plant's water requirements and to water it only as often as is necessary. Most plants (but not ferns and a few other water lovers) survive dry periods quite successfully but more indoor plants die from overwatering than from any other cause. If you do overwater your plant allow it to dry out naturally in an airy room. Do not try to hasten the process by putting it in a warmer place.

Flowering plants, with a few important exceptions, should be regarded as visitors to the home, either expendable after they have bloomed, like a cineraria, or taken back to the greenhouse to be nurtured for another season, like an azalea. Some true house plants do flower and also have attractive leaves.

Caring for your plant

Remembering that no plants grow in pots or containers naturally, there are certain operations that have to be carried out from time to time to keep them both healthy and under control.

The first is repotting. This is done to keep the root system healthy. You must first see whether the plant is pot-bound, that is, whether the soil is just a mass of roots with hardly any soil showing. You can sometimes guess from the plant's appearance when this has happened: it may look top-heavy for its pot, it may not produce new growth in spring or you may even see roots poking through the hole in the pot's base. However, the surest way to find out is by inverting the plant, tapping the top edge of the pot on a hard surface and gently sliding the pot off a little to inspect the roots. Always water a plant well before repotting and allow the surplus to drain away. It should not be watered immediately after repotting for two or three days; this is to encourage the roots to start to explore into the new compost in search of moisture. Always stand plants out of direct sunlight after repotting or protect them with a sheet of paper.

Despite repotting, some plants, particularly fast-growing ones, cannot always obtain enough nourishment from the compost in the pot. Alternatively, they may have grown too large for repotting to be feasible. It then becomes necessary to feed them when they are growing and producing flowers. The easiest method of giving them food is in the water and there are several proprietary foods on the market suitable for most house plants. It is also possible to feed with a foliar feed when spraying the plants. Never add more food than the instructions say; in many cases it is better to add less!

Most plants need to be pruned regularly. For some this is just a matter of hygiene and appearance involving simply the removal of dead and decaying leaves and flowers. More structural pruning is done for two reasons. Firstly, to keep a plant neat and tidy. Often in the house (or indeed the garden) a plant will get leggy and throw up a rogue stem. Such stems should be pruned off and leggy plants cut back to make them into an attractive shape and encourage more compact growth. The second reason is to encourage a plant to flower. By removing its growing point you encourage it to devote its energies to producing flowers and buds, instead of leaves. Keeping

plants in pots just a little too small for them sometimes produces the same results. Always use a sharp knife or secateurs to prune and do not be afraid to use them. If the cut stem oozes sap, smear it with petroleum jelly to seal the wound.

Choosing the right compost

What compost to use for what plant is a question vital to the welfare of some plants, while others get along with almost anything. Never use garden soil, it will contain weed seeds, perhaps pests and is likely to be badly drained. It is always best to buy a compost. Traditionally, potting composts have always been an art and a mystery. Old gardeners would guard with great secrecy their special mixtures for growing this or that—in fact some still do today. In older gardening books you will find a different compost for each plant. This worried plant growers very much, so an eminent horticultural research establishment, the John Innes Institute in Surrey, England, set out to develop a universal compost that would suit nearly all pot grown plants. Thus today we have the John Innes loam-based composts. The composition is 7 parts by volume of sterilized loam to provide plant foods, 3 parts peat to provide aeration and water retention and 2 parts grit to provide drainage. The seed compost contains no fertilizer but the composts No. 1, 2 and 3 contain base fertilizer. The numbers indicate the strength of the fertilizer, No. 1 being the weakest, No. 2 twice the strength, and No. 3 treble the strength. In the text they are referred to as loam-based composts Nos. 1, 2 or 3. Most commercial potting composts are based on the John Innes formulae. There are also peat-based, loamless varieties of compost which are suitable for many plants. Care should be taken not to firm these down too hard, and never to let them completely dry out. They are excellent for ferns but unsuitable for rapid growers which need a lot of food constantly available. Some plants need composts free of lime to grow well. These are available as ericaceous composts. They are usually peat-based. Finally, some plants, particularly the many bromeliads mentioned in this book, enjoy a light, well-aerated compost. For them use a peat-based compost lightened by sphagnum moss.

Pests and diseases

If you have maintained your plant well it is particularly disturbing when pests and diseases occur. They appear for a variety of reasons, not all of which are understandable. The most common reason is that they are contagious and travel from one plant to another, even from the garden to the house or from a newly bought plant to your existing collection. In other cases they are latent on the plant and the hot dry atmosphere in your home or the way you look after the plant brings them out. This is particularly true of diseases rather than pests. If you are worried, it is wise to carry out a policy of preventive disinfection by spraying with insecticide or fungicide diluted in water in a pressure sprayer every 14 to

There are a large number of tropical plants grown for their green foliage. Many of the popular ones come from two genera, *Ficus* and *Philodendron*.
Right: *Ficus diversifolia* the mistletoe fig. This relation of the common rubber plant has more unusual leaves and also produces small fruits. Like most green leaved plants it will put up with shady conditions. As its leaves are leathery it will also withstand dry atmosphere and even smoke and fumes.

House plants with variegated foliage generally require more light than their green counterparts. If they are confined to dark corners their foliage soon reverts to green.
Right: a cultivar of *Croton pictum*. All crotons require good sunlight.

Some species of flowering pot plants may be available all the year round. Others come onto the market seasonally.
Right: *Cyclamen persicum* is very popular at Christmas. Like many flowering plants it needs to be kept cool to flower well.

Ferns were very popular in Victorian times and are currently undergoing a revival. They are excellent for mixing with flowering plants or displaying in bathrooms.
Right: a frond of *Adiantum*, the popular maidenhair fern. As each leaflet is only a few cells thick, ferns are likely to shrivel in dry air.

Climbing plants can be trained up moss poles, wires and cane or string supports. Climbers can also double as trailers if they are left without support and many will do well in hanging baskets.
Right: *Ficus pumila*, the creeping fig.

21 days in the summer months.

Many pests and diseases of house plants can be avoided by buying only healthy plants and keeping them in the right conditions. Prevention is always better than cure. However, if problems do arise, first identify what they are from our 'What goes wrong' sections, so that you know how to treat the plant.

Most chemicals can be dangerous if improperly used. Always choose the safest option: derris and pyrethrum are the safest treatments as both are substances which occur in nature. Small infestations of pests can sometimes be killed by hand and mealy bug can often be wiped off with methylated spirits. Improving humidity will usually prevent red spider mite from recurring.

If you are forced to use something stronger you must follow the rules, both for your own safety and to avoid pollution.

Propagation

If your plants are growing well you are likely to want to produce more or you may find yourself getting requests from friends for young plants from your flourishing specimens. No-one can call himself or herself a gardener, indoor or outdoor, unless they know something about the art of propagation. There are various methods of reproducing plants, some more suitable and more successful than others. The best method varies from plant to plant and it is often possible to guess it from the plant's habit of growth.

The sowing of seed is the first and probably the most widespread method used by professional growers. In spite of some difficulties with hybrids (plants formed by crossing different species) it is often the cheapest method of production. Most palms, for example, are grown from seed as are all annual plants. More and more seeds of house plants are now being made available on the amateur market.

However, some plants will not come true from seed, meaning that they will not have the appealing characteristics of their parents. These must be propagated from a part of the parent plant itself, the most common method being by cuttings. Cuttings vary in type. The commonest is the stem tip type which has a length of stem, one or two leaves and a growing point. When such a cutting grows out of the base of a plant it is called a basal shoot cutting. With some plants, it is possible to cut the stem up into lengths about 2 in (5 cm) long and, provided there is an 'eye' or dormant bud, the stem will root and the bud will grow. The stem should normally be fairly woody for this method of reproduction, which is known as a stem section cutting. Several plants can be produced from one lengthy stem in this way. Many plants can also be propagated using leaf bud cuttings where a small piece of stem with a leaf and a bud are used.

Leaf and stem cuttings are better for some plants. Part of a leaf with its stem is placed into compost and a young plantlet will appear at the bottom of the leaf. Other plants require the leaf itself to be cut into

Danger! Insecticides

If you use insecticides, always follow the rules:

Do store your chemicals and sprayers in a dry, frost free place.

Do keep them them away from foodstuffs, children and animals.

Do follow the manufacturer's instructions when you mix the spray.

Do make up only the quantity you need immediately.

Do spray your plants outside.

Do spray in the evening when bees are not around. Malathion and some other chemicals are harmful to bees.

Do wash out the sprayer thoroughly, inside and out, when you have finished spraying.

Do wash out the product bottle when it is empty and dispose of all the washings on ground away from food crops and water sources.

Do dispose of old bottles, packets and sprayers in domestic waste.

Do wash thoroughly in hot water and detergent when you have finished spraying.

Don't decant chemicals into other bottles, particularly not into beer or soft drink cans.

Don't over or under dilute chemicals.

Don't mix chemicals.

Don't spray in windy weather.

Don't breathe the spray.

Don't allow spray to drift onto washing or into fishponds. Derris is harmful to fish.

Don't pour chemicals or the water in which you have washed out sprayers or product bottles down the sink or drains. This will directly pollute.

If any insecticide gets in your mouth or eyes, wash it out and **consult a doctor immediately.**

Loam-based potting composts

Standard loam-based compost
7 parts by volume of sterilized loam
3 parts peat
2 parts grit or coarse, washed sand
Base fertilizer
2 parts hoof and horn $\frac{1}{8}$in (4mm) grist
2 parts calcium phosphate
1 part potassium sulphate

Loam-based No. 1. Add 4oz (113g) base fertilizer and $\frac{3}{4}$oz (21g) powdered chalk to each bushel (8 gallons, 36 litres) loam-based compost.

Loam-based No. 2. Add 12oz (340g) base fertilizer and $1\frac{1}{2}$oz (42g) powdered chalk to each bushel (8 gallons, 36 litres) loam-based compost.

Loam-based No. 3. Add 12oz (340g) base fertilizer and $2\frac{1}{4}$oz (64g) powdered chalk to each bushel (8 gallons, 36 litres) loam-based compost.

pieces or the whole leaf to be laid on moist sand and its veins nicked with a sharp knife. Plantlets will grow on several of the pieces of leaf. These cuttings are known as leaf cuttings.

Some plants can be divided into two, three or sometimes four pieces by carefully pulling the plant and roots apart; sometimes a judicious cut with a sharp knife helps. This is an easy method of propagation known as division. With tuberous plants the tuber can be cut into pieces, each with a growing point. Some plants obligingly produce young plantlets that either drop off or that can be cut from stems. Air layering, a method of making the top of a plant form roots whilst it is still growing on the main stem, can be practised. More easily, some plants are propagated by layering a stem into another pot standing next to the main plant. Lastly, some plants, particularly bromeliads, are propagated by removing offsets or suckers which arise from the base.

The right tools help to make propagation easier and more effective. A sharp knife has been mentioned. Also important are hormone rooting powder, sulphur dust, petroleum jelly or Stockholm tar to put on any wounds on the donor plant, a compost that is 50% sharp sand and 50% peat or loam, and small sheets of glass or polythene to cover pots or boxes. Remember to turn the glass over, or let air into the tray each day, to stop the seedlings from damping off off as they germinate. A propagator is a useful but more expensive piece of equipment. It is a tray with a low voltage electrical element in the base to heat the rooting compost. On top there is a plastic hood to keep the moisture in. This is particularly useful for rooting cuttings that are difficult to get going. Many plants will also root in water, a method which invites experiment with the different species.

Growing plants in water

Recently a new method of cultivation has been introduced into the house plant market—hydroculture, or growing plants permanently in water. The actual concept has been around for some time, but the difficulty up to now has been to control the intake of fertilizer into the plant's root system. A method of releasing food elements by ionic exchange has now been developed. Fertilizer in the form of granules is put in the bottom of the container and the chemical additives in tap water (rain or soft water must not be used) react with these to release sufficient fertilizer for the plant as and when it wants it. The plant cannot be overwatered (the commonest cause of death among soil grown plants) or over/under fed. It is also possible to leave the plant for a long time without any attention. The plants are either grown from cuttings in this method or are converted from soil culture by a process which lasts about six weeks and involves washing the roots free of soil and promoting the growth of new water roots. The plants are supported in special open pots, in an inert material called Leca which is composed of expanded clay particles.

Like all methods, there are snags, the first being

that not all plants are suitable for this type of cultivation. It is particularly unfortunate that most flowering plants will not grow in this way. Another disadvantage is that in the winter water temperature can drop more quickly than compost temperature. In unheated buildings when a cold spell occurs, the plants' roots may be damaged. It is also difficult to pack a large number of plants into a tub or a trough and care must be taken to see that the pots are all the same size, otherwise there can be problems with water levels. Despite this it is an exciting new method of growing plants which has much to recommend it. In particular, it must appeal to those who are erratic waterers or who have to leave their plants unattended for considerable lengths of time. It is excellent for hot office environments.

Pots, troughs and other containers

Plants grown in hydroculture are anchored in pots which are heavy because of their water content. If you wish to make use of space other than floor areas it is best to use hanging baskets or hanging pots containing soil grown plants. If using green plants, it is best to use just one type of plant, and the plastic kind of container with a ready fixed drip tray is very suitable. The hanging woven containers generally called macramé make very attractive displays. These are available for single plants or for double and even triple displays. Plants suitable for hanging display make themselves obvious by their habit of growth. Remember that all climbers can also be grown as trailers.

If you are trying to grow plants in a particularly dry atmosphere remember that plants give off moisture, in fact they make their own moist microclimate which encourages growth. One of the best ways of containing this humidity is in a bottle garden. The old carboy used to transport chemicals makes a good container, but is very breakable and has a narrow neck, so any planting operation can only be made using special home-made tools. There are on the market nowadays special glass bottles with openings big enough to put one's hand into, making planting and maintenance much easier. Choosing plants for a bottle garden needs even more care for they must not be fast growing (ivy is completely banned) otherwise the whole garden is dominated by one or two plants which suffocate the others. Species suitable include *Chamaedorea, Cryptanthus, Fittonia* and small *Vriesia* offsets.

A second way of increasing the humidity around plants is to grow them in groups. Mixed bowls of plants are always a delight to see and add great interest in the home or office environment. They can be freshened up by using 'dot' plants in flower as temporary residents. However, considerable care must be exercised in choosing plants to grow together. Firstly, the container must be waterproof or have a satisfactory drainage tray to protect the surface on which it is placed. If the trough is waterproof, make sure that there is plenty of drainage material

Propagation

SEEDS e.g. *Solanum*

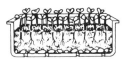

STEM TIP CUTTINGS

e.g. *Sinningia*

STEM SECTIONS

e.g. *Dracaena*

LEAF AND STEM CUTTINGS

e.g. *Saintpaulia*

DIVISION

e.g. *Anthurium*

DIVISION OF TUBERS
e.g. *Sinningia*

BASAL SHOOT CUTTINGS

e.g. *Aglaonema*

LEAF BUD CUTTINGS

e.g. *Ficus elastic*

LEAF CUTTINGS

i *Streptocarpus*

ii *Begonia rex*

iii *Sinningia*

PLANTLETS

i on parent leaf,
e.g. *Asplenium*

ii from stems,
e.g. *Chlorophytum*

AIR LAYERING
e.g. *Ficus elastica*

GROUND LAYERING
e.g. *Hedera*

OFFSETS
e.g. *Ananas*

The method of propagating a plant is often obvious from its habit of growth.
Right: *Saxifraga sarmentosa* produces young plantlets on the end of runners which can be rooted to make new plants.

Right: This *Vriesia*, like all bromeliads, will grow more quickly from offsets than from seeds.

Plants take up nutrients in different ways.
Left: *Dionaea muscipula*, the Venus fly trap, is an insectivorous plant.

Below: This *Dracaena deremensis* is growing in hydroculture. It feeds from a special fertilizer in the water.

(stones, broken bricks etc) at the bottom, together with some pieces of charcoal so that any surplus water does not become stagnant. The plants chosen must not only be suitable from an artistic point of view with a good variation of leaf shape, form and colour, a variation in plant habit (upright, climbing, trailing and squat); they must also have similar water requirements. To take two extreme cases, a cactus which needs very little water could not be mixed with *Cyperus* which can stand with its roots permanently immersed in water.

When planting, make sure that all plants are well firmed into position and that supporting sticks and canes are given, if required. The top of the container, be it large or small, can be top-dressed with moss, decorative stones, pieces of bark or driftwood.

All these recommendations for planting in bowls also apply to the grouping of plants in large displays. It may well be that you may wish to experiment with plant companions after successfully caring for single plants. Probably certain plants will have become firm favourites. Good luck with all your growing.

How and when to water a plant

More indoor plants die from overwatering than from any other cause. The special water needs of particular plants are explained in the pages that follow but a few general rules will help you to care for any plant you may obtain.

Always test the compost with your fingers before watering. It should feel dry and crumbly. Push a finger into the compost to check that it is not wet just below the surface. For ferns and a few other water-loving plants, the compost should always feel moist.

Remember that plants need less water in winter and more in the spring and summer, particularly in hot weather.

Most plants should have water added to the top of the compost. A few have leaves that rot if water gets on them and these must be watered in a different way, from below the pot.

When you add water to the top of the compost, fill the pot to the brim. Water will drain through the compost and the excess will collect in the saucer below. Allow this to be reabsorbed into the pot. If any remains after 15 minutes, empty the saucer. Never allow the pot to stand in water.

When you water from below you can simply add water to the saucer and allow it to be absorbed. A more effective method is to plunge the pot in a bowl or bucket of water to just below the pot rim. Leave it there for 15 minutes, then take it out and allow it to drain.

Avoid watering 'little and often'. Plants enjoy a good soak followed by a drier period when air can enter the soil. In this way the roots can breathe as well as drink.

15

MAIDENHAIR FERN

The maidenhair fern is perhaps the daintiest and most delicate in texture of all the ferns in this book. Its fine foliage used to be very popular in large wedding bouquets and was also used by florists in funeral wreaths. More recently it has fallen a little into disfavour because of its tendency to dry up and flop when cut.

Adiantums belong to a family of some two hundred tropical and temperate plants, the Polypodiaceae. Their pale green triangular leaves are like smaller versions of the leaves of the maidenhair tree and have given the plant its common name.

With a little care they are not difficult to grow in the house but they do dislike being moved from room to room. They flourish better if they are acclimatized to one position and left there. They must be kept damp but well drained at all times and in a centrally heated house they need a daily overhead spray, preferably with rainwater. If at any time the fronds do dry up, do not despair: cut them off, carry on spraying and soon new young shoots will appear.

Two varieties are commonly grown here. *A. capillus veneris* is the most easily obtainable and there are many forms on the market. The second is *A. cuneatum*. Its foliage is a little coarser but it is rather easier to keep.

When buying a new plant, choose one which is bushy, with new young fronds appearing.

Left: Spores of *Adiantum* appear under the fronds and turn brown as they mature.

Right: *Adiantum capillus veneris*, the common maidenhair fern. Its delicate texture makes it the most popular of all the ferns.

Below: *Adiantum cuneatum*, one of the most robust varieties.

Size: Normally grown in 5 in (12 cm) pots, they will grow to as much as 24 in (60 cm) across but are never more than 12–15 in (30–38 cm) high above the pot rim.

Growth: Fairly vigorous growers, they will easily double their size in a season.

Flowering season: None. Ferns do not flower.

Scent: None.

Light: They do not like direct sunshine but will do well on a north-facing windowsill. In the greenhouse, where it is very humid, they grow well under the staging.

Temperature: They are fairly tolerant and most of the commercial varieties will grow out of doors in summer. Do not let the temperature fall below 50°F (10°C) if you want them to grow all the year round. They dislike temperatures much above 70°F (21°C) unless humidity is high.

Water: Keep them damp at all times but do not let the pots stand in water. Water twice a week in summer, using rainwater if possible. Keep a little drier in winter, but never completely dry. Watering once a week should be sufficient. There are some deciduous varieties, not normally sold as house plants, which lose their leaves in winter. Do not let these dry out completely.

Feeding: Add half the recommended dose of liquid food to the water every 14 days during the summer.

Humidity: They love a high degree of humidity. Place the pot on a saucer of wet pebbles or put in an outer pot packed with damp peat or moss. In centrally heated houses, spray daily with rainwater.

Cleaning: The daily spray will keep the leaves clean. Never use leaf shine.

Atmosphere: They do not like gas fumes or cigar smoke.

Soil: A good, peat-based compost is the best. If you wish to prepare your own, equal parts of fibrous peat, loam and silver sand is a good mixture. Add a little base fertilizer.

Repotting: They prefer to be slightly underpotted – kept in pots that look too small. Repot in spring when they are becoming too large for their pot. Do not press the compost down too hard: ferns like to have some air around their roots.

Pruning: Remove only damaged or very old fronds. If by some mischance the plant dries out and fronds dry up, cut them all off and spray the stubble that is left twice daily with water. Young fronds will soon appear.

Propagation: Old plants can be divided in early summer but this is not always satisfactory as the two divisions often take time to grow vigorously again. It is better to grow young plants from the spores that are found under the fronds. Sow them in early spring at a temperature of 70°F (21°C), the heat being from below if possible. A simple propagator gives best results.

Life expectancy: Once established indoors, only neglect or dryness can kill it.

Plant companions: They do quite well in bowls of mixed house plants. However, they are best grown with other ferns or as individual plants. The Victorians had special fern cases which kept the humidity high.

Ease/difficulty: Quite an easy plant but it does not like to be moved. Find the place in which it grows best and leave it there.

Humidity

Two ways to provide the humidity adiantums love.

Put pot in outer container packed with damp peat.

or

Stand pot in saucer with water, pebbles or gravel. Make sure pot base is clear of water.

Root division

Divide large, old plants in early summer.

1 Prepare 2 pots with drainage layer and compost.

3 Gently pull roots and stems apart with your hands.

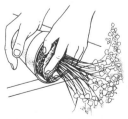 

2 Remove plant from pot and gently prise away compost.

4 Repot both sections in the usual way.

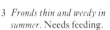

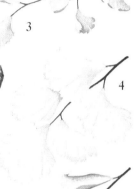

1 *Shrivelled leaves going brown at edges.* Needs water. Add water and spray. Dry leaves may also be caused by gas, smoke or lack of humidity.

2 *All leaves drop.* Much too dry. Cut plant down, add water and spray daily until new fronds appear.

3 *Fronds thin and weedy in summer.* Needs feeding.

4 *Leaves pale.* Too much direct sun. Move to a north window.

5 *Leaves curl but are not dry.* Too cold and wet. Move to a warmer place. Do not water until compost feels dry.

Growing from spores

1 Spores grow on the backs of the fronds and are ready to sow in spring.

2 Cut off a small frond and scrape spores onto a piece of foil or paper.

3 Prepare seed tray or propagator with drainage layer and sterilized seed compost. Water well and scatter spores on the surface, evenly if possible.

4 Cover with sheet of glass. Put in dark, warm place, heating from below if possible, at a temperature of 70 F (21 C)

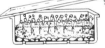

5 Turn glass each day to prevent rot but do not let the compost dry out. Keep dark until scales and shoots appear in 4–12 weeks.

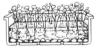

6 Bring into the light and remove glass.

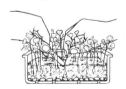

7 When plants are large enough to handle, thin out weaker ones, leaving 1in (2½cm) between each.

8 When rest are growing well, repot in small pots of peaty compost, 2 or 3 to a pot.

Repotting

1 Repot in spring when they begin to look too large for their pot. Water plant well.

2 Prepare pot 1 size larger with drainage layer and layer of damp, peat-based compost.

3 Hold old pot with one hand covering compost, fingers either side of stems. Tap edge of pot. Plant and compost will come out.

4 Carefully remove stale soil from roots, using stick or pencil. Do not damage roots.

5 Place plant in centre of new pot, root-ball on compost.

6 Add new compost to fill pot. Make sure that all the roots are covered but do not press it down too hard. Leave the plant in the shade without water for 2 days to encourage roots to grow into compost.

Watering

1 Test compost with fingers. If it is light and crumbly water at once. It must not dry out.

2 Add water at top of pot, using rainwater if possible. Empty excess from saucer after 15 minutes.

Spraying

Spray daily overhead with a fine mist spray, using rainwater if possible. Hold spray about 6in (15cm) from leaves.

URN PLANT

Aechmeas come from a large family of about 1400 species, the Bromeliaceae, and are closely related to the pineapple. Most bromeliads are epiphytes which means that in the wild they grow on other plants, usually trees, for support. They grow in hollows in the bark and absorb the water and nutrients from the decaying material which collects there. In the home they can be grown in compost in the normal way or, if kept well watered, may be fixed to a piece of cork bark as a hanging decoration.

A. fasciata (sometimes also known as *Aechmea* or *Billbergia rhodocyanea*) comes from Rio de Janiero, where it was discovered in 1826. Its common names of urn plant, Greek vase plant and bottle brush plant, come from the characteristic shape of its leaves and flower spike. The foliage is in the shape of a rosette, green but covered with a lime-like white deposit. This should not be wiped off for it contrasts well with the pink of the flower stem which emerges from the centre. The actual flowers are at the top of the spike and are purple. There are also rare varieties with green and yellow-green along the leaves.

A. fasciata has all the characteristics of the bromeliad family in that each rosette only flowers once, producing a succession of small blooms which last for some considerable time. After the flowers have died, the rosette itself slowly shrivels and dies but at the same time it produces at least two, sometimes three, baby rosettes to replace itself. Eventually the original rosette can be cut out and the 'babies' potted individually. It may then be a year or even longer before the new plants flower.

A. fulgens, another species available as a house plant, has bright green leaves and a red flower stem. The flowers are again purple but are more spread out along the stem.

Choose aechmeas with the flower spike just emerging from the rosette. Check that there is no rot at the base of the rosette and in the flower stem.

Left: *Aechmea fulgens discolor*. The opened flowers are purple and are followed by long lasting berries.

Right: The rosette of *Aechmea fasciata* forms a natural well to hold water in the centre. Its young flower (below) will stay in good condition for six weeks or more.

Size: A well grown plant can be up to 2 ft (60 cm) across with leaves 1 ft (30 cm) long.
Growth: Young rosettes severed from the parent plant will grow to flowering size in 2 years.
Flowering season: Mostly in summer although individual rosettes can flower at any time. It is said that an apple core placed in the centre of a young plant will release gases which help to bring it into flower.
Scent: None.
Light: Very tolerant. They do not mind direct sunlight or indirect light.
Temperature: Normal room temperature but not less than 55°F (12°C) and not more than 80°F (27°C).
Water: Keep fairly moist, particularly before flowering, watering about twice a week. The central rosette should also have about 1 in (2½ cm) water in it. This should be changed every 3 weeks. Use rainwater for preference. In the wild, tropical rain collects on the leaves and runs down into the centre.
Feeding: Not necessary.
Humidity: Very tolerant, no special needs.
Cleaning: Not necessary. Never use leaf shine.
Atmosphere: Very tolerant.
Soil: Any lime-free, porous compost.

Repotting: Put new rosettes into small pots after severing them from the parent plant. Pot once again before flowering. The pot is really only a means of keeping the plant upright and rosettes can equally well be wired onto a piece of cork bark.
Pruning: None necessary apart from cutting out the dead flower spike when it has died down completely.
Propagation: Most plants on the market have been grown from seed, but this is a job for the nurseryman. In the home propagation should be by potting up the new young offsets after the original rosette has died. It is very important to wait until the 'parent' leaves have completely shrivelled before dividing and potting up.
Life expectancy: The rosette dies gradually after flowering. The life span of each rosette can be 2–3 years, depending on how quickly it comes into flower.
Plant companions: They look best on their own in a ceramic pot but can be successfully used in mixed plantings of various green plants, such as philodendrons, *Ficus*, marantas etc.
Ease/difficulty: A very easy plant.

Propagation: Offsets

1 Wait until flowers and leaves of plant have died before removing offset. Offset should be about ½ size of parent.

3 Remove offset and roots from parent plant with sharp knife.

4 The offset must have its own small roots. If it has not, it will not grow.

2 Prepare small pot with drainage layer and damp, all peat compost.

5 Pot offset in new pot, firming compost around base. Water well.

1 *Rosette or flower stem rots.* Too much water in too low a temperature. Empty rosette and allow compost to dry out until recovered. Move to a warmer, more airy position.

2 *Leaves shrivel.* Too hot and dry. Add water to compost and check that central rosette is filled. Spray with rainwater if possible.

3 *Leaves distorted and sticky with green insects.* Greenfly. Spray with pyrethrum or a systemic insecticide.

4 *Leaves shrivel and die after flowering.* All aechmeas die after flowering. Propagate new plants from offsets.

5 *Flower spike and stem dry up and turn a dirty pink colour.* Too cold. Move to warmer position. The spike will also show these symptoms naturally after 7 to 8 weeks in flower.

Fixing a bromeliad to bark

Aechmeas look good fixed to bark or wood.

1 Choose suitable piece of cork bark, a branch or some well shaped driftwood.

2 If there is no natural hollow, chisel a shallow well where plant will rest.

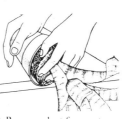

3 Remove plant from pot, keeping compost round the root ball.

4 Wrap roots in damp sphagnum moss and tie with plastic-coated wire.

5 Hold moss and root-ball firmly against wood or bark and bind in place with wire.

6 Fix bark to wall or prop it up, making sure the plant is growing upright. Dampen root ball and keep central well filled with water. Spray regularly.

Repotting

1 Repot young rosettes as they begin to look too large for their pot. A plant bought in flower will not need to be potted again.

2 Prepare pot 1 size larger with drainage layer and layer of lime-free compost. Water plant well.

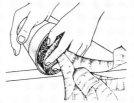

3 Hold old pot with one hand covering compost, fingers either side of stem. Tap edge of pot. Plant and compost will come out.

4 Carefully remove stale soil from roots, using stick or pencil. Do not damage roots.

5 Place plant in centre of new pot, root-ball on compost.

6 Add new compost to fill pot. Make sure that all the roots are covered but do not press it down too hard. Leave the plant in the shade without water for 2 days to encourage roots to grow into compost.

Watering and Removing flower stem

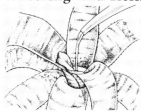

Keep about 1in (2½cm) of water in central funnel. Empty and refill every 3 weeks. Rainwater is best.

When the flowers have died, cut out central stem at base with secateurs.

CHINESE EVERGREEN

Aglaonemas are members of the Arum or Araceae family and there are some fifteen species recorded. The name comes from two Greek words – *aglaos*, bright and *nema*, a thread. Nearly all the species come from South-east Asia and the three mentioned here come from Malaysia. They were discovered in the late nineteenth century – the heyday of plant collection.

Aglaonemas are good house plants and really deserve to be more widely grown. They do not get too untidy and apart from the odd yellow leaf if underfed in summer or allowed to get too cold in winter, they present few problems. They are also very good plants to grow in hydroculture. Whilst it is possible to convert soil-grown plants to growing in water, plants propagated in water from the start will be more satisfactory.

A. trewbii 'Silver Queen' is probably the best variety for indoor conditions. The leaves, some 5 to 6in (12 to 15cm) long, are basically green with an overlay of silvery green markings. Next comes *A. pseudo-bracteatum*, which has a slightly bigger leaf, green again but with some golden markings top and bottom. *A. pictum* has more upright leaves than the other two varieties. They are green with little cream blotches, as if somebody had flicked paint onto them.

Aglaonemas are good examples of variegated plants that will put up with poor light and therefore make a change from philodendrons, *Ficus* and the other green leaved plants that are normally grown in the shade. Though once more delicate, they have now been bred and developed to cope fairly well with the dry atmosphere of most homes.

When buying a new plant, choose a young one which shows no signs of yellowing and has leaves that stand up firmly.

Right: *Aglaonema trewbii* 'Silver Queen' is the variety of *Aglaonema* most often available and is probably the finest in its leaf marking. It is often seen growing in hydro-culture and is an attractive plant to buy as an introduction to water culture.

Above left: *Aglaonema pseudobracteatum* is the only species with gold markings on its leaves.

Centre left: *Aglaonema roebelinii* has fine silver variegations and elegant young leaves.

Left: Other species and hybrids are sometimes available. All are excellent variegated plants which will tolerate shade. Use them to brighten mixed plantings of green plants in shady corners.

Size: They are not really very big plants – about 10in (25cm) tall – growing in a clump.
Growth: They produce about 5–6 leaves a year if they are growing well.
Flowering season: The white or yellow flowers are fairly insignificant and appear in a green sheaf during the summer months. *A trewbii* will go on to produce some dark red berries.
Scent: None.
Light: They grow well in most situations and will stand a fair amount of direct sunlight.
Temperature: They are fairly tolerant of low temperatures and will survive at 50°F (10°C) if they are kept fairly dry, but it is better to keep the temperature nearer 60°F (15°C). They enjoy temperatures up to 75°F (24°C) in summer, provided the humidity is high.
Water: In summer keep the soil damp, watering twice a week. In winter keep very much drier, watering not more than once a week. They do well in hydroculture.
Feeding: Add liquid food to the water every 14 days in the summer.
Humidity: They like a reasonable amount of humidity in summer and can be sprayed twice a week or put on a saucer of wet pebbles. In winter they will survive in a dry atmosphere.
Cleaning. By hand with tepid water. Do not use leaf shine.

Atmosphere: They do not like gas fires or oil fumes. They like a good flow of air but not icy draughts.
Soil: Loam-based No. 2 compost is ideal.
Repotting: Repot in spring every year. Do not firm the compost down too hard. Aglaonemas dislike compacted soil.
Pruning: Not necessary, but remove damaged leaves.
Propagation: By division. It is best to use young shoots with leaves and roots. Separate them in late spring – April to May is a good time – and keep them in a temperature of at least 70°F (21°C) until they are growing well. Cuttings using leafy stem tips are also possible but take a little longer. Use a propagator if possible, at a temperature of 75°F (24°C). Seeds are the slowest method. Sow them in spring at 81°F (27°C) and select the best plants for they will vary greatly in quality.
Life expectancy: After 2–3 years they become less vigorous and it is best to start again with stem tip cuttings.
Plant companions: They make very good mixers with most house plants – *Ficus*, cordylines, philodendrons, fatshederas etc. Their slightly unusual leaf shape and habit of growth is good in tubs or jardinières.
Ease/difficulty: A good, easy house plant.

Root division

Divide young shoots with leaves and roots in late spring.

1 Prepare 2 pots with drainage layer and compost.

3 Gently pull roots and stems apart with your hands.

2 Remove plant from pot and gently prise away compost.

4 Repot both sections and keep warm (70°F, 21°C) until they are growing again.

Cleaning the leaves

Wipe dust off leaves with soft cloth and sponge with tepid water. Support leaf with other hand.

Do not use leaf shine.

1 *Plant collapses.* Cold draughts. Move to a protected position.

2 *New leaves small.* Needs food.

3 *Leaves pale.* Not enough light or needs feeding. If in dark corner move to lighter position. If already in the light, feed.

4 *Leaves yellow.* Too wet and cold. Move to warmer, more airy position and allow to dry out until recovered.

5 *Leaves dry and brittle.* Too hot and dry. Move to more airy position and water regularly. Spray.

6 *White woolly patches under leaves and in leaf axils.* Mealy bug. Remove them individually with a swab dipped in methylated spirits or spray with malathion or a systemic insecticide.

7 *Leaves mottled with yellow especially along veins; brown scaly insects on underside of leaves and on stems.* Scale insect. Remove them individually with a swab dipped in methylated spirits or spray with a systemic insecticide.

8 *Leaves turn brown in patches.* Gas or other fumes. Move plant to a fume-free room.

Basal shoot cuttings

Aglaonemas really need a propagator but as their leaves are too big for most simple trays you can experiment using an ordinary pot covered with a polythene bag. Put it on a warm radiator or near a central heating boiler so that the temperature is constant and the heat comes from below.

1 Prepare pot with layer of drainage and mixture of ½ peat, ½ sharp sand.

2 Choose plant with several healthy stems and leaves and cut one with sharp knife just above compost.

3 Dip the cut surface in hormone rooting powder. Shake off surplus.

4 Make hole in compost with stick or pencil. It should be deep enough to take the length of stem to the base of the leaf.

5 Insert cutting so that end of stem is at bottom of hole and leaves are level with compost.

6 Water well and cover with polythene supported by wire. Remove polythene for 5 minutes a day to prevent rot. Do not let compost dry out. Keep warm (75 F, 24 C).

7 After 21 days remove the polythene. When the new plant is growing well, repot in loam-based No. 2 compost.

Repotting

1 Repot in spring as plant begins to look top-heavy. Water plant well.

2 Prepare pot 1 size larger with drainage layer and layer of damp, loam-based No. 2 compost.

3 Hold old pot with one hand covering compost, fingers either side of stems. Tap edge of pot. Plant and compost will come out.

4 Carefully remove stale soil from roots, using stick or pencil. Do not damage roots.

5 Place plant in centre of new pot, root-ball on compost.

6 Add new compost to fill pot. Make sure that all the roots are covered but do not press it down too hard. Leave the plant in the shade without water for 2 days to encourage roots to grow into compost.

PINEAPPLE

The pineapple plant is a very good house plant, particularly the variegated varieties, which always look bright and cheerful. A member of the bromeliad family, it comes from Brazil and was first introduced to Europe in the late seventeenth century. Some thirty years later it was successfully fruited in England and was then regularly cultivated in the glass house, next to the grapes and oranges, as a delicacy for the rich. Nineteenth-century gardening books give detailed instructions on how to arrange a succession of fruit but in the late 1860s commercial production was started outdoors in the Azores and private growing ceased. Today they are grown purely as decorative plants and if a small fruit appears that is a bonus. The flowers are small and insignificant but must be left on the plant if the fruit is to appear.

Unlike other bromeliads, the pineapple lives on the ground and absorbs food and water from the soil in the normal way. Great care should be taken when handling the plants for the leaves are sharply toothed and can easily tear both skin and clothing.

Three varieties are grown indoors. *A. comosus* is green with narrow leaves; it fruits well. *A. comosus* 'Variegatus' has smaller, wider leaves that are distinctly striped and form complete rosettes. This fruits much more rarely. Finally, *A. bracteatus* 'Striatus' is a much bigger plant than the other two and has variegated leaves. It often produces half pink fruits which contrast well with the yellow and green leaves.

When choosing a new plant, look for brightly coloured, vigorously growing leaves with no browning at the tips. A plant which is large and producing offsets has already flowered and will not do so again, although the offsets can be grown separately later on.

Above: The bright foliage of *Ananas comosus* 'Variegatus'.

Left: The fruiting spike of *Ananas bracteatus* 'Striatus' takes on attractive pink hues.

Right: The cultivated pineapple *Ananas comosus* needs warmth to fruit well. Young plants can be grown from the rosette on top of the fruit.

Size: *A. comosus* is a small plant, not much more than 10–12 in (25–30 cm) across. *A. bracteatus* 'Striatus' is much bigger, sometimes more than 3 ft (1 m) across.

Growth: Young plants will double their size in a year.

Flowering season: The flowers are small and almost insignificant; the fruit is the great attraction. This normally appears in spring.

Scent: Except when in fruit, none.

Light: Full sunlight is essential to ensure good colour in the leaves.

Temperature: They should be kept warm, particularly in winter. A temperature of 65–70°F (18–21°C) is ideal. If you want small plants keep the plants in pots that look too small and drop the temperature by about 10°F (5°C). 75°F (24°C) is the maximum.

Water: During the summer, the plant should be watered once or twice a week, according to the temperature. Let the plant dry out between waterings. In winter, keep drier, watering not more than once a week.

Feeding: Add liquid food to the water once a week when the fruit is forming.

Humidity: Spray twice a week in summer but only once a week in winter.

Cleaning: Wipe the leaves by hand. Wear gloves. Do not use leaf shine.

Atmosphere: Tolerant, but keep out of cold draughts.

Soil: Use a good loam-based compost. No. 2 is very suitable.

Repotting: Repot the growing plant twice before it is fully grown, once 3 months after the offset is separated and again a year later. Always wear gloves – the needle sharp leaves can really hurt. See that the pot is on the small side and well drained. Do not firm the compost down too hard.

Pruning: None necessary, but cut away damaged or dry leaves.

Propagation: It is easiest to propagate from offsets. If you keep them warm (75°F, 24°C) after potting, they will grow more quickly. Plants can sometimes be grown from freshly cut pineapples but these must have their full crown of leaves. The tops should be potted in peat and sand kept at 75°F (24°C). This is a much slower method than using offsets. Plants can also be grown from seed.

Life expectancy: Like all bromeliads the rosette dies after it has flowered and fruited. It will by this time have produced two or three offsets. The cycle from shoot to dying of the rosette takes about two years.

Plant companions: They look good in mixed plantings because their leaf colouring is different from most house plants. Use them as the focal point in arrangements.

Ease/difficulty: An easy plant.

Propagation

1 Choose fresh pineapple with full tuft of leaves, including central ones, which are sometimes removed by growers.

2 Prepare pot with layer of drainage and mixture of ½ peat, ½ sharp sand. Pot must be wide enough to take whole top of fruit.

3 Cut off tuft of leaves with about ½ in (1 cm) fruit.

4 Stand top in pot and firm compost round it so that tuft is upright and fruit base is well covered.

5 Water and cover with polythene supported by wire. Remove polythene for 5 minutes a day and do not let compost dry out. Keep warm at 75°F (24°C).

6 When new leaves grow in centre, remove polythene.

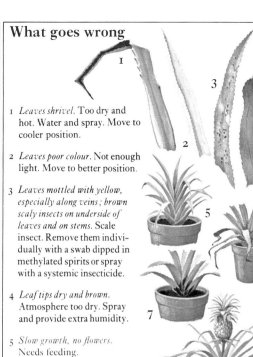

1 *Leaves shrivel.* Too dry and hot. Water and spray. Move to cooler position.

2 *Leaves poor colour.* Not enough light. Move to better position.

3 *Leaves mottled with yellow, especially along veins; brown scaly insects on underside of leaves and on stems.* Scale insect. Remove them individually with a swab dipped in methylated spirits or spray with a systemic insecticide.

4 *Leaf tips dry and brown.* Atmosphere too dry. Spray and provide extra humidity.

5 *Slow growth, no flowers.* Needs feeding.

6 *Lower leaves dry, shrivel and curl.* Draughts. Move to protected position.

7 *Rotting at base.* Too wet and cold. Move to warmer, airy position and allow to dry out until recovered. If the rot is advanced the plant will die.

8 *Leaves shrivel and die after flowering.* All *Ananas* die after flowering. Propagate new plants from offshoots.

Propagation: Offsets

1 Wait until flowers and leaves of plant have died before removing offset. Offset should be about $\frac{1}{2}$ size of parent.

2 Prepare small pot with drainage layer and damp, compost.

3 Remove offset and roots from parent plant with a sharp knife. Wear gloves. The leaves can hurt.

4 The offset must have its own small roots. If it has not, it will not grow.

5 Water well and cover with polythene supported by wire. Remove cover for 5 minutes a day and never let compost dry out. Keep at 75 F (24 C). Remove cover after 21 days.

Repotting

1 Repot young plant 3 months after separation and again a year later. Remember to wear gloves. Water plant well.

2 Prepare pot one size larger with good drainage layer and damp, loam-based No. 2 compost.

3 Hold old pot with one hand covering compost, fingers either side of plant. Tap edge of pot. Plant and compost will come out easily.

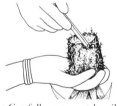

4 Carefully remove stale soil from roots, using stick or pencil. Do not damage roots.

5 Place plant in centre of new pot, root-ball on compost.

6 Add new compost to fill pot. Make sure that all the roots are covered but do not press it down too hard. Leave the plant in the shade without water for 2 days to encourage roots to grow into compost.

Cleaning and spraying

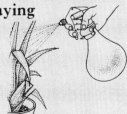

Wipe dust off leaves with soft cloth and sponge with tepid water. Support leaf with other hand – remember to wear gloves. Do not use leaf shine.

Spray with water twice a week in summer, once a week in winter. Hold the spray about 6in (15cm) from the leaves.

Trimming leaves

If the tips of the leaves are brown and dry, trim them off with sharp scissors, cutting just above healthy leaf tissue. Remember to wear gloves.

FLAMINGO FLOWER

Anthurium is a member of the Arum (Araceae) family, which includes so many of the lovely plants we cultivate in the home. This is a more difficult one to keep well but if you can give it the care it needs, it will amply repay you. It requires a fairly high constant temperature and also needs a high degree of humidity.

There are some five hundred species of anthuriums, coming mainly from Columbia in central tropical America. The name comes from the Greek words *athos*, a flower and *oura*, a tail – if you look at the photographs you will see why.

Three varieties are generally grown as indoor plants. The most popular is *A. scherzerianum*, a rather untidy plant whose long, narrow leaves come out of the centre of the plant at all angles. The flowers, usually red but sometimes rose, white or spotted, are the plant's main attraction. They emerge from the centre as a red spear and once the plant has started to flower will appear continuously. The flowers are sometimes too heavy for their stems so a discreet stake helps to display them better.

The other two varieties are really for the expert and both need a warmer atmosphere. *A. andreanum* has larger flowers than *A. scherzerianum*, formed with a straight spadix in the centre. They last a long time as cut flowers, and are much prized for flower arrangements. *A. crystallinum* is grown for its beautiful leaves which are heart-shaped, deep, velvety green in colour with veins of silver. Like *A. andreanum* it is rather difficult to keep. A slight bonus is that most anthuriums do well in hydroculture.

Plants are normally sold in flower. Ensure that there are buds still to open and that the leaves are firm and glossy. Limp leaves show that this moisture loving plant has dried out.

The spectacular foliage of *Anthurium crystallinum*.

Right: *A. scherzerianum*.

Below: Flowers of *A. andreanum* (left) and *A. scherzerianum* (right).

Size: *A. scherzerianum* is a fairly small plant reaching 9–10 in (22–25 cm) high with a spread of 15 in (38 cm) at most. The other two can be much bigger, up to 20 in (50 cm) across by 24 in (60 cm) high.

Growth: Not very fast in the house. Be satisfied to keep them safely alive.

Flowering season: All the year round, but more prolific in summer.

Scent: None.

Light: A good, light position is essential. However, protect from direct sunlight.

Temperature: An even temperature, particularly in winter, is essential. They do not like sharp drops at night. *A. scherzerianum* needs a minimum temperature of 60°F (15°C) and the other two 70°F (21°C). Maximum 85°F (29°C) with high humidity.

Water: Keep well watered in summer, watering at least twice a week. Keep drier in winter, watering only once a week. Rainwater is best.

Feeding: Add liquid food to the water every 14 days when the plant is growing and flowering heavily in the summer.

Humidity: A high degree of humidity is essential. Stand the pot on damp pebbles or pack it into an outer pot packed with damp peat or moss. Spray daily with rainwater.

Cleaning: Wipe the leaves by hand. Leaf shine can be used every 2 months.

Atmosphere: Cold draughts can kill but it is otherwise tolerant.

Soil: It is very important to get the right mixture. Use one of the peat-based composts with the addition of 1 part of chopped sphagnum moss to 3 parts of compost.

Repotting: This is normally carried out every second year. Make sure that the crown of the plant is well above the soil. As the plant grows it will tend to push its crown up, and the exposed roots should be covered up with moss.

Pruning: Not necessary.

Propagation: Really this is a job for the expert but you can try division in January or February. The plant should be kept very warm (70°F, 21°C) after the operation. They can also be grown from seed at 75°F (24°C).

Life expectancy: Indefinite if all conditions are right. Under a year if not.

Plant companions: It is probably best to grow anthuriums on their own unless they are in a warm greenhouse, where crotons and some orchids go well with them.

Ease/difficulty: These are not beginner's plants and will only do well when all the conditions are right for them.

Repotting

1 Repot in spring when roots grow out of compost at the top and through pot base. Water well.

4 Carefully remove stale soil from roots, using stick or pencil. Do not damage roots.

2 Prepare pot 1 size larger with drainage and compost. Use 3 parts peat-based to 1 part sphagnum moss.

5 Place plant in centre of new pot, root-ball on compost.

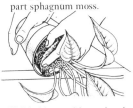

3 Hold old pot with one hand covering compost, fingers either side of stems. Tap edge of pot. Plant and compost will come out.

6 Add new compost to fill pot. Make sure that all roots are covered. Press down well. Leave in the shade without water for 2 days to encourage roots to grow into compost.

1 *Leaves turn yellow and droop in winter.* Too cold and wet. Move to warmer, more airy position and allow to dry out until recovered. Also caused by a sudden drop in temperature.

2 *Leaves dry and papery, possibly yellowish.* Too dry. Water and provide humidity.

3 *Leaves droop and collapse.* Draughts. Move to protected position.

4 *Roots exposed at base of stem.* Needs repotting. Cover with moss until repotted.

5 *New leaves small, no flowers.* Needs feeding.

6 *Brown spots on leaves.* Fungus. Spray leaves with a systemic fungicide.

7 *White woolly patches under leaves and at leaf axils.* Mealy bug. Remove them individually with a swab dipped in methylated spirits or spray with malathion or a systemic insecticide.

Watering

1 Test compost with fingers. If it is light and crumbly, the plant needs water.

2 Add water at top of pot, using rainwater if possible. Empty excess from saucer after 15 minutes.

Cleaning the leaves

Wipe dust off leaves with soft cloth and sponge with tepid water. Support leaf with other hand.

Use leaf shine but not more than once every 2 months.

Spraying

Spray daily overhead with a fine mist spray, using rainwater if possible. Hold spray about 6in (15cm) from leaves.

Humidity

Stand pot in saucer with water, pebbles or gravel. Make sure pot base is clear of water.

Put pot in outer container packed with damp peat.

Root division

1 Prepare 2 pots with drainage layer and compost.

2 Remove plant from pot and gently prise away compost.

3 Gently pull roots and stems apart with your hands.

4 Repot both sections in the usual way.

ZEBRA PLANT

Left: The flower spike of the *Aphelandra* often takes several weeks to open.

Right: The dramatic foliage and flower of *Aphelandra squarrosa* 'Louisae'. Young plants can be grown from the side shoots below the flowers.

Below: Some hybrid aphelandras have silvered leaves.

This is a most striking plant, with its crisp, well formed leaves, the veins distinctly marked out by cream stripes. The flowers, which are bright yellow, come out of greenish-yellow bracts formed in a many-sided, pyramid shaped head.

Aphelandras are members of the Acanthaceae family and are found mainly in the tropics. There are some sixty species. Their name comes from two Greek words meaning sessile and male and refers to botanical characteristics of the flowers. The only species normally available as a house plant is *A. squarrosa* but there are several varieties in cultivation. It comes from Brazil and must have been collected first by a Belgian for one of the varieties is called after a queen of the Belgians ('Louisae'), another after a king ('Leopoldi').

A. squarrosa 'Louisae' is the usual variety grown. *A. squarrosa* 'Dania' is an improved strain which grows more compactly and has shorter leaves. There is also a silver variety (the leaves striped with silver instead of cream) but this does not flower quite so well as the others.

The plant is generally bought either in or about to flower and is often regarded as expendable. However, with a little care, it is possible to keep it from year to year, to bring it into flower again and to grow young plants from the original. It is most important never to let it dry out – otherwise it will lose some if not all of its leaves.

Choose plants with firm, glossy foliage without any browning. Avoid plants with limp leaves. They are likely to have dried out or been chilled.

Size: About 1 ft (30 cm) tall and 7–8 in (18–20 cm) across when flowering for the first time. Will grow to twice this size with 4–5 shoots in the second year.

Growth: They grow quite quickly. Cuttings struck in March will flower in the late summer.

Flowering season: All through the summer, depending on when the cuttings were struck.

Scent: None.

Light: They like plenty of light but should be kept out of direct sunshine as this can easily burn the leaves.

Temperature: A temperature of around 60°F (15°C) suits them well, a little higher will do no harm. After they have flowered, keep cooler, at about 55°F (12°C). Maximum is 75°F (24°C) when humidity must be high.

Water: They must be kept well watered all the time they are growing. Water at least twice a week for if they ever dry out they will lose some or all of their leaves. After flowering, water not more than once a week and allow them to rest for 4–6 weeks. Start twice weekly watering again when you want them to begin growing once more.

Feeding: As soon as the flower spike appears, add liquid food to the water every 14 days.

Humidity: As jungle plants, they enjoy plenty of moisture. Spray overhead every day and stand the pot on a saucer of wet pebbles or pack it around with peat. Once in flower, reduce the humidity by removing the peat pack or wet pebbles. This will make the blooms last longer.

Cleaning: The spray will keep the leaves clean. Leaf shine can be used every 2 months.

Atmosphere: Tolerant, except of draughts. They can even stand gas or oil fumes.

Soil: Loam-based No. 3 will suit this plant.

Repotting: Repot cuttings once or twice before they come into flower. Always repot the mature plant after the resting period, removing most of the spent soil.

Pruning: After flowering, snap off the flower head. In the spring the plant will have produced several shoots. These should be reduced to 3 or 4.

Propagation: Use the removed shoots as cuttings in spring. Dust them with hormone rooting powder and place them in compost of sharp sand and loam at a temperature of 75°F (24°C).

Life expectancy: Most people keep them for one year only but they should live for a second and flower a second time. After that it is best to start again with new cuttings.

Plant companions: They do well in mixed plantings of all green plants such as *Ficus*, hederas, philodendrons and bromeliads. Remove after flowering.

Ease/difficulty: Medium – not as difficult as many people imagine.

Repotting

1 Repot in spring. If plant looks top-heavy with only small new leaves and roots growing out of pot at base, it needs a larger pot.

2 Prepare pot 1 size larger with drainage layer and layer damp, loam-based No. 3 compost. Water plant well.

3 Hold old pot with one hand covering compost, fingers either side of stems. Tap edge of pot. Plant and compost will come out.

4 Carefully remove stale soil from roots, using stick or pencil. Do not damage roots.

5 Place plant in centre of new pot, root-ball on compost.

6 Add new compost to fill pot. Make sure that all roots are covered. Press down well. Leave in the shade without water for 2 days to encourage roots to grow into compost.

1 *Leaves drop, Too hot and dry.* Water and spray. Move to more airy position.

2 *Leaves limp, plant collapses.* Draughts. Move to protected position.

3 *Rotting at base.* Too wet and cold. Move to warmer position and allow to dry out until recovered.

4 *New leaves small, no flowers.* Needs feeding.

5 *Brown spots on leaves.* Too much sun. Move out of direct sunlight.

6 *Leaves turn brown.* Gas or other fumes. Move to fume-free room.

7 *White woolly patches under leaves and at leaf axils.* Mealy bug. Remove them individually with a swab dipped in methylated spirits or spray with malathion or a systemic insecticide.

8 *Leaves mottled with yellow, especially along veins; brown scaly insects on underside of leaves and on stems.* Scale insect. Remove them individually with a swab dipped in methylated spirits or spray with a systemic insecticide.

9 *Leaves distorted and sticky, with green insects.* Greenfly. Spray with pyrethrum or a systemic insecticide.

10 *Leaves yellowed and fall. Webs underneath.* Red spider mite. Spray with derris, malathion or a systemic insecticide. Improve the humidity.

Stem tip cuttings

1 In spring plant produces new shoots which can be used for cuttings. Prepare small pot with drainage layer and mixture of sharp sand and loam-based compost.

2 Choose shoot or stem tip with at least 2 pairs of healthy leaves and a growing point. Cut off below second pair of leaves, close to main stem. Cuttings should be 3–4in (8–10cm) long.

3 Prepare cuttings by trimming off stem just below a leaf.

4 Remove the lowest pair of leaves.

5 Dip the cut surface in hormone rooting powder. Shake off the surplus.

6 Make hole in compost with stick or pencil.
Insert cutting so that end of stem is at bottom of hole and leaves are level with compost.

7 Water well and cover with polythene supported by wire. Remove cover for 5 minutes a day and never let compost dry out. Keep at 75 F (24 C). Remove cover after 21 days and when cuttings are growing well, repot in normal compost.

Removing dead flowers

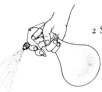

When flower has died, cut off flower stem just above the top pair of leaves.

Humidity

Three ways to provide the humidity aphelandras love.

1 Stand pot in saucer with water, pebbles or gravel. Make sure pot base is clear of water.

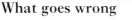

2 Spray overhead every day.

3 Put pot in outer container packed with damp peat. Remove the saucer or peat pack while the plant is flowering but continue to spray the leaves.

27

FALSE CASTOR OIL PLANT

The aralias are a small group of plants which make very good house dwellers. They belong to the family Araliaceae and are a genus of some twenty species of hardy or nearly hardy plants coming from Asia, America and Australia.

We are concerned with two species. The first is *Aralia japonica*, also known as *Aralia sieboldii* and *Fatsia japonica*. *Aralia japonica* is a very tolerant plant which can also be grown outdoors in warmer temperate areas and does particularly well on a terrace or patio in town gardens. The leaves are bright green and sharply cut rather like fingers. As its name suggests it comes from Japan and was collected in 1838. There is an alternative variegated form, in which the tips of the leaves are cream.

The second variety is *A. elegantissima*, the finger aralia otherwise known by the almost unpronounceable name of *Dizygotheca elegantissima*. Another good plant but not quite so tolerant as *A. japonica*, its leaves are bronze in colour, making it a good plant to contrast with others. It is interesting botanically for it is often possible to have three different leaf forms on the same plant. Firstly there are the cotyledons or seed leaves just above the soil, then the juvenile leaves which are very pointed and serrated, and then above them the adult leaves which are like the other aralias but bronze in colour. It comes from the New Hebrides in the South Pacific.

When choosing aralias look for rich colour and a gloss on the leaves. Select shapely plants and beware of any sign of leaf drop. *A. japonica* may need acclimatising before being planted outdoors. Do this by standing the pot outside for 2 or 3 days before planting.

Above: A young plant of *Aralia elegantissima* showing its juvenile foliage.

Aralia japonica is a nearly hardy plant often used outside in town gardens. It is also an easy house plant.

Left: The variegated form.

Right: *Aralia* (or *Fatsia*) *japonica*.

Size: In the house *A. japonica* will grow to about 3 ft (1 m). *A. elegantissima* 4 ft (120 cm). The first has a spread of some 18 in (46 cm), the second 12 in (30 cm). *A. japonica* when growing outside will become quite a big shrub 6 to 7 ft (2 m) tall and nearly as wide.

Growth: Fairly rapid, will easily double in height in a year.

Flowering season: *A. japonica* will only flower outside or if allowed to grow mature in a conservatory. It carries clusters of white flowers in autumn and early winter. *A. elegantissima* is unlikely to flower.

Scent: None.

Light: Will survive in quite dark places away from natural light. *A. japonica* 'Variegata', and *A. elegantissima* require more light but not direct sunlight.

Temperature: *A. japonica* will survive a wide range of cool temperatures. 50-55°F (10-12°C) is ideal, but it will take a drop to nearly freezing. It dislikes temperatures above 65°F (18°C). *A. elegantissima* needs 60°F (15°C) in winter and a maximum of 70°F (21°C) in summer.

Water: Keep moist at all times during the summer with at least twice weekly watering. In the winter keep drier, watering only once a week, but never let the pot completely dry out.

Feeding: Add liquid food to the water every 14 days in the growing season.

Humidity: Both species appreciate daily overhead sprays of soft water. This is essential for *A. elegantissima*.

Cleaning: Only the leaves of *A. japonica* are large enough to sponge. A daily spray of water will keep *A. elegantissima* clean. Use leaf shine every 2 months for *A. japonica* but never for *A. elegantissima*.

Atmosphere: Both are tolerant. *A. japonica* likes good ventilation.

Soil: A good loam-based compost such as No. 2.

Repotting: In the spring at the start of the growing season. Do not use too large a pot.

Pruning: Cut back to size leggy plants or ungainly stems after repotting.

Propagation: Both *A. japonica* and *A. elegantissima* can be grown from seed in spring, or from cuttings. *A. japonica* 'variegata' can only be propagated by cuttings. *A. elegantissima* needs a temperature of 70°F (21°C); *A. japonica* needs 55°F (13°C).

Life expectancy: 3-4 years at least.

Plant companions: *A. japonica* is best grown as a single plant. *A. elegantissima* does better in a mixed grouping where humidity is higher e.g. with philodendrons, *Ficus*, and hederas.

Ease/difficulty: *A. japonica* is a very easy plant and should be on every beginner's list. *A. elegantissima* needs a little more attention.

Cleaning the leaves

Wipe dust off *A. japonica's* leaves with a soft cloth and sponge with tepid water, supporting leaf with other hand. Keep *A. elegantissima's* leaves clean with a daily spray of soft water.

Humidity

Aralia elegantissima needs a daily spray of soft water to provide humidity and keep the leaves clean.

Pruning a leggy plant

1 A plant that has grown leggy with long stems and widely spaced leaves needs pruning to regain its shape.

3 Dust with sulphur dust.

2 After repotting, cut stem right back, cutting just above a leaf stem or bud.

4 New shoots will grow to make a more vigorous, compact plant.

What goes wrong

A. elegantissima

1 *Leaves dry and brittle.* Too hot and dry. Move to cooler place, water and spray.

2 *Leaves droop.* Soil waterlogged. Allow to dry out until recovered. Then water less often.

3 *Leaves drop.* Too cold or too hot, with not enough humidity. Check temperature. Spray and provide extra humidity.

4 *Slow growth, small new leaves.* Needs feeding.

Leaves distorted and sticky, with green insects. Greenfly. Spray with pyrethrum or a systemic insecticide.

Aralia japonica

1 *Long, weak stems with gaps between leaves.* Too hot, not enough ventilation. Move to cooler, more airy place.

2 *Leaves pale.* Needs feeding.

3 *Leaves droop.* Too dry or too wet. Test compost and either water or allow to dry out.

4 *Whole plant flops, young leaves at top go black.* Frost. Plant will die.

Repotting

1 Repot in spring as the growing season starts and the pot begins to fill with roots. Water plant well.

2 Prepare pot 1 size larger with drainage layer and layer of damp, loam-based No. 2 compost.

3 Hold old pot with one hand covering compost, fingers either side of stem. Tap edge of pot. Plant and compost will come out.

4 Carefully remove stale soil from roots, using stick or pencil. Do not damage roots.

5 Place plant in centre of new pot, root-ball on compost.

6 Add new compost to fill pot. Make sure that all roots are covered. Press down well. Leave in the shade without water for 2 days to encourage roots to grow into compost.

Growing from seed

1 Prepare a seed tray or propagator with a drainage layer and sterilized, seed-growing compost. Scatter seeds evenly and add thin layer of compost, no thicker than depth of seed. Water well.

2 Cover with glass and put in dark place or cover with dark cloth. Make sure the compost never dries out and turn glass over daily. Keep warm.

3 When seeds germinate, bring them into light and remove the glass cover.

4 When seedlings are large enough to handle, thin out the weaker ones, leaving about 1in (2½cm) between each one.

5 When remaining ones are growing well, repot in separate small pots.

Stem tip cuttings

Aralia elegantissima can be propagated from stem cuttings. It needs a temperature of 70 F (21 C) and a propagator will give best results. If you have no propagator, try using a polythene bag cover.

1 Prepare pot with layer of drainage and mixture of ½ peat, ½ sharp sand.

2 Choose shoot or stem tip with at least 2 pairs of healthy leaves and a growing point. Cut off below second pair of leaves, close to main stem. Cuttings should be 3–4in (8–10cm) long.

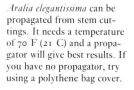

3 Prepare cuttings by trimming off stem just below a leaf.

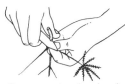

4 Remove the lowest pair of leaves.

5 Dip the cut surface in hormone rooting powder. Shake off the surplus.

6 Make small holes in compost around edge of pot and insert cuttings. Base of stem should rest on bottom of hole, lowest leaf level with the compost.

7 Water well and cover with polythene supported by wire. Remove cover for 5 minutes a day and never let compost dry out. Keep at 70°F (21°C). Remove cover after 21 days and when cuttings are growing well, repot in normal compost.

NORFOLK ISLAND PINE

Araucaria excelsa is an evergreen conifer, one of the few conifers which can be grown as a house plant. It is really a handsome, aristocratic plant which in its native habitat will grow up to 200 ft (60 m). Fortunately, it is a very slow grower and you would be lucky to get one reaching even to 5 ft (150 cm) indoors. It is commonly called the Norfolk Island pine, after the South Pacific Island where it was discovered in 1793. Its pine-like branches stick out horizontally from the stem rather like the cedar of Lebanon and it makes a very good table-top Christmas tree. However, don't dress it up with electric lights: they might burn the tender needles.

It is very much a specimen plant and, whatever its size, always looks at its best when grown alone. Placed alone it is also more likely to benefit from free circulation of air. They are not to be recommended for central heating, especially if the temperature is kept above 70°F (21°C), but are very suitable for a light, unheated room or a conservatory. If they are grown in too high a temperature they become weak and are likely to be attacked by mealy bug. An invasion of these tiny sucking insects can kill even a 6 ft (2 m) specimen.

A. excelsa has a very well known cousin which is often seen in old and well established gardens. This is *A. araucana*, the monkey puzzle tree, which comes from the mountains of Chile. Both species share the characteristic of shedding their lower branches as they mature but the foliage of *A. excelsa* is paler and softer in texture than that of its prickly relative.

Araucarias are becoming increasingly popular but are sometimes difficult to obtain. When choosing one, ensure that it has a good, rich green foliage, supple leaves and shows no sign of leaf drop on its lower branches. It is normal to buy the plant at 1 ft (30 cm) although seedlings can sometimes be obtained. Plants over 4 ft (120 cm) are very expensive.

Right: A young plant of *Araucaria excelsa*.

Left: The top branches, showing how they grow in tiers.

Below: Young foliage is pale green, deepening in colour as it matures.

Size: Usually bought at about 1 ft (30 cm) they will grow to about 5 ft (150 cm).

Growth: They grow very slowly, about 6 in (15 cm) or one layer of branches per year.

Flowering season: None.

Scent: None.

Light: They like a south facing window, but keep them away from the midday sun in summer. Will tolerate a fair amount of shade if moved from time to time to a lighter place.

Temperature: Almost hardy, in fact could be grown outdoors in warmer areas. Minimum winter temperature of about 40°F (5°C). Maximum summer temperature 55°F (13°C).

Water: Water twice a week during summer, just keep the soil damp in the winter, watering not more than once a week. Always use lime-free water.

Feeding: They like a dilute liquid feed every 14 days in the summer. Add half the recommended dose to the water.

Humidity: They appreciate a spray of lime-free water at least twice a week in summer, and once a week in winter if they are in a centrally heated room.

Cleaning: Unnecessary. Spraying for humidity is sufficient to clean the needles. Never use leaf shine.

Atmosphere: Tolerant of most things except icy draughts from open front doors and lack of ventilation.

Soil: Use a fairly rich compost, such as loam-based No. 2.

Repotting: Every other year when young. Once over 3 ft (1 m) leave in same pot and just change the topsoil.

Pruning: Not necessary, unless shedding from the lower branches becomes unsightly. In this case remove dead branches. Do not remove the growing point at the top.

Propagation: From seed in autumn or spring normally, at a temperature of 50–55°F (10–13°C). It is possible to root stem cuttings in a propagator with high humidity at a temperature of 60°F (18°C).

Life expectancy: With care, almost everlasting. Remember they grow to 200 ft (60 m) in their native habitat.

Plant companions: Best grown alone. However, older plants which have shed their lower branches may look more attractive with younger specimens of the same species placed in front.

Ease/difficulty: Very easy provided it is given a little care and attention and the winter temperature is not too high.

Repotting

1 Repot every other year in spring while the plant is young. Water well first.

2 Prepare pot 1 size larger with drainage layer and layer of damp, loam-based No. 2 compost.

3 Hold old pot with one hand covering compost, fingers either side of stem. Tap edge of pot. Plant and compost will come out.

4 Carefully remove stale soil from roots, using stick or pencil. Do not damage roots.

5 Place plant in centre of new pot, root-ball on compost.

6 Add new compost to fill pot. Make sure that all roots are covered. Press down well. Leave in the shade without water for 2 days to encourage roots to grow into compost.

What goes wrong

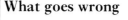

1 *Dry, yellow needles. Needles fall.* Too hot and dry with poor ventilation. Water and move to cooler, more airy room.

2 *Slow growth, pale colour.* Needs feeding.

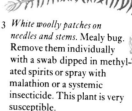

3 *White woolly patches on needles and stems.* Mealy bug. Remove them individually with a swab dipped in methylated spirits or spray with malathion or a systemic insecticide. This plant is very susceptible.

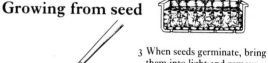

4 *Green insects and sticky coating on needles.* Greenfly. Spray with pyrethrum or a systemic insecticide.

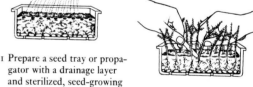

Growing from seed

3 When seeds germinate, bring them into light and remove the glass cover.

1 Prepare a seed tray or propagator with a drainage layer and sterilized, seed-growing compost. Scatter seeds evenly and add thin layer of compost, no thicker than depth of seed. Water well.

4 When seedlings are large enough to handle, thin out the weaker ones, leaving about 1in (2½cm) between each one.

2 Cover with glass and put in dark place or cover with dark cloth. Make sure the compost never dries out and turn glass over daily. Keep at 50–55°F (10–13°C).

5 When remaining ones are growing well, repot in separate small pots.

Replacing the topsoil

1 When plant is over 3ft (1m) tall, do not repot. Water, then remove top inch (2½cm) of old compost. Do not damage roots.

2 Add new compost to fill pot.

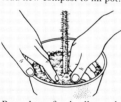

3 Press down firmly all round, making sure roots are all well covered.

4 Leave in shade without water for 2 days to encourage roots to grow into new compost.

Pruning

1 As araucarias grow older, the lower branches lose their needles and become bare and unsightly.

2 Cut the bare branch off cleanly, close to the main trunk. There should be no jagged end remaining. Dab the cut with sulphur to prevent any fungal infections.

3 If sap runs, use cotton wool dipped in vaseline to stop the 'bleeding'.

Spraying

Clean the leaves by spraying them all over with tepid water from a mist sprayer. Hold the spray about 6in (15cm) from leaves.

ASPARAGUS FERN

Most people refer to *Asparagus* as a fern but they are quite wrong. Though fern like, the leaves resemble needles and are known botanically as phyllocades. *Asparagus* is a genus of about a hundred species and belongs to the Lily family. They make handsome house plants, are easier to keep than most true ferns and are particularly suitable for growing in hanging baskets. They come from South Africa and were first collected at the end of the nineteenth century.

There are several commonly available varieties of *Asparagus*. *A. plumosus* has soft, feathery fronds like its relative the edible asparagus, *A. officinalis*, and both are prized for floral decoration. This plant grows in an upright shape and when the plant is young it looks rather sparse and twiggy. Fuller specimens make better plants and the dwarf, dense *A. plumosus* 'Nanus' is the form usually supplied.

A. sprengeri is the easiest variety to grow as a room plant and in the summer it will also grow outdoors. It makes a bushy plant with its fronds falling naturally and looks very well in window boxes or hanging baskets. The foliage is prickly. *A. sprengeri* 'Meyerii' is similar but the needles are soft, very close together and the fronds look rather like bottle brushes. It grows much more slowly but is a striking plant when mature.

Lastly, *A. falcatus* is a very hardy species with upright stems and foliage widely spread apart. It deserves to be more widely known and grown.

Buy asparagus ferns when the foliage is bushy, of a good colour and preferably when new growth is appearing. Beware of yellowing foliage.

Above: The bamboo-like foliage of *Asparagus falcatus*. Beware of the thorns on this species.

Below: *Asparagus meyerii* is slow growing. Here it is producing a young, pale frond.

Above: *Asparagus sprengeri* is an easy, bushy plant.

Right: *A. plumosus* has the most delicate foliage of all the species. Use it where you have difficulty growing true ferns.

Size: Usually grown in 3½in (8cm) to 5in (12cm) pots with fronds up to 18in (46cm) long or in hanging baskets of 12in (30cm) diameter.

Growth: If kept well watered one year old plants will produce 12 or more new fronds during the season.

Flowering season: They have insignificant white flowers but produce red berries which are quite attractive.

Scent: None.

Light: They will tolerate quite shady positions in the house. *A. sprengeri* can be grown outdoors in summer and this improves the colour of the foliage.

Temperature: Will take quite low temperatures in winter – down to 45°F (8°C). In summer a higher temperature of 55–60°F (12–15°C) is needed. They are unhappy above 70°F (21°C) unless the ventilation is excellent.

Water: In the summer water 2–3 times a week. They should never be allowed to dry out. Only water once a week in winter, less if the temperature is lower.

Feeding: Add half the recommended dose of liquid food to the water every 14 days in summer.

Humidity: Like most plants they enjoy an overhead spray, and flourish when interplanted with other plants in a bowl or trough which increases moisture around the foliage.

Cleaning: Overhead spraying is sufficient.

Leaf shine is obviously inappropriate.

Atmosphere: They tolerate most conditions.

Soil: Either loam- or peat-based composts, but not too strong in fertilizer, e.g. No. 1.

Repotting: They like to grow in small pots so wait until the roots come through the bottom of the pot before repotting. Clay pots are better for them than plastic.

Pruning: Apart from cutting out old or dead fronds, no other pruning is necessary. If the plant has been allowed to dry out all the top foliage can be cut off, the plant soaked and growth will start again.

Propagation: Preferably by seed sown in April. Propagation can also be by division of old plants into 5–6 small plants but these can be slow to grow.

Life expectancy: After 3 or 4 years the plants become less vigorous and look tired. It is therefore better to start again from seed. However, old plants will survive even if they do not look so good.

Plant companions: They grow and look well in mixed plantings because the foliage contrasts well with other plants, especially with broad-leaved species. Particularly useful for indoor troughs, tubs and window boxes.

Ease/difficulty: Easy plants for beginners provided they are not allowed to dry out.

Reviving a dried-up plant

1 If plant is very straggly or has dried out it can be revived quite easily.

3 Soak plant well in bucket of water, leaving it there until all air bubbles have stopped rising. Allow to drain.

2 Cut off all top foliage with sharp scissors, just above the compost.

4 Keep it cool (55°F, 13°C) until new shoots appear.

Spraying

Spray daily overhead with a fine mist spray, using rainwater if possible. Hold spray about 6in (15cm) from leaves.

1 *Leaves yellow and spines drop.* Too dry or too hot, and/or lack of food and light. Check compost, position and feeding.

2 *Leaves mottled with yellow, especially along veins; brown scaly insects on underside of leaves and on stems.* Scale insect. Remove them individually with a swab dipped in methylated spirits or spray with a systemic insecticide.

3 *Leaves yellowed and fall. Webs under leaves.* Red spider mite. Spray with derris, malathion or a systemic insecticide. Improve the humidity.

4 *Leaflets drop, if plant is outside.* Too cold, frost. Plant can be revived if brought into 55°F (13°C) and top growth cut off.

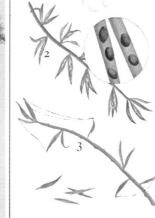

Growing from seed

Sow *Asparagus* seeds in spring.

1 Prepare a seed tray or propagator with a drainage layer and sterilized, seed-growing compost. Scatter seeds evenly and add thin layer of compost, no thicker than depth of seed. Water well.

2 Cover with glass and put in dark place or cover with dark cloth. Make sure the compost never dries out and turn glass over daily. Keep warm (60°F, 16°C).

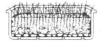

3 When seeds germinate, bring them into light and remove the glass cover.

4 When seedlings are large enough to handle, thin out the weaker ones, leaving about 1in (2½cm) between each one.

5 When remaining ones are growing well, repot in separate small pots.

Repotting

1 When roots show through pot and no new fronds appear, plants needs repotting. Water well.

4 Carefully remove stale soil from roots, using stick or pencil. Do not damage roots.

Watering

1 Test compost with fingers. If it is light and crumbly, the plant needs water.

2 Add water at top of pot, using rainwater if possible. Empty excess from saucer after 15 minutes.

Root division

1 Prepare 2 pots with drainage layer and compost.

2 Remove plant from pot and gently prise away compost.

3 Gently pull roots and stems apart with your hands.

4 Repot both sections in the usual way.

2 Prepare pot 1 size larger with drainage layer and layer of loam-based compost No.1.

3 Hold old pot with one hand covering compost, fingers either side of stems. Tap edge of pot. Plant and compost will come out.

5 Place plant in centre of new pot, root-ball on compost.

6 Add new compost to fill pot. Make sure that all roots are covered.

7 Press down well. Leave in the shade without water for 2 days to encourage roots to grow into new compost.

CAST IRON PLANT

The aspidistra was the joke of old time music halls and is even now often associated with dark, neglected rooms. But when well grown it is an elegant and beautiful room plant. Known as the cast iron plant because it is so easy to keep, it is currently enjoying great popularity along with cane furniture and other Victoriana.

Aspidistras are members of the Liliaceae family; there are four species known and they come from Himalaya, China and Japan. The only one in cultivation is *A. elatior* (or *lunida*) which was first found in China in 1822. There is a variegated variety which is a naturally occurring mutation but its variegation only appears when the plant is grown in poor soil and is rather pot-bound. It needs more light than its green counterpart. An *Aspidistra* flower is bright purple, fleshy and cupshaped. It very rarely appears and shows at ground level with hardly any stem. It only lasts a day or so.

The *Aspidistra* is a slow grower but an extremely tolerant plant which will suffer a lot of neglect and even positive ill-treatment. It will withstand gas fumes, cigar smoke, violent changes of temperature and even being abandoned during holiday periods. However, do not spray the foliage with leaf shine. These products are recommended for plants with thick, leathery leaves but, surprisingly, aspidistras dislike them.

As aspidistras are best grown as lone specimens it is appropriate to choose a plant for its shape and the elegance of its arched leaves. Avoid plants with split leaves or with leaf margins which have been trimmed back by the grower. Plants with speckled leaves of a poor colour may be infected with red spider mite.

Left: *Aspidistra* flowers are rare, appearing at ground level.

Right: A large plant of *Aspidistra elatior*. After another growing season this plant could be divided.

Below: *Aspidistra elatior* 'Variegata' needs less food and more light than the green form, to retain its variegation.

Size: Leaves are about 12-18 in (30-46 cm) depending on the variety. A lot of leaves can be contained in a 5 in (12 cm) pot as the plant does better if pot-bound.

Growth: Four or five leaves per year.

Flowering season: The flowers appear irregularly, normally in the summer months.

Scent: None.

Light: They will survive in dark places. The leaves scorch in the full sun.

Temperature: 50-60°F (10-15°C) is best, but they will survive in much lower temperatures provided they are kept frost-free.

Water: Keep well watered (twice a week) during the summer. In the winter water not more than once a week.

Feeding: It is easy to overdo feeding. Add liquid food to the water once every month or two in summer but do not feed the variegated variety. If the leaves split, stop feeding altogether that season.

Humidity: They appreciate and respond to overhead spraying with soft water once a week but will tolerate dry air.

Cleaning: Sponge the leaves with soft water whenever they appear dusty. Never use leaf shine.

Atmosphere: Will survive any atmosphere that is not directly poisonous to human beings.

Soil: For normal repotting use loam-based compost No. 2. However if you have a variegated plant use seed compost.

Repotting: Should be done not more than every 2-3 years. If left, the plant will show it needs repotting by breaking its pot. As a member of the Lily family, the *Aspidistra* has rhizomes. When repotting make sure these are buried completely under the compost and not left half in, half out.

Pruning: None necessary.

Propagation: By division of old plants in spring.

Life expectancy: One of the longest lived house plants.

Plant companions: Normally grown alone as a specimen plant, especially if you are trying to create a Victorian atmosphere. However, they do well in mixed arrangements of moisture-loving plants.

Ease/difficulty: The easiest of all houseplants.

Root division

Divide large, old plants in early spring.

1 Prepare 2 pots with drainage layer and compost.

3 Gently pull roots and stems apart with your hands.

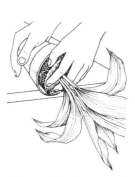

2 Remove plant from pot and gently prise away compost.

4 Repot both sections in the usual way.

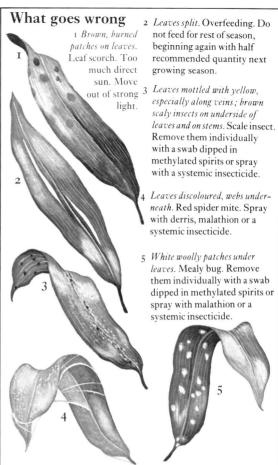

1 *Brown, burned patches on leaves.* Leaf scorch. Too much direct sun. Move out of strong light.

2 *Leaves split.* Overfeeding. Do not feed for rest of season, beginning again with half recommended quantity next growing season.

3 *Leaves mottled with yellow, especially along veins; brown scaly insects on underside of leaves and on stems.* Scale insect. Remove them individually with a swab dipped in methylated spirits or spray with a systemic insecticide.

4 *Leaves discoloured, webs underneath.* Red spider mite. Spray with derris, malathion or a systemic insecticide.

5 *White woolly patches under leaves.* Mealy bug. Remove them individually with a swab dipped in methylated spirits or spray with malathion or a systemic insecticide.

Watering

1 Test compost with fingers. If it is light and crumbly, the plant needs water.

2 Add water at top of pot, using rainwater if possible. Empty excess from saucer after 15 minutes.

Cleaning and spraying

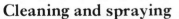
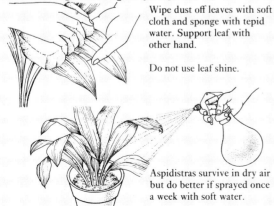

Wipe dust off leaves with soft cloth and sponge with tepid water. Support leaf with other hand.

Do not use leaf shine.

Aspidistras survive in dry air but do better if sprayed once a week with soft water.

Repotting

1 Repot only once every 2–3 years. If left in the same pot the strong roots may crack the pot open. Water well.

2 Prepare pot 1 size larger with drainage layer and layer of damp, loam-based No. 2 compost.

4 Carefully remove stale soil from roots, using stick or pencil. Do not damage roots.

6 Add new compost to fill pot. Make sure that all roots are covered.

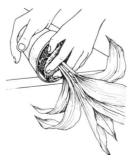
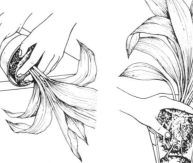

3 Hold old pot with one hand covering compost, fingers either side of stems. Tap edge of pot. Plant and compost will come out.

5 Place plant in centre of new pot, root-ball on compost.

7 Press down well. Leave in the shade without water for 2 days to encourage roots to grow into new compost.

BIRD'S NEST FERN

The aspleniums form a large family of ferns (Aspleniaceae) numbering nearly seven hundred species. They are found all over the world from tropical Africa to temperate New Zealand. The name is derived from the Greek and means 'spleen medicine' as fibre from the plant was used in herbal remedies years ago.

There are two varieties which make attractive and interesting room plants. They are also particularly suitable for bottle gardens and fern cases and for the damp conditions of bathrooms. The first is *Asplenium nidus avis*, the bird's nest fern – the reason for the common name is obvious when you look at the leaf formation. The leaves are bright green, somewhat leathery in texture and have a raised, brown vein along the centre which is especially well developed towards the base and on the back of the leaves. The species is an epiphyte and comes from northern Australia where the leaves can grow to nearly 5 ft (150 cm).

The other *Asplenium* grown indoors is *A. bulbiferum*, not quite so attractive but equally interesting. This plant comes from New Zealand and the foothills of India. It is known as the mother spleenwort, for young plantlets appear on the edge of adult fronds. These can easily be detached and will soon grow if planted in a sandy compost.

Like all ferns, aspleniums require a damp, partly shady position. *A. nidus avis* looks superb in dappled shade where light can shine through its light green leaves.

Choose plants with fresh rather than tired foliage and avoid those with malformed leaves or browned tips.

Asplenium bulbiferum produces new plantlets on its fronds (above). An attractive plant (below), it will tolerate low temperatures.

Asplenium nidus avis (above and right) produces young fronds from its centre. In nature it lives on trees as an epiphyte, collecting water and food in its central funnel.

Size: The fronds grow up to 2 ft (60 cm) long and 8 in (20 cm) wide, although most plants are sold at about half this size. The plants stay smaller if restricted to small pots.
Growth: They grow fairly quickly. Plants will reach adult size in one season.
Flowering season: None.
Scent: None.
Light: They like a semi-shaded position. *A. nidus avis* will stand full sun, but the leaves go pale and lose their brightness.
Temperature: Fairly tolerant. An average winter temperature of 60°F (15°C) is ideal. *A. bulbiferum* is almost hardy and will tolerate 34°F (1°C). In summer *A. nidus avis* should not be kept at more than 70–75°F (21–24°C), *A. bulbiferum* not more than 64°F (18°C).
Water: Keep damp at all times unless the temperature drops below about 50°F (10°C) in winter. This will probably mean watering once or twice a week. In cool temperatures keep drier, watering once every 7–10 days.
Feeding: Add half the recommended dose of liquid food to the water in the summer months.
Humidity: They both appreciate the damp atmosphere associated with ferns. If grown as specimens, stand pot on saucer full of damp stones to increase the local humidity.
Cleaning: Spraying of the foliage with lime-free water is sufficient. Do this daily if possible. Never spray ferns with leaf shine. *A. nidus avis* has a very bad reaction to this

and will become blackened.
Atmosphere: They are tolerant of most conditions except cold draughts in winter. They dislike being moved around.
Soil: Peat-based composts are best for these ferns.
Repotting: Should be done once a year only, preferably in spring. Avoid pressing down the compost too firmly in the pot.
Pruning: Except for cutting out damaged or dried fronds, none.
Propagation: *A. nidus avis* by spores from the undersides of the fronds. This is really a specialist's job. *A. bulbiferum* is much easier and can be propagated by the novice. Young plantlets form at the edge of the fronds. These should be detached and potted up into a mixture of sharp sand and peat, preferably in the spring.
Life expectancy: They are long lived but if after a few years they begin to look down at heart, start again with plantlets or new stock.
Plant companions: *A. nidus avis* is a good plant to grow in mixed tubs and troughs where it appears to enjoy the humidity of other plants. Its light green colour and shuttlecock shape contrast excellently with other plants. *A. bulbiferum* is a loner, and it is better to grow this by itself.
Ease/difficulty: Neither is difficult. *A. bulbiferum* is the easier of the two.

Humidity

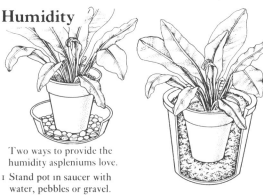

Two ways to provide the humidity aspleniums love.

1 Stand pot in saucer with water, pebbles or gravel. Make sure pot base is clear of water.

2 Put pot in outer container packed with damp peat.

Spraying

Spray daily overhead with a fine mist spray, using lime-free or rainwater. Hold spray about 6in (15cm) from the leaves.

What goes wrong

1 *Leaves pale.* Too much sun. Move out of direct light. Or needs feeding.

2 *Brown patches on leaves, starting at tips.* Too cold. Move to warmer position out of draughts.

3 *Leaf edges black, leaves shrivel.* Too hot. Move to cooler place and provide humidity.

4 *Leaves dull and lifeless.* Too dry or poor ventilation. Check compost for dryness and move to more airy position.

5 *Leaves mottled with yellow, especially along veins; brown scaly insects on underside of leaves and on stems.* Scale insect. Remove them individually with a swab dipped in methylated spirits or spray with a systemic insecticide.

Making a fern garden

Aspleniums grow well when planted together or with other ferns in a larger container.

1 Prepare container with a layer of drainage and layer of damp, peat-based compost. If there is no drainage hole, add some charcoal and sphagnum moss. The moss will soak up excess moisture and the charcoal will prevent water from becoming stagnant.

2 Knock plants from pots and remove stale soil from roots.

3 Place first fern in container. Add compost to cover roots.

4 Arrange other plants around it, leaving space for growth.

5 Add compost to cover roots and hold them upright but do not press it down too firmly.

6 Leave in the shade without water for 2 days.

Repotting

1 Repot in spring. If plant looks top-heavy and only small new leaves appear, plant needs repotting. Water plant well.

2 Prepare pot 1 size larger with drainage layer and layer of damp, peat-based compost.

3 Hold old pot with one hand covering compost, fingers either side of stems. Tap edge of pot. Plant and compost will come out.

4 Carefully remove stale soil from roots, using stick or pencil. Do not damage roots.

5 Place plant in centre of new pot, root-ball on compost.

6 Add new compost to fill pot. Make sure that all the roots are covered but do not press it down too hard. Leave the plant in the shade without water for 2 days to encourage roots to grow into compost.

Propagation: plantlets

1 The plantlets which appear on the fronds of *A. bulbiferum* will grow into new plants.

2 Prepare small pot with layer of drainage and damp compost made of ½ sharp sand, ½ peat. Make hole in top with stick or pencil.

3 Choose a well developed plantlet. Pull it gently away with your fingers and place in in prepared pot. Press compost lightly around it.

AZALEA

Azaleas are perhaps the most sophisticated of the winter-flowering plants that can be brought indoors. The plants we buy at Christmas time are usually called *Azalea indica* although their correct name is *Rhododendron simsii*. They come from China and were first collected in 1708. Like other azaleas they are members of the Rhododendron family which includes some five hundred known species spread across Europe, Asia, North America and Australia. With care they can be kept indoors for some time but they need a humid atmosphere and will soon drop their leaves if they are not sprayed with lime-free water at least once a day.

Most plants are raised in areas with rich, peaty soil which suits their culture. They flower naturally in spring but are usually forced into bloom for Christmas and during the early months of the year. They are not hardy and cannot be grown permanently in the garden if there is any danger of frost. However, they must be planted out of doors during the summer months if there is to be any chance of keeping them from year to year. They are very slow growing plants and this is why they are usually expensive. The larger plants can be clipped to all sorts of shapes – pyramids, standards and half standards are quite often available.

The other variety grown as an indoor plant is *A. japonica* or *Rhododendron obtusum*. This is a rather spindly plant with sparse leaves but it has beautifully delicate flowers in soft pastel colours. It is slightly hardier than its more flamboyant cousin *A. indica*. *A japonica* is not so easy to force into flower as *A. indica* and is not normally available in the shops until nearer its natural flowering time, from February onwards. Some varieties are hardy and can be grown outdoors even in cooler climates.

Choose well-budded azaleas of an even shape, with flowers about to open. Make sure that the leaves are not dropping off.

Left: The flowers of *Azalea indica* are available in both deep and pastel colours.

Right: A young, well-budded plant of *Azalea indica*.

Below: *Azalea obtusum* is available in pastel shades. It may survive winters outside in sheltered areas if planted out in May.

Size: Plants are normally sold from 5–15 in (12–38 cm) diameter across the flower head on a stem from 3–12 in (7–30 cm). Specimen plants can be much bigger, particularly the trained pyramids and standards.
Growth: Very slow, the smallest plants sold are at least two years old.
Flowering Season: Naturally in April/May but can be forced from autumn onwards.
Scent: None, although perfumed azaleas are common in the garden varieties.
Light: A good light position not in sun.
Temperature: In the winter 55°F (13°C) is ideal. In a room hotter than this azaleas tend to dry out and the flowers die quickly.
Water: When in flower they need a lot of lime-free water, usually every second day. A plant should never dry out and should be checked at least twice a week. If it becomes too dry plunge into a bucket of tepid water until the bubbles stop rising from the pot.
Feeding: Add liquid food to the water when in flower and when growing in the summer about every 14 days. Use lime-free water.
Humidity: Spray at least once a day overhead with lime-free water, and stand pot on a saucer of wet pebbles.
Cleaning: Azaleas often need grooming by

having dead and dropped leaves removed. Never use leaf shine.
Atmosphere: For a short time they will stand most things. Avoid severe draughts, especially when they have just been watered.
Soil: A good proprietary peat compost. If you want to mix it yourself, use equal parts of peat, leaf mould and sharp sand with a sprinkling of fertilizer.
Repotting: After the summer resting period is the time to repot. However, it is better to keep the plants in smaller pots and to feed them well. Clay pots are better than plastic, although they take more water.
Pruning: Only necessary to keep plant in good shape. Remove lanky stems and green shoots that appear among the flower buds.
Propagation: By stem tip cuttings, but this is best left to the experts.
Life expectancy: Many seasons if carefully planted out in summer.
Plant companions: Small azaleas look well in mixed bowls, but the larger plants are better displayed as specimens.
Ease/difficulty: In an unheated greenhouse it is easy to grow, but it is difficult to keep long in the house as it misses the essential humidity and most houses are kept too warm. If possible return to the greenhouse as soon as the flowers start to wilt.

Planting out

1 After flowering, pick off dead flowers and put plant in cool, frost-free place. Water only once a week.

2 In early June, dig a hole in the garden in a place shaded from direct afternoon sun. The hole should be large enough to take plant and pot together. Plunge pot and plant into hole and cover with soil.

3 Water every other day and spray overhead when it is very hot.

4 In early September, dig up plant and pot. If roots are growing out of pot, repot. If not, replace the topsoil.

5 Remove dead leaves and twigs.

6 Place in cool room until flower buds begin to open.

What goes wrong

1 *Leaves dry and fall.* Too hot and dry. Spray with lime-free water. Water regularly and move to cooler place.

2 *Flowers fail to open.* Plant waterlogged or standing in a draught after watering. Allow to dry out in draught free place until recovered. Then water less often.

3 *Yellow speckling on leaves with webs underneath.* Red spider mite. Spray with derris, malathion or a systemic insecticide. Improve the humidity.

4 *White tunnels and markings on leaves, sometimes caterpillars.* Azalea leaf miner. Spray with malathion.

5 *New leaves small, no flowers.* Needs feeding.

Repotting

1 Inspect the plant when you bring it indoors after the summer. If it looks top-heavy and roots are growing through the pot, it needs repotting.

2 Prepare clay pot 1 size larger with drainage and layer of peat-based, lime-free compost. Water plant.

3 Hold old pot with one hand covering compost, fingers either side of stems. Tap edge of pot. Plant and compost will come out.

4 Carefully remove stale soil from roots, using stick or pencil. Do not damage roots.

5 Place plant in centre of new pot, root-ball on compost.

6 Add new compost to fill pot. Make sure that all roots are covered.

7 Press down well. Leave in the shade without water for 2 days to encourage roots to grow into new compost.

Watering

1 Test compost. If it feels light and crumbly, add water.

2 Place plant in bucket and fill bucket with water to just below the rim of the pot. Leave for 15 minutes then allow it to drain.

Pruning

1 An overgrown, untidy plant needs pruning to shape.

2 Make cuts with secateurs just above a bud or side shoot, cutting at an angle.

3 The plant will grow into a more even, bushy shape.

4 If you are training plant as a standard, remove side stems that grow low down as they appear.

FOLIAGE BEGONIAS

Begonia is a genus of some nine hundred species of the family Begoniaceae from which a multitude of hybrids have been raised for indoor use. They are native to most tropical and subtropical countries and were named after a French amateur botanist Michel Begon who was at one time Governor of Canada.

The genus is divided into three main types: tuberous rooted, fibrous rooted and rhizomatous. *B. rex* is rhizomatous. It was introduced from Assam in 1858 and many varieties were developed for Victorian collectors by the famous nineteenth-century nurseryman James Veitch. From the names of varieties such as 'König Heinrich' and 'Isolde', it seems likely that a number were also bred in Germany.

B. rex is grown solely for its beautifully coloured and shaped leaves and nearly all its varieties have multicoloured leaves with delicate patterns. *B. masoniana*, another rhizomatous species, is known as Iron Cross because of the black markings on its bright green leaves which strongly resemble the shape of the German war medal. It was introduced from Malaya in the late 1940s and named after Maurice Mason, a well known collector. *B. masoniana* is a little more delicate than *B. rex* but needs the same basic care. Both are good room plants but can also be used in greenhouses as ground cover plants under the staging, for they flourish in very shady positions.

Buy begonias with undamaged leaves and signs of new growth. Examine them to ensure there is no rot or browned patches on the stems and leaves. Choose the plant for the appeal of its leaf as these markings will be retained if you propagate by leaf cuttings or root division.

Above, right and below: leaf markings of *Begonia rex* vary considerably. Healthy leaves have a lustrous sheen.

Above: The leaves of *Begonia masoniana* 'Iron Cross' are hairy. Never try to clean them.

Size: They do not grow very large indoors, reaching 12in (30cm) and spreading to 18in (46cm) at the most. *B. masoniana* grows to about 9in (23cm).

Growth: About 5 to 6 new leaves a year indoors.

Flowering season: Summer. The plant produces small pale pink flowers but to improve the leaves, remove flowers as soon as they appear.

Scent: Very faint, if flowers are allowed to appear.

Light: Keep in a good, light position but out of direct sunlight. Do not place in a window unless it faces due north.

Temperature: A minimum of 55°F (13°C) in winter and 60°F (15°C) in summer. *B. masoniana* likes a slightly higher temperature in winter and should not be kept in rooms at less than 60°F (16°C). Providing the air is not too dry, they are unlikely to get too hot in temperate climates.

Water: Water twice a week in summer with lime-free water. In winter keep the compost just moist, watering probably once every 10 days. Keep water off the leaves.

Feeding: Add liquid food to the water every 2 weeks from April to September.

Humidity: Keep humid in warm weather either by spraying or by placing the pot on damp pebbles or peat. In cold weather too much humidity can cause stem rot.

Cleaning: Unnecessary. Never use leaf shine.

Atmosphere: They enjoy movement of air but not draughts and will deteriorate if left in an airless room. Gas fumes will kill them.

Soil: They like a light, open mixture. The proprietary peat composts are suitable or a compost of two parts of loam and two of peat to one part of leaf mould and one of sharp sand.

Repotting: They grow well in small pots but when they are very pot-bound they can be repotted in spring into a slightly larger size. Avoid damaging the delicate leaves.

Pruning: Not necessary.

Propagation: By leaf cuttings in late spring. Keep cuttings at 70°F (21°C), in a propagator if possible.

Life expectancy: Plants tend to get damaged and sometimes rather gnarled in the home and seldom last more than about 2 years. They live longer in a greenhouse.

Plant companions: They do well in mixed bowls and will adapt to most other plants. Peperomias, hederas and small palms such as *Chamaedorea* all grow well with begonias.

Ease/difficulty: Relatively easy plants which grow well if given the right care and attention. Avoid direct light and draughts. The leaves are extremely fragile so great care must be taken when moving them.

Propagation: Leaf cuttings 1

1 Prepare a seed tray or propagator with layer of drainage, layer of compost and ½in (1cm) of sharp sand.

2 Choose a healthy leaf and cut it off at base.

3 Lay leaf upside down on a hard surface and trim off edges all round.

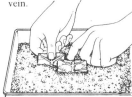

4 Cut trimmed leaf into 2in (5cm) squares. Each square must include part of a main vein.

5 Insert each cut section half into the sand. The part covered must be the part of the leaf that was closest to the stem of the original leaf.

6 Water well and keep warm (70 F, 21 C). Cover with polythene and keep moist. Remove cover for 5 minutes a day. New plantlets will grow from cut sections.

7 When the new plants have 2 or 3 new leaves, lift them from the compost and pull them gently away from the old leaf section. Pot separately in small pots.

1 *Leaves curl and dry at edges.* Too hot and dry. Water and move to cooler place.

2 *Leaf drop in winter.* Too cold. Move to warmer place.

3 *Plant droops, leaves limp.* Gas fumes. These will kill the plant. Move to fume-free room at once.

4 *New leaves small.* Needs food.

5 *Leaves dull, webs underneath.* Red spider mite. Spray with derris, malathion or a systemic insecticide.

6 *Stem and crown rotting at base of plant.* Too wet. Allow to dry out until recovered. Water less frequently.

7 *Leaves discoloured, swellings on roots.* Eel worms. No cure. Destroy plant.

8 *Greyish brown powdery blotches on leaves and flowers.* Grey mould. Spray with benomyl-based fungicide and keep plant in drier, more airy place.

9 *White powdery patches on leaves and stems.* Powdery mildew. Spray with benomyl-based fungicide and keep plant in drier, more airy place.

10 *Yellow rings and mottling on distorted leaves.* Cucumber mosaic virus. No cure. Destroy plant immediately.

11 *Roots black and rotting.* Black root rot. Spray with benomyl-based fungicide. Caused by overwatering.

Repotting

1 Repot in spring. If plant looks top-heavy with only small new leaves and roots growing out of pot at base, it needs a larger pot.

2 Prepare pot 1 size larger with drainage layer and layer of damp, peat-based compost.

3 Hold old pot with one hand covering compost, fingers either side of stems. Tap edge of pot. Plant and compost will come out.

4 Carefully remove stale soil from roots, using stick or pencil. Do not damage roots.

5 Place plant in centre of new pot, root-ball on compost.

6 Add new compost to fill pot. Make sure that all roots are covered. Press down well. Leave in the shade without water for 2 days to encourage roots to grow into compost.

Propagation : Leaf cuttings 2

1 Leaf cuttings can also be taken using complete leaves. Lay leaf upside down on hard surface and cut the thick veins below vein junctions.

2 Lift leaf carefully and lay face upwards on the sand. Peg it down in several places with wire. Make sure veins touch sand closely.

3 Water well and keep at 70°F (21°C). Cover with glass or polythene and never let the compost dry out. New plants will grow from cut veins.

4 When new plants have 2 or 3 new leaves lift them from the sand, pull them gently away from old leaf and pot them separately in small pots.

Removing flowers

Small flowers may appear in the summer. Pinch them out to improve leaf growth.

Humidity

Stand pot in saucer with water, pebbles or gravel. Make sure pot base is clear of water.

FLOWERING BEGONIAS

The majority of the flowering begonias are tuberous and fibrous rooted. For years at Christmas time we have been delighted by the fibrous rooted *'Gloire de Lorraine'* varieties and their successors. They are beautiful plants some 15 in (38 cm) tall with a mass of small pink and white flowers, surrounded by a collar of glossy green foliage. Over recent years the *Schwabenland* hybrids (also fibrous rooted) have been introduced. These flower practically all the year round and make excellent room plants.

Many of the tuberous begonias (*Begonia* x *tuberhybrida*) are only suitable for summer display outdoors but the *semperflorens* varieties, although also used as summer bedding, make good room plants. They are compact and go on flowering the whole summer.

Lastly there are the shrubby begonias which are now rather collectors' items. They have large, heart-shaped leaves and in summer produce clusters of soft pink flowers. *B. haageana* has green, hairy leaves which are purplish underneath; *B. coccinea* 'President Carnot' has silver spotted leaves and *B. metallica* has smaller leaves marked with silver hairs. They are beautiful plants but because they are difficult to market commercially they are not widely available. Though not often seen in the shops, the shrubby species tend to have a cult interest and are passed as cuttings from friend to friend. The cuttings can often be rooted successfully in water.

Begonias are very susceptible to fungal disease because their succulent stems contain a very high proportion of water. If they are kept for a second year it is best to spray *'Lorraine'* and *'Schwabenland'* types with a benomyl-based fungicide regularly before they come into flower. It is a good idea to take cuttings and have a stream of young plants coming along to replace victims of fungal disease.

The *Schwabenland* hybrid begonias are available throughout the year and come in a variety of colours.

All parts of these plants are fleshy and easily damaged so care is needed to prevent damage and infection by rot.

Size: They vary from 2–3 in (5–8 cm) up to 18 in (46 cm). Some of the shrubby species can grow to 6 ft (2 m) and usually need staking as they grow bigger.

Growth: All varieties grow quickly. Whether from cuttings or seed, they often come into flower the same season.

Flowering season: Once they have reached flowering size they all tend to flower more or less continuously. The shrubby types are mostly summer flowering.

Scent: None.

Light: They need and enjoy plenty of light but not direct sun. Do not leave water on the leaves when in sun; scorching could result.

Temperature: A minimum winter temperature of 60°F (15°C) will suit most. Keep at 65°F (18°C) in the summer. They dislike temperatures over 70°F (21°C).

Water: Water once or twice a week in summer but take care not to overwater in winter for if the temperature drops too low they can rot. Water every 10 days will probably suffice.

Feeding: Add liquid food to the water once a month when the plants are in flower.

Humidity: They will stand normal room humidity although they appreciate standing on dampened stones. Spray once a week but do not spray the flowers or they will mark and rot.

Cleaning: Unnecessary. The leaves are too brittle, succulent or furry to take cleaning.

Atmosphere: They don't like living in a closed room without any movement of air. Stagnant air will encourage fungal disease very quickly. Avoid gas fumes.

Soil: Loam-based compost No. 2.

Repotting: Once in flower, repot only once. Use care as most species have delicate, succulent stems.

Pruning: If the plant gets too straggly cut down to about 1½ in (4 cm) above the pot and it will regrow.

Propagation: Mostly from seed in spring although leaf and stem tip cuttings root easily in spring and summer. Keep cuttings at a temperature of 70°F (21°C).

Life expectancy: About a year is a good average although many will live longer. *Begonia semperflorens* should be treated as an annual.

Plant companions: Smaller plants can be used in mixed bowls. Larger varieties such as *Schwabenland* and the large-flowered tuberous varieties are best grown on their own.

Ease/difficulty: All are really quite easy provided they are in airy conditions.

Repotting

1 Most begonias have delicate, succulent stems, so take care. Repot only once after they have reached flowering size.

2 Prepare pot 1 size larger with drainage layer and layer of damp, loam-based compost No. 2. Water plant well.

3 Hold old pot with one hand covering compost, fingers either side of stems. Tap edge of pot. Plant and compost will come out.

4 Carefully remove stale soil from roots, using stick or pencil. Do not damage roots.

5 Place plant in centre of new pot, root-ball on compost.

6 Add new compost to fill pot. Make sure that all the roots are covered but do not press it down too hard. Leave the plant in the shade without water for 2 days to encourage roots to grow into compost.

What goes wrong

1 *No flowers, new leaves small.* Needs feeding.

2 *Leaves dry and droopy.* Too hot and dry. Water and move to a cooler room.

3 *Leaves yellowed and limp.* Too cold and wet. Allow to dry out until recovered and then keep in warmer room.

4 *Small blister-like spots which join up. Leaf turns black.* Bacterial wilt. Spray with a systemic fungicide.

5 *Soft, white patches on leaves.* Mildew. Spray with a systemic fungicide.

6 *Brown/black patches on leaves with rotting.* Botrytis. Plant too wet and not airy enough. Spray with benomyl-based fungicide. Keep plant drier and in a better ventilated room.

7 *Yellow rings or mottling on leaves.* Cucumber mosaic or tomato spotted wilt virus. No cure, destroy plant.

8 *Rot at base of stems.* Over-watering. Allow to dry out until recovered. Then water less often.

9 *Rot on leaves, flowers or buds.* Overhead spraying. Do not spray.

Stem cuttings

1 In spring plant produces new shoots which can be used for cuttings. Prepare small pot with drainage layer and mixture of sharp sand and loam-based compost.

2 Choose shoot or stem tip with at least 2 pairs of healthy leaves and a growing point. Cut off below second pair of leaves, close to main stem. Cuttings should be 3–4in (8–10cm) long.

3 Prepare cuttings by trimming off stem just below a leaf.

4 Remove the lowest pair of leaves.

5 Dip the cut surface in hormone rooting powder. Shake off the surplus.

6 Make hole in compost with stick or pencil. Insert cutting so that end of stem is at bottom of hole and leaves are level with compost.

7 Water well and cover with polythene supported by wire. Remove cover for 5 minutes a day and never let compost dry out. Keep at 70°F (21°C). Remove cover after 21 days and when cutting is growing well, repot in normal compost.

Growing from seed

1 Prepare a seed tray or propagator with a drainage layer and sterilized, seed-growing compost. Scatter seeds evenly and add thin layer of compost, no thicker than depth of seed. Water well.

2 Cover with glass and put in dark place or cover with dark cloth. Make sure the compost never dries out and turn glass over daily. Keep warm (70°F, 21°C).

3 When seeds germinate, bring them into light and remove the glass cover.

4 When seedlings are large enough to handle, thin out the weaker ones, leaving about 1in (2½cm) between each one.

5 When remaining ones are growing well, repot in separate small pots.

43

Beloperone guttata

SHRIMP PLANT

This plant is one of sixty tropical evergreen shrubs from central America that belong to the family Acanthaceae. The name comes from the Greek *belos* an arrow and *perone* a bond, and refers to the arrow shape of the leaves as they emerge from the stems. Only one species is commonly grown as a house plant. This is *B. guttata* which comes from Mexico and was introduced as recently as 1936. It is a good house plant which likes plenty of light, will tolerate full sun and enjoys the company of other plants. It is commonly known as the shrimp plant because the dull pink bracts that shield the white flowers resemble a shrimp's body. The flowers are produced fairly continuously during the summer months. When not in flower in winter it is a fairly uninteresting plant and will benefit from a resting period in a cool room. During this season it may well drop its leaves. Don't worry, this is quite natural.

There is also a variety with yellow bracts but this is rare and difficult to obtain. Sometimes leggy plants with pale leaves, long spaces between the leaves and pale yellow flowers are marketed. This is not the yellow variety (*B. lutea*), but a poorly grown plant. Its flowers have never produced the usual brick red coloured bracts because of poor light conditions. *Pachystachys lutea* (see page 136) is very similar in appearance to *Beloperone* and is sometimes popularly known as the yellow shrimp plant.

Buy plants which have a good rich colour to their bracts and are of a compact size and shape. Plants should not have blackened bracts or yellowed and dropping leaves or any trace of mildew in the centre. You will sometimes find the plant marketed under the name *Drejerella guttata*.

Above: The yellow form of *Beloperone guttata*.

Left: The true flower of the shrimp plant is white and emerges from the coloured bracts. It is the shape of the bracts which give the plant its common name.

Right: A well grown, compact plant of *Beloperone guttata*.

Size: They are best grown as small plants some 5–6 in (12–15 cm) tall and 4–5 in (10–12 cm) across. They look untidy if allowed to grow too tall.

Growth: A slow grower, producing 3–4 in (8–10 cm) a year. Shorter plants flower better.

Flowering season: All through the summer.

Scent: None.

Light: Will take plenty of light including full sun in summer to encourage good colour in the bracts. When resting in winter, place away from the window.

Temperature: Normal room temperature in summer but not above 75°F (24°C). They are better kept cooler in winter when resting: 45°F (7°C) is sufficient.

Water: They like to be kept very moist during the summer but it is essential that the plant drains well so that the compost does not become waterlogged. Water once or twice a week. In the winter keep compost just moist, watering once every 14 days, but never allow to dry out.

Feeding: Add liquid food to the water every 21 days in summer and not at all in winter.

Humidity: They enjoy standing on damp pebbles or in a dish full of damp peat. Never spray overhead when in flower, as this will cause the bracts to rot.

Cleaning: Unnecessary. Remove spent bracts. Do not use leaf shine.

Atmosphere: Will stand most atmospheres. They enjoy good ventilation.

Soil: A good loam-based compost such as No. 2 is suitable.

Repotting: Adult plants require repotting every spring, normally to replace the spent soil rather than to enlarge the pot size. Always make sure the drainage is good.

Pruning: Clip back into a neat shape in spring or, if very straggly, cut right down to 1–2 in (2½–5 cm) and allow the plant to start again.

Propagation: Take young cuttings in spring when they are about 3–4 in (8–10 cm) long and pot into sharp sand with a little peat added. Place in a propagator or cover with a polythene bag and keep at 64–70°F (18–21°C) until rooted. Then pot them 5 to a 3½ in (9 cm) pot and, as they grow, pinch out each growing tip to encourage bushiness.

Life expectancy: They will survive for a long time but, as with many small shrubby plants, it is better to restock with young cuttings taken every other year.

Plant companions: They like the company of other plants and do well in mixed bowls provided these can be placed in a light position. Lack of light can result in the bracts going a little pale.

Ease/difficulty: A good plant for a person who has got over the first stages of indoor gardening. It is not really challenging to maintain but demands a little skill to keep it in tip-top condition.

Stem tip cuttings

1 Take cuttings from stems 3–4 in (8–10 cm) long in spring. Prepare small pot with drainage layer and mixture of sharp sand and a little peat.

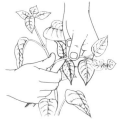

2 Choose shoot or stem tip with at least 2 pairs of healthy leaves and a growing point. Cut off below second pair of leaves, close to main stem.

3 Prepare cuttings by trimming off stem just below a leaf.

4 Remove the lowest pair of leaves.

5 Dip the cut surface in hormone rooting powder. Shake off the surplus.

6 Make small holes in compost around edge with stick or pencil.

What goes wrong

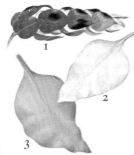

1 *Bracts turn black.* Caused by overhead spraying. Pick off blackened bracts.

2 *Leaves yellow.* Too much water. Allow to dry out until recovered. Then water less often.

3 *Leaves drop.* Too dry or, in winter, too cold. Test compost and water if dry. If damp, move plant to warmer place.

4 *Leaves pale.* Needs feeding.

5 *Bracts pale.* Needs more light. Move to lighter place but not into direct sunlight.

6 *Leaves yellowed with webs underneath.* Red spider mite. Spray with derris, malathion or a systemic insecticide. Improve the humidity.

7 *Leaves distorted and sticky, with green insects.* Greenfly. Spray with pyrethrum or a systemic insecticide.

8 *Lanky growth.* Too hot. Move to a cooler place.

Pruning for shape

7 Insert cutting so that end of stem is at bottom of hole and leaves are level with compost.

1 A badly shaped plant can be clipped back in spring, before it comes into flower.

2 Make cuts just above a leaf stem.

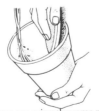

3 A well shaped plant with flowers and bracts.

Removing dead bracts

Pinch off dead bracts with thumb and forefinger.

8 Water well and cover with polythene supported by wire. Remove polythene for 5 minutes a day to prevent rot. Do not let compost dry out. Keep warm (64 F, 18 C)

Repotting

1 Repot mature plants each spring. Water running straight through shows compost is exhausted.

3 If you are using the same pot again, wash it out well, and prepare as above.

4 Hold old pot with one hand covering compost, fingers either side of stems. Tap edge of pot. Plant and compost will come out.

5 Carefully remove stale soil from roots, using stick or pencil. Do not damage roots.

7 Add new compost to fill pot. Make sure all roots are well covered.

9 After 21 days remove polythene. When plants are growing well, repot in normal compost.

2 Prepare new pot of same size with drainage layer and layer of damp, loam-based No.2 compost.

6 Place plant in centre of new pot, root-ball on compost.

8 Press down firmly around stems. Leave plant in the shade without water for 2 days to encourage the roots to grow into new compost.

BOUGAINVILLEA

The name *Bougainvillea* conjures up memories of romantic novels and warm, Mediterranean gardens. In cooler climates this beautiful plant is grown best in a conservatory or sun room. However, it can be grown equally successfully as a small pot plant if trained and pruned correctly and given enough sun to ripen the wood and encourage flower buds.

Named after the French admiral Louis Antoine de Bougainville, *Bougainvillea* is a small genus of seven or eight shrubs or small trees of which only two species concern us. They come from Brazil from where they were introduced in the mid-nineteenth century. They belong to the family Nyctaginaceae.

The most well known is *B. glabra* with its brilliant mauve bracts and small yellow flowers. It will flower profusely all through the summer. The second species is *B. spectabilis* and its hybrids 'Mrs Butt' which has bright rose bracts and 'Kiltie Campbell' with bracts that are orange in colour. These bracts are longer (as are the leaves) but not as prolific as those of *B. glabra*.

It is possible to grow *B. glabra* out-of-doors in very sheltered parts of temperate regions particularly if the stem is well protected by straw or polythene in the winter. *B. spectabilis* is much more tender.

Bougainvilleas are generally supplied in flower and trained around wire hoops. Choose plants with glossy, deep green foliage. Plants in clay pots are less likely to suffer from over-watering and yellowing of the foliage.

Left: The true flowers of the bougainvillea are small and yellow. The spectacular colouring comes from the bracts or modified leaves surrounding them.

Right: *Bougainvillea glabra* needs full sun to flower well.

Below: *Bougainvillea* 'Mrs Butt' has orange bracts which fade to lilac.

Size: Will grow to 9–13 ft (3–4 m) if planted in a conservatory bed, and indeed make a good show trained along the roof. In a pot they are better trained round wires or canes. Normally grown in a 5 in (12 cm) pot to a height of 15–18 in (38–46 cm).

Growth: They will put on 12–18 in (30–46 cm) of growth early in the season even in a pot.

Flowering season: Summer. Although the flowers tend to come in flushes, there are normally some present throughout the period.

Scent: None.

Light: They must have plenty of light. If it is too dark they will lose their leaves and fail to flower at all the following summer.

Temperature: They are tolerant of a low temperature when resting in winter. It can be as low as 40–45°F (5–7°C) in which case they will lose their leaves until re-shooting the following spring. In summer, a maximum of 70°F (21°C).

Water: Keep very moist in summer, watering at least 3 times a week. The drainage must be good. In winter keep the compost barely damp, especially if the temperature is low. Watering once a week will probably be enough. They like lime and thus prefer 'hard' tap water.

Feeding: Add half the recommended dose of liquid food to the water every 14 days.

Humidity: Spray well every few days as they are about to come into flower. Do not spray onto flowers. Stand the pot on wet pebbles.

Cleaning. Unnecessary. Never use leaf shine.

Atmosphere: Tolerant for a short while of any atmosphere in which we live. They appreciate good ventilation.

Soil: They like rich soil, such as loam-based No. 3.

Repotting: For adult plants this should be done every spring to replace spent soil, but replace them in the same sized or an only slightly larger pot as they flower better if rather pot-bound.

Pruning: Cut back straggly growth in the spring. Do not be too severe as the plants flower on wood made and ripened by the sun in the previous summer.

Propagation: Really a job for the expert. Young cuttings are taken in the spring and rooted at a temperature of 70–75°F (21–24°C) and in high humidity.

Life expectancy: In a conservatory bed 20–30 years. In a pot up to about 5 years, then the plant becomes too woody and is shy to flower.

Plant companions: Best grown on its own as a specimen.

Ease/difficulty: It is easier to grow in a conservatory but it will do quite well on a very sunny windowsill.

Training round a hoop

1 Push one end of flexible cane or wire hoop into compost at side of pot, stopping when end of cane is ⅔ down pot.

4 If necessary, tie some twine to lower part of hoop. Thread it along hoop, looping it around the stem as you go.

2 Bend hoop to other side of pot and push into compost.

3 Gently twine plant stem around hoop, taking care not to damage stem or leaves.

5 The plant will continue to grow along the hoop and can be trained to circle the hoop again or to retrace its steps.

What goes wrong

1 *Stunted growth*. Pot badly drained, compost compacted. Repot with good drainage layer.

2 *No flowers*. Too dark and stuffy or overwatering. Move to lighter more airy position. If wet, allow to dry out until recovered. Old plants with woody stems will not flower indoors.

3 *Leaves fall*. Normal in winter when plant is resting. Move to warmer place. In summer, too dark. Move to a lighter, airy place.

4 *Leaves and flowers dry up and fall, leaving only bracts*. Too hot and dry. Water and spray.

5 *New leaves small*. Needs feeding.

6 *Leaves yellow*. Too wet. Make sure pot has good drainage layer. Allow to dry out until recovered. Then water less often.

7 *Soft, white patches on leaves*. Mildew. Too damp from spraying in a badly ventilated room. Move to a more airy position.

8 *White woolly patches on leaves*. Mealy bug. Remove them individually with a swab dipped in methylated spirits or spray with malathion or a systemic insecticide.

9 *Leaves yellowed and fall, webs underneath*. Red spider mite. Spray with derris, malathion or a systemic insecticide.

10 *Leaves mottled with yellow, especially along veins. Brown scaly insects under leaves and on stems*. Scale insect. Remove them individually with a swab dipped in methylated spirits or spray with a systemic insecticide.

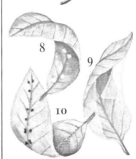

Pruning

grow more bushily. Cut the growing tip back so that only 2 or 3in (5–7cm) of new growth remains. You can tell new growth from old because the old stem is thicker and more woody. Cut weak, spindly side stems right off and trim other side shoots to the first leaf beyond the main stem. Always make the cut cleanly just above a leaf or leaf bud.

Prune bougainvilleas in February to restrict their size and to encourage them to

Repotting

1 Repot in spring to replace spent soil. If plant is too big for pot and roots show through, choose larger pot. Water well.

2 Add layer of drainage and damp, loam-based No. 3 to new pot. If you use the same pot again, wash it out.

3 Loosen compost with knife around top edge of pot.

4 Remove plant, holding it firmly by base of stem and supporting the upper part.

5 Lay plant on table and remove old compost from roots with stick or pencil. Do not damage roots.

6 If plant is too big for pot, prune the longest roots with secateurs.

7 Place plant in centre of new pot, root-ball on compost. Add new compost to fill pot.

8 Press down well. Leave in the shade without water for 2 days to encourage roots to grow into new compost.

Watering

1 Test compost with fingers. If it is light and crumbly, the plant needs water.

2 Add water at top of pot, using rainwater if possible. Empty excess from saucer after 15 minutes.

ANGEL WINGS

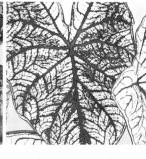

This is a member of the Arum family, so many of which are grown solely for the beauty of their leaves. The leaves of *Caladium* are arrow shaped and almost papery thin. The colours are very distinctive in shades of white, pink, red and green. The veins are usually highlighted and there is sometimes a delicate edging of pale green at the leaf margins. They have a flower like a green arum in the late summer, but it is very insignificant.

The plant was found in Brazil and its common name comes from a South American Indian word *kelady*. There are some sixteen known species, although *C. bicolor* and its hybrids are the plants most commonly available.

They should not really be regarded as long-term house plants for they need high humidity and are extremely difficult to keep from year to year. They are grown from rhizomes which are started into growth in the spring in a high temperature, and at the end of the summer the whole plant dies down and the rhizomes have to be carefully overwintered. For this reason they should be bought in full leaf, preferably during late spring and early summer, so that you can enjoy their beauty for the maximum length of time.

Choose caladiums for the appeal of their foliage. Ensure that none of the long stalks are broken and that there is no sign of greenfly. Make sure that they are wrapped carefully to protect them from draughts on the way to your home.

Varieties of *Caladium bicolor* have spectacular colouration. Usually the deepest pigments follow the veins. They are the most delicate members of the Arum family and occasionally produce a flower spathe, like the plant on the right.

Size: Normally grown in a 5 in (12 cm) pot with 2–3 rhizomes per pot. This produces a plant rising to 18 in (46 cm) tall with a 12 in (30 cm) diameter spread.

Growth: Will make about 10–12 leaves per season.

Flowering season: The green arum flower is unspectacular and comes at the end of the summer.

Scent: None.

Light: They like plenty of light to maintain the colour of the leaves but avoid placing them in direct sunlight during the middle of the day as the papery leaves will scorch.

Temperature: 60–65°F (15–18°C) at least during the summer and a minimum of 55°F (13°C) if you are trying to overwinter the rhizomes. The summer maximum is 75°F (24°C), when humidity must be kept high.

Water: Should be kept well watered, probably 2–3 times a week whilst they are growing. Reduce the watering gradually to once a week when fresh leaves stop appearing. During the winter just keep the soil moist, watering perhaps once a fortnight.

Feeding: Add half the recommended dose of liquid food to the water once every 21 days during the growing period.

Humidity: They need high humidity and enjoy the company of other plants, but do not take too kindly to overhead spraying.

Cleaning: Do not attempt to wipe the leaves as they are paper thin. Remove shrivelled leaves. Never use leaf shine.

Atmosphere: Keep out of draughts.

Soil: A rich peaty compost, such as loam-based No. 2, with extra peat added.

Repotting: Once the rhizomes have been placed in a pot it is best not to disturb for that season.

Pruning: None necessary.

Propagation: The expert can grow from seed but the easiest way is to split the over-wintered tubers. Sometimes the plant produces little plantlets during the growing season which can be potted up separately. When starting the rhizomes into growth in the spring it is essential to maintain a temperature of at least 70°F (21°C).

Life expectancy: One summer season for the average person, several seasons for the expert.

Plant companions: They enjoy the humidity of other plants, provided their companions can stand plenty of light and the drainage is good. However their leaves are so spectacular that they deserve a place of honour of their own, particularly if displayed well below eye-level where the upper surfaces of the leaves can best be seen.

Ease/difficulty: It is not an easy plant to overwinter. When the leaves die down in the autumn the rhizomes must be kept slightly moist and in a fairly warm temperature. It is better for the average person to regard the plant as an annual. The plant is easier to grow in a greenhouse where high humidity can be provided.

Overwintering and Repotting

1 When leaves begin to die down at end of summer, and no new ones appear, gradually reduce watering. In winter keep the soil just moist, watering once a fortnight. Keep temperature at least 55 F (13 C).

4 Carefully remove stale soil from roots, using stick or pencil. Do not damage roots.

2 In spring, mix loam-based No. 2 compost with ⅓ by volume extra peat. Prepare new pot with drainage layer and compost.

5 Place plant in centre of new pot, root-ball on compost.

3 Water plant thoroughly. Hold old pot with one hand covering compost, fingers either side of stems. Tap edge of pot. Plant and compost will come out.

6 Add new compost to fill pot. Make sure that all roots are covered. Press down well. Leave in the shade without water for 2 days to encourage roots to grow into compost.

What goes wrong

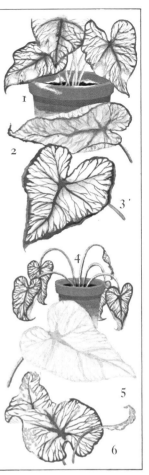

1 *Mould on leaves and top of pot.* Overwatering and cold draughts. Allow to dry out and move to draught-free place. Water less often.

2 *Leaves shrivel.* Too hot and dry or draughts. Test compost for dryness. Water, spray and provide humidity. Move to draught-free place.

3 *Leaves brown at edges and crisp.* Slightly too cold. Raise temperature to at least 60°F (15°C).

4 *Leaves collapse, curl up and die.* No growth. Too cold. Move to warmer place.

5 *Leaves poor colour.* Not enough light. Move to lighter place, but not direct sun.

6 *Leaves and shoots distorted and sticky, with green insects.* Greenfly. Spray with pyrethrum or a systemic insecticide.

Dividing rhizomes

You can divide *Caladium* rhizomes as they are just starting to shoot again after the winter. They need a temperature of at least 70°F (21°C) and high humidity so without a propagator they are unlikely to grow.

3 Carefully remove stale soil from roots, using stick or pencil.

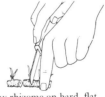

1 Prepare the propagator with a drainage layer, compost and an inch (2½cm) sharp sand.

4 Lay rhizome on hard, flat surface and cut through it in several places. Each section must have at least one leaf.

2 Remove plant from pot.

5 Push each section into the sharp sand. Water well and cover. Keep moist, removing cover for 5 minutes a day. When they are growing well repot in small pots.

Removing dead leaves

When dead leaf is quite dry cut it off with secateurs where leaf stem joins plant.

Watering

Test compost. If it feels light and crumbly, add water.

Caladiums need to be kept well watered, probably 2–3 times a week when they are growing. When the leaves die down, allow them to get gradually drier.

Humidity

Two ways of providing the humidity caladiums need.

Put pot in outer container packed with damp peat.

Stand pot in saucer with water, pebbles or gravel. Make sure pot base is clear of water.

Do not spray their delicate leaves and never use leaf shine.

49

BELL FLOWER

Campanula isophylla is a member of a group of plants which is more familiar in the herbaceous border or the rock garden, where the Canterbury bell and the harebell add much to our enjoyment of our gardens. The family Campanulaceae contains some 250 species, coming mostly from the northern coasts of the Mediterranean, although some are found growing wild in more northern areas. *C. isophylla* is a good summer-flowering plant from northern Italy.

By habit *C. isophylla* is a trailing plant and is excellent in a hanging basket. By carefully pinching out the growing buds and providing support it is also possible to train it upright. There are both white and blue varieties, the former being the stronger.

It is a delightful plant, covered with a mass of bell-shaped flowers which give it its common name and which will continue all through the summer if they are picked off as they fade. It is sometimes also called star of Bethlehem.

This plant is a useful addition to our limited stock of trailing house plants, but is only available between July and August when it is sold in full flower. At that time it is usually expensive, although once obtained further plants are easy to propagate. Choose plants with a good shape, plenty of buds and showing new, young growth. Avoid straggly, woody plants with yellowed leaves.

Campanula isophylla is a very popular summer flowering, trailing plant. Above: The white form, *Campanula isophylla* 'Alba'. Left and right: The blue form flowers just as freely. Always pick off dying flowers to keep the plant covered in bloom throughout the summer. It can also be planted in a hanging basket.

Size: Best grown in a 5 in (12 cm) pot with 5–6 cuttings growing to make a sizeable plant.
Growth: About 12–15 in (30–38 cm) each summer. Growth must be pruned back each spring if the plant is to keep its compact habit.
Flowering season: They will flower on their young growth throughout the late summer, provided the dead flowers are removed.
Scent: None.
Light: To give of its best this plant must have plenty of light. It loves a light windowsill or a place out of doors in the summer. However, avoid a south-facing windowsill with full sun in the height of the summer.
Temperature: Very tolerant of a range of cool temperatures below 60°F (16°C). It can live outside in the summer time, and as long as water is withheld the winter temperature can drop as low as 43°F (8°C).
Water: In the growing season water often, depending on its position. If it is near a warm window, at least once a day, if facing north every 2–3 days. In the winter just keep the soil damp by watering every 7–10 days depending on the temperature. They prefer tap water, as they are lime lovers.
Feeding: Add liquid food to the water every 14 days when growing.
Humidity: They like a moist atmosphere and weekly spraying but do not spray overhead when in flower.

Cleaning: Unnecessary, but groom the plant by removing dead flowers and leaves. Do not use leaf shine.
Atmosphere: Tolerant of most conditions.
Soil: A good loamy compost with a little fertilizer, e.g. loam-based No. 1.
Repotting: Once rooted cuttings have been potted up no other potting that season is required. With older plants it is as well to replace some of the soil at the start of each season, but keep the same sized pot.
Pruning: Cut back in late winter to one pair of leaves above the soil. When growing, pinch out the central buds of each growth if you require a compact upright plant.
Propagation: The prunings may be used as cuttings. Shorten the tips to about 3–4 in (8–10 cm). Put 5–6 stem tip cuttings in a 5 in (12 cm) pot and keep covered in a propagator or plastic bag until growth starts.
Life expectancy: If the plant is cut back during the winter it will produce vigorous new growth in the spring. It is best to renew your stock with young cuttings every 2–3 years as the older plants become rather woody.
Plant companions: They do quite well in 10–12 in (25–30 cm) diameter bowls of mixed plants, provided they are placed in plenty of light. They do not do well in big planters.
Ease/difficulty: An easy plant but only really attractive during the flowering season.

Pruning

1 *Campanula's* long, trailing stems become woody as they grow older. To stimulate new, strong shoots, the plant should be pruned hard in late winter.
2 Cut back to one pair of leaves above the compost. Make cut just above a leaf joint. Use the cuttings for propagation.

Replacing the topsoil

1 Older plants should be kept in the same size pot but their topsoil should be changed in spring. Water, then remove top inch (2½ cm) compost. Do not damage roots.

2 Add new compost to fill pot.

3 Press down firmly all round, making sure roots are all well covered.

4 Leave in shade without water for 2 days to encourage roots to grow into new compost.

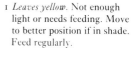
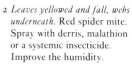

1 *Leaves yellow.* Not enough light or needs feeding. Move to better position if in shade. Feed regularly.

2 *Leaves yellowed and fall, webs underneath.* Red spider mite. Spray with derris, malathion or a systemic insecticide. Improve the humidity.

3 *Lanky growth, no flowers.* Too hot and stuffy. Move to cooler, more airy place.

4 *Leaves yellow, dry and shrivelled. Flowers die.* Too dry. Water regularly.

5 *Rotting at base.* Too wet. Allow to dry out until recovered.

6 *No new growth, leaves die.* Too cold. Move to warmer place.

7 *Flowers rot and do not open.* Too wet and cold. Move to warmer place and allow to dry out until recovered.

8 *Leaves turn black.* Frost in spring or autumn.

Stopping for bushiness

1 A plant will grow more bushily if the growing tips are pinched from the end of the main stem.

2 A well pruned plant.

Removing dead flowers

Pinch off dead flowers with thumb and forefinger.

Watering

1 Test compost with fingers. If it is light and crumbly, the plant needs water.

2 Add water at top of pot, using rainwater if possible. Empty excess from saucer after 15 minutes.

Stem tip cuttings

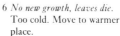

1 Prepare pot with layer of drainage and mixture of ½ peat, ½ sharp sand.

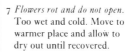

2 Choose shoot or stem tip with at least 2 pairs of healthy leaves and a growing point. Cut off below second pair of leaves, close to main stem. Cuttings should be 3–4in (8–10cm) long.

3 Prepare cuttings by trimming off stem just below a leaf.

4 Remove the lowest pair of leaves.

5 Dip the cut surface in hormone rooting powder. Shake off the surplus.

6 Make small holes in compost around edge with stick or pencil.

7 Insert cutting so that end of stem is at bottom of hole and leaves are level with compost. Water well and keep at 55–60 F (13–16 C).

8 When cuttings are growing well repot separately in loam-based No. 1 compost. Use small pots.

ORNAMENTAL CHILLI PEPPER

This is an annual from tropical America and is much valued for its bright fruit, which brings an extra touch of colour in autumn. It is a member of the Solanaceae. The name comes from the Greek *kapto*, to bite, and refers to the hot taste of the edible fruit. It is strains of this plant that are grown commercially to produce chilli peppers and, when the fruits are dried, to give cayenne pepper and paprika.

Unless you have a greenhouse it is not an easy plant to raise, so it is better to buy plants that are already in fruit in the autumn. There are several varieties available, all being derivatives of *C. annuum*. Among the cultivars 'Christmas Greeting' has green, violet, yellow or red fruits; 'Fiesta' has pointed fruits which ripen through yellow and orange to red; and 'Rising Sun' has red fruits like tomatoes. All the varieties are annuals and must be discarded at the end of the season, which is usually around Christmas time. At about the same time another similar plant becomes available. This is *Solanum pseudocapsicastrum* which unlike *Capsicum*, is a perennial plant and lives from year to year.

Always be sure which plant you are buying for although the fruits of *Capsicum* are edible those of *Solanum pseudocapsicastrum* are very poisonous and must never be eaten.

Choose bushy plants well set with fruit. The leaves should not be dropping and the foliage should be bright green.

Hybrids of *Capsicum annuum* carry brightly coloured fruits in the autumn months. Right: The fruits ripen from yellow through orange to red. They are useful to display temporarily among other plants, as among the group of young cinerarias, below.

Size: Best grown in 3½ in (9 cm) pots. They grow to about 8–9 in (20–23 cm) above the top of the pot.
Growth: They grow, flower and fruit in one season.
Flowering season: The small white or greeny white flowers come in early summer but are not really significant. The fruit comes in late summer or early autumn and quickly colours to give the plant its attractive appearance.
Scent: None.
Light: They need plenty of light and a few hours of morning sun daily.
Temperature: Normal room temperature, not below 50°F (10°C) and not above 70°F (21°C).
Water: Keep well watered twice a week when growing but nearly every day if the temperature is high. Do not allow to dry out if standing in full sun. When the fruits set, reduce watering to 2–3 times a week.
Feeding: Add liquid food to the water every 7 days when growing. Stop feeding as soon as fruits set.
Humidity: They appreciate overhead spraying once a week. After the plant has flowered, spraying helps the fruit to set.

Cleaning: Unnecessary. Do not use leaf shine.
Atmosphere: They are tolerant of most conditions provided there is a circulation of air.
Soil: Loam-based No. 1.
Repotting: Only once during the growing season after the original potting from the seedling stage.
Pruning: Not when growing. However, if your plant should lose its leaves through dryness, cut off the stems and use the fruits in dried arrangements for Christmas.
Propagation: From seed in early spring in a propagating frame under glass. Better left to the professional. They need a temperature of 65°F (18°C).
Life expectancy: One season – it's an annual.
Plant companions: Can be used as a temporary 'dot' plant to lend colour to mixed bowls. Can also do well in window boxes out-of-doors for seasonal display in late summer and autumn.
Ease/difficulty: It is not difficult to raise if you have the right equipment. However, if only a few plants are required it is better to buy them fully grown in the late summer.

Growing from seed

Capsicum seeds do not need a high temperature but they are difficult to germinate successfully. A propagator or propagating frame will give the best chance of success.

1 Sow seeds in early spring. Prepare a seed tray or propagator with a drainage layer and sterilized, seed-growing compost. Scatter seeds evenly and add thin layer of compost, no thicker than depth of seed. Water well.

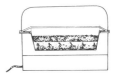

2 Cover and put in dark place or cover with dark cloth. Make sure the compost never dries out and remove the cover for 5 minutes a day. Keep at 65 F (18 C).

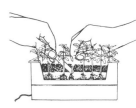

3 When seeds germinate, bring them into light and remove the glass cover.

4 When seedlings are large enough to handle, thin out the weaker ones, leaving about 1 in (2½ cm) between each one.

5 When remaining ones are growing well, repot in separate small pots.

Repotting

1 Repot in the growing season in midsummer as plant becomes big for its pot. Water well.

2 Prepare pot 1 size larger with drainage layer and layer of damp, loam-based No.1 compost.

3 Hold old pot with one hand covering compost, fingers either side of stems. Tap edge of pot. Plant and compost will come out.

4 Carefully remove stale soil from roots, using stick or pencil. Do not damage roots.

5 Place plant in centre of new pot, root-ball on compost.

6 Add new compost to fill pot. Make sure that all roots are covered.

7 Press compost down well around base of stem.

8 Leave in the shade without water for 2 days to encourage roots to grow into compost.

Watering

In summer it will need water almost every day and it should never dry out. When the fruit appears, water less often. Two or three times a week will be enough at this time.

Add water at top of pot, using rainwater if possible. Empty excess from saucer after 15 minutes.

Spraying

Spray once a week overhead with a fine mist spray. Hold spray about 6in (15cm) from leaves.
This will keep the leaves clean and will help the fruit to set.

53

PARLOUR PALM

This is a dwarf, slow-growing palm suitable for rooms of any size and well meriting its common name. Its graceful fronds are between 12 and 24 in (30-60 cm) long. *Chamaedorea elegans* is sometimes also called *Neanthe bella* and is a native of Mexico from where it was first introduced in 1873.

The demands of this plant are really very modest, the most crucial being water. It must be kept damp throughout summer and winter. It will tolerate most living conditions and its fronds have a timeless look about them that blend well into any decor, either modern or traditional. One remarkable feature is that it grows a flower quite early in its life. This is a green frond covered with rather delicate, mimosa-like flowers and is an attractive contrast to the leaf fronds. The flowers are followed by small fruits which resemble berries.

In its native habitat it grows almost as a ground cover plant under very tall trees, so is well used to shady places and grows indoors in most positions. When small it is also a good plant for a bottle garden and suitable seedlings are often available. It grows well in hydroculture.

Choose plants with fresh foliage and new growth. There should be no browning of the leaf tips. It is possible to buy three plants and pot them together if a thicker specimen is required. It is freely and cheaply available as a small plant in $3\frac{1}{2}$ in (9 cm) pots but like all palms it is expensive to buy as a large plant because it grows so slowly.

Chamaedorea elegans is one of the easiest palms to grow in the house. It does not grow fast but produces a flower frond (below) early in its life. The flowers will be followed by berries.

Right: Two plants potted together to form a bushy plant. The young fronds are pale green and deepen in colour as they mature.

Size: Their maximum height is 4 ft (120 cm) but specimens are not usually sold at more than 2 ft (60 cm). The individual fronds are normally from 12-24 in (30-60 cm) long depending on the age of the plant. Often 2 or 3 plants are potted up together to make a more bushy plant.
Growth: A slow grower, it produces perhaps 2 or 3 fronds per year. As the plant gets older the fronds get longer.
Flowering season: The flower spike is delicate in contrast to the formal palm leaves and is likely to appear at any time.
Scent: None.
Light: They appreciate a reasonable amount of light without being in direct sunlight. They will tolerate a dark position, but will then grow even more slowly.
Temperature: Keep in a coolish position in summer at 60°F (16°C) and at a minimum of 55°F (13°C) in winter. Maximum summer temperature is 65°F (18°C).
Water: This plant must be kept moist at all times which will probably mean watering 2 or 3 times a week in summer and once a week in winter.
Feeding: During the summer add half the recommended dose of liquid food to the water every 14 days.
Humidity: Improve humidity by wiping the foliage at least once a week.
Cleaning: Gently wipe the fronds with a damp cloth to remove dust. Never use leaf shine. It is harmful to all palms, producing browning of the fronds.
Atmosphere: They are tolerant of most conditions including gas fumes and smoke, but they appreciate a circulation of air.
Soil: They like a very peaty compost, e.g. 3 parts loam-based No. 1 to one part of granulated peat.
Repotting: Best done in March of each year. Do not use too large a pot, for they grow better if slightly pot-bound.
Pruning: Not necessary, except to remove dead lower fronds.
Propagation: From seeds in the spring. A high temperature of at least 80°F (27°C) is required for germination, plus high humidity. Unless you can provide these conditions the job is best left to the growers. A propagator with bottom heat may give successful results.
Life expectancy: At least 5 or 6 years.
Plant companions: Fits in well with most green plants and contrasts well with many broad-leaved species such as *Ficus*, philodendrons, cordylines and *Fatshedera*. Young plants can be used in bottle gardens.
Ease/difficulty: An easy plant for the beginner provided it is kept moist.

Three plants in one pot

1 Prepare large pot with drainage layer and layer of compost.

4 Place other plants around it, allowing a little space between each for the root balls.

2 Remove plants from pots as for repotting.

5 Fill up with compost so that all roots are covered. Firm it between and around the root balls.

3 Place first plant in centre of new pot.

6 Water thoroughly in a bucket of water.

What goes wrong

1 *Leaf tips turn brown.* Too dry and sunny. Water, spray and move out of direct sunlight.

2 *Leaves yellowed and fall, webs underneath.* Red spider mite. Spray with derris, malathion or a systemic insecticide.

3 *Fronds dry up, shrivel and die.* Too hot. Move to cooler place. Spray.

4 *Leaves rot at soil level and fall off.* Too cold and wet. Move to warmer place and allow to dry out until recovered.

5 *No growth.* Too cold and wet or in spring, needs feeding. Move to warmer place and allow to dry out until recovered.

Removing dead leaves

If lower fronds turn brown and die, cut them off with seca-teurs, cutting as close to the main stem as possible.

Repotting

1 Repot in early spring when plant looks top-heavy for pot and roots grow out through the base. Water well.

2 Prepare compost of 3 parts loam-based No. 1 with 1 part peat. Use pot 1 size larger and add drainage layer and layer of compost.

3 Hold old pot with one hand covering compost, fingers either side of stems. Tap edge of pot. Plant and compost will come out.

4 Carefully remove stale soil from roots, using stick or pencil. Do not damage roots.

5 Place plant in centre of new pot, root-ball on compost.

6 Add new compost to fill pot. Make sure that all roots are covered. Press down well. Leave in the shade without water for 2 days to encourage roots to grow into compost.

Watering

1 Test compost. If it feels light and crumbly, add water.

2 Place plant in bucket and fill bucket with water to just below the rim of the pot. Leave it there for 15 minutes, then allow it to drain.

Trimming

If leaf tips brown, cut new point just above edge of healthy leaf. Do not cut into green tissue.

Cleaning and spraying

Wipe dust off leaves with soft cloth and sponge with tepid water. Support leaf with other hand.

Do not use leaf shine.

Spray daily overhead with a fine mist spray, using rain-water if possible. Hold spray about 6in (15cm) from leaves.

SPIDER PLANT

This is one of the easiest and most accommodating of house plants. It is a member of the Liliaceae family and there are some forty known species. The one commonly grown as a house plant has three specie names, *Chlorophytum elatum, comosum* and *capense*. The latin name *Chlorophytum* means simply 'green plant' and the original species does in fact have all green leaves. The variety always seen is technically *C. comosum* 'Variegatum'. Its common names are spider plant (for reasons that are obvious when you see a well grown plant) and St. Bernard's lily. In the States it is sometimes known as the airplane plant – perhaps because of its 'aerial' way of reproducing itself. It comes originally from South Africa and was first introduced as an indoor plant in the middle of the nineteenth century.

Chlorophytum has narrow, strap-like leaves some 12 to 18in (30-46cm) long and up to 1in (2½cm) wide, normally green with a broad band of off-white down the middle, although sometimes this order is reversed. Very insignificant white flowers are borne on long cream stems. These flowers soon give way to young plantlets which can in time be potted up to become independent plants. However, if several of the stems are left on, the plant looks most attractive in a hanging basket as the stems arch over with the weight of the young plants. It can even be used as an attractive outdoor summer bedding plant. Four or five young plants potted together in a 12in (30cm) diameter hanging basket make a very full, spectacular display.

Being such a tolerant plant it is very good for a beginner to start with. It also grows well in water and converts easily to hydroculture.

Chlorophytums can be bought throughout the year. Choose plants with slightly glossy, succulent leaves. If the midribs of some of the leaves are damaged they will not recover and the plant will soon look untidy.

Size: Good plants will fill a 5in (12cm) pot, although 'mother plants' can be much bigger, about 18in (46cm) tall and as much across.
Growth: From a rooted cutting to a fully grown plant in a 5in (12cm) pot in one year.
Flowering season: Flowers, shoots and new plantlets may appear at any time, but are more likely in the summer.
Scent: None.
Light: Very tolerant of dark places. However, the white leaf marking is much more pronounced in a well lit position.
Temperature: They will tolerate a wide variety of temperatures as long as they are above freezing. In the summer they can be planted out and used as a bedding plant. Maximum summer temperature indoors is 65°F (18°C).
Water: Water 2-3 times a week in the summer and once a week in the winter. They are tolerant of drought and will not die if you occasionally forget them. In fact dryness may encourage them to produce more stems, flowers and plantlets.
Feeding: Add liquid food to the water every 14 days in summer.
Humidity: Spray overhead daily in summer. Remove the plant from direct sunlight first to avoid scorching.

Cleaning: A mister spray is sufficient. An occasional 'flick' with a duster also helps. The leaves are rather too brittle to wipe and the plant reacts badly to leaf shine.
Atmosphere: Very tolerant. They appreciate good ventilation.
Soil: Loam-based No. 2. They also grow well in hydroculture.
Repotting: When grown in soil, about twice a year is usually necessary. The white swellings on the roots are rhizomes, not a gall or root infection.
Pruning: Cut out damaged leaves.
Propagation: Young plantlets emerge on stems from the centre of the plant. These can be potted into 3in (8cm) pots or put into hydroculture. It is possible to divide a big plant, but this must be done with care otherwise the leaves get damaged.
Life expectancy: Plants will go on indefinitely but it is better to renew the stock every 3-4 years as the mature plants can get tired and shabby.
Plant companions: Will grow with practically any other indoor plant.
Ease/difficulty: An excellent plant for a beginner to start with.

Chlorophytum comosum 'Variegatum' is a common and very easy plant. It is excellent in a hanging pot or basket (right) where the young plantlets on the end of their runners can best be seen. It is possibly this habit of aerial reproduction that has given the plant a common name of the airplane plant.
Below: the young plantlets.

Repotting

1 Roots growing from bottom of pot and crowded leaves and stems show plant needs repotting. Water plant well.

2 Prepare pot 1 size larger with drainage layer and layer of damp, loam-based No. 2 compost.

3 Hold old pot with one hand covering compost, fingers either side of stems. Tap edge of pot. Plant and compost will come out.

4 Carefully remove stale soil from roots, using stick or pencil. Do not damage roots.

5 Place plant in centre of new pot, root-ball on compost.

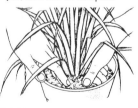
6 Add new compost to fill pot. Make sure that all roots are covered. Press down well. Leave in the shade without water for 2 days to encourage roots to grow into compost.

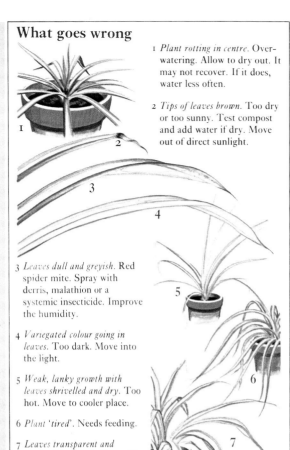

What goes wrong

1 *Plant rotting in centre.* Over-watering. Allow to dry out. It may not recover. If it does, water less often.

2 *Tips of leaves brown.* Too dry or too sunny. Test compost and add water if dry. Move out of direct sunlight.

3 *Leaves dull and greyish.* Red spider mite. Spray with derris, malathion or a systemic insecticide. Improve the humidity.

4 *Variegated colour going in leaves.* Too dark. Move into the light.

5 *Weak, lanky growth with leaves shrivelled and dry.* Too hot. Move to cooler place.

6 *Plant 'tired'.* Needs feeding.

7 *Leaves transparent and mushy. No growth.* Too cold, probably frosted.

Spraying

Clean the leaves by spraying them all over with tepid water from a mist sprayer. Hold the spray about 6in (15cm) from leaves.

Propagation

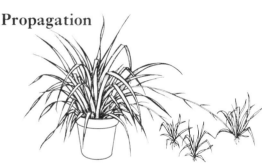

2 Place new pot next to main plant and gently bend stem with plantlet until plantlet rests on compost in new pot. Peg stem to compost with plastic wire and press compost lightly around plantlet.

Removing dead leaves

Cut cleanly with scissors where damaged area meets healthy leaf. Take care not to cut into green, living tissue.

If leaf tips brown, cut new point just above edge of healthy leaf. Do not cut into green tissue.

Chlorophytums are amongst the easiest of all plants to propagate. After flowering, they produce small plantlets on the end of long, tough stems. These can be left hanging for a while and will look most attractive. As the plantlets grow larger leaves and roots they can be planted beside the parent and eventually severed completely.

1 Prepare a small pot with drainage layer and compost. Use loam-based No. 2.

3 When plantlet grows new leaves, sever it from the stem with sharp knife.

Root division

1 Prepare 2 pots with drainage layer and compost.

2 Remove plant from pot.

3 Carefully remove stale soil from roots.

4 Gently pull roots and stems apart with your hands.

5 Repot both sections in the usual way.

KANGAROO VINE

Cissus is one of the few genera of the Vine family which we can grow as house plants. There are some two hundred known species but only three or four are widely cultivated. The name comes from the Greek word for an ivy.

Three varieties are commonly available. *C. antarctica* comes from Australia, as its common name suggests. It was first cultivated in 1790. This plant is a strong climber with tendrils which grip onto a support such as a trellis. Its leaves are oval in shape, rough in texture, bright green, some 2–3 in (5–8 cm) in size and are borne on brownish stalks from the main stem. It is a tolerant house plant which grows well, especially in indirect light but must not be overwatered, particularly in winter. It appreciates growing up a trellis or strings and will quickly cover a wall or room divider if it is happy in its position. All *Cissus* varieties do well in hanging baskets.

C. striata is a much smaller leaved plant, but is very similar in its habits to *C. antarctica*. It comes from Chile and was first collected in 1878. The leaves are small, 1–2 in (3–4 cm) long and are borne in clusters of five, each with its own tendril with which to climb and grip.

By far the most attractive *Cissus* is *C. discolor*, but it is also the most difficult to keep indoors. The leaves are quite smooth-edged in comparison with *C. antarctica's*, green and purple with patches of silver on the veins and crimson underneath. This species comes from Java and Cambodia. It tends to lose its leaves in winter if the temperature drops too low and it needs some humidity.

Choose your plants with bushy, vigorous growth. Avoid any which are dropping their foliage or developing brown papery leaves. *C. discolor* is unfortunately rarely available.

Cissus discolor (above) is a superb climbing plant but one that needs warmth and humidity. *Cissus antarctica* (below and right) is easier.

Size: *C. antarctica* will grow to at least 9–10 ft (3–3½ m). The other varieties are much smaller.
Growth: 2–3 ft (60–100 cm) a year.
Flowering season: They do not normally flower in the house.
Scent: None.
Light: They like a position which faces north or east, preferring not to be in direct sunlight.
Temperature: 55–60°F (12–16°C) in winter 65–70°F (18–21°C) in summer.
Water: Twice a week in summer but check soil condition before watering. Overwatering will cause leaf damage, producing brown papery spots. In winter keep just moist, watering about every 14 days.
Feeding: Add liquid food to the water every 14 days in summer.
Humidity: They like a weekly spray in summer. Stand the pot on damp pebbles. *C. discolor* should be sprayed every day.
Cleaning: A mister with rain-water weekly is best. Do not use a liquid leaf shine more than once every 2 months. Do not use leaf shine at all on *C. discolor*, which has very delicate leaves.
Atmosphere: Tolerant of most conditions. *C. discolor* does not like gas fumes.
Soil: Loam-based No. 2.

Repotting: Once or twice a year according to strength of growth until the plant has reached its required size, then rely on regular feeding to maintain vigour.
Pruning: Pinch out the leading growths from time to time in the growing season to keep the plant dense and bushy. If the plant gets straggly, cut down to within 9 in (23 cm) of the pot and allow to shoot again.
Propagation: Young stem tips with a bud and two leaves will root in a mixture of half compost and half sharp sand in spring and early summer. Use a propagator if possible, at 61–64°F (16–18°C).
Life expectancy: At least 5 or 6 years, but can collapse and die in old age.
Plant companions: Most other green plants. They do well in mixed plantings if care is taken when watering.
Ease/difficulty: Except for *C. discolor* they are comparatively tolerant and easy plants.

Repotting

1 Repot in spring when plant looks too big for pot but produces no new leaves. Old leaves may look faded. Water well.

4 Carefully remove stale soil from roots, using stick or pencil. Do not damage roots.

2 Prepare pot 1 size larger with drainage layer and layer of damp, loam-based No. 2 compost.

5 Place plant in centre of new pot, root-ball on compost.

3 Hold old pot with one hand covering compost, fingers either side of stems. Tap edge of pot. Plant and compost will come out.

6 Add new compost to fill pot. Make sure that all roots are covered. Press down well. Leave in the shade without water for 2 days to encourage roots to grow into compost.

What goes wrong

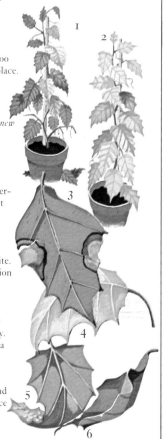

1 *No growth, leaves drop.* Too cold. Move to a warmer place.

2 *Leaves poor colour and no new growth in spring.* Needs feeding.

3 *Brown papery patches on leaves and leaves drop.* Over-watering. Allow to dry out until recovered and then water less frequently.

4 *Leaves yellowed with webs underneath.* Red spider mite. Spray with derris, malathion or a systemic insecticide. Improve the humidity.

5 *Leaves distorted and sticky with green insects.* Greenfly. Spray with pyrethrum or a systemic insecticide.

6 *Leaves shrivel.* Too hot and dry. Move to a cooler place and water and spray regularly.

Stem tip cuttings

1 In spring plant produces new shoots which can be used for cuttings. Prepare small pot with drainage layer and mixture of sharp sand and loam-based compost.

2 Choose shoot or stem tip with at least 2 pairs of healthy leaves and a growing point. Cut off below second pair of leaves, close to main stem. Cuttings should be 3–4in (8–10cm) long.

3 Prepare cuttings by trimming off stem just below a leaf.

4 Remove the lowest pair of leaves.

5 Dip the cut surface in hormone rooting powder. Shake off the surplus.

6 Make small holes in sand around edge with stick or pencil.

7 Insert stem as far as base of leaf. End of stem must rest on bottom of hole. Firm sand around cutting. Add other cuttings in the same way.

8 Water well and cover with polythene supported by wire. Remove cover for 5 minutes a day and never let compost dry out. Keep at 61–64 F (16–18 C). Remove cover after 21 days and when cuttings are growing well, repot in normal compost.

Humidity

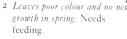

Cissus likes a weekly spray of water in summer.

Tying to a cane

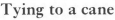

Cissus climbs strongly and needs a cane or trellis.

1 Push cane gently into compost a few inches away from the main stem, stopping when cane is ⅔ down the pot.

2 Cut a 9in (23cm) length of string and tie firmly around cane on stem side.

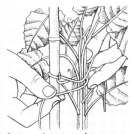

3 Loop string around stem as shown.

4 Tie a firm knot against the cane. Repeat at intervals up the stem.

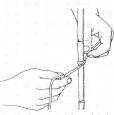

59

CALAMONDIN ORANGE

Left: The flowers of *Citrus mitis* are very fragrant. They should be pollinated to ensure the production of fruit.

Right: A well pruned plant of *Citrus mitis* with immature fruit.

Below: The fruit changes from green to orange as it ripens.

There is something exotic and extravagant about growing oranges. I suppose it goes back to when the landed gentry built large orangeries beside their mansions to protect their expensive specimens during the winter. The large orange and lemon trees were grown in tubs so that they could be placed on the terraces in the summer time and easily moved by the gardeners into the orangery in the winter. Today these varieties are quite unsuitable to grow in the house because of their size. Instead we grow the Calamondin orange, *Citrus mitis* which is a miniature plant from the Philippines, introduced to the west as long ago as 1595. It is a member of the Rutaceae family.

In all but size the characteristics of the Calamondin are exactly the same as those of its bigger relations. It has lovely white, highly scented flowers, and the fruits are edible, although somewhat bitter. They can be sliced like lemons and used in drinks. It will carry flowers, green and ripe fruit on its branches all at the same time. It likes to be out of doors in the summer and indoors in the winter.

Plants already bearing fruit are often on sale at Christmas but some care should be taken when purchasing at that time. Firstly, try to ascertain whether the plant is well rooted, for some plants are grown outdoors in Florida and have very few roots to sustain them indoors. Secondly, select a plant with a good shape. It should not be dropping its leaves. Lastly, ensure that the plant doesn't get cold on its way to your home.

Size: This is a miniature plant so rarely grows above 2-3 ft (60-100 cm) tall.

Growth: A very slow grower, putting on about 4-5 in (10-12 cm) per year.

Flowering season: Mostly in the summer months but can produce buds at any time. If they flower indoors away from insects they will have to be pollinated with a brush.

Scent: A strong perfume is always associated with opened orange blossom.

Light: They need a good light position and will deteriorate if too far away from a window.

Temperature: In winter they only require to be above freezing point, but will appreciate a temperature of 55° to 60°F (13-15°C). In summer they are better grown out-of-doors. If indoors in summer, the maximum temperature should be 65°F (18°C) and the ventilation good.

Water: Almost daily in the summer. In the winter about every 10 days, unless in a very warm room. Then increase the frequency to every 5 days. However, plants do not like to be waterlogged and good drainage is essential. They are lime lovers so prefer 'hard' tap water.

Feeding: When growing in the summer add liquid food to the water every 14 days.

Humidity: Enjoys frequent spraying overhead – every day if possible.

Cleaning: Rely on the spraying to keep clean. Do not use leaf shine.

Atmosphere: They like a good movement of air, but not direct draughts. They do not like gas fumes.

Soil: Loam-based No. 2. Ensure that the drainage at the bottom of the pot is good.

Repotting: When adult, once a year in spring. Either repot or replace the topsoil in the same pot.

Pruning: Not really necessary as this is a slow growing plant. If necessary remove any branch that is out of shape or too long.

Propagation: Normally done with cuttings in a warm greenhouse and best left to the experts. Orange and lemon trees can be grown from normal fruit pips but the plants can become very large and will only flower and fruit when they are at least 5-6 ft (1½-2 m). Grafting onto a dwarfing rootstock is possible – but again this is a specialist's work.

Life expectancy: Very long provided that the plant is given regular attention.

Plant companions: Best grown on its own.

Ease/difficulty: A moderately easy plant, but not one for the complete novice.

Spraying and Cleaning the leaves

Clean the leaves by spraying them all over with tepid water from a mist sprayer. Hold the spray about 6 in (15 cm) from leaves.

Do not use leaf shine.

Pruning for shape

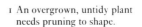

1 An overgrown, untidy plant needs pruning to shape.

2 Make cuts with secateurs just above a bud, leaf or side shoot, cutting at an angle.

3 The plant will grow into a more even, bushy shape.

Repotting

1 Repot young plants in spring when roots growing through pot and lack of new leaves show compost is exhausted. Water plant well.

2 Prepare pot 1 size larger with drainage layer and layer of damp, loam-based No. 2 compost.

3 Hold old pot with one hand covering compost, fingers either side of stems. Tap edge of pot. Plant and compost will come out.

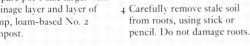

4 Carefully remove stale soil from roots, using stick or pencil. Do not damage roots.

5 Place plant in centre of new pot, root-ball on compost.

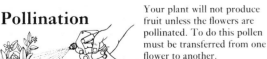

6 Add new compost to fill pot. Make sure that all roots are covered. Press down well. Leave in the shade without water for 2 days to encourage roots to grow into compost.

Pollination

Your plant will not produce fruit unless the flowers are pollinated. To do this pollen must be transferred from one flower to another.

1 Spray daily with soft water while the plant is in flower OR

2 Brush the stamens of a fully opened flower with a soft brush. Carry the pollen to another flower and brush this gently in the same way.

Continue until you have treated all the flowers.

What goes wrong

1 *Leaves drop*. Too dry and not enough humidity. Or too wet, soil badly drained and roots saturated. Test compost to see whether to allow plant to dry out or to water and spray immediately.

2 *Lanky growth*. Too hot with poor ventilation. Move plant to cooler, more airy place. If no flowers appear it may be too dark. Move to a lighter place.

3 *Growth stops, leaves fall*. Too cold. Move to a warmer position.

4 *Leaves curl and turn brown at tips*. Cold draughts. Keep in a protected position.

5 *Leaves pale*. Needs feeding.

6 *White woolly patches on leaves*. Mealy bug. Remove them individually with a swab of cotton wool dipped in methylated spirits or spray with a systemic insecticide or malathion.

7 *Brown scaly insects under leaves and on stems*. Scale insect. Remove them individually with a swab of cotton wool dipped in methylated spirits or spray with a systemic insecticide.

8 *Yellow mottling on leaves*. Leaf hoppers. Spray with a systemic insecticide.

9 *Leaves yellowing. White insects fly away from plant when touched*. Whitefly. Spray with derris or a resmethrin-based insecticide.

10 *Leaves covered with sooty mould*. Wipe off mould with damp cloth. Spray with a systemic fungicide.

Propagation

1 Keep the pips from a large ripe orange.

2 Prepare 3in (8cm) pots with drainage layer and seed compost.

3 Press one pip into top of compost in each pot. Cover them with half their depth of compost.

4 Keep moist, at a temperature of 61°F (16°C) until seedlings appear. Repot in loam-based No. 2 compost when plants are growing well.

KAFFIR LILY

An old fashioned plant, the *Clivia* was often seen in association with the heavy velvet curtains of the Victorian drawing-room. It is, however, an excellent house plant for modern decor with elegant strap-like leaves which shine all the year round. Once a year in early spring it produces a stem with a cluster of brilliant orange, trumpet-shaped flowers which transform it from a rather ordinary green foliage plant to an exotic tropical showpiece.

The *Clivia* is a native of Natal in South Africa from where it was introduced at the beginning of the nineteenth century. It is a member of the Amaryllidaceae family and was named, for reasons long since lost, after a Duchess of Northumberland whose maiden name was Clive.

Hybridizers and plant breeders have worked with this plant and produced flowers ranging from pale yellow to deep orange. In some strains the trumpets are also more open than others but there are no variety names for these improvements. The species which is supplied is *Clivia miniata* with a variety *C. miniata* 'Variegata' which has leaves striped in cream along their length.

Clivias are sold in spring and early summer with the bud just emerging from the centre of the plant. Ensure that the bud is undamaged and that the leaves are dark and glossy. Once obtained, a particularly attractive strain can be propagated by division or by offsets. Plants grown from seed will not necessarily produce flowers the same colour as their parent and will vary considerably in quality. If you allow your plant to produce seed it will probably prevent it from flowering the following year. Sow home produced seed while the fruit is red, bought seed as soon as it can be obtained.

Left: *Clivia miniata* var. citrina, a pale yellow flowered form.

Right: A young plant of *Clivia miniata*, probably flowering for the first time. This plant will be happy for years in this size of pot and the flower spike (below) should increase in size.

Size: An adult plant is usually not more than 20 in (50 cm).

Growth: 5–6 leaves per year on a healthy specimen.

Flowering season: Beginning of February/March. After flowering the heads should be removed before the plant produces seeds, to conserve its strength.

Scent: None.

Light: Tolerant of most positions. They produce better flowers if kept in a north-facing window.

Temperature: Must be kept cool, at 45–50°F (7–10°C) when resting in the early winter. Raise the temperature to 60°F (15°C) when the flower bud appears. Maximum summer temperature is 70°F (21°C).

Water: Keep on the dry side with compost barely moist in the resting period, watering once a fortnight. Water freely when the plant is flowering and afterwards when it is growing. This will probably mean at least once a week.

Feeding: Add liquid food to the water once a week when the plant is growing in the summer.

Humidity: Like most plants they like moisture in the atmosphere. Stand the pot on damp pebbles.

Cleaning: Clean the leaves by hand with a damp cloth. Do not use leaf shine.

Atmosphere: Tolerant of most conditions.

Soil: Loam-based compost No. 2.

Repotting: Young plants should be re-potted every year in the spring. Established plants are best left alone for as long as possible but the topsoil should be changed every 2–3 years. When repotting, avoid damaging the fleshy roots and never use too large a pot.

Pruning: Not necessary, apart from the removal of the lower leaves as they die.

Propagation: By division of big plants or by separation of the young offsets after flowering. Plants can be raised from seed germinated at 60°F (18°C) provided it has been allowed to set and ripen. However, this seed ripening process may take 10 months.

Life expectancy: Very long lived.

Plant companions: Can be used in large mixed plantings with any combination of green plants. More often grown as a specimen plant.

Ease/difficulty: A very easy amenable plant, but it will produce better flowers if well cared for.

Repotting

1 Clivias grow better if slightly pot-bound. Repot when many roots grow from pot and new young growth does not appear. Water well first.

4 Carefully remove stale soil from roots, using stick or pencil. Do not damage the fleshy roots.

2 Prepare pot 1 size larger with drainage layer and layer of damp, loam-based No. 2 compost.

5 Place plant in centre of new pot, root-ball on compost.

3 Hold old pot with one hand covering compost, fingers either side of stems. Tap edge of pot. Plant and compost will come out.

6 Add new compost to fill pot. Make sure that all roots are covered. Press down well. Leave in the shade without water for 2 days to encourage roots to grow into compost.

What goes wrong

1 *Leaves brown and scorched.* Direct sun on wet leaves. Move out of sun. Avoid watering in sunlight.

2 *White woolly patches on leaves.* Mealy bug. Remove them individually with a swab of cotton wool dipped in methylated spirits or spray with a systemic insecticide or malathion.

3 *Leaves shrivel.* Too dry. Water and spray immediately and water more regularly.

4 *New growth weak, no flowers.* Too hot. Move to a cooler place.

5 *No growth.* Too cold. Move to a warmer place.

6 *Leaves poor colour and few flowers.* Needs feeding.

7 *Plant rots at base.* Too wet from overwatering. Allow to dry out until recovered and then water less frequently.

Propagation : Offsets

1 Young offsets appear next to the parent plant as the flowers die down.

2 Prepare small pot with drainage layer and damp, loam-based No. 2 compost.

3 Hold old pot with one hand covering compost, fingers either side of stems. Tap edge of pot. Plant and compost will come out.

4 Remove offset and roots from parent plant with sharp knife.

5 The offset must have its own small roots. If it has not, it will not grow.

6 Pot offset in new pot, firming compost around base. Water well.

Humidity

Stand pot in saucer with water, pebbles or gravel. Make sure pot base is clear of water.

Cleaning

Wipe dust off leaves with soft cloth and sponge with tepid water. Support leaf with other hand.
Do not use leaf shine.

Root division

Divide large, old plants in early spring.

1 Prepare 2 pots with drainage layer and compost.

2 Remove plant from pot and gently prise away compost. Do not damage delicate roots.

3 Gently pull roots and stems apart with your hands.

4 Repot both sections in the usual way.

Removing flower

When flowers have withered, cut stem at base.

DWARF COCONUT PALM

This is a plant which is a member of the Palmaceae family and one of the few which does not have a name derived from Greek. *Coco* is the Portuguese word for monkey and refers to the likeness of the nut to a monkey's head. The commercial coconut, *Cocos nucifera*, came originally from tropical Central and South America and was first collected in 1690. It is now found all over the tropics either because man has transported it or because it has floated naturally from shore to shore.

Only two species are grown as house plants, one large and one small. The larger species is the true coconut, *Cocos nucifera*, which makes an attractive and unusual room plant, particularly when young. It grows out of a nut which rests half buried in the pot. When young the leaves are fine and slender and a trunk only appears when the plant is mature. The chances of getting any nuts on a mature plant indoors (even in a tropical palm house) are very remote.

The smaller species is *C. weddeliana*, a neat miniature palm with slender fronds of thin leaflets. When small it makes a good plant for a bottle garden. It is sometimes listed as *Microcoelum* or *Syagrus weddeliana*.

When buying *C. nucifera* ensure that the shoot is vigorous and there is no rot in the nut or at the base of the shoot. *C. weddeliana* is generally trouble free but avoid plants where the soil seems very dry and the foliage is browned and brittle from dryness. Neither variety is very easy to keep for a long time in the house but both do well in the more humid atmosphere of a greenhouse or conservatory.

Above: A young plant of *Cocos nucifera*. At this stage the fronds are shaped like fish tails.

Left: The nut of *Cocos nucifera* should not be buried. Here the adult trunk is just beginning to form.

Right: The delicate fronds of *Cocos weddeliana*, the dwarf coconut palm.

Size: In the tropics *C. nucifera* will grow up to 100ft (30m). In the house about 10ft (3m) is possible. *C. weddeliana* has a maximum height of 4ft (120cm) and is normally bought at 1 to 1½ft (30-40cm). It may take 20 years to reach its full size.

Growth: Slow – a matter of a few inches per year.

Flowering season: None. It will not produce coconuts indoors.

Scent: None.

Light: They like plenty of light and will take direct sunlight provided the leaves are not wet.

Temperature: About 65°F (18°C) in winter, 70°F (21°C) in summer.

Water: Keep well moist in summer, watering at least twice a week. In winter water more moderately, depending on the room temperature. Once a week will probably be enough but never let the root ball dry out.

Feeding: Add half the recommended dose of liquid food to the water every 3 weeks when growing in the summer.

Humidity: They enjoy a moist atmosphere. Stand on damp pebbles or put the plant into an inner pot surrounded by wet peat.

Cleaning: Spray with tepid water. Do not use leaf shine.

Atmosphere: Fairly tolerant, but warm dry air in winter will cause the leaflets to go brown and die.

Soil: Loam-based No. 2, but add ¼ measure by volume of extra granulated peat.

Repotting: About once a year in the spring when young. If you are able to keep the plant growing to adulthood cease repotting and rely on feeding and changing the topsoil.

Pruning: None necessary, except to remove the occasional leaf that has died.

Propagation: From nuts or seeds in a temperature of 75°F (24°C) and high humidity in spring. This is really a job for professional growers.

Life expectancy: The first year or two is the most difficult. If the plant survives that period it is likely to be long lived.

Plant companions: *C. nucifera* is best on its own because of its size. *C. weddeliana* likes being in a mixed planting and does well in small bowls with hederas, crotons and ferns. Because it is small and slow growing it will also do well in bottle gardens.

Ease/difficulty: Moderately difficult, requiring some care.

Repotting

1 Repot in spring when roots growing through pot and lack of new fronds show soil is used up.

2 Prepare pot 1 size larger with damp, loam-based No.2 compost with ¼ extra peat by volume. Palms prefer tall, narrow pots.

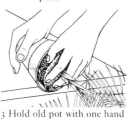

3 Hold old pot with one hand covering compost, fingers either side of stems. Tap edge of pot. Plant and compost will come out.

4 Carefully remove stale soil from roots, using stick or pencil. Do not damage roots.

5 Place plant in centre of new pot, root-ball on compost.

6 Add new compost to fill pot. Make sure that all roots are covered. Press down well. Leave in the shade without water for 2 days to encourage roots to grow into compost.

What goes wrong

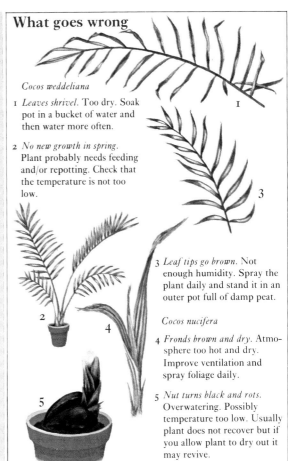

Cocos weddeliana

1 *Leaves shrivel*. Too dry. Soak pot in a bucket of water and then water more often.

2 *No new growth in spring*. Plant probably needs feeding and/or repotting. Check that the temperature is not too low.

3 *Leaf tips go brown*. Not enough humidity. Spray the plant daily and stand it in an outer pot full of damp peat.

Cocos nucifera

4 *Fronds brown and dry*. Atmosphere too hot and dry. Improve ventilation and spray foliage daily.

5 *Nut turns black and rots*. Overwatering. Possibly temperature too low. Usually plant does not recover but if you allow plant to dry out it may revive.

Planting a bottle garden

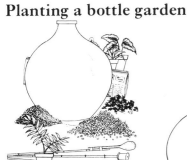

1 You will need a large glass bottle or carboy; pea gravel and charcoal for drainage; damp compost; newspaper; a wooden kitchen spoon, cotton reel and soft paintbrush, all tied to lengths of cane. Several small plants, e.g. *Cocos, Begonia, Cryptanthus.*

2 Add drainage and compost to bottle through a paper chute.

3 Make planting holes with the wooden spoon.

4 Knock plants from pots and gently remove compost from roots. If root ball is too large, gently pull part away.

5 Drop plant into bottle, aiming for planting hole.

6 Firm soil around plant with cotton reel tied to cane. Add more plants until bottle garden is finished.

7 Dust leaves with paintbrush.

8 Add spray of water. Put in light position and water only when the plants begin to droop. They will provide their own humidity.

Replacing the topsoil

1 When plant is over 3ft (1m) tall, do not repot. Water, then remove top inch (2½cm) of old compost. Do not damage roots.

2 Add new compost to fill pot.

3 Press down firmly all round, making sure roots are all well covered.

4 Leave in shade without water for 2 days to encourage roots to grow into new compost.

65

Codiaeum variegatum

CROTON

This is one of the most colourful of all the house plants and is often aptly named Joseph's coat. *Codiaeum variegatum pictum*, to give it its full botanical name, comes from Malaysia and the East Indies and is a member of the Euphorbiaceae family. The name comes from the native word for the plant, *Kodiho*. It was introduced to the west in the first half of the nineteenth century. Many variations are now being grown, some with leaves that are laurel shaped, some shaped like oak leaves, some strap like and many others. All have strong, yellow veined markings with bright colours in between. They are very frequently known as crotons, though this in fact is the proper name for another genus of plants. Another name sometimes found is *Croton-codiaeum*, combining the two latin names.

Until recently crotons were always thought to need high temperatures to survive and were therefore quite unsuitable to bring into the house except for short periods. Now they are grown in very much cooler temperatures and have become popular house plants. However they are still difficult to overwinter without losing some bottom leaves and for this reason some people regard them as expendable plants. An even temperature at all times is one of the keys to success.

Crotons are useful as one of the few house plants which really need a bright position. Select them for the appeal of their foliage. The plant should be well furnished with leaves to the base and the leaves should not be faded or dull. Do not allow the plant to be chilled or in a draught on its way to your home in winter.

The leaves of crotons vary in shape and colouration. Although very attractive they are not easy to keep.

Above: *Croton poullini*.
Above left: *Croton 'Brava'*.
Right: a cultivar of *Croton variegatum pictum*.

Below: *Croton holufiana*.

Size: To about 10 in (25 cm) in 3½ in (9 cm) pots, and to 20 in (50 cm) in 5 in (13 cm) pots. They will grow to quite large shrubs, often 3–4 ft (1 m) tall and as much across.
Growth: 8–10 in (20–25 cm) per year per stem.
Flowering season: A slender spike of small flowers is produced during the summer on mature plants. It is not very significant.
Scent: None.
Light: The better the light, the better the colour in the leaves. They will stand direct sun but don't spray overhead in direct sunlight or the leaves will scorch.
Temperature: The temperature must not fluctuate wildly. This is the key to success. The ideal in winter is around 60°F (15°C) but can fall to 55°F (13°C) if this is kept steady. They will tolerate up to 80°F (27°C).
Water: Keep well watered in the summer, at least 2–3 times a week. Never let the plant dry out. In winter, every 4–5 days should suffice. Use tepid water in winter.
Feeding: Add liquid food to the water regularly every 14 days during the summer growing season.
Humidity: They benefit from a daily overhead spray during the summer, but don't do this in direct sunlight. Alternatively stand the plant on dampened pebbles.
Cleaning: Either by spraying with water or spraying with leaf shine not more than once a month.

Atmosphere: Keep out of draughts at all times and away from gas fires.
Soil: Loam-based No. 2.
Repotting: Best done in April or May. Do not put in too large a pot.
Pruning: Plants that have become leggy and lost leaves can be cut back in the spring when they will make new growth. The cuts should be dusted with charcoal to stop the sap bleeding.
Propagation: Take stem tip cuttings in the spring at a temperature of about 75°F (24°C) and in humidity. If possible use a propagator.
Life expectancy: Mature specimens in good growing conditions will go on for years. To the novice in the home they should be regarded as expendable.
Plant companions: It is worthwhile putting them in mixed groups which show off their colours to the full.
Ease/difficulty: Experience with plants is needed if you wish to keep this plant from season to season.

Repotting

1 Repot in April or May when roots are crowded and new leaves are small. Water well. Prepare pot 1 size larger with drainage and loam-based No. 2 compost.

4 Lay plant on table and remove old compost from roots with stick or pencil. Do not damage roots.

2 Loosen compost with knife around top edge of pot.

5 Place plant in centre of new pot, root-ball on compost.

3 Remove plant, holding it firmly by base of stem and supporting the upper part.

6 Add new compost, firming it until the pot is filled. Make sure all roots are covered. Leave in the shade without water for 2 days to encourage roots to grow into compost.

66

Stem tip cuttings

1 Take young stem tip cuttings in spring. Use a propagator if possible. Prepare it with drainage and mixture of $\frac{1}{2}$ sand, $\frac{1}{2}$ loam-based compost. Wear gloves, the sap is irritating.

2 Choose shoot or stem tip with at least 2 pairs of healthy leaves and a growing point. Cut off below second pair of leaves. Cuttings should be 3–4in (8–10cm) long.

3 Prepare cuttings by trimming off stem just below a leaf.

4 Remove the lowest pair of leaves.

5 Dip the cut surface in hormone rooting powder. Shake off the surplus.

6 Make small holes in compost with stick or pencil.

7 Insert cutting so that end of stem is at bottom of hole and leaves are level with compost.

8 Water well and cover. Remove cover for 5 minutes a day to prevent rot and make sure the compost does not dry out. Keep at 75°F (24°C).

9 Remove cover after 21 days and when cuttings are growing well, repot in normal compost.

What goes wrong

1 *Bottom leaves drop*. Atmosphere too dry, too cold. Move to warmer place and provide humidity. Spray.

2 *Leaves faded and dull or revert to green*. Lack of light. Move to a better, lighter place.

3 *Leaves brown and scorched*. Direct sun on wet leaves. Do not spray in sunlight.

4 *Leaves spotted and collapse*. Gas fumes. Move to fume-free room.

5 *Leaves shrivel*. Too hot and dry. Move to cooler place and provide humidity and spray.

6 *Leaves droop and collapse. Stem rots*. Overwatering. Allow to dry out until recovered and then water less frequently.

7 *New leaves small and distorted*. Needs feeding.

8 *Leaves drop*. Fluctuating temperature. Try to keep at even temperature.

9 *Leaves yellowed with webs underneath*. Red spider mite. Spray with derris, malathion or a systemic insecticide. Improve the humidity.

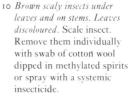

10 *Brown scaly insects under leaves and on stems. Leaves discoloured*. Scale insect. Remove them individually with swab of cotton wool dipped in methylated spirits or spray with a systemic insecticide.

11 *White woolly patches on leaves and in leaf axils*. Mealy bug. Remove them individually with swab of cotton wool dipped in methylated spirits or spray with malathion or a systemic insecticide.

Watering and Humidity

1 Spray daily overhead with a fine mist spray, using rainwater if possible. Hold spray about 6in (15cm) from leaves.

Test compost. If it feels light and crumbly, add water. Never let your plant dry out. In winter use tepid water.

2 Stand pot in saucer with water, pebbles or gravel. Make sure pot base is clear of water.

Columnea microphylla

GOLDFISH VINE

Columneas are handsome evergreen trailing plants which, if well cultivated, reward their owners with spectacular orange flowers in the spring. A member of the Gesneriaceae family, there are some hundred known species, most of which come from tropical America. The name is in honour of the Italian Fabius Columna who published one of the earliest botanical books with engraved illustrations in Naples in 1592.

Columneas are particularly suitable for growing in hanging baskets. They are epiphytes, that is in nature they grow on trees and dead wood, depending on these hosts for support but not nourishment. The leaves are small, oval and appear in pairs on hanging stems which can be 2 or more feet (60 cm) long. The flowers are bright orange to scarlet and appear in the spring. They are tubular shaped with a wide open throat at the lower end, and it is these which give the plant its common name of goldfish vine. Whilst they are not particularly difficult plants, they require good light to flourish.

There are two species commonly grown. *C. microphylla* has longer growth, smallish leaves and orange flowers. *C. gloriosa* has darker, longer leaves, shorter growth and scarlet flowers. There are also many modern hybrids, some, such as *C. gloriosa* 'Purpurea', with purple leaves. The care is the same for all varieties.

A closely related group of plants called *Aeschynanthus* (or *Trichosporum*) require the same treatment as *Columnea*. They flower later (May to September) and all come from Java. The commonest is *Aeschynanthus lobbianus* which has crimson flowers emerging as buds from long sheaths – giving it the common name of lipstick vine. The two genera look so similar that they are often confused but *Aeschynanthus* is usually rather more expensive.

Columneas are sold in the spring as they come into flower. Choose plants with luxuriant, rather fleshy, growth and plenty of buds. They are often available in individual pots or planted together in a basket and sold complete.

Left: The neatly paired leaves of *Columnea microphylla*. This is possibly the most attractive of all the species.

Right: *Columnea microphylla*. These trailing plants are best displayed in hanging baskets.

Below: Columneas have very unusual flowers. This is *Columnea gloriosa*.

Size: The trailing growth will lengthen to between 18 in (46 cm) and 3 ft (1 m).
Growth: 15–20 in (38–50 cm) per year.
Flowering season: March and April, but a winter resting period followed by a period in a warm moist atmosphere is needed to induce good flowering.
Scent: None.
Light: To flourish, they require to be near a window or in a similar light position, but protected from full midday sun in summer. Do not let the foliage touch the glass.
Temperature: 55°–60°F (13–15°C) is ideal. If warmer, increase the humidity by spraying daily. They will not enjoy temperatures above 75°F (24°C).
Water: Apart from a resting period during the winter of about one month, these plants should be kept very moist. Water at least twice a week in summer, even more if it is hot. Water once a week in winter, even less in the resting period.
Feeding: Add liquid food to the water every 14 days in summer.
Humidity: A high degree of humidity is desirable if these plants are to flower well. If grown in pots stand them on dampened stones, or in a secondary pot of wet peat. If grown in plastic hanging baskets, keep some water in the drip tray. Spray the foliage with tepid, lime-free water.
Cleaning: Spraying is sufficient. As the leaves are rather hairy, do not use leaf shine.
Atmosphere: Keep out of draughts.
Soil: Loam-based No. 1 with a quarter measure by volume of extra peat added.
Repotting: Not very often, at the most every second year in June. Make sure that the drainage is good. Take care when handling as the long trails can easily snap off.
Pruning: Shorten stems to about half their length after flowering to encourage new bushy growth.
Propagation: Stem tip cuttings inserted in sandy compost will root in early summer. Keep covered with polythene or glass until rooted or use a propagator at 70°F (21°C).
Life expectancy: About 5 or 6 years. Then it is necessary to propagate new stock as the parent plants become untidy.
Plant companions: Although they will mix well with most green plants, it is too difficult to provide enough trailing space in a bowl. Grow them singly as specimen plants.
Ease/difficulty: Not a difficult plant provided it has the right conditions of light and humidity. It is easier to grow it well in a glasshouse or conservatory.

Repotting

1 Repot only every other year after flowering. Make sure you remove all dead flowers. Water plant well.

2 Prepare pot 1 size larger with drainage and compost (loam-based No. 1 and $\frac{1}{4}$ peat).

3 Hold old pot with one hand covering compost, fingers either side of stems. Tap edge of pot. Plant and compost will come out.

4 Carefully remove stale soil from roots, using stick or pencil. Do not damage roots.

5 Place plant in centre of new pot, root-ball on compost.

6 Add new compost to fill pot. Make sure that all roots are covered. Press down well. Leave in the shade without water for 2 days to encourage roots to grow into compost.

1 *Leaves dry, plant looks tired.* Not enough humidity. Spray regularly.

2 *Thin, weedy growth.* Needs feeding.

3 *Stems elongated and thin.* Not enough light. Move to a better, lighter place.

4 *No flowers. Not enough light.* Move to a lighter place.

5 *Leaves drop, plant stems rotting.* Too cold and wet. Move to a warmer place and allow to dry out until recovered. Then water less often.

6 *Leaves shrivel.* Compost too dry. Water immediately.

7 *Leaves shrivel, weedy growth and no flowers.* Too hot with poor ventilation. Move to a cooler, more airy place.

8 *Leaves yellowed with webs underneath.* Red spider mite. Spray with derris, malathion or a systemic insecticide. Improve the humidity by spraying regularly with water.

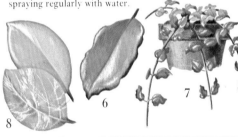

Humidity

Plants in a hanging basket can be kept humid with a daily spray of tepid, lime-free water.

Plants in pots also need constant humidity.

Stand pot in saucer with water, pebbles or gravel. Make sure pot base is clear of water.

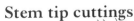

Watering

Test compost with fingers. If it is light and crumbly, the plant needs water. Empty excess from saucer after 15 minutes.

Pruning

After flowering, cut back trailing stems by half to encourage more bushy growth. Make cuts just above a leaf joint.

Stem tip cuttings

1 Take stem tip cuttings after flowering has finished. Prepare pot with drainage, ½ sand, ½ loam-based compost.

2 Cut stem tip about 4in (10cm) long. Cut off just above a pair of leaves.

3 Prepare cuttings by trimming off stem just below a leaf.

4 Remove the lowest leaves so that there is sufficient stem to insert in compost.

5 Dip the cut surface in hormone rooting powder. Shake off the surplus.

6 Make small holes in compost around edge of pot and insert cuttings. Base of stem should rest on bottom of hole, lowest leaf level with the compost.

7 Water well and cover with polythene supported by wire. Remove cover for 5 minutes a day and never let compost dry out. Keep at 70°F (21°C). Remove cover after 21 days and when cuttings are growing well, repot in normal compost.

CORDYLINE

The name *Cordyline* means 'club' and refers to the thick roots of some species. Cordylines are members of the Liliaceae family. The genus contains a dozen evergreen trees and shrubs which come from tropical South America, temperate New Zealand, Australia and tropical Polynesia, Malaysia and India. They are closely related to the dracaenas, and there is much confusion in naming the varieties.

The cordylines are very popular as indoor or conservatory plants and have bright colourful leaves. They are by and large very easy to keep going and the dark green ones will tolerate bad light conditions. Whilst they will eventually grow tall, the majority of plants are supplied fairly short – 2 ft (60 cm) tall at the most.

There are several named varieties. *C. terminalis* 'Prince Albert' has bright red and dark red leaves which make a beautiful contrast amongst green plants. *C. terminalis* 'Red Edge' is similar in colouring to 'Prince Albert', but is a miniature with leaves about 5 in (13 cm) long and ¾ in (2 cm) wide. They look particularly well if grown three in a pot and do well in mixed bowls. *C. terminalis* 'Lord Robertson' has red, cream and green leaves. It grows slightly bigger than 'Prince Albert' but is not so hardy and its leaves mark rather easily. *C. rubra congesta* is one of the most robust of the cordylines. Its leaves are narrower and dark green.

Choose cordylines with clear colour in their leaves. The leaves should not be marked with brown spots or have browned tips. Plants which have not dropped their lower leaves are to be preferred.

Left: The tough and durable *Cordyline volkartii* will put up with shady conditions.

The coloured cordylines share the characteristic of producing bright young leaves which darken as they mature. Below left: *Cordyline* 'Lord Robertson'. Below: The aptly named *Cordyline terminalis* 'Red Edge'. Right: A good, unmarked young plant of *Cordyline terminalis* 'Prince Albert'.

Size: Normally 12–24 in (30–60 cm) tall when grown in the house. The leaf spread is up to 18 in (46 cm).

Growth: They do not grow very quickly, about 4–6 in (10–15 cm) per year.

Flowering season: Only mature plants flower. Creamy white, star-shaped flowers appear on a long stem during the summer months.

Scent: The flowers have a heavy tropical scent.

Light: Plenty of light is needed to maintain the colour in the leaves. They should not be in the midday sun in summer. The green varieties need less light.

Temperature: They like a fairly high temperature of 65–70°F (18–21°C) in winter, but will tolerate 55°F (13°C) if water is reduced. Maximum summer temperature is 75°F (24°C) in which case humidity should be high.

Water: Keep moderately watered in summer, once or twice a week and once a week in winter. Never allow the plant to stand in water or dry out completely.

Feeding: Add liquid food to the water every 14 days.

Humidity: They enjoy a twice weekly spray with a mister, except when in direct sunlight.

Cleaning: Leaves can be cleaned by hand using a damp cloth. Leaf shine may be used but not more than every 2 months. Do not use it on 'Red Edge' variety as it marks badly.

Atmosphere: Fairly tolerant of most conditions but they dislike cold draughts.

Soil: Loam-based No. 2 mixed with peat, or a peat-based compost.

Repotting: Best done in March every 2–3 years at the most. Make sure that the drainage is good.

Pruning: None necessary, except to remove dried or damaged leaves. Leggy plants can be cut down in spring and they will re-shoot.

Propagation: By stem tip cuttings and stem sections cut to about 3 in (8 cm) long. Place these in a humid propagator or cover in polythene in early spring, at a temperature of 75°F (24°C).

Life expectancy: Cordylines will survive for a very long time, although the lower leaves may be shed leaving the stem bare. This is due to dryness in the air.

Plant companions: They do well in mixed plantings and enjoy the company of most other green plants. With their colourful and variegated leaves they provide a good contrast to green *Ficus*, philodendrons, hederas etc.

Ease/difficulty: Not difficult plants but easier to keep going if you have some basic knowledge of plant needs.

Repotting

4 Carefully remove stale soil from roots, using stick or pencil. Do not damage roots.

1 Roots growing from bottom of pot and crowded leaves and stems show plant needs repotting. Water plant well.

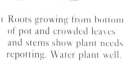

2 Prepare pot 1 size larger with drainage layer and layer of damp, peat-based compost or loam-based No. 2 mixed with ¼ peat.

5 Place plant in centre of new pot, root-ball on compost.

3 Hold old pot with one hand covering compost, fingers either side of stem . Tap edge of pot. Plant and compost will come out.

6 Add new compost to fill pot. Make sure that all roots are covered. Press down well. Leave in the shade without water for 2 days to encourage roots to grow into compost.

What goes wrong

1 *Leaf tips brown, lower leaves drop.* Lack of humidity—usually too hot and dry from central heating. Provide humidity and spray regularly.

2 *Leaves lack colour.* Not enough light. Move to lighter position.

3 *Leaves drop and may rot. No new growth.* Too cold and wet. Move to a warmer place and allow to dry out until recovered. Water less often.

4 *New growth distorted or small.* Needs feeding.

5 *Leaves yellowed with webs underneath.* Red spider mite. Spray with derris, malathion or a systemic insecticide. Improve the humidity.

6 *Brown scaly insects under leaves and on stems.* Scale insect. Remove them individually with a swab of cotton wool dipped in methylated spirits or spray with a systemic insecticide.

7 *Leaves distorted and sticky with green insects.* Greenfly. Spray with pyrethrum or a systemic insecticide.

Cleaning the leaves

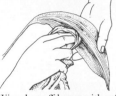

Wipe dust off leaves with soft cloth and sponge with tepid water. Support leaf with other hand.

Humidity

Stand pot in saucer with water, pebbles or gravel. Make sure pot base is clear of water.

Spray twice a week with a mister.

Stem sections

1 Prepare pot with layer of drainage and mixture of ½ peat, ½ sharp sand.

2 Remove plant from pot.

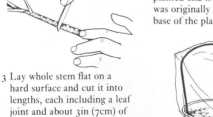

3 Lay whole stem flat on a hard surface and cut it into lengths, each including a leaf joint and about 3in (7cm) of the stem.

4 Dip the lower cut surface of each section in hormone rooting powder.

5 Place each section upright in the compost, making sure the planted end is the end that was originally nearest the base of the plant.

6 Water well and cover with polythene supported by wire. Remove polythene for 5 minutes a day to prevent rot and make sure the compost does not dry out. Keep warm (75°F, 24°C).

Trimming the leaves

If the tips of the leaves are brown and dry, trim them off with sharp scissors, cutting just above healthy leaf tissue.

7 New shoots will grow from each section. When they are growing well, repot them in the usual way.

Pruning

1 A leggy plant that has lost its lower leaves can be cut down in spring.

2 Cut stem 4in (10cm) above base, making cut above an old leaf joint.

3 New leaves will grow from lower down the stem.

CROSSANDRA

This is a small, pretty plant with dark green pointed leaves and spikes of bright orange flowers which look like ears of corn. It comes from the East Indies and was introduced to the west in the early nineteenth century. There are about twelve known species, members of the Acanthaceae family.

Unfortunately it is not the easiest house plant to keep going and to some is best regarded as expendable. It is very prone to damping off, especially in winter. However it presents a surmountable challenge to the more experienced and once the technique of keeping it has been mastered it can then be overwintered. It is advisable to propagate young specimens each spring for replacements as old plants tend to become rather untidy.

A well kept plant will flower over a long period – perhaps continually from May to September. The flowers open one after the other from the base of the spike to the top, the lower ones dropping off as they finish.

Only *C. undulaefolia* (or *C. infundibuliformis* as it is sometimes known) is cultivated, although there are several improved strains of this species in existence and the cultivar most commonly supplied is 'Mona Walhed'.

Choose plants with unmarked, glossy leaves. There should be no sign of rot on the flower spikes, leaves or at the base of the stems. Limp foliage is a sign of overwatering and such a plant will rarely recover.

Crossandra undulaefolia has an attractive combination of dark, glossy leaves and an unusual flower colour. The flower spike (below) resembles an ear of corn. Many flowers emerge from it in succession.

Right: The cultivar *Crossandra undulaefolia* 'Mona Walhed'.

Size: Normally fairly small at 6–10 in (15–25 cm) tall although they will reach 3 ft (1 m) if kept from year to year.
Growth: Will grow from cuttings to flowering size in one growing season.
Flowering season: From May to September.
Scent: None.
Light: They need good light, ideally in a south facing window. Protect from midday sun in summer.
Temperature: 65°F (18°C) is ideal but will tolerate 55°F (13°C) in winter if kept on the dry side. Maximum summer temperature 70°F (21°C).
Water: At all times use tepid water. Cold water from the tap can kill. Water sparingly always, only when the soil feels dry. This will probably mean about once a week in summer and every 14–16 days in winter. Overwatering will kill.
Feeding: Add liquid food to the water every 14 days in summer.
Humidity: They like to be dry. Do not spray overhead.
Cleaning: Dust gently or wipe with a cloth. If sprayed with water, shake surplus off afterwards. Do not use leaf shine.
Atmosphere: They do not like fumes from gas fires. Keep out of draughts.
Soil: Loam-based No. 2.
Repotting: In spring. Make sure the drainage is very good.

Pruning: Pinch out leaf shoots during the growing period to encourage flower production. Remove all dropped flowers to avoid rotting.
Propagation: Take stem tip cuttings 3 to 4 in (8–10 cm) long in March and insert into a mixture of leaf mould and sand in a pot or propagator at 70°F (21°C). When rooted after about 3 weeks pot into 3½ in (9 cm) pots with 3 cuttings per pot. They can also be grown from seed sown in March at 61°F (16°C).
Life expectancy: Crossandras are best regarded as expendable and fresh stock propagated each spring. The plants get straggly after a couple of years and are then best discarded.
Plant companions: Best grown on their own because of their tendency to rot in humid conditions. However, it is worth trying to grow them with saintpaulias on a temporary basis. They are compatible in size and contrast well in colour though their water requirements are different.
Ease/difficulty: Expertise is needed to overwinter this plant successfully.

Repotting

1 Repot in spring before flowering when plant is too tall for pot and leaves pale. Water plant well.

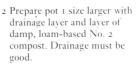

2 Prepare pot 1 size larger with drainage layer and layer of damp, loam-based No. 2 compost. Drainage must be good.

3 Hold old pot with one hand covering compost, fingers either side of stems. Tap edge of pot. Plant and compost will come out.

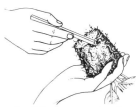

4 Carefully remove stale soil from roots, using stick or pencil. Do not damage roots.

5 Place plant in centre of new pot, root-ball on compost.

6 Add new compost to fill pot. Make sure that all roots are covered. Press down well. Leave in the shade without water for 2 days to encourage roots to grow into compost.

What goes wrong

1 *Rot on leaves, flower spikes and at base of stems.* Too wet and humid. Spray with a systemic fungicide and move to a drier atmosphere. Allow plant to dry out until recovered and then water less often.

2 *Leaves limp.* Overwatering. Allow to dry out until recovered, then water less often.

3 *No growth, leaves may drop.* Too cold. Move to a warmer place. If growth dwarfed in spring, needs food.

4 *Leaves shrivel.* Too hot and dry. Move to a cooler place. Water and spray regularly.

5 *Plant wilts, leaves drop.* Draughts. Move to a protected position.

6 *Leaves spotted, plant wilts and collapses.* Gas fumes. Move to a fume-free room.

Pruning a leggy plant

1 Crossandras tend to become straggly after 2 years. Cut them back by ⅓ in spring to encourage new, more bushy growth.

2 As the plant grows it produces side shoots that will not flower. Pinch these out by hand so that all the plant's energy goes to producing flowers.

Stem tip cuttings

1 Take stem tip cuttings in March. Prepare pot with drainage layer and mixture of ½ leaf mould, ½ sharp sand.

2 Choose shoot or stem tip with at least 2 pairs of healthy leaves and a growing point. Cut off below second pair of leaves, close to main stem. Cuttings should be 3–4in (8–10cm) long.

3 Prepare cuttings by trimming off stem just below a leaf.

4 Remove the lowest pair of leaves.

5 Dip the cut surface in hormone rooting powder. Shake off the surplus.

6 Make small holes in compost around edge of pot and insert cuttings. Base of stem should rest on bottom of hole, lowest leaf level with the compost.

7 Water well and cover with polythene supported by wire. Remove cover for 5 minutes a day and never let compost dry out. Keep at 70°F (21°C).

8 Remove cover after 21 days and when cuttings are growing well, repot 3 to a pot in normal compost.

Removing dead flowers

When flower has died, cut off flower stem just above the top pair of leaves.

Cleaning the leaves

Wipe dust off leaves with soft cloth and sponge with tepid water. Support leaf with other hand.
Do not use leaf shine.

Watering

1 Test compost with fingers. If it is light and crumbly, the plant needs water.

2 Add a little tepid water. Empty excess immediately. Crossandras must never be overwatered.

STAR FISH

Cryptanthus plants are the smallest of all the bromeliads and because of their shape are commonly called star fish or earth stars. The name *Cryptanthus* comes from the Greek words *krypto,* to hide and *anthos,* a flower, for the plant has a few small flowers low down in its centre which are often difficult to see. Primarily they are grown as foliage plants. They come mostly from Brazil and were introduced in the mid to late nineteenth century.

These plants are real sun lovers. The more light they have, the brighter the colour on their flat leaves. Unlike most bromeliads *Cryptanthus* do not retain water in the centre of the rosette. Nevertheless they should be watered overhead. They have a poor root system and are easy to wire onto bark or logs to make an arrangement that imitates their natural habitat. They look well in the front of bowls and are even used in flower arrangements. They also do particularly well in bottle gardens.

There are three species commonly grown. *C. bivittatus* has dark green stripes running down the centre of the leaf. *C. tricolor,* is the brightest species, being mostly cream with pink and green markings. *C. fosterianus* is the largest, with spectacular red and grey horizontal stripes across the leaves. All species are propagated by small offsets which are produced in the axils of the leaves. They are easily detached in April and should then be potted into soil, covered with polythene and left in a very warm atmosphere to root for about three weeks. Unlike other bromeliads the parent plant does not die back after producing offsets.

There is very little that can go wrong with *Cryptanthus* and they are usually marketed in good condition. Plants already producing offsets are often sold and this is a good way to increase your stock immediately. Alternatively, small plants are often sold quite cheaply in 2 in (5 cm) pots.

Cryptanthus are small bromeliads grown for their foliage. They have shallow root systems and look good displayed on bark.

Above: *Cryptanthus bivittatus.*
Right: The spectacular *Cryptanthus fosterianus.*
Below: *Cryptanthus tricolor.*

Size: These are mostly small plants with leaves varying from about 4 in (10 cm) long in the case of *C. bivittatus* to about 15 in (38 cm) long in *C. fosterianus.*

Growth: They grow slowly in the house, making 2–3 new leaves a year.

Flowering season: Summer. The flowers are few and far between, low and often hidden under the leaves in the centre of the plant.

Scent: None.

Light: The more light the better the plants like it and this shows in the bright colouring of the leaves.

Temperature: Will tolerate 60°F (15°C) but prefer 65°F (18°C) in the winter if possible. Maximum summer temperature 75°F (24°C).

Water: Water freely in the summer, 2–3 times a week according to temperature. Keep on the dry side in winter, watering perhaps every 10 days.

Feeding: Not really necessary, but an occasional feed once every 21 days in the summer can be beneficial. Add the liquid food to water.

Humidity: On hot days spray overhead. Lack of humidity will cause the leaf tips to turn brown.

Cleaning: The spraying should be sufficient. Do not use leaf shine.

Atmosphere: Tolerant of most conditions.

Soil: They like a peaty compost with a little sphagnum moss added.

Repotting: As they have a small root system these plants are usually grown in small pots and do not often require repotting. Alternatively they can be tied onto pieces of bark or tree trunks to make a group. Provided they are not left to dry out they will do well. Put a little moss around the roots before wiring them on.

Pruning: None.

Propagation: Like all bromeliads, from offsets detached in Spring. These need not have roots and may simply fall off the plant. Plant them in a mixture of compost and sharp sand in a propagator at 75°F (24°C) or in a pot covered with polythene. Keep in a warm place and remove the polythene for 5 minutes each day. When they begin to grow, repot them separately in small pots.

Life expectancy: Will survive virtually forever.

Plant companions: They do well with other small plants and ferns in bottle gardens or in the front of mixed planted bowls.

Ease/difficulty: Easy.

Fixing a bromeliad to bark

1 Choose suitable piece of cork bark, a branch or some well shaped driftwood.

2 If there is no natural hollow, chisel a shallow well where plant will rest.

3 Remove plant from pot, keeping compost round the root ball.

4 Wrap roots in damp sphagnum moss and tie with plastic-coated wire.

5 Hold moss and root-ball firmly against wood or bark and bind in place with wire.

6 Fix bark to wall or prop it up, making sure the plant is growing upright. Spray regularly. Keep root-ball damp

What goes wrong

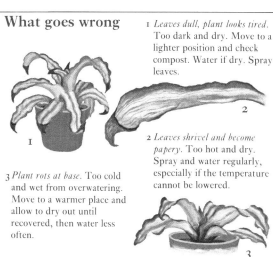

1 *Leaves dull, plant looks tired.* Too dark and dry. Move to a lighter position and check compost. Water if dry. Spray leaves.

2 *Leaves shrivel and become papery.* Too hot and dry. Spray and water regularly, especially if the temperature cannot be lowered.

3 *Plant rots at base.* Too cold and wet from overwatering. Move to a warmer place and allow to dry out until recovered, then water less often.

Trimming the leaves

Cryptanthus grows slowly and does not need pruning. However, the tips of its leaves may turn brown if it is too hot and dry. Cut a new point just above the edge of the healthy leaf. Do not cut into the healthy part of the leaf or this will form scar tissue and turn brown again.

Planting a bottle garden

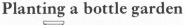

1 You will need a large glass bottle or carboy; pea gravel and charcoal for drainage; damp peat-based compost; newspaper; a wooden spoon, cotton reel and paintbrush, tied to cane. Small plants e.g. *Cryptanthus, Cocos, Begonia.*

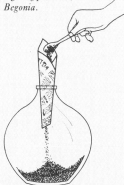

2 Add drainage and compost to bottle through a paper chute.

3 Make planting holes with the wooden spoon.

4 Knock plants from pots and gently remove compost from roots. If root ball is too large, gently pull part away.

5 Drop plant into bottle, aiming for planting hole.

6 Firm soil around plant with cotton reel tied to cane. Add more plants until bottle garden is finished.

7 Dust leaves with paintbrush.

8 Add spray of water. Put in light position and water only when plants begin to droop. They will provide their own humidity.

Watering

1 Test compost with fingers. If it is light and crumbly, the plant needs water.

2 Add water at top of pot, using rainwater if possible. Empty excess from saucer after 15 minutes.

Unlike many other bromeliads, *Cryptanthus* does not need to be watered in the centre. If you are growing it fixed to bark, spray it regularly and make sure that the moss around its roots does not dry out.

CYCLAMEN

This is surely the most beautiful of all the winter flowering plants and to those who succeed in keeping it, also the most satisfying. But to many people it can be the most frustrating of plants, for it can virtually die before your eyes.

The secret of success is to get the plant acclimatized to your own home. Keep it in a cool room permanently at first, maintaining a high level of humidity by standing it on a saucer of wet sand or packing damp peat around the pot. The cooler you keep it the longer it will last.

The cyclamen we buy from shops is *Cyclamen persicum,* one of a family of 16 known plants which come mainly from the Mediterranean area. *Cyclamen persicum* comes from Asia Minor, where it was discovered in 1731. The name comes from the Greek *kyclos,* meaning circular, from the way the flower stalk of some species twists into a spiral when the seed is formed.

The original species has small, dainty flowers and practically all green leaves. Modern varieties have a wide range of colours from pure white through shades of pink, rose purple, even salmon, to scarlet and dark red. Their leaves are beautifully marbled in silver in different patterns. These modern varieties are often easier to keep indoors than the older types and have been developed by carefully selecting and breeding from plants which show suitable characteristics.

A good plant will have been grown 'hard' in very cool conditions and should have such firm foliage that it should take standing upside down on its leaves. Floppy plants will soon collapse in the home. Cyclamen should have plenty of buds coming along deep in the crowns of the plant. The corm should project slightly out of the compost and you can check for any sign of rot near the corms by gently parting the leaves.

All varieties of *Cyclamen persicum* grow best in cool conditions. Flower colours range from white to scarlet and dark red.

Below: The flowers of the popular white hybrid.

Right: A modern hybrid of the silver leaf strain. This is a well grown plant.

Bottom: Leaf patterns on a green leaved hybrid.

Below: A mature plant of the miniature species, which is now very popular.

Size: Maximum height 12–15 in (30–38cm) including the flowers.
Growth: All plants throw up a profusion of flowers and leaves in proportion to the size of the corm. Dies down after flowering.
Flowering season: Autumn to spring. Seeds sown in the summer of one year will flower in the autumn of the following year.
Scent: Only the original species has a scent.
Light: Likes plenty of light but must be protected from full sun. An east-facing windowsill is ideal.
Temperature: Ideally, keep at about 45–60°F (7–15°C) during the day, falling by about 10°F (5°C) at night. They are therefore better suited to the hall or bedroom than to the warmer living room. They can be planted outside in the summer.
Water: The compost should be kept moist but they must never stand in water. Always water from below so that the corm does not get wet. Water twice a week when the plant is growing and flowering. When the flowers die down, allow the plant to rest in a cool but frost-free place. Water less often (once a week is enough) but do not let the compost dry out completely. When new leaves begin to sprout, start to water more frequently again and keep in a cool, airy place.
Feeding: Add liquid food to the water every 14 days during the growing/flowering season.

Humidity: They must be kept humid if they are to survive indoors. Stand the pot on wet pebbles or in an outer pot of peat. Do not spray.
Cleaning: Use a soft brush if the leaves get dusty. Never use leaf shine.
Atmosphere: Keep away from fires, especially gas fires, and strong cigar smoke. Protect from draughts.
Soil: Loam-based compost No. 2
Repotting: Repot after flowering, when the old leaves have died down and new ones begin to appear. Carefully remove dead flowers or leaves. Cyclamen flower better if they are slightly pot-bound, so do not use too large a pot.
Pruning: Not necessary.
Propagation: From seeds kept at a temperature of 55–60°F (13–16°C). Old corms can be divided after the leaves and flowers have died down.
Life expectancy: They will continue for several years in the right conditions. The flowers tend to get smaller as the plant grows older.
Plant companions: They are best grown as single plants but smaller ones can be put in mixed bowls for short periods.
Ease/difficulty: Not the easiest plant for the beginner. More cyclamen die over the Christmas period than any other plant.

Dividing corms

1 Divide old corms when leaves have died down. Prepare 2 small pots with drainage and loam-based No. 2 compost.

2 Remove corm from pot and gently prise away old soil.

3 Lay corm on flat surface and cut it in two with a sharp knife. Each section must have leaf buds. Dust with sulphur dust.

4 Repot both in usual way. Keep cool (55–60°F, 13–16°C).

Humidity

Cyclamen must be kept humid indoors, but do not spray.

Stand pot in saucer with water, pebbles or gravel. Make sure pot base is clear of water.
or Put pot in outer container packed with damp peat.

What goes wrong

1 *New leaves small, no flowers.* Needs feeding.

2 *Leaves shrivel and collapse.* Too hot and dry. Add water. Move to a cooler place.

3 *Leaves turn yellow and fall apart.* Too hot and too dark. Move to a lighter, cooler and more airy place. Gas or smoke fumes may also cause yellowing of the leaves.

4 *Scorched leaves.* Direct sun and water on leaves. Move plant out of direct sunlight and make sure watering is done from below.

5 *Leaves distorted and sticky with green insects.* Greenfly. Spray with pyrethrum or a systemic insecticide.

6 *Grey mould on leaves.* Botrytis. Spray with benomyl-based fungicide.

7 *Corm rotting.* Caused by water getting into the corm. If plant is resting without leaves, try cutting out rot with sharp knife and dusting with sulphur dust. If plant is growing there is nothing to be done.

Watering

1 Test compost with fingers. If it is light and crumbly, the plant needs water.

2 Place plant in bucket and fill bucket with water to just below the rim of the pot. Leave it there for 15 minutes, then allow it to drain. Water must never get on the corm.

Cleaning the leaves

Brush leaves gently with soft, dry paintbrush. Never add water or leaf shine.

Growing from seed

1 Prepare a seed tray or propagator with a drainage layer and sterilized, seed-growing compost. Scatter seeds evenly and add thin layer of compost, no thicker than depth of seed. Water well.

2 Cover with glass and put in dark place or cover with dark cloth. Make sure the compost never dries out and turn glass over daily. Keep cool (55–60 F, 13–16 C).

3 When seeds germinate, bring them into light and remove the glass cover.

4 When seedlings are large enough to handle, thin out the weaker ones, leaving about 1in (2½cm) between each one.

5 When remaining ones are growing well, repot in separate small pots. Remember to keep them in a cool place.

Repotting

1 Repot young cyclamen grown from seed or corms when their roots begin to be congested. Older plants should be repotted after the leaves and flowers have died down, just as the new leaves start to appear. Remove all the old leaves and flowers before repotting.

2 For young plants use a pot 1 size larger. For old plants use the same size of pot. Prepare it with drainage layer and loam-based No. 2 compost.

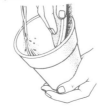

3 If you use the same pot again, wash it out.

4 Hold old pot with one hand covering compost, fingers either side of stems. Tap edge of pot. Plant and compost will come out.

5 Do not disturb root ball by prising away stale soil. You may damage the roots.

6 Place plant in centre of new pot, root-ball on compost.

7 Add new compost to fill pot. The corm should be covered around its base but should have about half its depth above the compost. Leave in the shade without water for 2 days to encourage roots to grow into compost.

Cyperus diffusus

UMBRELLA GRASS

The Cyperaceae are a family of some four hundred species which come from all over the subtropical and tropical world. They are mostly perennial, rush- or grass-like plants. One species, the papyrus, was known to the ancient Egyptians and was used to make parchment. Another produces groundnuts. They are all water lovers and in nature live in swamps and at the edges of slow moving rivers and lakes. They prefer to stand in water and are a boon to heavy-handed amateurs for they cannot be overwatered. They do well in hydroculture.

Their common name, umbrella grass, is an obvious allusion to the way the leaves curve out at the top of the stem. The flowers, fascinating but not particularly beautiful, are brown and spiky and come up above the leaves.

The two species grown as house plants both come from Madagascar and were introduced as indoor plants in the 1870s. *Cyperus alternifolius* is the more compact of the two, not normally being more than 12 to 18 in (30–46 cm) tall. *C. diffusus* is more striking, with stems up to 3 ft (1 m) tall and a wider spread of leaves. *C. alternifolius* has a variegated form *C. alternifolius* 'Albo Variegata' which has white stripes along the leaves.

Both are easy to propagate and are plants to be recommended to any beginner. However, they are sometimes difficult to find in the shops. As they tend to die back in winter they are most often available in the summer months. Choose lush looking plants. Those with yellowed or browned foliage will have dried out at some stage.

The *Cyperus* species are graceful bog plants.

Left: The grass-like flowers of *Cyperus alternifolius*.

Right: The young, pale green fronds of *Cyperus diffusus* arise from soil level.

Below: *Cyperus alternifolius* has narrow leaflets.

Size: *C. alternifolius* grows to 18 in (46 cm) and has a spread of about 10 in (25 cm) in a 5 in (12 cm) pot. *C. diffusus* grows to 3 ft (1 m) and has a spread of at least 18 in (46 cm). Young plants of *C. alternifolius* should be staked as the fronds will bend over and crease if knocked. If this happens they will not recover.
Growth: They grow fairly quickly and will normally produce 5 or 6 new leaves per growing season.
Flowering season: All through the summer.
Scent: None.
Light: They do not like the hot midday sun in summer but do need a very light position. A north or east-facing windowsill is ideal.
Temperature: A minimum winter temperature of 55°F (12°C) suits them but they will stand higher temperatures if the humidity is increased. Summer temperatures should be 68°F (20°C) with a maximum of 77°F (25°C).
Water: Keep them wet at all times. In fact the pot can actually stand in water. If they dry out they will go yellow within 24 hours.
Feeding: Add liquid food to the water every 14 days during the summer.
Humidity: They love water so spray frequently, daily if possible. Either let the plant stand in water or pack the pot round with wet peat.
Cleaning: Rely on spraying to keep them

clean. Do not use leaf shine. In summer put them outside in the rain.
Atmosphere: Keep away from fires, radiators etc.
Soil: Loam-based compost No. 2.
Repotting: Once a year in spring. Do not use too large a pot.
Pruning: Just cut away any leaves that have died through old age.
Propagation: By dividing a pot-bound plant in spring. Carefully separate the plant into two parts and pot each one separately. You can also propagate in warm water using leaves still attached to the parent plant. Try this after the flowers have died off. The temperature you need is 61°F (16°C). They can be raised from seed at 64–70°F (18–21°C). Sow seeds in spring.
Life expectancy: They live for a long time, producing a succession of new leaves to replace those that die. In winter they may die down if they are in a cold room. The stem will turn yellow and the leaves will drop. If this happens, cut them right down. They will reshoot in spring.
Plant companions: They do well in mixed bowls, provided there is enough moisture.
Ease/difficulty: A good plant for the beginner or for anyone who tends to overwater their plants.

Repotting

1 Repot in spring when stems are overcrowded, plant looks top-heavy and new shoots do not appear. Water plant well.

4 Carefully remove stale soil from roots, using stick or pencil. Do not damage roots.

2 Prepare pot 1 size larger with drainage layer and layer of damp, loam-based No. 2 compost.

5 Place plant in centre of new pot, root-ball on compost.

3 Hold old pot with one hand covering compost, fingers either side of stems. Tap edge of pot. Plant and compost will come out.

6 Add new compost to fill pot. Make sure that all roots are covered. Press down well. Stand repotted plant in water.

What goes wrong

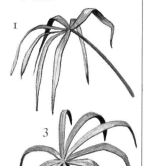

1 *Leaves turn rapidly yellow or brown.* Plant dried out. Water well immediately. Stand pot in water.

2 *Leaves die in winter, stem yellow.* Too cold. Cut right down. Plant will reshoot in spring.

3 *Leaves look dull and tired.* Lack of light. Move to a lighter position.

4 *Leaves sticky with green insects.* Greenfly. Spray with pyrethrum or a systemic insecticide.

5 *White insects fly from leaves when they are touched.* Whitefly. Spray with derris or a resmethrin-based insecticide.

Humidity

Cyperus are bog plants and need a constant supply of water and humidity. Stand the pot in a saucer of wet pebbles. The water should cover the pot base. Keep it at this level always.

Spraying

Spray daily overhead with a fine mist spray, using rainwater if possible. Hold spray about 6in (15cm) from leaves.

Root division

Divide large, old plants in early spring.

1 Prepare 2 pots with drainage layer and compost.

3 Gently pull roots and stems apart with your hands.

2 Remove plant from pot and gently prise away compost.

4 Repot both sections in the usual way.

Propagation

1 Choose a stem which has finished flowering and trim the leaves to half their length.

2 Prepare a wide, shallow jar with tepid water and a few grains of charcoal.

3 Bend the stem so that the cut leaflets are completely submerged in water. It does not matter if the stem of the parent plant is damaged but it should not be completely severed.

4 Keep jar and plant in a warm place and change the water every 4–5 days. New plantlets appear at the leaf axils.

5 When they have 3 or 4 leaves each, pull them gently away from the old leaf and pot them in small pots. Stand pots in saucers of water. Cut off old leaf stem at base.

Pruning

1 If temperature falls too low in winter stems may die down. Cut off just above the compost. Keep the pots standing in water.

2 In spring the stems will reshoot.

Dieffenbachia amoena

DUMB CANE

The *Dieffenbachia* is a most attractive plant which comes from Brazil and owes its name to a Herr Dieffenbach who was gardener to the Imperial palace at Schönbrunn, Austria in 1830. There are about twenty species in the genus, which belongs to the Arum (Araceae) family.

Dieffenbachias have broad, well defined leaves with distinctive, variegated markings which vary according to the species. Until recently they could only be grown in the tropical houses of collectors but with a little knowledge and care the varieties now available can be successfully grown in the house. They can also be successfully grown in hydroculture. Like the *Aglaonema* (page 20) they are more tolerant of semi-shaded positions than most other variegated plants. They are therefore useful to mix with the green, thick-leaved species normally grown in darker corners.

The sap of a *Dieffenbachia* is reputed to be highly poisonous and gives the plant its common name – dumb cane. If the sap touches the lips or mouth it affects the tongue which swells and makes speech difficult. It is advisable to wash your hands after handling the plant.

As dieffenbachias grow it is natural for them to lose their bottom leaves. Eventually the trunk may become too tall and unmanageable. The plant can then be cut down and will reshoot.

Most of the plants grown for sale are hybrids or varieties of *Dieffenbachia picta*. The large leaved ones come from *D. amoena*. Choose stocky plants with unfaded colour in the leaves. Plants whose lower leaves are beginning to yellow are not recommended. Avoid any with damaged leaves or broken midribs.

Above: *Dieffenbachia* 'Exotica Perfecta'.

Above: The most variegated cultivar, *Dieffenbachia* 'Pia'.

Below: *Dieffenbachia* 'Tropic Snow' has thick, succulent leaves.

Right: A large, bushy specimen of *Dieffenbachia amoena*.

Size: The smaller varieties are usually bought in 5 in (12 cm) pots and will grow to about 2 ft (60 cm). Larger varieties can easily reach 4 ft (120 cm).

Growth: Fairly fast, 12–18 in (30–46 cm) per year in the house, depending on the variety.

Flowering season: Some of the more mature plants will produce a flower. This resembles an arum lily, is green, thin and not very significant. They are often removed by professional growers.

Scent: None.

Light: Whilst they do not need to stand in a window, they like light. This applies particularly to the more variegated species.

Temperature: Much more tolerant than growers used to think. They prefer 60–64°F (15–18°C) but for short periods can survive in temperatures as low as 50°F (10°C) although this sometimes makes them lose their lower leaves. Maximum summer temperature 75°F (24°C) when humidity should be high.

Water: Use rainwater for preference. In winter it should be tepid. Water well in spring and summer – 2 to 3 times a week. Keep barely damp in winter, watering not more than every 7 to 8 days.

Feeding: Add liquid food to the water once a month in summer.

Humidity: Stand pot on wet pebbles but do not let it actually stand in water.

Cleaning: Sponge the leaves every 2–3 weeks. Take care to support them as they can easily snap.

Atmosphere: They appear to be tolerant of most conditions except oil fumes and cold draughts.

Soil: Loam-based compost No. 3.

Repotting: Once a year in spring. Put into a pot 2 sizes larger each time.

Pruning: Remove the bottom leaves as they die. If the plant gets too straggly, cut it down to about 4 in (10 cm) from the bottom and it will shoot again. Use the top as stem tip and stem section cuttings to propagate new plants. Use gloves to keep the sap off your hands.

Propagation: Some varieties are propagated from shoots that grow from the base in summer. Most are rooted from top cuttings and stem sections 3 in (8 cm) long. These are allowed to dry for about 2 days and then put in compost in a warm propagator at about 70–75°F (21–24°C) and kept well moistened. Wear gloves.

Life expectancy: Will live for a long time. However, as the bottom leaves die off naturally, the plants can get a little leggy and it is as well to replace them every 3–4 years.

Plant companions: The smaller varieties do well in mixed plantings with most other green plants. Grow the larger plants by themselves as specimens.

Ease/difficulty: They require some experience of growing plants.

Repotting

1 Repot in spring when plant looks top-heavy and no new leaves appear. Water plant well.

4 Carefully remove stale soil from roots, using stick or pencil. Do not damage roots.

2 Prepare pot 2 sizes larger with drainage and layer of loam-based No. 3 compost.

5 Place plant in centre of new pot, root-ball on compost.

3 Hold old pot with one hand covering compost, fingers either side of stems. Tap edge of pot. Plant and compost will come out.

6 Add new compost to fill pot. Make sure that all roots are covered. Press down well. Leave in the shade without water for 2 days to encourage roots to grow into compost.

What goes wrong

1 *Lower leaves drop.* Too cold. Move plant to warmer place.

2 *Lower leaves yellow.* Over-watered. Allow plant to dry out until recovered. Then water less often, especially in winter.

3 *Parts of leaves and stems rot and become slimy.* Overhead spraying when temperature low. Stop spraying. Dust areas with flowers of sulphur.

4 *Leaves at top small.* Insufficient light. Move to a lighter place.

5 *White woolly patches on leaves.* Mealy bug. Remove them individually with a swab dipped in methylated spirits or spray with malathion or a systemic insecticide.

6 *Leaves yellow with webs underneath.* Red spider mite. Spray with derris, malathion or a systemic insecticide. Improve the humidity.

Stem sections

An old plant that has lost most of its leaves can be used for propagation.

1 Prepare seed tray or propagator with a compost of ½ peat, ½ sand.

2 Remove plant from pot. Wear gloves, the sap is very poisonous.

3 Lay whole stem flat on a hard surface and cut it into lengths, each including a leaf joint and about 3in (7cm) of the stem.

4 Dip the lower cut surface of each section in hormone rooting powder.

5 Place each section upright in the compost, making sure the planted end is the end that was originally nearest the base of the plant.

6 Water well and cover. Remove cover for 5 minutes a day to prevent rot and make sure the compost does not dry out. Keep at 70–75°F (21–24°C).

7 New shoots will grow from each section. When they are growing well, repot them in the usual way.

Humidity

Stand pot in saucer with water, pebbles or gravel. Make sure pot base is clear of water.

Cleaning the leaves

Wipe dust off leaves with soft cloth and sponge with tepid water. Support leaf with other hand.

Do not use leaf shine.

Dieffenbachia sap is very poisonous. If it touches your lips or mouth it causes swelling and may make you choke. Always wear gloves if you are pruning or cutting the plant in any way and wash your hands well after handling it.

Pruning

1 A leggy plant that has lost its lower leaves can be cut down in spring.

2 Cut stem 4in (10cm) above base, making cut above an old leaf joint.

3 Keep well watered and at a temperature of not less than 60°F (15°C). New leaves will grow from the stem.

PINK ALLAMANDE

This is a climbing plant for the greenhouse which, with careful pruning, can be kept as a small, bushy house plant. A member of the Asclepiadaceae, there are some forty species, most of which come from tropical South America. The name is derived from two Greek words: *diploos*, meaning double and *aden* meaning gland. It refers to the two glands in the ovary of the flower. The leaves are oval and grow in pairs up the stem. The flowers are trumpet shaped, curled back at the edges. They normally open at the end of a stem which may produce three or four flowers in succession.

Dipladenias are essentially twining or climbing plants and if left alone will quickly grow long stems which need to be trained round a trellis or wire mesh. If they are cut back after flowering it is possible to keep them bushy and compact for some years.

Two varieties are usually sold. *Dipladenia sanderi* 'Rosea' has pretty pink flowers up to 3 in (8 cm) across with a yellow marked 'throat'. *D. boliviensis* has smaller, white flowers with quite a strong fragrance. *D. sanderi* is sometimes listed as *Mandevilla splendens*.

These are not the easiest plants to keep in the house for they need a high degree of humidity. They are also sometimes difficult to obtain. Choose them from June onwards with lush foliage and flower buds still to open. Avoid plants with dull or yellowed leaves.

Left: The white flowers of *Dipladenia boliviensis* are perfumed.

Right: Dipladenias are climbing plants and need some support and training if grown in a pot.

Below: *Dipladenia sanderi* 'Rosea' has pink and yellow flowers.

Size: By careful pruning they can be kept to about 18 in (46 cm). However, if left to twine without pruning they will soon reach 15 ft (5 m).

Growth: Unpruned, they can easily put on 2 ft (60 cm) or more of growth in a year.

Flowering season: From early summer to early autumn.

Scent: The white variety, *D. boliviensis*, has a pleasant perfume.

Light: They need plenty of light and will stand some sun.

Temperature: A minimum of 55°F (13°C) in winter if kept almost dry but they prefer 60°F (15°C) if they are to stay really healthy. 65°F (18°C) in summer. If the temperature rises above 70°F (21°C) ensure that the humidity is high.

Water: Water well in summer, probably 2–3 times a week. In winter give hardly any water at all. Wait until the plant is almost limp before watering. It is advisable to use tepid water at all times.

Feeding: In summer add half the recommended dose of liquid food to the water every 14 days.

Humidity: They like a very humid atmosphere. Stand the pot on wet pebbles. If possible, spray with tepid water every day, all the year round.

Cleaning: The daily spray should keep the leaves clean. Do not use leaf shine.

Atmosphere: Fairly tolerant of most conditions provided the humidity is kept up.

They like some ventilation while they are in flower.

Soil: Either loam-based No. 2 or peat based compost.

Repotting: May need repotting 2 or 3 times in the first year if growing rapidly. After this, repot or change the top of the soil every spring.

Pruning: If you want to keep the plant bushy, cut back growth to 2 in (5 cm) of new wood each year after flowering. If you are keeping it as a climber, leave the main stem and trim back the side shoots to keep it tidy.

Propagation: Take stem tip cuttings about 3–4 in (8–10 cm) long in the spring and root them at 77°F (25°C) with bottom heat in a propagator. These rooted cuttings will start to flower the same year.

Life expectancy: With care and attention they will last for a long time: without proper care they can be dead within a month of purchase. Keeping a high humidity is the key to success.

Plant companions: Whilst best grown on their own, they can be used when in flower as a temporary patch of colour in a mixed bowl.

Ease/difficulty: Not a plant for the beginner. It is really best in a conservatory or greenhouse.

Humidity

Stand pot in saucer with water, pebbles or gravel. Make sure pot base is clear of water.

or
Put pot in outer container packed with damp peat.

Pruning

1 If dipladenias are cut back after flowering they can be kept as more bushy plants. Cut them back so that only about 2 in (5 cm) of new wood remains.

2 Make cuts with small secateurs or scissors, cutting newly grown stem just above a leaf joint.

3 New side shoots will grow from further down the stem.

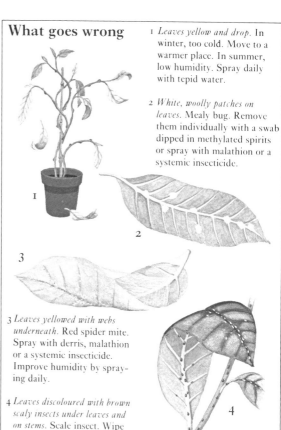

1 *Leaves yellow and drop.* In winter, too cold. Move to a warmer place. In summer, low humidity. Spray daily with tepid water.

2 *White, woolly patches on leaves.* Mealy bug. Remove them individually with a swab dipped in methylated spirits or spray with malathion or a systemic insecticide.

3 *Leaves yellowed with webs underneath.* Red spider mite. Spray with derris, malathion or a systemic insecticide. Improve humidity by spraying daily.

4 *Leaves discoloured with brown scaly insects under leaves and on stems.* Scale insect. Wipe off with methylated spirits or spray with a systemic insecticide.

Stem tip cuttings

1 Prepare propagator with compost of ½ peat, ½ sand.

2 Choose shoot or stem tip with at least 2 pairs of healthy leaves and a growing point. Cut off below second pair of leaves, close to main stem. Cuttings should be 3–4in (8–10cm) long.

3 Prepare cuttings by trimming off stem just below a leaf.

4 Remove the lowest pair of leaves.

5 Dip the cut surface in hormone rooting powder. Shake off the surplus.

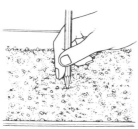

6 Make small holes in compost with stick or pencil.

7 Insert cutting so that end of stem is at bottom of hole and leaves are level with compost.

8 Water well and cover. Remove cover for 5 minutes a day to prevent rot and make sure the compost does not dry out. Keep at 77°F (25°C),

9 Remove cover after 21 days and when cuttings are growing well, repot in normal compost.

Repotting

1 Repot in spring when roots show through base of pot and plant does not produce new growth. Water plant well.

2 Prepare pot 1 size larger with drainage layer and layer of damp, loam-based No. 2 compost.

3 Hold old pot with one hand covering compost, fingers either side of stem. Tap edge of pot. Plant and compost will come out.

4 Carefully remove stale soil from roots, using stick or pencil. Do not damage roots.

5 Place plant in centre of new pot, root-ball on compost.

6 Add new compost to fill pot. Make sure that all roots are covered. Press down well. Leave in the shade without water for 2 days to encourage roots to grow into compost.

DRAGON TREE

The dracaenas are members of the Liliaceae family and their name derives from the Greek word *drakania*, meaning female dragon. The genus contains some forty species of tropical palm-like plants from Africa and Asia. They are very popular and fairly robust house plants, standing a variety of temperatures. Some will grow outside in milder temperate climates. The dracaenas are related to the cordylines, the names being often interchanged. There is considerable confusion about the naming of the two genera and they are sometimes wrongly labelled. Dracaenas on the whole have less spectacularly coloured leaves than cordylines, being mainly green or variegated.

In nature they can grow up to 20 ft (6 m) tall, with large trunks. However house plants are normally about 18 to 24 in (46 to 60 cm) tall. Recently there has been a tendency to import canes over 1 in (2½ cm) in diameter and between 1 and 4 ft (to 1 m) long and to bring them on under glass so that they sprout a head of fresh rosettes of growth at the top.

D. deremensis has pretty green and grey striped leaves. There is also a yellow and green variety, *D. schryveriana*. *D. fragrans*, so named for the heavily scented flower which appears on a mature plant, has broad green leaves. This species is suited to the cane culture described above. The variegated version is *D.f.* 'Massangeana'. *D. marginata* has very thin, almost coppery leaves which do well in mixed plantings. *D.m.* 'Tricolor' is very pretty but also rather tender. *D. sanderiana* is a miniature variety with cream and green striped leaves. It is very suitable for small mixed table bowls.

There are also two species which are suitable for use on patios or in sheltered gardens. These are *D. parrii* and *D. indivisa*, which both have strap-like leaves bending outwards from the centre.

Choose plants well furnished with unmarked leaves. The variegated varieties should have clear, unfaded colouring.

Above: *Dracaena fragrans.*

Below: A multi-headed example of *Dracaena marginata.*

Above: A highly variegated form of *Dracaena schryveriana.*

Right: *Dracaena schryveriana.*

Size: Normally 18–24 in (46–60 cm) tall. When grown on mature canes, from 18 in (46 cm) to 4 ft (120 cm) tall. The leaf span varies with variety, and can be as much as 3 ft (1 m) across.

Growth: They grow quite slowly, usually about 4–6 in (10–15 cm) per year.

Flowering season: During the summer months mature plants may flower. A stem is produced with many star-shaped cream flowers.

Scent: The flowers have a heavy tropical scent.

Light: Plenty of light is needed to maintain colour in the leaves. Avoid midday sun in summer.

Temperature: They like a fairly high temperature of 65–70°F (18–21°C) but will tolerate down to 55°F (13°C) if water is reduced. The summer maximum is 75°F (24°C).

Water: Moderate in summer, watering once or twice a week and once a week in winter. Never allow the plant to stand in water or to dry out completely.

Feeding: Add liquid food to the water every 14 days in summer.

Humidity: Plants enjoy a twice weekly spray with a mister, except when in direct sunlight.

Cleaning: Leaves can be cleaned by hand using a damp cloth. Leaf shine may be used but not more than every 2 months.

Atmosphere: Fairly tolerant of most conditions. They do not like cold draughts.

Soil: Loam-based No. 2 is suitable or a peat-based compost can be used.

Repotting: Best done in March, every 2–3 years at the most. Make sure the drainage is good.

Pruning: None necessary, except to remove dried or damaged leaves.

Propagation: By stem tip cuttings and also stem sections cut to about 3 in (8 cm) long. Root these in a humid propagator in early spring at 75°F (24°C).

Life expectancy: At least 5 or 6 years. However the bottom of the stem may become bare due to dryness in the air.

Plant companions: They do well in mixed plantings and enjoy the company of most other greenhouse plants. With their colourful and variegated leaves they provide a good contrast to green *Ficus*, philodendrons, hederas etc.

Ease/difficulty: Not really a difficult plant.

Repotting

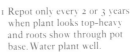

1 Repot only every 2 or 3 years when plant looks top-heavy and roots show through pot base. Water plant well.

2 Prepare pot 1 size larger with good drainage layer and damp, loam-based No. 2 or peat-based compost.

3 Hold old pot with one hand covering compost, fingers either side of stem. Tap edge of pot. Plant and compost will come out.

4 Carefully remove stale soil from roots, using stick or pencil. Do not damage roots.

5 Place plant in centre of new pot, root-ball on compost.

6 Add new compost to fill pot. Make sure that all roots are covered. Press down well. Leave in the shade without water for 2 days to encourage roots to grow into compost.

1 *Lower leaves drop.* Too dry and hot. Water and spray.

2 *Leaves fade.* Not enough light. Move to lighter place.

3 *Leaves discoloured with brown scaly insects under leaves and on stems.* Scale insect. Remove them individually with a swab dipped in methylated spirits or spray with malathion or a systemic insecticide.

4 *Leaves yellowed with webs underneath.* Red spider mite. Spray with derris, malathion or a systemic insecticide. Improve humidity.

5 *Greyish brown spots on leaves.* Leaf spot fungus. Spray with a systemic fungicide.

6 *Plant sheds leaves and stops growing.* Too cold. Move to warmer place.

7 *Plant flops, leaves rot and roots may rot.* Too wet. Allow to dry out until recovered. Then water less often.

8 *New leaves small and distorted, no new growth in spring.* Needs feeding.

Stem tip cuttings

A propagator is best for this plant but you can experiment with a polythene cover if you can keep the plant on a warm radiator with heat coming from below.

1 Prepare propagator with compost of ½ peat, ½ sand.

2 Choose shoot or stem tip with at least 2 pairs of healthy leaves and a growing point. Cut off below second pair of leaves. Cuttings should be 3–4in (8–10cm) long.

3 Prepare cutting by trimming off stem just below a leaf.

4 Remove the lowest pair of leaves.

5 Dip the cut surface in hormone rooting powder. Shake off the surplus.

6 Make small hole in compost with stick or pencil.

7 Insert cutting so that end of stem is at bottom of hole and leaves are level with compost.

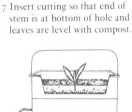

8 Water well and cover. If you have no propagator, cover with polythene supported by wire and keep on a warm radiator. Keep at 75°F (24°C). Remove cover for 5 minutes a day and never let the compost dry out.

9 Remove cover after 21 days and when cutting is growing well, repot in normal compost.

Trimming the leaves

If leaf tips brown, cut new point just above edge of healthy leaf. Do not cut into green tissue.

Spraying

Spray twice a week overhead with a fine mist spray. Hold spray about 6in (15cm) from leaves.

CAPE HEATH

There are some five hundred known species of the genus *Erica* of which no less than 470 come from South Africa, some seven or eight from tropical Africa and the rest from Europe. Unfortunately the Cape heaths that are sold as pot plants can only be regarded as transient plants in the house: most homes are too warm in winter for them. On the other hand they do not like frost and most will not survive outside all the year round in a cold climate. They are best accepted as a flowering plant produced by the nurserymen, enjoyed for a few weeks in the house and then discarded. In this way they bring a delightful interlude of colour in the late autumn and early winter before the azaleas come into flower.

If you wish to keep the plant from year to year, keep it in your coolest room while it is in flower and when the flowers have finished let it rest at 45°F (7°C). Plant it out in the garden in May, bringing it in again in late September before the flower buds appear.

E. gracilis, introduced in 1774, has flowers that are a deep rose pink in colour. The white form is called *E. gracilis* 'Alba' or sometimes *E. nivalis*. These two appear first in the shops, followed just before Christmas by *E. hyemalis* which has longer pink and white bells. Individual flowers of all varieties are very long lasting.

E. gracilis is now also used for winter bedding outside. Even when it has finished flowering the whole plant turns a rust colour with the cold and this contrasts well with the green of other plants around it.

Choose Cape heaths as they come into flower. Make sure that the flowers are fresh and the foliage is supple. Brittle plants will have dried out and may not recover. Shake the plant to make sure the foliage does not fall off.

The Cape heaths are best kept in a cool room. Several hybrids (below) can be grown from seed.

Above: *Erica* 'Limelight'.

Right: *Erica hyemalis*.

Size: About 18 in (46 cm) tall for *E. gracilis* and about 2 ft (60 cm) for *E. hyemalis*.

Growth: Will make 10 in (25 cm) of growth in one season.

Flowering season: Late autumn and early winter. *E. gracilis* flowers first, followed by *E. hyemalis*.

Scent: None.

Light: They need a very light position. Keep on a windowsill if you are trying to keep it from one year to the next.

Temperature: An ideal temperature is 45°F (7°C). 60°F (15°C) is the maximum. The cooler the temperature, the longer the plant will last.

Water: Always use rainwater or other lime-free water. Keep the root ball very moist at all times, watering 2–3 times a week.

Feeding: Not necessary if kept as a short term plant. If it survives longer, add liquid food to the water every 14 days while it is making new growth.

Humidity: Stand the pot on wet pebbles or pack moist peat around it.

Cleaning: Not necessary although a weekly spray with soft water will help. Do not use leaf shine.

Atmosphere: They do not like a hot dry atmosphere and need good ventilation. In summer the plant should be put out of doors and sprayed overhead weekly.

Soil: A very peaty compost. It must be lime free.

Repotting: Once a year in spring. Use plastic pots as the plants are less likely to dry out in these. Firm the compost down well over the roots.

Pruning: Cut back quite hard after flowering, to about half its height.

Propagation: In late summer, take stem tip cuttings and insert in a box of peat and sand. Keep covered with plastic or glass and maintain humidity. The temperature should be about 60°F (15°C). A propagator gives best results.

Life expectancy: Treat as an expendable plant to be enjoyed and discarded. If planted outside in summer they may survive for a second year.

Plant companions: They look well in any planted bowl of green plants as a 'visitor'.

Ease/difficulty: Easy to keep for a short time. As a long-term plant, more suited to conditions in a nursery than in the house.

Repotting

1 Repot in spring after flowering when plant looks top-heavy and does not produce new growth. Water plant well.

2 Prepare pot 1 size larger with drainage layer and layer of damp, peat-based, lime-free compost. Plastic pots are best as the plant is less likely to dry out.

3 Hold old pot with one hand covering compost, fingers either side of stems. Tap edge of pot. Plant and compost will come out.

4 Carefully remove stale soil from roots, using stick or pencil. Do not damage roots.

5 Place plant in centre of new pot, root-ball on compost.

6 Add new compost to fill pot. Make sure that all roots are covered. Press down well. Leave in the shade without water for 2 days to encourage roots to grow into compost.

What goes wrong

1 *Whole plant goes brittle.* Too dry. Soak plant in bucket of water. It may not survive.

2 *Brown scaly insects under leaves and on stems.* Scale insect. Remove them individually with a swab dipped in methylated spirits or spray with a systemic insecticide.

3 *Plant drops leaves, soil smells dank.* Saturation leading to root rot. No cure.

Stem tip cuttings

1 Take stem tip cuttings in late summer. A propagator gives best results as they need humidity to root. Prepare a propagator with $\frac{1}{2}$ peat, $\frac{1}{2}$ sand.

2 Choose healthy stem without flowers and cut off the tip. It should be about 1in ($2\frac{1}{2}$cm) long.

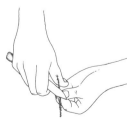

3 Prepare cutting by trimming the leaves off its lowest third.

4 Dip the cut surface in hormone rooting powder. Shake off the surplus.

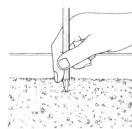

5 Make small holes in compost with stick or pencil.

6 Insert cutting so that end of stem is at bottom of hole and leaves are level with compost.

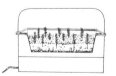

7 Water well and cover. Remove cover for 5 minutes a day to prevent rot Do not let compost dry out. Keep at 60°F (15°C).

8 Remove cover after 21 days and when cuttings are growing well, repot in normal compost.

Humidity

Stand pot in saucer with water, pebbles or gravel. Make sure pot base is clear of water.

or

Put pot in outer container packed with damp peat.

Pruning

1 Cut plant back hard after it has flowered, especially if it has grown straggly. Do not cut into the old wood.

2 Cut evenly all round the plant with secateurs. Shears can be used.

3 The plant will grow into a more even shape and you will have a better chance of keeping it for the following year. After pruning, put it outside for the summer, or keep it on a windowsill where it will receive good light.

POINSETTIA

Poinsettias are known all over the world as the flower of Christmas, from the brilliant red colouring they produce at this time of the year. In fact the flowers themselves are relatively insignificant, small, yellow pods with black stamens emerging in the centre. The real colour comes from the large modified leaves or bracts which surround these flowers.

Euphorbias are a large genus of plants, including nearly a thousand species. They include plants of many types, some annuals, some perennials, some shrubs, others trees and even succulents. They all have a milky sap or latex which oozes out when the stem is damaged and is said to be poisonous.

Euphorbia pulcherrima (*pulcherrima* means 'most beautiful') comes from Mexico, where it was discovered in 1834. In its natural habitat it is a shrub which will grow up to 16ft (5m) tall.

Until the late 1950s poinsettias were very much specialists' plants and had a very limited life in the home: the leaves would drop off almost as soon as it came into a dry atmosphere. However, Paul Ekke of California USA developed a strain that would stand room conditions and would indeed survive in temperatures very much lower than those found in a normal house or flat. The leaves did not fall and with minimum care it would keep its coloured bracts for many weeks. Today these varieties have been developed further and there are several different colours available.

Buy poinsettias when they are in full colour. A healthy plant will have bright green, fresh looking leaves. One with 5 to 9 heads is probably the best size for most homes. Avoid plants which are dropping their leaves.

Poinsettias bear small yellow flowers surrounded by bracts of brilliant colours. Varieties are now available in white (above) and pink as well as red.

Left: The flowers with their collar of bracts.

Right: A well grown, branched example of *Euphorbia pulcherrima*.

Size: They vary greatly from small single headed plants to large multibranched ones carrying some 20-30 heads of colour. These may be up to 20 in (50 cm) tall.

Growth: When bought in flower, they will not grow any more that season. However, they grow strongly before flowering and will easily grow 12-18 in (30-46 cm) before forming their final bracts.

Flowering season: From late autumn into winter and sometimes early spring. They are short day plants – they need long periods of darkness for the bracts to colour fully.

Scent: None.

Light: They like a good, natural light position and in winter can stand direct sunshine. When they are growing, keep them shaded from direct sun.

Temperature: Keep at normal room temperature when in colour (not less than 55°F (12°C), not more than 70°F (21°C)). At other times they will stand cooler temperatures, but they will not survive frost.

Water: Keep the compost quite moist during the growing season and while the plant is in flower. Water twice a week, from the top of the pot, never letting the plant dry out. After flowering allow the plant to rest for several weeks, watering only once a week to keep it on the dry side. Start to give more water again after pruning and repotting.

Feeding: Add liquid food to the water every 14 days while growing and flowering.

Humidity: Spray daily with water to keep the leaves fresh.

Cleaning: Not necessary. The spray will remove dust and dirt. Do not use leaf shine.

Atmosphere: Fairly tolerant but keep out of cold draughts. May be affected by gas fires.

Soils: They do well in loamless composts.

Repotting: If the plant is being kept for the next season, repot after pruning back in midsummer. Take care, stems and roots are brittle. Repot again a month to 6 weeks later, before it reaches flowering size. If the stem has been rooted into a small, inner pot by the grower, do not remove it. Repot inner pot as if it is the root ball. Never firm down the soil.

Pruning: Cut off top shoots in spring, after flowering and before repotting. This will encourage new shoots to grow.

Propagation: Tiny shoots can be rooted in small pots in the summer. The earlier the cuttings are taken, the bigger the plants will be when flowering in the winter. Use a propagator at 70°F (21°C).

Life expectancy: Unless you are an experienced grower with a greenhouse, it is best to treat poinsettias as one season plants. Flowering time can last as long as 3 months.

Plant companions: Large specimens are best on their own. Small, single stem plants look well in mixed bowls of green plants.

Ease/difficulty: Easy to keep for several months but difficult to retain from one season to the next. Commercial growers repropagate each year, using a growth retardant to keep the plants compact.

Repotting

1 Repot in midsummer after pruning, if plant is too big for its pot and roots look crowded. Water plant well.

2 Prepare pot 1 size larger with drainage layer and layer of loamless compost.

3 Hold old pot with one hand covering compost, fingers either side of stems. Tap edge of pot. Plant and compost will come out. Take care, the stems are brittle.

4 Do not remove stale soil and if plant is in a rooting pot do not remove it.

5 Place plant in centre of new pot, root-ball on compost.

6 Add new compost to fill pot. Make sure that all the roots are covered but do not press it down too hard. Leave the plant in the shade without water for 2 days to encourage roots to grow into compost.

1 *Leaves turn yellow and curl, then fall.* Too hot and dry and too dark. Water and spray regularly. Feed regularly and keep in a light place.

2 *Leaves shrivel and dry.* Gas fires. Move to fume-free room.

3 *Whole plant droops.* Draughts. Move to protected position.

4 *Leaves distorted and sticky with green insects.* Greenfly. Spray with pyrethrum or a systemic insecticide.

5 *Leaves marbled with silver.* Silver leaf virus. No cure. Destroy plant.

Stem tip cuttings

1 Take stem tip cuttings in summer. Prepare lattice pots with mixture ½ sand, ½ loamless compost. Wear gloves, the sap can irritate the skin.

2 Choose shoot or stem tip with at least 2 pairs of healthy leaves and a growing point. Cut off below second pair of leaves, close to main stem. Cuttings should be 3–4in (8–10cm) long.

3 Prepare cuttings by trimming off stem just below a leaf.

4 Remove the lowest pair of leaves.

5 Dip the cut surface in hormone rooting powder. Shake off the surplus.

6 Poinsettias have delicate roots and hate root disturbance. Put each cutting into a 2in (5cm) lattice pot or rooting block.

7 Place pots in propagator, water and cover. Keep at 70°F (21°C). Remove cover for 5 minutes a day to prevent rot. Do not let the pots dry out.

8 Remove cover after 21 days. When cuttings are growing, place them pot and all into their next pot and add compost. Do not press it down.

9 Cuttings taken in mid-summer will flower the following winter.

Humidity

Stand pot in saucer with water, pebbles or gravel. Make sure pot base is clear of water.

Spray daily overhead with a fine mist spray, using rainwater if possible. Hold spray about 6in (15cm) from leaves. Do not spray the bracts.

Pruning for growth

1 Prune the plant at the end of the flowering season, to encourage new growth. Remember to wear gloves.

2 Make cuts just above a leaf stem. If sap runs, dab cuts with cotton wool dipped in petroleum jelly.

IVY TREE

The *Fatshedera* is a rare example of a hybrid which has been given its own genus name instead of being listed under the names of its two parents. It is what is known as a bigeneric hybrid, the result of a cross between plants belonging to different genera – the *Fatsia* or *Aralia* (false castor oil plant) and the *Hedera* (ivy). The actual varieties involved were *Fatsia japonica* 'Moseri' and *Hedera helix* 'Hibernica'. The cross was made in France in 1910 and has added a worthy member to our list of houseplants. Its common name is ivy tree and it is a member of the Araliaceae.

The leaves are smaller than those of the *Aralia* although they are the same shape. It grows as an upright climber, like an ivy and normally requires some support. It looks well when three plants are grown together round a moss pole and it is a good plant for that slightly darker position.

Whilst both aralias and hederas are hardy, the *Fatshedera* is not. It can be placed outside in the summer on a patio or terrace but must be brought back indoors in the winter. Take care not to overwater it for this can cause the plant to drop its leaves.

The green form is the stronger plant but there is also an attractive variegated version with cream edges to the leaves. However, this does tend to get brown tipping to the leaves in winter.

Buy bushy plants which will probably have several cuttings per pot. None of the leaves should be yellowed and there should not be sections of the stem bare of leaves.

Size: Will easily grow up to 10ft (250cm).
Growth: Fairly fast. They will put on 1ft (30cm) or more in the house. Grown in a greenhouse they will double this rate.
Flowering season: Flowers appear in late summer on mature plants. They are like the green flowers of an ivy and are not very impressive.
Scent: None.
Light: Tolerant of bad conditions. Whilst it flourishes better in direct light, it will survive and even grow in a dark corner.
Temperature: They prefer a cool place and will be happy in a temperature as low as 45°F (7°C). Maximum summer temperature 65°F (18°C).
Water: In summer they like plenty of water, 2 or 3 times a week. Do not let your plant stand in water. In winter keep it on the dry side, watering every 7–10 days, especially if the temperature is low. Never let the root ball dry out.
Feeding: Add liquid food to the water every 14 days in summer.
Humidity: They appreciate a regular spraying with water – every week at least.
Cleaning: If spraying does not remove the dust, the leaves should be cleaned by hand. Leaf shine can be used but not more than once every two months.
Atmosphere: They are tolerant of most conditions except dry heat. They are therefore not plants for a centrally heated house.
Soil: Loam-based No. 2.

Repotting: Once a year in March or April.
Pruning: If the plant gets too leggy it can be cut back to about 12in (30cm) above the compost. The top can be used for propagating new plants.
Propagation: By rooting stem tip cuttings in spring in compost and sharp sand. The cuttings should be about 6in (15cm) long. No propagator is required and a minimum temperature of (55–60°F (13–15°C)) is sufficient in spring and summer. It is also possible to air layer the top of the plant.
Life expectancy: 6–7 years at least.
Plant companions: They enjoy the company of all indoor green plants and look well in mixed tubs and jardinières.
Ease/difficulty: This is a plant that a beginner should try.

Adding a moss pole

1 Three fatshederas can be planted in the same pot and trained up a moss pole to give a good display.

4 Place plants beside it, spacing them to allow room for their roots to grow.

2 Knock plants from pots and remove a little soil from around the roots.

5 Add new compost to fill pot. Make sure all roots are well covered.

3 Position moss pole and add a little compost around it to hold it firm.

6 Tie stems to moss pole with twine or raffia.

The *Fatshedera* is a hybrid which has the leaf shape of the *Fatsia* and the climbing habit and vigour of the *Hedera* (ivy).

Right: A well grown example of a *Fatshedera*, well supported by a moss pole.

Left: Plain green leaves of *Fatshedera lizei*.

Left: The variegated form, *Fatshedera lizei* 'Variegata' has different shades of green on its leaves.

What goes wrong

1 *Leaves turn yellow.* Over-watering. Allow to dry out and then water less often.

2 *Shoots elongated, long spaces between leaves.* Too dark. Move to a lighter place. Possibly too hot: check temperature.

3 *Leaves yellowed with webs underneath.* Red spider mite. The plant is very susceptible. Spray with derris, malathion or a systemic insecticide and move to a cooler position. Spray daily with water to improve humidity.

Repotting

1 Repot in spring when plant looks top-heavy, leaves are a poor colour and no new growth appears. Water plant well.

2 Prepare new pot 1 size larger with drainage and damp, loam-based No. 2 compost.

3 Loosen compost with knife around top edge of pot.

4 Remove plant, holding it firmly by base of stem and supporting the upper part.

5 Lay plant on table and remove old compost from roots with stick or pencil. Do not damage roots.

6 If plant is too big for pot, prune the longest roots with secateurs.

7 Place plant in centre of new pot, root-ball on compost.

8 Add new compost, firming it until the pot is filled. Make sure all roots are covered. Leave in the shade without water for 2 days to encourage roots to grow into compost.

Stem tip cuttings

1 Take stem tip cuttings in spring. Prepare pot with ½ sand, ½ loam-based compost.

2 Choose shoot or stem tip with at least 2 pairs of healthy leaves and a growing point. Cut off below second pair of leaves. Cuttings should be about 6in (15cm) long.

3 Prepare cuttings by trimming off stem just below a leaf.

4 Remove the lowest pair of leaves.

5 Dip the cut surface in hormone rooting powder. Shake off the surplus.

6 Make small holes in compost around edge with stick or pencil.

7 Insert cutting so that end of stem is at bottom of hole and leaves are level with compost.

8 Water well and cover with polythene supported by wire. Remove cover for 5 minutes a day and never let compost dry out. Keep at 55–60 F (13–16 C).

9 Remove cover after 21 days and when cuttings are growing well, repot in normal compost.

WEEPING FIG

The *Ficus* or fig is found all over the warmer parts of the world and is a member of the Moraceae family. Because the family includes a large number of important and popular house plants, three sections are devoted to it here. The first is about the small leaved species, the second covers the larger leaved ones and the third the climbers and trailers.

Ficus benjamina is perhaps the best known of the small leaved varieties. Commonly known as the weeping fig, it has branches which droop gracefully, particularly as the plant gets big. Like the other small leaved species it can grow over 15 ft (5 m) tall indoors. The leaves are bright green and are up to 3 in (8 cm) long and about 1 in (2½ cm) wide. Many are carried on each stem. It needs a good, light position to flourish and is particularly susceptible to cold draughts. Like other *Ficus*, it is tolerant of dry air because of its leathery, waxy leaves.

F. nitida or *rubinginosa* has leaves of a similar size and shape but grows more upright. Its stem is like that of a birch tree. *F. australis* has a much more spreading habit of growth. It branches readily and the leaves are similar to those of the rubber plant (*F. elastica*) but smaller, being not more than 4–5 in (10–12 cm) long. It makes a good specimen plant.

F. diversifolia, the mistletoe fig, is one of the hardiest of the family. The leaves are small, almost round and grow sparsely on branches of an upright stem. The plant produces green berries which turn a yellow orange before dropping off. It is not a difficult plant but is not widely grown. It is sometimes known as *F. deltoidea*.

Choose plants with a bushy, elegant shape. Avoid those which are dropping leaves or have yellowed leaves on the lower part of the plant.

The small leaved figs are graceful plants and may produce fruit when still young. *Ficus diversifolia* (left) fruits when 1 ft (30 cm) high.

Below: *Ficus nitida* is similar to *F. benjamina* but grows more upright.

Size: All these small leaved *Ficus* are trees and will easily grow to 15–20 ft (5–6 m) and even more. They should be staked when they are young.

Growth: A little difficult to generalize but some varieties can grow 18 in (46 cm) in a year. *F. diversifolia* grows most slowly.

Flowering season: Except for *F. diversifolia*, these plants do not flower or fruit indoors.

Scent: None.

Light: *F. benjamina* needs plenty of light or the leaves will drop. The others need less light and *F. diversifolia* is a good plant for a dark situation.

Temperature: All except *F. diversifolia* need a minimum temperature of 55–60°F (13–15°C). *F. diversivolia* can stand temperatures as low as 45°F (7°C) provided water is reduced. Maximum summer temperature 75°F (24°C).

Water: Like most *Ficus*, these do not like to be overwatered, otherwise the leaves turn yellow and drop off. Water not more than twice a week in summer and every 7–10 days in winter. Never let the plants stand in water.

Feeding: Add liquid food to the water every 14 days in the growing season.

Humidity: All these species will benefit from a daily spray with tepid water.

Cleaning: If the spraying does not keep them clean, use leaf shine but not more than once every two months.

Atmosphere: Tolerant of most conditions except draughts.

Soil: Loam-based No. 2.

Repotting: Once a year at most in spring. When caring for mature plants, just change the topsoil in the pot or tub in spring.

Pruning: Prune if the plant is getting out of hand. Do this in spring time, just as growth starts and remember to dust the wounds with charcoal to stop bleeding. *F. benjamina* and *F. nitida* develop aerial roots as they age, like the philodendrons. These must never be cut off.

Propagation: From stem tip cuttings taken in spring in a propagator at about 75°F (24°C). It is possible to propagate some species (e.g. *F. australis*) by air layering.

Life expectancy: Very long lasting. Space is more likely to be the problem if the plants have survived the first year or so.

Plant companions: All *Ficus* are good mixers. However, a tall plant makes an excellent specimen plant.

Ease/difficulty: Once established in the house (i.e. after the first three months) all these species are easy.

Replacing topsoil

1 When plant is over 3 ft (1 m) tall, do not repot. Water, then remove top inch (2 cm) of old compost. Do not damage roots.

2 Add new compost to fill pot.

3 Press down firmly all round, making sure roots are all well covered.

4 Leave in shade without water for 2 days to encourage roots to grow into new compost.

Watering

1 Test compost with fingers. If it is light and crumbly, the plant needs water.

2 Add water at top of pot, using rainwater if possible. Empty excess from saucer after 15 minutes.

Right: *Ficus benjamina*, the weeping fig. Very large examples of this plant weep elegantly like a willow tree.

Below: The leaves of *Ficus australis*.

What goes wrong

1 *Leaves drop.* Insufficient light, or draughts. Move to a lighter place, protected from draughts.

2 *Leaves discoloured with brown scaly insects under leaves and on stems.* Scale insect. This plant is susceptible. Remove them individually with a swab dipped in methylated spirits or spray with a systemic insecticide.

3 *Leaves turn yellow.* Plant overwatered. Allow to dry out until recovered, then water less often.

4 *Leaves yellowed with webs underneath.* Red spider mite. Spray with derris, malathion or a systemic insecticide. Improve humidity.

Tying to a cane

1 Push cane gently into compost a few inches away from the main stem, stopping when cane is $\frac{2}{3}$ down the pot.

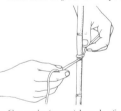

2 Cut a 9in (23cm) length of string and tie firmly around cane on stem side.

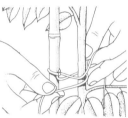

3 Loop string around stem as shown.

4 Tie a firm knot against the cane. Repeat at intervals up the stem.

Stem tip cuttings

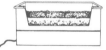

1 Prepare seed tray or propagator with a compost of $\frac{1}{2}$ peat, $\frac{1}{2}$ sand.

2 Choose shoot or stem tip with at least 2 pairs of healthy leaves and a growing point. Cut off below second pair of leaves. Cuttings should be 3–4in (8–10cm) long.

3 Prepare cuttings by trimming off stem just below a leaf.

4 Remove the lowest pair of leaves.

5 Dip the cut surface in hormone rooting powder. Shake off the surplus.

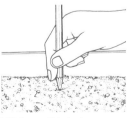

6 Make small holes in compost with stick or pencil.

7 Insert cutting so that end of stem is at bottom of hole and leaves are level with compost.

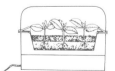

8 Water well and cover. Remove cover for 5 minutes a day to prevent rot and make sure the compost does not dry out. Keep at 75°F (24°C). Remove cover after 21 days and when cuttings are growing well, repot in normal compost.

Spraying

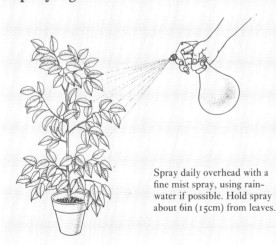

Spray daily overhead with a fine mist spray, using rainwater if possible. Hold spray about 6in (15cm) from leaves.

93

RUBBER PLANT

The large leaved figs usually need staking. Left: The hairy leaves of *Ficus benghalensis*.

Below: *Ficus lyrata* is an imposing plant with leaves shaped like the back of a violin.

Ficus elastica is probably the best known (and most abused) of all house plants. The genus has some six hundred species, including the edible fig, and is spread across the warmer parts of the world. *F. elastica* comes from India, where it grows in the wild to heights of 100 ft (30 m) or more.

The plants most commonly seen today are the cultivated varieties *F. elastica* 'Decora' and *F. elastica* 'Robusta'. They are ideal room plants with their broad, leathery, dark green leaves. New leaves grow from a pointed red sheath, emerging an attractive bronze colour and becoming green as they mature. The plants grow quite quickly into large branching trees. They have a natural tendency to drop some of their lower leaves as they age.

Two other large-leaved species are popular, *F. lyrata* (or *F. pandurata*) often called the banjo or fiddle-back fig and *F. benghalensis*, the Banyan fig. *F. lyrata* is a most imposing plant, particularly when mature. The leaves are some 12 in (30 cm) long and 9 in (23 cm) across and resemble the body of a violin. It branches well and large plants are often used by interior designers. Whilst still an easy plant, it grows more slowly than *F. elastica* and needs more care. It should always be well staked when young.

F. benghalensis has rough hairy leaves, slightly smaller than the leaves of *F. elastica*. It is a fast grower and branches well. However, it can be greedy for space and may soon appear to take over a small room.

There are several variegated varieties on the market, *F. doescheri* and *F. schryveriana* being the two best known. *F. doescheri* has pretty pink and cream markings on a green background whilst *F. schryveriana* has delicate shades of green interspersed with cream. Both are slower growers than the all green varieties and need good light to preserve the colours of their leaves.

Choose plants well furnished with undamaged leaves of a good colour.

Size: Most plants are sold when they are about 18 in (46 cm) tall with 5 to 8 well formed leaves. More mature plants, already some 3 ft (1 m) tall, can also be obtained. Indoors they will grow to about 30 ft (10 m).

Growth: In good conditions *F. elastica* and *F. benghalensis* may grow 2 to 3 ft (60 cm to 1 m) a year; *F. lyrata* and the variegated types 1 ft (30 cm).

Flowering season: Only very large, old plants flower and produce a fruit rather like a fig.

Scent: None.

Light: Grows better in good light but will also tolerate darker positions. Insufficient light restricts growth.

Temperature: A minimum of 60°F (15°C) in winter. In summer it will tolerate temperatures well above 60°F (15°C), but not above 85°F (29°C).

Water: In winter keep the soil barely moist, watering not more than once a week. In summer water liberally, at least twice a week.

Feeding: Add liquid food to the water every 14 days in summer.

Humidity: Will tolerate central heating but spray overhead at least once a week and sponge leaves monthly.

Cleaning: Clean smooth-leaved varieties by hand. Brush hairy leaves with a soft brush. Leaf shine can be used every 2 months on *F. elastica* but never on *F. lyrata* or *F. benghalensis*.

Atmosphere: They like movement of air but no direct draughts.

Soil: They grow well in either a proprietary peat compost or in loam-based No. 2 potting compost. Good drainage is essential.

Repotting: This is necessary when either the plant is much too tall for its pot and becomes top heavy, or the water runs right through from top to bottom, showing that the soil is exhausted. Repot in spring.

Pruning: Not necessary except to restrict growth. Stake young plants well. If a leaf or stem is torn it will 'bleed' a white sticky substance. The wound should be covered with petroleum jelly or a tissue to seal it.

Propagation: In spring or early summer by air layering or leaf bud cuttings, using 3 in (8 cm) lengths of stem, each with a leaf attached. Use a propagator at 77°F (25°C).

Life expectancy: A well cared for plant will live and grow until it reaches the ceiling! Overwatered plants may die in 6 months.

Plant companions: Best grown alone because of their size.

Ease/difficulty: Easy plants, requiring minimum care. Be careful not to overwater, especially in winter.

Propagation

1 A large plant that has lost its lower leaves may be given a new lease of life by air layering the stem.

2 Make shallow upward cut in stem below leaf or leaf scar, using a sharp knife.

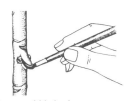

3 Insert pebble in the cut to hold it open and dust the cut surface with hormone rooting powder.

4 Wrap damp moss around the cut and tie with string.

5 Wrap polythene around moss and secure top and bottom with thread or string.

6 When roots begin to show through moss, prepare new pot. Cut straight across main stem below polythene. Remove polythene and moss and repot plant as usual. If you want to keep the old plant, seal the cut stem with damp cotton wool dipped in petroleum jelly. The plant may reshoot from dormant buds lower down the stem.

The rubber plants include species with attractive variegations.

Above: The young growth of *Ficus schryveriana*.

Right: *Ficus elastica* 'Robusta', with leaves growing right to the base of the stem.

Below: A leaf of *Ficus doescheri*.

What goes wrong

1 *Leaves hang down and seem limp*. Plant in urgent need of water. Soak in a bucket and allow to drain.

2 *Lower leaves yellow and then drop, especially in winter*. Overwatering. Allow to dry out and then water less often.

3 *Leaves pale and new growth small and distorted*. Plant needs feeding or repotting.

4 *Leaves drop suddenly, brown patches on other leaves*. Too cold. Move to a warmer position.

5 *White woolly patches on leaves*. Mealy bug. Remove them individually with a swab dipped in methylated spirits or spray with malathion or a systemic insecticide.

6 *Leaves peppered with yellow spots with webs underneath*. Red spider mite. Spray with derris, malathion or a systemic insecticide. Improve the humidity.

7 *Brown scaly insects under leaves and on stems*. Scale insect. Remove them individually with a swab dipped in methylated spirits or spray with a systemic insecticide.

Repotting

1 Repot in spring when new leaves are dwarfed and a poor colour. Roots may grow through the pot base. Water plant well.

2 Prepare pot 1 size larger with either peat-based compost or loam-based No. 2. Make sure there is a good drainage layer in the bottom.

3 Loosen compost with knife around top edge of pot.

4 Remove plant, holding it firmly by base of stem and supporting the upper part.

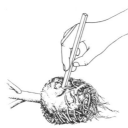

5 Lay plant on table and remove old compost from roots with stick or pencil. Do not damage roots.

6 If plant is too big for pot, prune the longest roots with secateurs.

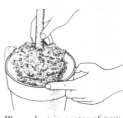

7 Place plant in centre of new pot, root-ball on compost.

8 Add new compost, firming it until the pot is filled. Make sure all roots are covered. Leave in the shade without water for 2 days to encourage roots to grow into compost.

Tying to a cane

1 Push cane gently into compost a few inches away from the main stem, stopping when cane is $\frac{2}{3}$ down the pot.

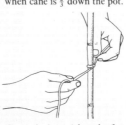

2 Cut a 9in (23cm) length of string and tie firmly around cane on stem side.

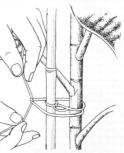

3 Loop string around stem as shown.

4 Tie a firm knot against the cane. Repeat at intervals up the stem.

CREEPING FIG

The third section on *Ficus* is about the two climbing or trailing varieties, the first of which, *Ficus pumila*, is extremely popular.

F. pumila (meaning 'small') otherwise known as *F. repens* (meaning 'creeping') is the better known plant of the two. Its small, almost round leaves of about $\frac{1}{2}$ in (1 cm) across are carried on wiry stems which trail everywhere. If allowed to climb up a wall in the greenhouse it will adhere quite neatly and soon form a dense green tapestry. It can also be successfully trained up a stake or moss pole. It loves shade and needs a moist atmosphere. If it is left to dry out, it will die immediately. It grows well in hanging baskets (if kept well watered) and in large bottle gardens where it flourishes in the humid atmosphere. It grows wild in both China and Japan and was first introduced into the West in 1721. A variegated variety is sometimes available.

F. radicans 'Variegata', the rooting fig, is the other climbing species available. The variegated leaves are bigger, up to 2 in (5 cm) long, and are pointed. It comes from the East Indies and was introduced more than 150 years later than *F. pumila*. Again, it needs a humid atmosphere to survive and grow, but it likes more light to preserve the markings in its leaves.

Buy these plants with lush, bushy growth. None of the leaves should be shrivelled and new growth should be appearing.

Below: The variegated form *Ficus pumila* 'Variegata' grows more slowly than its all green relative and is not so commonly available.

Right: *Ficus pumila* is the most popular of the trailing figs. It is easy to keep provided it never dries out. It can be grown as either a trailer or a climber, trained up a moss pole.

Size: Being climbers, they will spread over a large area, so it is difficult to give sizes. Up a moss pole they will reach about 4 ft (120 cm).

Growth: *F. pumila* will grow several trails of 12-18 in (30-46 cm) in a year. *F. radicans* grows much more slowly, at 6 in (15 cm) a year. The leaves of *F. pumila* become larger and oblong when the plant is mature.

Flowering season: Neither normally flowers in the house, although flowering can occur in summer if the plant is growing in a bed in a greenhouse.

Scent: None.

Light: *F. pumila* is a good, shade-loving plant and does not like direct sunlight. *F. pumila* 'Variegata' and *F. radicans* like a little more light.

Temperature: *F. pumila* will stand temperatures as low as 45°F (7°C). *F. radicans* prefers 55°F (12°C). Neither minds the summer heat as long as they are never allowed to dry out.

Water: Both require plenty of water and should never be allowed to dry out. Water 2-3 times a week in summer and once a week in winter if the temperature is below 50°F (10°C).

Feeding: Add liquid food to the water every 14 days when growing.

Humidity: Spray every day in summer to keep up humidity. Spray every other day in winter. In high central heating, spray every day all the year round.

Cleaning: The spraying will be sufficient. Unlike some of the larger *Ficus* species, these plants do not like leaf shine.

Atmosphere: Neither plant likes it too hot and dry.

Soil: Loam-based No. 2 or peat based.

Repotting: Once a year in spring. When mature, change the topsoil in spring.

Pruning: Trim back in spring if they get untidy and to encourage bushy growth.

Propagation: In spring, take stem tip cuttings about 4 in (10 cm) long and place in a propagator or under a polythene bag at about 61-64°F (16-18°C). *F. radicans* 'Variegata' can be propagated by layering. Prepare a small pot with drainage and a mixture of $\frac{1}{2}$ compost, $\frac{1}{2}$ sharp sand. Choose a healthy side stem and with the stem still attached to the parent plant peg it to the compost in the small pot so that one of the leaf joints touches the surface closely. New roots will form at the point where the leaf stem joins the main stem and when these are growing well and new leaves show above as well, sever the new plant from the parent.

Life expectancy: Long lived provided they are kept moist and in a humid atmosphere.

Plant companions: They do well in the front of mixed bowls or containers and also in the moist atmosphere of bottle gardens or terrariums.

Ease/difficulty: Follow the rules and they are easy.

Repotting

1 Repot in spring when water goes straight through pot, roots are crowded and new leaves do not appear. Water plant well.

2 Prepare pot 1 size larger with drainage layer and layer of damp, loam-based No. 2 or peat-based compost.

3 Hold old pot with one hand covering compost, fingers either side of stems. Tap edge of pot. Plant and compost will come out.

4 Carefully remove stale soil from roots, using stick or pencil. Do not damage roots.

5 Place plant in centre of new pot, root-ball on compost.

6 Add new compost to fill pot. Make sure that all roots are covered. Press down well. Leave in the shade without water for 2 days to encourage roots to grow into compost.

1 *Leaves go yellow and drop.* Plant saturated or standing in water. Allow to dry until recovered. Water less often.

2 *White, woolly patches on leaves.* Mealy bug. Remove them individually with a swab dipped in methylated spirits or spray with malathion or a systemic insecticide.

3 *Leaves dry up.* Too dry. Soak plant in a bucket and then water more frequently. If very dry, the plant will die.

4 *Leaves discoloured with brown scaly insects under leaves and on stem.* Scale insect. Remove them individually with a swab dipped in methylated spirits or spray with a systemic insecticide.

5 *Leaves yellow with webs underneath.* Red spider mite. Spray with derris, malathion or a systemic insecticide. Improve humidity by spraying daily.

Adding a moss pole

1 Prepare new pot with drainage and layer of damp, loam-based No. 2 compost.

4 Place plant in pot beside moss pole.

2 Position moss pole and add a little compost around it to hold it firm.

5 Add new compost to fill pot. Make sure that all roots are covered. Press down well.

3 Remove plant from pot.

6 Tie plant stem to moss pole with raffia or twine at intervals.

Stem tip cuttings

1 Take stem tip cuttings about 4in (10cm) long in spring. Prepare shallow pot or seed tray with drainage and ½ sand, ½ loam-based compost.

2 Choose shoot or stem tip with at least 2 pairs of healthy leaves and a growing point.
As leaves are small and close together you may need more than 2 pairs. Cut off above a pair of leaves.

3 Prepare cuttings by trimming off stem just below a leaf.

4 Remove the lowest pair of leaves.

5 Dip the cut surface in hormone rooting powder. Shake off the surplus.

6 Make small holes in compost around edge with stick or pencil.

7 Insert cutting so that end of stem is at bottom of hole and leaves are level with compost.

8 Water well and cover with polythene supported by wire. Remove cover for 5 minutes a day and never let compost dry out. Keep at 61–64°F (16–18°C).
Remove cover after 21 days and when cuttings are growing well, repot in normal compost.

Fittonia verschaffeltii

PAINTED NET LEAF

Fittonias are beautiful creeping plants for the expert. They are named after two ladies, Elizabeth and Sara Fitton who wrote a book together called *Conversations on Botany*. The *Fittonia* is a member of the Acanthaceae family and comes from Peru, from where it was introduced in 1867.

They are popular plants but are not the easiest to keep going, requiring a warm atmosphere and plenty of humidity. Should either of these be lacking, they will immediately begin to deteriorate. Whilst they will flourish in bottle gardens and terrariums they are best grown in a warm greenhouse and brought into the house for short periods. In Victorian times they were stove house plants, grown in the warmest part of the greenhouse, next to the boiler. They do well in shady places and will even grow up damp walls. Watering well is the secret of success with fittonias: they must never dry out.

Fittonia argyroneura is probably the more difficult of the two species that are available. The leaves are olive green with very distinct white markings. Indeed, the species name means 'with silver nerves' and it is easy to see where its common names of silver net leaf and snakeskin plant come from. There is a miniature form of *F. argyroneura* which is probably now more common and more popular than the original variety.

F. verschaffeltii (named after a Belgian who was also an expert on camellias) has similar leaves, about 3 or 4 in (8–10 cm) long, but they are slightly darker green and the vein markings are carmine red.

Choose bushy plants without any curled or dropped leaves. If you can keep them flourishing then you are an accomplished house plant grower.

Fittonias are popular plants but they are not easy because of their need for humidity.

Right: *Fittonia verschaffeltii.*

Left: Although primarily foliage plants both species do produce small flowers.

Below: The miniature form of *Fittonia argyroneura.*

Size: Normally available in 3½ in (9 cm) pots, but they will spread to 10–12 in (25–30 cm) across.
Growth: 3–4 in (8–10 cm) per year is normal.
Flowering season: They have green flower heads which stand upright from the foliage. These appear at any time during the summer, but the plants are primarily grown for their foliage and if the flowers are removed it will improve the quality of the leaves.
Scent: None.
Light: These are shade-loving plants. Too much light (even indirect light) is bad for them.
Temperature: They need a warm temperature. A minimum of 65°F (18°C) at all times but 70°F (21°C) is preferred. Maximum summer temperature is 80°F (27°C) in which case the humidity must be high.
Water: Keep plants well watered in summer which will probably mean watering 2–3 times a week. In winter reduce this by half but never let the plants dry out. Softened or rainwater is best.
Feeding: Add half the recommended dose of liquid food to the water every 14 days in the summer.
Humidity: Fittonias must have a humid atmosphere. Spray overhead with tepid water daily.
Cleaning: Rely on the daily spraying to keep them clean. Do not use leaf shine.

Atmosphere: They are very susceptible to draughts. They also dislike fumes from gas fires.
Soil: Loam-based No. 2 or peat-based compost.
Repotting: Once a year in the spring. Make sure that the drainage is good. Use shallow pots or half pots as the roots do not grow deep.
Pruning: Cut back straggly growths in early summer. Young cuttings should have their growing tips pinched out 2 or 3 times to make them grow more bushy.
Propagation: By stem tip cuttings in spring in a propagator at about 75°F (24°C). Large old plants can be divided in the summer but as young plants are the most attractive it is best to root cuttings at least every other year.
Life expectancy: If you are an expert, this plant will be long lived. If not, 4–6 months.
Plant companions: Does well in bottle gardens and terrariums with *Pilea, Cryptanthus, Hedera,* and small ferns.
Ease/difficulty: Definitely for the green fingered.

Repotting

1 Repot in spring if plant has spread all over the sides of the pot and there is no new growth. Water plant well.

2 Prepare pot 1 size larger with drainage layer and layer of damp, peat-based compost or loam-based No. 2.

3 Hold old pot with one hand covering compost, fingers either side of stems. Tap edge of pot. Plant and compost will come out.

4 Carefully remove stale soil from roots, using stick or pencil. Do not damage roots.

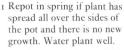

5 Place plant in centre of new pot, root-ball on compost.

6 Add new compost to fill pot. Make sure that all roots are covered. Press down well. Leave in the shade without water for 2 days to encourage roots to grow into compost.

1 *Leaves shrivel.* Plant too dry and/or in direct sunlight. Soak plant immediately and allow to drain. Stand in a semi-shaded position. Never allow to dry out.

2 *Leaves lack lustre and shrivel at edges.* Lack of humidity. Spray daily and place in outer pot packed with damp peat.

3 *Leaves drop. No new growth.* Too cold. Move to a warmer position. Check that there are are no draughts.

4 *Lower leaves turn yellow.* Waterlogging. Check that plant is not standing in water. Check drainage in the pot. Allow to dry out until recovered, then water less often.

5 *Leaves distorted and sticky with green insects.* Greenfly. Spray with pyrethrum or a systemic insecticide.

Humidity

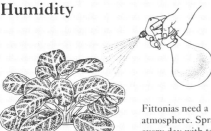

Fittonias need a humid atmosphere. Spray them every day with tepid water.

Stand pot in saucer with water, pebbles or gravel. Make sure pot base is clear of water.

Root division

Divide large, old plants in early summer.

1 Prepare 2 pots with drainage layer and compost. Water plant well.

2 Remove plant from pot and gently prise away compost.

3 Gently pull roots and stems apart with your hands.

4 Repot both sections in the usual way.

Stem tip cuttings

1 Take stem tip cuttings in spring. Prepare propagator or pot with $\frac{1}{2}$ sand, $\frac{1}{2}$ loam-based compost. A propagator will give the best results, but if you can keep the cuttings humid and at the right temperature you may succeed without one.

2 Choose shoot or stem tip with at least 2 pairs of healthy leaves and a growing point. Cut off below second pair of leaves, close to main stem. Cuttings should be 3–4in (8–10cm) long.

3 Prepare cuttings by trimming off stem just below a leaf.

4 Remove the lowest pair of leaves.

5 Dip the cut surface in hormone rooting powder. Shake off the surplus.

6 Make small hole in compost with stick or pencil.

7 Insert cutting so that end of stem is at bottom of hole and leaves are level with compost.

8 Water well and cover with polythene supported by wire. Remove cover for 5 minutes a day and never let compost dry out. Keep at 75°F (24°C). Remove cover after 21 days and when cutting is growing well, repot in normal compost.

GARDENIA

This is the plant that produces the beautiful white flowers once so much in demand for gentlemen's buttonholes, brides' bouquets and for girls to wear in their hair for 'coming out' balls. The scented double flowers still have great appeal.

Regretably, gardenias are difficult plants to grow in the house for they require quite a high temperature and high humidity if they are to flower properly. They are ideally greenhouse or conservatory plants. However, if they are treated as visitors to the house, brought in for a week or two and then returned to the greenhouse, it is possible to enjoy their beauty and scent for short periods.

The gardenia is named after a Dr Alexander Garden, an eminent botanist who lived in Charleston, Carolina, in the late eighteenth century. It is a member of the Rubiaceae family. There are some sixty species of this evergreen shrub, growing wild in Asia and Africa. Only one species is generally cultivated, that is *Gardenia jasminoides*, which comes from both China and Japan and was introduced in 1754. The leaves are bright dark green, narrow, pointed and about 4 in (10 cm) long and 1 in ($\frac{1}{2}$ cm) wide. The original wild species is single flowered but the various cultivated forms all have double flowers with several layers of petals. There is one variety that flowers in winter, *G. jasminoides* 'Veitchiana'.

Gardenias are sold as they come into flower. Choose a plant with glossy green leaves, a well-balanced shape and plenty of buds still to open.

Below: Occasionally slightly different forms of this plant are available. This is *Gardenia jasminoides* 'Rothmanii'.

Right: *Gardenia jasminoides* has a superb heavy perfume. However it is difficult to keep long in the house and grows best in a conservatory. The flowers are pure white, fading to rich cream as they age.

Size: They are normally bought as small bushes, about 1 ft by 1 ft (30 cm) but will grow in a pot to about 4 ft (120 cm) tall and 3 ft (1 m) wide.
Growth: Slow, not more than 6 in (15 cm) per year.
Flowering season: The waxen flowers appear all through the summer from May to September. There is no real main flowering period: flowers appear one after another. They bruise very easily so great care should be taken when handling them. They tend to yellow with age. *G. j.* 'Veitchiana' flowers in winter.
Scent: A beautiful, heavy perfume which resembles that of jasmine.
Light: They need plenty of light, but should be protected from direct sunlight in midsummer.
Temperature: They will stand temperatures down to 50°F (10°C) in winter while resting but require a minimum of 60–65°F (15–18°C) in summer to flower properly. Maximum summer temperature 75°F (24°C), with high humidity. *G.j.* 'Veitchiana' needs winter warmth of 64–71°F (18–22°C).
Water: They must be well watered, at least 3 times a week in summer, with rainwater. In winter give less water, only about once a week. It should then be tepid, again lime-free water or rainwater.
Feeding: Add half the recommended dose of liquid food to the water every 14 days during the flowering season.
Humidity: Regular spraying with tepid rainwater throughout the year (preferably every day) is essential if they are to flower well. Avoid spraying the flowers as this will mark or discolour them. If the plant is in a greenhouse, damp down the floor to keep the humidity high.
Cleaning: Spraying should keep the plant clean. If not, leaf shine can be used once every 2 months but avoid spraying the flowers.
Atmosphere: Whilst hating draughts, they like good ventilation. They dislike gas fumes.
Soil: A rich, lime-free compost.
Repotting: In spring, depending on the amount of growth. Yearly repotting may not be necessary if the plant has not outgrown its pot.
Pruning: Keep the plant in a neat shape by removing untidy branches in March. Established plants can be clipped back after flowering. With young plants, pinch out the growing tips in summer to encourage branching.
Propagation: By young stem tip cuttings taken in late winter and early spring, placed in a propagator or under polythene using a compost of sand and loam. The temperature should be about 64–70°F (18–21°C).
Life expectancy: As they flower better while young, it is better not to keep them more than about 3–4 years. Keep a succession of young plants coming on.
Plant companions: Because they dislike room conditions, it is better to treat gardenias as single specimens.
Ease/difficulty: If you have a heated greenhouse or conservatory it is quite easy. In the house alone it is difficult.

Repotting

1 Repot in spring if plant has grown top-heavy and roots show through pot base. Do not disturb in the growing season. Water plant well.

2 Prepare pot 1 size larger with drainage layer and layer of damp, lime-free loam or peat-based compost.

3 Hold old pot with one hand covering compost, fingers either side of stem. Tap edge of pot. Plant and compost will come out.

4 Carefully remove stale soil from roots, using stick or pencil. Do not damage roots.

5 Place plant in centre of new pot, root-ball on compost.

6 Add new compost to fill pot. Make sure that all roots are covered. Press down well. Leave in the shade without water for 2 days to encourage roots to grow into compost.

What goes wrong

1 *Flower buds drop before opening.* Lack of humidity. Stand pot on damp pebbles; spray daily with soft water.

2 *Flowers discoloured.* Marking by water from overhead spraying. Don't spray flowers.

3 *White woolly patches on leaves.* Mealy bug. Remove with a swab dipped in methylated spirits or spray with malathion or a systemic insecticide.

4 *Leaves, especially young ones, become yellow but veins stay green.* Chlorosis from using limy water. Water once with sequestered iron and thereafter with lime-free water.

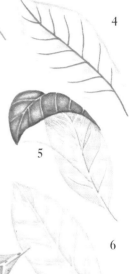

5 *Leaves yellowed with webs underneath.* Red spider mite. Spray with derris, malathion or a systemic insecticide. Keep humidity higher. This plant is very susceptible.

6 *Leaves become pale and yellowed.* Lack of light. Move to lighter position.

7 *Leaves discoloured with brown scaly insects under leaves and on stems.* Scale insect. Remove them individually with a swab dipped in methylated spirits or spray with a systemic insecticide.

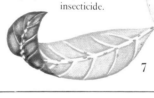

Stem tip cuttings

1 Take stem tip cuttings in late winter and early spring. Use a heated propagator if you can; if not, prepare a pot with drainage layer and ½ sand, ½ loam-based compost.

4 Remove the lowest pair of leaves.

7 Insert cutting so that end of stem is at bottom of hole and leaves are level with compost.

2 Choose shoot or stem tip with at least 2 pairs of healthy leaves and a growing point. Cut off below second pair of leaves. Cuttings should be 3–4in (8–10cm) long.

5 Dip the cut surface in hormone rooting powder. Shake off the surplus.

8 Water well and cover with polythene supported by wire. Remove cover for 5 minutes a day and never let compost dry out. Keep at 64–70 F (18–21 C). Remove cover after 21 days and when cuttings are growing well, repot in normal compost.

3 Prepare cuttings by trimming off stem just below a leaf.

6 Make small holes in compost around edge with stick or pencil.

Pruning

Pinch out growing tips of young plants to make them grow more bushily.

Clip back untidy branches in March, cutting just above a leaf stem.

Humidity

Spray every day with tepid rainwater. Do not spray the buds or flowers as this may mark them.

Put pot in outer container packed with damp peat.

SCARLET STAR

The *Guzmania* is another member of the Bromeliaceae family. There are some eighty or ninety known species, found mostly in the West Indies and in south-western South America. Named after A. Guzman, a Spanish naturalist and plant collector, they were introduced at the beginning of the nineteenth century.

Like many bromeliads they are epiphytes: they grow on the branches of other plants but are not dependent on their hosts for sustenance. In the house they are usually grown in pots. However, some varieties do well if tied onto pieces of bark or wood, with their roots bound into sphagnum moss – in imitation of their natural habitat.

Guzmanias, like their close relation the *Tillandsia*, are medium sized bromeliads but all have striking bracts surrounding their small flowers. *Guzmania* has bright orange or red star-shaped bracts, which stay coloured for a long time. The actual flowers are insignificant and soon fade away. They are usually white or yellow.

Guzmanias are easy and striking house plants. Whilst they can be grown on their own they perhaps look their best in mixed plantings in tubs and troughs. Like other bromeliads they die after they have produced their flowers but new plants can easily be propagated from the offsets that appear on the stem during the flowering period.

Choose guzmanias with fresh, light green leaves and rich, red bracts. The tips of the leaves should not be browned.

Guzmanias are bromeliads which produce brightly coloured bracts lasting up to two months. The true flowers are small, and rarely emerge.

Right: *Guzmania minor*, the species which is most commonly available.

Below: *Guzmania lingulata*.

Size: This varies according to variety but most are about 12–15 in tall (30–38 cm), including flowering spike, and some 10 in (25 cm) across.

Growth: When in flower they usually produce 2 or 3 offsets per plant. The complete cycle from offset to flowering stage can well take 2 years.

Flowering season: Normally in summer but they can produce a flower spike at any time. Whilst the brightly coloured bracts will last a long time, the actual flowers only last a day or so.

Scent: None.

Light: They enjoy a very light position but protect them from strong sunshine during the middle of the day in summer.

Temperature: 60–64°F (15–18°C) in winter, 65–75°F (18–24°C) in summer. If the temperature falls, the plant may rot at the base. Maximum summer temperature 80°F (27°C) in which case humidity should be high.

Water: Keep very moist, watering 2–3 times a week during summer. In winter water about once a week. Soft rainwater is best. Keep about 1 in (2½ cm) of water in the central well.

Feeding: Not necessary.

Humidity: Spray frequently in summer, every day if possible.

Cleaning: Not really necessary if spraying is carried out regularly. Do not use leaf shine.

Atmosphere: Fairly tolerant of most conditions except cold draughts.

Soil: A good, peat-based compost, with some sphagnum moss added.

Repotting: Young plants should only need repotting once after they have been separated from the old plant. The pot is really only the medium for holding the plant firm and upright as guzmanias have very small roots. Do not press the compost down too hard.

Pruning: None necessary, except to remove damaged leaves.

Propagation: By young offsets produced as the mother plant is in flower. It is best to wait until the offsets are fairly well developed and have roots of their own before separating them. By this time the mother plant will have begun to deteriorate. Spring is the best time. No propagator is required. Just pot up the rooted offsets at room temperature.

Life expectancy: The plant has a life cycle of between 2 and 3 years, depending on how quickly it develops.

Plant companions: They do well in any mixed planting of green plants, provided the container is in a light position.

Ease/difficulty: Like all bromeliads they are easy to keep going with a minimum amount of care.

Fixing a bromeliad to bark

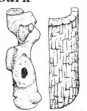

Guzmanias grow well fixed to bark or wood.
1 Choose suitable piece of cork bark, a branch or some well shaped driftwood.

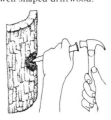

2 If there is no natural hollow, chisel a shallow well where plant will rest.

3 Remove plant from pot, keeping compost round the root ball.

4 Wrap roots in damp sphagnum moss and tie with plastic-coated wire.

5 Hold moss and root-ball firmly against wood or bark and bind in place with wire.

6 Fix bark to wall or prop it up, making sure the plant is growing upright. Dampen root ball and spray regularly.

What goes wrong

1 *Lower leaves go brown and dry.* Plant needs water. Keep moist but not waterlogged.

2 *After flowering, plant dies back.* Normal for bromeliads. Offsets should begin to appear if temperature is not too low.

3 *Tips of leaves turn brown.* Lack of humidity. Spray daily and place in an outer pot packed with damp peat.

4 *Leaves distorted and sticky with green insects.* Aphids. Spray with pyrethrum or a systemic insecticide.

5 *Plant goes black and rotten at base.* Waterlogging. Allow to dry out but plant unlikely to recover.

Humidity

Stand pot in saucer with water, pebbles or gravel. Make sure pot base is clear of water.

Spraying

Spray daily overhead with a fine mist spray, using rainwater if possible. Hold spray about 6in (15cm) from leaves.

Watering

Keep about 1in (2½cm) of water in central funnel. Empty and refill every 3 weeks. Rainwater is best.

Offsets

1 Wait until flowers and leaves of plant have died before removing offset. Offset should be about ½ size of parent.

2 Prepare small pot with drainage layer and damp, all peat compost mixed with an equal quantity of sphagnum moss.

3 Knock plant from pot and remove offset and roots from parent plant with sharp knife.

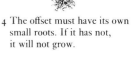

4 The offset must have its own small roots. If it has not, it will not grow.

5 Pot offset in new pot. Water well and cover with polythene cover for a few days to give extra humidity.

Removing the flower stem

When flowers have withered, cut stem at base.

Cleaning the leaves

Wipe dust off leaves with soft cloth and sponge with tepid water. Support leaf with other hand.
Do not use leaf shine.

Removing dead leaves

When dead leaf is quite dry cut it off with sharp scissors, cutting just above healthy leaf tissue.

VELVET PLANT

This is a plant which resembles a rather superior nettle. The leaves are nettle shaped, bright purple and look as if they are made of velvet. Actually both the leaves and the stems are covered with fine purple hairs and it is these that give the plant this luxurious appearance.

Gynuras are members of the Compositae family and there are some twenty known species, all of which come from India or the Far East. The name is from the Greek *gyne*, meaning female and *oura*, meaning tail, referring to the stigma which is long and rough.

Gynuras are grown purely for their leaves. They have rather insignificant orange flowers resembling those of groundsel but these should be removed as soon as they appear, for if the plant is allowed to bloom it will deteriorate rapidly. The flowers also have a rather unpleasant smell. It is one of the few plants that can be grown in full sun all the year round.

These plants root easily from cuttings. As they get very untidy after about two years it is best to discard and replace them. Two species are commonly available. *G. aurantiaca* is an upright bushy plant. *G. sarmentosa* is low and squat and is best described as a creeper although it can also be trained as a climber. Several plants of this species can be put together in a hanging basket to make a good display.

Choose bushy plants with plenty of young growth of a good, deep purple. Pale plants are suffering from lack of light. Check that the plants are not flowering. It is best to buy them in early spring or autumn.

Left: Gynuras are covered with fine purple hairs which give them their common name. The hairs are more plentiful on the young growth which is why young, bushy plants are preferable.

Right: *Gynura sarmentosa*.

Below: *Gynura aurantiaca* has oval leaves and grows as a shrub.

Size: They grow to about 18 in (46 cm).
Growth: They are fairly quick growers and will make full size plants in one season. They need staking in their second year.
Flowering season: Spring and summer. The flowers are best removed as they seem to take all the strength out of the plant. If the plant has deteriorated rapidly after flowering it is best discarded.
Scent: The flowers have an unpleasant smell.
Light: They appreciate lots of light, even full sun, which deepens the purple colour of the leaves. Also give as much light as possible in winter.
Temperature: 60°-65°F (15-18°C) is a suitable winter temperature. Will tolerate 55°F (13°C) if water is reduced. Maximum summer temperature is 70°F (21°C).
Water: Water freely in summer. This will probably mean 2-3 times a week. In winter water much less, at the most once a week.
Feeding: Does not require much food. Add liquid food to the water once a month in summer only.
Humidity: The plant appreciates being stood on wet pebbles, but this is not a necessity.
Cleaning: Spray with tepid water occasionally on a dull day when there is no danger of sunlight scorching the leaves. Shake surplus moisture from the leaves afterwards. This is a hairy leaved plant so never use leaf

shine. Dust on the leaves can be removed with a small brush.
Atmosphere: They like a good airy position in the summer when they are growing.
Soil: Loam-based compost No. 2.
Repotting: Plants will require repotting at the start of the second year. Use a pot 2 or 3 sizes bigger.
Pruning: Trim back in March of the second year to neaten plant. The trimmings can be used as cuttings.
Propagation: Stem tip cuttings root easily either singly or 3 to a pot. Keep them about 65 to 70°F (18-21°C)
Life expectancy: This is a plant which is at its most attractive when the leaves are young. It should therefore be grown on a 2 year cycle so that the plants are always fresh and healthy looking.
Plant companions: Can be grown in mixed bowls. The purple leaves contrast well with the green of other plants.
Ease/difficulty: This is a good plant for the beginner. But do not forget to pinch out the flower buds as they appear.

Repotting

1 Repot young plants when their roots are crowded. They will also need repotting at the beginning of their second year. Water plant well.

2 Prepare pot 2 sizes larger with drainage and layer of damp, loam-based No. 2 compost.

3 Hold old pot with one hand covering compost, fingers either side of stems. Tap edge of pot. Plant and compost will come out.

4 Carefully remove stale soil from roots, using stick or pencil. Do not damage roots.

5 Place plant in centre of new pot, root-ball on compost.

6 Add new compost to fill pot. Make sure that all roots are covered. Press down well. Leave in the shade without water for 2 days to encourage roots to grow into compost.

What goes wrong

1 *Leaves more green than purple.* Too little light. Move to a brighter position.

2 *Black blotches on leaves.* Water has been allowed to remain on leaves after spraying. Spray only with the mister adjusted to fine spray. Do not stand sprayed plant in sun.

3 *Leaves distorted and sticky with green insects.* Greenfly. Spray with pyrethrum or a systemic insecticide.

4 *Plant produces evil smelling orange flowers and leaves deteriorate.* Remove flowers and all flower buds that appear in future.

5 *Plant tired and ragged.* Needs replacing by young plant. Propagate from strong shoots.

Stem tip cuttings

1 Old plants look straggly so it is best to take cuttings. Take them in spring. Prepare pot with drainage layer and mixture of sharp sand and loam-based compost.

4 Remove the lowest pair of leaves.

7 Insert cutting so that end of stem is at bottom of hole and leaves are level with compost.

2 Choose shoot or stem tip with at least 2 pairs of healthy leaves and a growing point. Cut off below second pair of leaves, close to main stem. Cuttings should be 3–4in (8–10cm) long.

5 Dip the cut surface in hormone rooting powder. Shake off the surplus.

8 Water well and cover with polythene supported by wire. Remove cover for 5 minutes a day and never let compost dry out. Keep at 65–70 F (18–21 C).
Remove cover after 21 days and when cuttings are growing well, repot in normal compost.

3 Prepare cuttings by trimming off stem just below a leaf.

6 Make small holes in compost around edge with stick or pencil.

Training round a hoop

1 Push one end of flexible cane or wire hoop into compost at side of pot, stopping when end of cane is $\frac{2}{3}$ down pot.

3 Gently twine plant stem around hoop, taking care not to damage stem or leaves.

2 Bend hoop to other side of pot and push into compost.

4 If necessary, tie some twine to lower part of hoop. Thread it along hoop, looping it around the stem as you go.

Removing flowers

Small flowers may appear in the summer. Pinch them out to improve leaf growth.

The flowers have an unpleasant smell.

IVY

The common ivy, *Hedera helix*, is one of the few plants native to Europe that can be grown as a house plant. It is a member of the Araliaceae family. There are only seven known species and only two of these are commonly grown as house plants: *Hedera helix* with its almost countless varieties and *H. canariensis*, Canary ivy.

New varieties of *H. helix* are constantly being introduced with variations in leaf size, shape and colouration. They are all good plants in the house and do quite well in dark places, although sometimes they lose colour if they are kept too dark. One important point to remember is that whilst hederas enjoy a moist atmosphere and should be sprayed regularly, they do not like to be overwatered, particularly in winter time. They also do not like situations that are excessively hot and dry. This is not surprising since all *H. helix* varieties are hardy and even *H. canariensis* will survive outdoors in all but the most severe of winters.

If you wish to put any ivy grown in the house into the garden it is best to do so in early summer so that it has time to harden to outdoor life. If put out in the middle of winter it will perish at the first hard frost.

Most hederas are self branching, that is if the growing point is removed, the plant will immediately produce two or three new growing points lower down the stem. This is how properly pruned ivies make such full and bushy plants. Left unpruned they will grow tall and straggly.

Always buy bushy plants which are showing new growth. Choose the leaf shape and pattern you like best.

Size: Most of the *H. helix* varieties are fairly small but can grow to 2 ft (60 cm). If pinched out they will make bushier plants 18 in (46 cm) across. *H. canariensis* will easily grow up to 6 ft (2 m) in the house.

Growth: They are fast growers, but the growing points should be pinched out to encourage bushy growth. 12–18 in (30–46 cm) in a year is possible.

Flowering season: They never flower in the house.

Scent: None.

Light: Like most plants they prefer plenty of light but full sun can bleach the leaves. *H. helix* will tolerate and grow in very dark positions. *H. canariensis* needs plenty of light at all times.

Temperature: Very flexible. In the winter plants indoors should not drop below 45°F (7°C). They prefer not to be above 60°F (15°C) but if this is unavoidable, spray daily.

Water: Do not overwater ivies. Once or twice a week in the summer according to the weather is sufficient and once a week or even less in the winter.

Feeding: In the summer months they will appreciate a regular fortnightly liquid feed.

Humidity: Spray with tepid water once or twice a week or stand on damp pebbles in a saucer.

Cleaning: The spraying will help do this but also wipe the plants over with a damp cloth every 2–3 weeks. They do not like dust on their leaves. Leaf shine can be used but not more than once every 2 months.

Atmosphere: They are very tolerant of gas fumes, oil fumes, cigars etc.

Soil: Loam-based No. 2 or a peat based compost.

Repotting: This is best done in the spring, although young plants may require to be re-potted twice in a year. When in large pots it is best just to change the top soil in the spring.

Pruning: Prune to keep the plant in a neat shape and to increase bushiness. Nip out the leading shoots once or twice a year to encourage this.

Propagation: This is easy. Take young stem tip cuttings about 3–4 in (7.5–10 cm) long and put 2 or 3 together into pots in a propagator or under a polythene bag at 60°F (15°C). This is best done in the spring or early summer. Shoots root readily in water and the plants can also be layered.

Life expectancy: Long. If they get too big or untidy put them out into the garden. Remember to do this in early summer so that they have time to acclimatize.

Plant companions: They will grow with most plants but are not recommended for bottle gardens as they can smother everything else.

Ease/difficulty: An ideal plant for the beginner. Very easy to keep.

Repotting

1 Repot in spring when roots show through pot base. Water plant well first.

2 Prepare pot 1 size larger with drainage layer and layer of damp, peat or loam-based No. 2 compost.

3 Hold old pot with one hand covering compost, fingers either side of stems. Tap edge of pot. Plant and compost will come out.

4 Carefully remove stale soil from roots, using stick or pencil. Do not damage roots.

5 Place plant in centre of new pot, root-ball on compost.

6 Add new compost to fill pot. Make sure that all roots are covered. Press down well. Leave in the shade without water for 2 days to encourage roots to grow into compost.

Ivies are popular plants which can be grown indoors or outside. Indoors it is best to keep them cool or they may become infested with red spider mite. They mutate very easily and dozens of varieties are available.

Left: *Hedera helix* 'Lutzii'.

Below left: *Hedera helix* 'Little Diamond'

Far left, below: *Hedera helix* 'Chicago'.

Right: The larger leaved Canary Ivy, *Hedera canariensis*.

Below: All ivies climb by means of tendrils and suckers on the stems.

What goes wrong

1 *Variegated varieties turn green.* Overfeeding and insufficient light. Cease feeding and move to a lighter spot.

2 *Leaves go pale in summer.* Too much direct sun. Move to a slightly shaded spot.

3 *Leaves go black.* Overwatering. Allow to dry out until recovered and then water less often.

4 *Leaves dry up.* Too hot and dry. Reduce temperature and spray daily.

5 *Leaves go yellow with webs underneath.* Red spider mite. Ivies are very susceptible. Spray with derris, malathion or a systemic insecticide. Lower temperature and spray daily to improve humidity.

6 *Silvery marks on leaves.* Thrips. Spray with pyrethrum.

7 *Leaves distorted and sticky with green insects.* Greenfly. Spray with pyrethrum or a systemic insecticide.

8 *Leaves discoloured with brown scaly insects under leaves and on stems.* Scale insect. Remove them individually with a swab dipped in methylated spirits or spray with a systemic insecticide.

9 *Sooty deposits on leaves.* Sooty mould. Usually follows a greenfly or scale attack. Kill pest and wipe away mould.

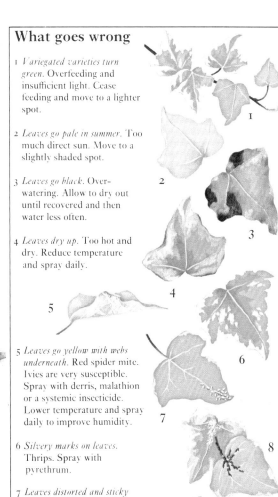

Cleaning

Wipe dust off leaves with soft cloth and sponge with tepid water. Support leaf with other hand.

Spraying

Spray twice a week with tepid water to provide humidity. This is important to prevent attacks of red spider mite.

Tying to a cane

1 Push cane gently into compost a few inches away from the main stem, stopping when cane is $\frac{2}{3}$ down the pot.

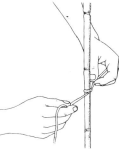

2 Cut a 9in (23cm) length of string and tie firmly around cane on stem side.

3 Loop string around stem as shown.

4 Tie a firm knot against the cane. Repeat at intervals up the stem.

5 If well supported, *H. canariensis* may grow up to 6ft (2m) tall.

Propagation

1 Prepare pot with drainage layer and compost of $\frac{1}{2}$ loam-based, $\frac{1}{2}$ sharp sand.

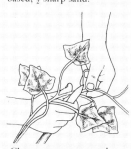

2 Choose strong stem and make slit in outer skin on lower surface, below a leaf joint.

3 Bend stem so that cut surface lies on compost in new pot. Weight the stem with a small pebble or peg it closely to the compost. Contact must be close.

4 Roots will grow from the cut and when these are well formed the stem can be cut away from the parent plant and potted on its own.

CHINESE ROSE

Hibiscus is a genus of about 150 species in the plant family Malvaceae. They are trees or shrubs, mostly sub-tropical, with varieties spread across the world. In their natural habitat they are often used for hedging as they produce dense, prickly growth. Nearly all have attractive though short-lived flowers. *H. rosa-sinensis* is the most popular indoor variety.

Hibiscus was introduced to Europe by plant explorers in 1731 and by 1786 at least three varieties were known. Today many new ones are being produced. Their flowers are always bright – red, yellow and orange being the predominant colours. *H. mutabilis,* from Asia, has thick, coarse branches covered with soft hairs. The leaves are wide with long stalks and are up to 8 in (20 cm) long. Its flowers are white or white and red and the plant grows to around 12 ft (4 m). *H. archeri,* from the West Indies, also grows to 12 ft (4 m). It is similar to *H. rosa-sinesis* but has larger leaves and its flowers are smaller and nearly always red. *H. schizopetalus,* a hybrid from tropical Africa, has smaller leaves and flowers not more than $2\frac{1}{2}$ in (6 cm) across, dark red inside and light red outside.

Flowers are the *Hibiscus's* main attraction so it is particularly annoying when they fall off while they are still in bud. This can be prevented by increasing humidity and there are now two new hybrids on the market (*H.* 'Weekend' and *H.* 'Moonlight') which have been developed specifically not to drop buds.

Good specimens of this plant will have a branched shape, glossy leaves and plenty of buds. Check that buds have not been dropped from the lower part of the plant, leaving unsightly stalks.

Hibiscus have either double (above) or single flowers (below). New hybrids with rounder leaves (above right) do not drop their buds.

Right: A well grown young plant of *Hibiscus rosa-sinensis.*

Size: Normally about 12–15 in (30–38 cm) when purchased. Will grow to 4–5 ft (120–150 cm) in a pot.

Growth: May double in size in one season.

Flowering season: Continuously from late spring through the summer until late autumn. The number of flowers at one time depends on the size of the plant. Each flower lasts only about 36 hours.

Scent: No strong scent.

Light: Keep in good light position but not direct sunlight. Ideal for conservatories or shaded greenhouses. Keep by a north window if indoors.

Temperature: 65–70°F (18–21°C) during the growing season. If temperature falls below 50°F (10°C) in winter the leaves will drop. Maximum summer temperature 80°F (27°C).

Water: During the growing season water at least twice a week, more if the weather is warm and dry. Do not allow compost to become waterlogged or the roots may rot. Water only once a week in winter, especially if the temperature is low, allowing the compost to become quite dry on the top before adding water.

Feeding: During the growing season only, add liquid food to the water every 14 days.

Humidity: They need plenty in summer and appreciate a daily overhead spray, otherwise buds may drop. In winter keep drier but spray every other day in centrally heated rooms.

Cleaning: The spray will keep leaves clean but if they get dusty, clean carefully by hand.

Atmosphere: Give plenty of fresh air in summer. Avoid gas fumes.

Soil: Adult plants grow well in loam-based compost No. 3. Use a lighter compost with extra peat for younger plants.

Repotting: Ideally done in spring immediately after pruning, when the plant is beginning to grow. Do not put into too large a pot as it will flower better if slightly pot-bound.

Pruning: Prune vigorously each spring to give a compact shape with plenty of flowering buds. Cut back in the growing season if it gets too leggy.

Propagation: From cuttings, though with large plants layering is possible. Cuttings taken in spring should flower the same year. Root them at a temperature of 64°F (18°C).

Life expectancy: Indefinite if well pruned – 3 to 4 years is an average.

Plant companions: Choose plants that by their leaf structure act as a foil to the brilliant flowers. *Rhoicissus,* philodendrons and green dracaenas are suitable.

Ease/difficulty: An easy plant but it must never be overwatered.

Repotting

1 Repot in spring as plant starts to grow and looks top-heavy for pot. New leaves may look pale. Water plant well.

2 Prepare pot 1 size larger with drainage layer and layer of damp, loam-based No. 3 compost.

3 Hold old pot with one hand covering compost, fingers either side of stems. Tap edge of pot. Plant and compost will come out.

4 Carefully remove stale soil from roots, using stick or pencil. Do not damage roots.

5 Place plant in centre of new pot, root-ball on compost.

6 Add new compost to fill pot. Make sure that all roots are covered. Press down well. Leave in the shade without water for 2 days to encourage roots to grow into compost.

What goes wrong

1 *Leaves drop.* In summer, plant waterlogged from over-watering. Allow to dry out until recovered and move to more airy position. Then water less often. In winter, too cold or cold draughts. Move to warmer place and water less often.

2 *Buds drop.* Not enough humidity. Spray daily with soft water. Try to raise the temperature a little.

3 *New leaves small, no flowers.* Needs feeding.

4 *Leaves distorted and sticky with green insects.* Greenfly. Spray with pyrethrum.

5 *Plant wilting.* Too hot and dry. Water and spray.

Stem tip cuttings

1 Take stem tip cuttings in spring. Prepare pot with drainage layer and ½ sand, ½ loam-based compost.

2 Choose shoot or stem tip with at least 2 pairs of healthy leaves and a growing point. Cut off below second pair of leaves, close to main stem. Cuttings should be 3–4in (8–10cm) long.

3 Prepare cuttings by trimming off stem just below a leaf.

4 Remove the lowest pair of leaves.

5 Dip the cut surface in hormone rooting powder. Shake off the surplus.

6 Make small holes in compost around edge with stick or pencil.

7 Insert cutting so that end of stem is at bottom of hole and leaves are level with compost.

8 Water well and cover with polythene supported by wire. Remove cover for 5 minutes a day and never let compost dry out. Keep at 64°F (18°C).

9 Remove cover after 21 days and when cuttings are growing well, repot in normal compost.

Humidity

Stand pot in saucer with pebbles or gravel and water. *Hibiscus* buds may drop if the atmosphere is not sufficiently humid. Spray every day when in bud. In winter spray every other day if the central heating is high.

Pruning for shape

1 Prune each spring to give a compact plant.

2 Make cuts with secateurs just above a bud or side shoot, cutting at an angle.

3 Dust lightly with sulphur. If sap runs, use cotton wool dipped in petroleum jelly to stop the bleeding.

4 The plant will grow into a more even, bushy shape.

WAX FLOWER

Here is a climbing plant named after an Englishman. Thomas Hoy was head gardener to the Duke of Northumberland at Syon House, Middlesex, at the end of the eighteenth century. Hoyas are members of the Asclepiadaceae family and there are some seventy known species. They come from the Far East including tropical Australia and are commonly known as wax flowers because of the waxy texture of their leaves and flowers.

Only two species are commonly available. *H. carnosa* is the more common of the two and the easiest to keep. This species makes a good plant for training to climb up a wall and will often cling to the wall without artificial support. It has pairs of fleshy, oval leaves about 2 in (5 cm) long and 1 in (2½ cm) wide. The star-like flowers come in bunches of about 12 to 15 and are flesh coloured with red centres. A good plant can be smothered with blooms. There is also an attractive variegated form which is equally easy to grow but does not flower so often or so much. When mature the plants often produce long leafless shoots about 18 in (46 cm) long. Do not remove these as the leaves will follow later.

H. bella is a slightly more delicate plant. The leaves are much smaller and the stems are smaller and pendulous. It is best grown in a hanging basket. The flowers are similar to those of *H. carnosa* except that the petals are pure white with a red centre.

Hoyas should be bought with firm, fleshy leaves and new growth. They are sometimes supplied trained up sticks or around wires and are not often available in flower.

Size: *H. carnosa* will make quite a big plant, given support and time. It can grow up to 4 ft (120 cm) tall and 18 in (46 cm) across. *H. bella* is much smaller, about 12 in (30 cm) tall and 8 in (20 cm) across. In a conservatory *H. carnosa* may reach 15 ft (5 m).

Growth: *H. carnosa* can grow 18 in (46 cm) or more in one year. *H. bella* about 5–6 in (12–15 cm) only.

Flowering season: All through the summer, although a main flush is produced in June followed sometimes by a secondary one in September. Never remove the dead flower stalks as the next set of blooms will come on the old stalks. Do not move them around or the buds may drop.

Scent: A faint but distinct perfume. The flowers will drop a sticky honey-like liquid.

Light: They need a good light position but protect them from the midday sun as this can mark the leaves.

Temperature: *H. carnosa* will tolerate a low winter temperature of 50°F (10°C) and will survive at 5°F (2°C) lower. *H. bella* requires a winter maximum of 60°F (16°C) and should not drop below 50°F (10°C). Summer maximum for both is 75°F (24°C).

Water: They do not like being overwatered. Once a week in summer is enough unless the weather is very hot. Water once a fortnight in winter. Rainwater is preferred.

Feeding: Add half the recommended dose of liquid food to the water every 3–4 weeks in summer.

Humidity: They enjoy a spray with tepid water about once every 14 days. Avoid spraying the flowers. They also appreciate standing on wet pebbles. Keep them drier in their cool winter resting period.

Cleaning: The spraying should keep them clean but you can clean them by hand with a damp cloth if they get dusty. Do not use leaf shine.

Atmosphere: Avoid severe draughts.

Soil: Loam-based No. 2. Crushed brick in the bottom of the pot aids flowering.

Repotting: Do not repot too often, not more than every 2–3 years. The plants flower better if pot-bound. Make sure that they have good drainage. They prefer clay pots.

Pruning: Hoyas dislike surgery but remove any damaged leaves.

Propagation: Root stem tip cuttings in the spring in a mixture of sand and peat. Dust the base of the cuttings with rooting hormone and place under polythene at 70°F (21°C). Not easy for the amateur to do. They can also be layered.

Life expectancy: *H. carnosa* is very long lived. *H. bella* is not so easy and will probably last about 2–3 years.

Plant companions: They are probably best grown on their own. Because of their way of growing they do not blend very well with other plants.

Ease/difficulty: *H. carnosa* is an easy plant for the beginner. *H. bella* is for the more experienced.

Repotting

1 Repot in late spring when roots grow from base of pot and there is no new growth.

2 Prepare pot 1 size larger with drainage layer and layer of damp, peat-based compost or loam-based No. 2. Some crushed brick in the bottom will encourage flowering.

3 Hold old pot with one hand covering compost, fingers either side of stems. Tap edge of pot. Plant and compost will come out.

4 Carefully remove stale soil from roots, using stick or pencil. Do not damage roots.

5 Place plant in centre of new pot, root-ball on compost.

6 Add new compost to fill pot. Make sure that all roots are covered. Press down well. Leave in the shade without water for 2 days to encourage roots to grow into compost. Replace hoop.

Left: The waxen flowers of *Hoya bella*. The flowers hang downwards so the plant is best displayed in a hanging basket.

Left: *Hoya bella* has smaller leaves than *Hoya carnosa* and is a slightly more delicate plant.

Right: *Hoya carnosa* 'Variegata' is an attractive climbing plant. Young plants need training to their support but later in life they cling by themselves. The leaves are obviously fleshy: this indicates that they dislike being overwatered.

What goes wrong

1 *Leaves turn yellow and rot.* Overwatering. Allow to dry out until recovered and then water less often.

2 *Leaves develop brown scorch marks.* Too much direct sun. Move to shaded position.

3 *White woolly patches on leaves.* Mealy bug. Remove them individually with a swab dipped in methylated spirits or spray with malathion or a systemic insecticide.

4 *Leaves dry and curl.* Too hot and dry. Water and spray.

5 *New growth small, no flowers.* Needs feeding.

6 *Buds drop.* Plant has been moved about. Keep in one place until new buds form.

Stem tip cuttings

1 Take stem tip cuttings in spring. Prepare pot with drainage layer and ½ sand, ½ peat mixture.

2 Choose shoot or stem tip with at least 2 pairs of healthy leaves and a growing point. Cut off below second pair of leaves, close to main stem. Cuttings should be 3–4in (8–10cm) long.

3 Prepare cuttings by trimming off stem just below a leaf.

4 Remove the lowest pair of leaves.

5 Dip the cut surface in hormone rooting powder. Shake off the surplus.

6 Make small holes in compost around edge with stick or pencil.

7 Insert cutting so that end of stem is at bottom of hole and leaves are level with compost.

8 Water well and cover with polythene supported by wire. Remove cover for 5 minutes a day and never let compost dry out. Keep at 70°F (21°C). Remove cover after 21 days and when cuttings are growing well, repot in normal compost.

Training round a hoop

1 Push one end of flexible cane or wire hoop into compost at side of pot, stopping when end of cane is ⅔ down pot.

3 Gently twine plant stem around hoop, taking care not to damage stem or leaves.

2 Bend hoop to other side of pot and push into compost.

4 If necessary, tie some twine to lower part of hoop. Thread it along hoop, looping it around the stem as you go.

Spraying

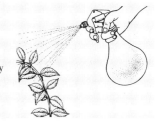

Spray with tepid water every 14 days to clean the leaves and provide humidity. Do not spray the flowers.

HYDRANGEA

The hydrangea has a limited life in the house but it makes an excellent spring and summer gift, for after it has passed its best indoors it can go on to give years of pleasure in the garden. If allowed to rest in a cool place during the dormant period it can be kept in the pot and brought into flower the following year.

There is much controversy about the hydrangea's botanical family, some placing it with the saxifrages, others in the family Hydrangeaceae. *Hydrangea macrophylla* is the species grown for house decoration. It comes from Japan and was introduced to Europe in 1790. The flowers are mostly sterile, producing no seeds but forming the lovely 'mop caps' that we all admire. It is a most tolerant plant but gets very limp when it needs water. It soon revives when it has been watered but do not let it flop too many times from dryness for this weakens the plant and eventually it will not recover.

The *Hydrangea's* flowers are naturally pink but if the plant is watered with alum (aluminium sulphate) the flowers will turn lovely shades of blue. However, they will quickly revert to pink if the chemical is not given. There is also a pure white variety. The recent 'Lace Cap' varieties are most attractive, particularly the whites. These have flatter flower heads where the outer florets open while the inner ones are still in bud, giving a delicate, lacy appearance.

Hydrangeas are usually supplied in bud with some colour just showing. Make sure that the plant chosen is a good shape, that none of the stems is broken and that the foliage is a good green.

Left: The flowers of *Hydrangea macrophylla* can be turned blue by watering with alum.

Right: Young mop cap hydrangeas should have their heavy flowering stems staked. The flowers are naturally pale green before they colour.

Below: The dainty lace cap variety 'Lanarth White'.

Size: As pot plants they will grow to about 2 ft (60 cm) tall and as much wide. In the garden they grow to 3–4 ft (over 1 m) tall and as much wide.

Growth: Cuttings taken in spring or summer will flower the following year.

Flowering season: From early April to early June indoors, but from June to August in the garden.

Scent: None.

Light: They like plenty of light, otherwise the leaves will turn yellow. Do not place in direct sunlight or the plant may dry out.

Temperature: Normal room temperature when flowering. In winter when dormant they should be kept at about 45°F (7°C). Raise this to 55°F (13°C) in February when the plants are brought into growth for spring or early summer flowering. Maximum summer temperature indoors 65°F (18°C).

Water: Keep well watered when growing and when in flower. In the house it is as well to immerse the whole pot in a bucket of water for 10 minutes every other day, or more often if the plant shows signs of wilting. Keep plants on the dry side (watering every 10 days) when dormant in the winter. The blue varieties need lime-free water.

Feeding: Add liquid food to the water once a week when the plant is growing and flowering.

Humidity: Spray overhead every day in the summer particularly when they are making fresh growth.

Cleaning: The spraying should be sufficient. Do not use leaf shine.

Atmosphere: When in flower in the house they will temporarily tolerate any conditions.

Soil: Either loam- or peat-based compost as long as it is rich and lime free. The acidity helps to bring out the strong colours.

Repotting. They should be repotted after flowering. Make sure the drainage is good for whilst they are thirsty plants they do not like to stand in water. Bigger plants in pots only need to have the top soil changed.

Pruning: Whether the plant is being grown in a pot or planted out, it should be pruned after flowering. Cut it back to two pairs of leaves of new growth. This is easily recognizable, for the new growth is green and speckled and the old is woody.

Propagation: The top 4–6 in (10–15 cms) of the prunings can be used as stem tip cuttings. Insert into sharp sand mixed with a little peat, keep moist and in a temperature of 55–61°F (13–16°C).

Life expectancy: In a pot 3–4 years is probably long enough for any *Hydrangea*. It is best to keep a cycle of young plants going. In the garden they are very long lived.

Plant companions: They are best grown on their own although they can be added to a trough of green plants as temporary residents to make a splash of colour.

Ease/difficulty: Treated as a visitor to sitting rooms and put out-of-doors in the summer, it is an easy plant to keep going. It is not so easy to keep permanently indoors.

Repotting

1 Repot the plant at the end of the flowering season. Water plant well.

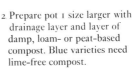

2 Prepare pot 1 size larger with drainage layer and layer of damp, loam- or peat-based compost. Blue varieties need lime-free compost.

3 Hold old pot with one hand covering compost, fingers either side of stems. Tap edge of pot. Plant and compost will come out.

4 Carefully remove stale soil from roots, using stick or pencil. Do not damage roots.

5 Place plant in centre of new pot, root-ball on compost.

6 Add new compost to fill pot. Make sure that all roots are covered. Press down well. Leave in the shade without water for 2 days to encourage roots to grow into compost.

2 *Leaves turn yellow.* Lack of light. Move to a lighter place.

3 *Young growth turns yellow, on older growth veins show prominently.* Chlorosis caused by lime in the water. Water once with sequestered iron and then water only with lime-free or rainwater.

4 *Plant fails to produce new growth in spring or after flowering.* Soil exhausted. Plant needs repotting or feeding.

5 *Blue flowers revert to pink.* Water with aluminium sulphate sold as hydrangea colourant or blueing compound. Only necessary if you prefer blue flowers.

6 *Brown spots on leaves.* Fungal infection. Dust these areas with flowers of sulphur or spray with a systemic fungicide.

7 *Leaves yellowed with webs underneath.* Red spider mite. Spray with derris, malathion or a systemic insecticide. Improve humidity.

8 *Young leaves distorted and sticky with green insects.* Greenfly. Spray with pyrethrum or a systemic insecticide.

Stem tip cuttings

1 Take step-tip cuttings after flowering. You can use prunings. Prepare pot with drainage layer and compost of $\frac{1}{2}$ sand, $\frac{1}{2}$ peat.

2 Choose shoot or stem tip with at least 2 pairs of healthy leaves and a growing point. Cut off below second pair of leaves, close to main stem. Cuttings should be 4–6 in (10–15cm) long.

3 Prepare cuttings by trimming off stem just below a leaf.

4 Remove the lowest pair of leaves.

5 Dip the cut surface in hormone rooting powder. Shake off the surplus.

6 Make small holes in compost around edge with stick or pencil.

7 Insert cutting so that end of stem is at bottom of hole and leaves are level with compost.

8 Water well and cover with polythene supported by wire. Remove cover for 5 minutes a day and never let compost dry out.
Remove cover after 21 days and when cuttings are growing well, repot in normal compost.

Watering

Hydrangeas need plenty of water and flop down when they are thirsty. It is better to water them before they reach this stage.

Place plant in bucket and fill bucket with water to just below the rim of the pot. Leave it there for 30 minutes, then allow it to drain.

Pruning

If you are keeping the plant for a second year indoors, cut each stem back to two pairs of leaves after it has flowered.

FRECKLE FACE

The two beautiful species of *Hypoestes* are much sought after by collectors. They were originally classified as stove house plants and had to be kept in high temperatures but now, like many other indoor plants, varieties have been bred to grow well in cooler temperatures.

Members of the Acanthaceae family, they came originally from Madagascar and were first imported in 1874. They have in all some forty relations, mostly found in southern Africa.

Hypoestes sanguinolenta is the better known plant. It has downy, oblong leaves of about 2–3 in (5–8 cm) long with coloured veins and markings that make the leaf appear to be dotted with pink spots. These give it its common names of freckle face and polka dot plant. It has delicate purple and white flowers but these only appear on mature plants and it is primarily grown as a foliage plant.

H. aristata is a larger plant, up to 2 ft (60 cm) tall with larger, more sharply pointed leaves which are pale green and spread out along the stem. The flowers are bright purple and have a downy 'throat'.

H. sanguinolenta can be raised from seeds available on the amateur market. Plants are normally available from late spring onwards and it is best to select bushy plants with the deepest and most attractive markings. Both varieties are best regarded as short lived and it is as well to propagate new ones each year.

Left: The flowering spike of *Hypoestes aristata*. This species is rare; it does not have variegated leaves.

Right and below: *Hypoestes sanguinolenta* produces many side shoots. It can therefore be pruned back to make a bushier plant.

Size: *H. sanguinolenta* does not grow more than 12 in (30 cm) high. *H. aristata* grows to just over 2 ft (60 cm). If they have been well grown they will be bushy plants.

Growth: Both will grow to their maximum size in one season.

Flowering season: Midsummer. The flowers are lilac, and purple in *H. aristata*. However, they are rather insignificant compared to the leaves.

Scent: None.

Light: They need plenty of light. A north or east facing windowsill away from the direct sun is ideal. In poor light *H. sanguinolenta* may lose some of its variegation.

Temperature: Maintain 65° to 70°F (18–21°C) throughout summer and winter. Maximum summer temperature is 75°F (24°C) in which case the ventilation should be good.

Water: Keep well watered, probably every other day in summer. Once a week in winter should be enough.

Feeding: Add half the recommended dose of liquid food to the water every 14 days in summer.

Humidity: Maintain a high humidity at all times by keeping the plant on a saucer of wet pebbles. This is better than spraying.

Cleaning: Dust carefully with a soft cloth. Do not use leaf shine.

Atmosphere: They are not very tolerant and do not like smoke, gas fumes or too dry an atmosphere. They appreciate some ventilation but not draughts.

Soil: Loam-based compost No. 2.

Repotting: Once a year in spring if they are being kept from year to year.

Pruning: None necessary unless the plants are being kept for a second year, in which case cut them down by half in early spring.

Propagation: Take young cuttings about 2–3 in (5–8 cm) long in spring and place in a propagator with bottom heat or inside a polythene bag. They appreciate a temperature of 70°F (21°C) at least. They can also be raised from seed sown in spring at 70°F (21°C). Both cuttings and seedlings should be 'stopped' twice (their growing tips removed) to encourage bushiness.

Life expectancy: These plants can get leggy and untidy, so it is as well to propagate new plants each spring. They are much more attractive when they are young.

Plant companions: Because they are delicate in looks as well as care they are best kept by themselves.

Ease/difficulty: Rather difficult.

Repotting

1 Repot in spring when plant looks top-heavy and roots grow through pot base. Water plant well.

4 Carefully remove stale soil from roots, using stick or pencil. Do not damage roots.

2 Prepare pot 1 size larger with drainage layer and layer of damp, loam-based No. 2 compost.

5 Place plant in centre of new pot, root-ball on compost.

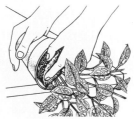

3 Hold old pot with one hand covering compost, fingers either side of stems. Tap edge of pot. Plant and compost will come out.

6 Add new compost to fill pot. Make sure that all roots are covered. Press down well. Leave in the shade without water for 2 days to encourage roots to grow into compost.

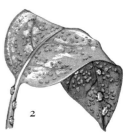

1 *Plant droops and looks tired.* Too cold and/or too wet. Allow to dry out in a warmer spot until recovered, then water less often.

2 *Leaves discoloured with brown scaly insects under leaves and on stems.* Scale insect. A common pest. Remove them individually with a swab dipped in methylated spirits or spray with a systemic insecticide.

Stem tip cuttings

1 *Hypoestes* becomes straggly after a year and it is best to take cuttings each year. Prepare pot with drainage and mixture ½ peat, ½ sand.

5 Dip the cut surface in hormone rooting powder. Shake off the surplus.

2 Choose shoot or stem tip with at least 2 pairs of healthy leaves and a growing point. Cut off below second pair of leaves.

6 Make small holes in compost around edge with stick or pencil.

3 Prepare cuttings by trimming off stem just below a leaf.

7 Insert cuttings so that end of stem is at bottom of hole and leaves are level with compost. Water well and cover with polythene supported by wire. Remove cover for 5 minutes a day and never let compost dry out. Keep at 70°F (21°C).

4 Remove the lowest pair of leaves.

8 Remove cover after 21 days and when cuttings are growing well, repot in normal compost. Pot rooted cuttings 3 per pot.

Growing from seed

Sow seeds in spring.
1 Prepare a seed tray or propagator with a drainage layer and sterilized, seed-growing compost.

2 Scatter seeds very evenly and add thin layer of compost, no thicker than depth of seed. Water well.

3 Cover with glass and put in dark place or cover with dark cloth. Make sure the compost never dries out and turn glass over daily. Keep at 70°F (21°C).

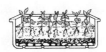

4 When seeds germinate, bring them into light and remove the glass cover.

5 When seedlings are large enough to handle, thin out the weaker ones, leaving about 1in (2½cm) between each one.

6 When remaining ones are growing well, repot in separate small pots.

Stopping

Pinch out the growing tips when cuttings have 2 pairs of leaves and are about 5in (12½cm) tall.

Humidity

Stand pot in saucer with water, pebbles or gravel. Make sure pot base is clear of water.

Watering

Add water at top of pot, using rainwater if possible. Empty excess from saucer after 15 minutes.

BUSY LIZZIE

The ubiquitous busy Lizzie is a must for any novice indoor gardener. It practically thrives on mis-treatment and if the worst comes to the worst it can be cut down to start again with cuttings rooted to make more plants.

Impatiens means impatient and this refers to the tendency of the ripe seed pod to burst and scatter its seeds everywhere. They are members of the balsam family which contains some five hundred species, most of which are annuals or biennials from subtropical Asia and Africa.

The common species available are *Impatiens sultanii* or *I. holstii* and both come from Zanzibar. The flowers are bright, flat and spurred, and plenty of them will be produced provided the plants are given sufficient light. These plants will grow out-of-doors in the summer time and can be used as bedding plants like the half-hardy annual balsam to which they are closely related.

Recently the New Guinea hybrids have been introduced. These are slightly larger plants with bigger flowers and prettily marked foliage varying from bronze green with red veins to green and yellow variegations. They must be propagated from cuttings to retain their characteristics. They are a little more tender than the original varieties and should not be put out-of-doors.

The last common species is *I. petersiana* which has reddish brown foliage and bright red flowers. It is a most striking plant when grown well. All these varieties are easily propagated and are bright and cheerful.

Buy compact plants just beginning to flower in the spring and summer. Inspect them for infestations by aphids and choose plants with good colour in their leaves.

Above: One of the New Guinea hybrid *Impatiens.* Below: *Impatiens sultanii* 'Variegata'.

Right: A very free flowering plant of *Impatiens sultanii.*

Size: Up to 15in (38cm) is a good size, though they will easily grow to twice that. However, like a number of plants they are most attractive and produce more flowers when they are small.

Growth: Quick growers, they will easily make 10in (25cm) growth in a year.

Flowering season: All through the summer and on into the autumn. It pays to disbud young plants as this helps to prolong the flowering season as well as to bring a heavier first flush of flowers.

Scent: None. They rely on their colour to attract.

Light: They require plenty of light to flower well and will even stand direct sun.

Temperature: They enjoy a high temperature in winter of 65–70°F (18–21°C) but will survive in 55–60°F (13–15°C). Normal room temperature in summer if not planted out between June and September. Summer maximum indoors should be 65°F (18°C).

Water: Water very freely in summer, 2–3 times a week. Water every 10 days in winter and keep the soil on the dry side as the plants are succulent and they can rot when not growing actively.

Feeding: They benefit from plenty of dilute liquid food. Add this to the water at least once a week.

Humidity: Do not spray the leaves as this can produce a fungus or cause rot. It will also mark the flowers.

Cleaning: Dust occasionally with soft cloth or feather duster. Never use leaf shine.

Atmosphere: They are tolerant of nearly anything humans can survive.

Soil: They like a rich soil such as loam-based No. 3.

Repotting: Once a year is enough. They flower better when pot-bound.

Pruning: Straggly plants should be cut back in summer to 3in (8cm) stumps.

Propagation: Place stem tip cuttings about 3–4in (8–10cm) long either in water or in soil in the spring. Except for the New Guinea hybrids they can also be grown easily from seed sown in spring at a temperature of 61–64°F (16–18°C).

Life expectancy: They will go on for a long time. However, as the plants get straggly it is better to re-propagate every year to produce new stock. The plants look neater and flower better when young.

Plant companions: As the plant tends to spread it is probably better on its own. It can however be planted as a temporary visitor to brighten up a planted bowl provided there is good light.

Ease/difficulty: A good beginner's plant.

Repotting

1 Repot in spring when roots show through pot base, leaves are pale and plant looks top-heavy. Water plant well.

2 Prepare pot 1 size larger with drainage layer and layer of damp, loam-based No. 3 compost.

3 Hold old pot with one hand covering compost, fingers either side of stems. Tap edge of pot. Plant and compost will come out.

4 Carefully remove stale soil from roots, using stick or pencil. Do not damage roots.

5 Place plant in centre of new pot, root-ball on compost.

6 Add new compost to fill pot. Make sure that all roots are covered. Press down well. Leave in the shade without water for 2 days to encourage roots to grow into compost.

What goes wrong

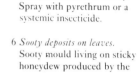

1 *No flowers.* Too dark. Move to a lighter place.

2 *Leaves drop.* Too cold. Move to a warmer place.

3 *Fungus on leaves or stems.* Too cold and dark. Move to a warmer, lighter place and spray with a systemic fungicide.

4 *White insects under leaves, fly away if plant is touched.* Whitefly. Spray with derris or a resmethrin-based insecticide.

5 *Leaves distorted and sticky with green insects.* Greenfly. Spray with pyrethrum or a systemic insecticide.

6 *Sooty deposits on leaves.* Sooty mould living on sticky honeydew produced by the greenfly. Kill greenfly and wipe off mould.

7 *Leaves become pale, mottled with webs underneath.* Red spider mite. Spray with derris, malathion or a systemic insecticide. Improve the humidity.

Watering

1 Test compost with fingers. If it is light and crumbly, the plant needs water.

2 Add water at top of pot, using rainwater if possible. Empty excess from saucer after 15 minutes.
Water freely in summer but less often in winter when they are not growing.

Stem cuttings in water

Take cuttings in spring, before the flowers appear.
1 Put 3 or 4 small pieces of charcoal in shallow jar and fill ⅔ with water.

2 Cover with kitchen foil held in place with a rubber band or string.
Pierce several small holes in foil with a pencil or stick.

3 Remove a shoot of about 3in (8cm) from plant.

4 Push the stem through foil into the water. Repeat with other shoots.

5 When new roots form, remove the shoots from water and repot them in small pots. Be careful not to damage the delicate roots.

6 Water well and cover with polythene cover for a few days to give extra humidity.

Growing from seed

1 Prepare a seed tray or propagator with a drainage layer and sterilized, seed-growing compost. Sow seed in spring.

2 Scatter the seeds very evenly and add thin layer of compost, no thicker than depth of seed. Water well.

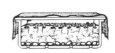

3 Cover with glass and put in dark place or cover with dark cloth. Make sure the compost never dries out and turn glass over daily.   Keep at 61–64 F (16–18 C).

4 When seeds germinate, bring them into light and remove the glass cover.

5 When seedlings are large enough to handle, thin out the weaker ones, leaving about 1in (2½cm) between each one.

6 When remaining ones are growing well, repot in separate small pots.

JASMINE

Jasminum polyanthum is a winter flowering plant that is really best in a conservatory but can be brought into the home for a short time while it is in flower. It has a heavy perfume and this is one of its great attractions. A vigorous climber, it is normally grown and sold around a hoop of wire some 15 in (38 cm) tall. If planted into a bed in a conservatory or greenhouse and tied to a trellis it will soon cover a wall. As a pot plant it is best placed outside in summer to give it good ventilation and kept in full sun to allow the shoots to ripen. This will ensure good flowering the following winter. Bring it indoors again in early autumn.

Jasmines are members of the olive family (Oleaceae) and the name comes from Persia, having at some stage been latinized. There are in all some twenty species, all native to subtropical or temperate countries. The summer flowering *Jasminum officinale* is well known out-of-doors. *J. polyanthum*, the indoor species, comes from China and was first introduced in 1891.

When purchasing a plant look for good, clean, bright green foliage without any brown leaves. The bunches of flower buds should be well formed, and some buds should be just showing white. If the flowers are well out and some are dropping off, it has been in stock too long. If the flower buds are browned the plant has been kept too hot or dry in the shop and the buds may never open.

Jasminum polyanthum is normally available in late winter or early spring when few other white, scented flowers are available.

Below: The flowers are pure white and scented. They turn brown as they fade. If they are kept cool they last much longer.

Right: A plant covered in a mass of flowers. Usually plants are supplied staked or trained around a wire hoop which helps to support the weight of the blooms.

Size: They are climbers and will grow up to 15 ft (4½ m). However, they are normally trained around a wire hoop some 15 in (38 cm) tall or up a 3 ft (1 m) cane.

Growth: They will put out long growths very quickly. Cuttings struck in the spring will be at flowering size 10 months later.

Flowering season: Beautiful clusters of white flowers appear from January to March.

Scent: The flowers have the sweet perfume that is typical of all jasmines.

Light: They require plenty of light but not too much direct summer sunshine indoors. They do best grown in the greenhouse or conservatory and just brought into the house when they are about to flower.

Temperature: They do not like to be too hot in the winter as the leaves soon dry up and the flowers fail to open. Keep them at about 55°F (13°C). They will stand 60–65°F (15–21°C) in the summer but there should be good ventilation.

Water: Once every 4 or 5 days in the winter and when flowering. Every other day in summer when growing.

Feeding: Add liquid food to the water every 14 days when the plant is growing.

Humidity: Spray with water, particularly when in the house, but try to avoid spraying the flowers as this can mark them.

Cleaning: Spraying will keep the leaves clean. Do not use leaf shine.

Atmosphere: They do not like a hot dry centrally heated atmosphere and they need plenty of air in the summer.

Soil: Loam-based No. 2.

Repotting: In the spring after flowering.

Pruning: It is as well to prune them back after flowering and when repotting. Cut back the leading growths by some 6–12 in (15–30 cm) depending on the growth. The growth buds should be pinched out once a month from spring to October to develop a bushy and more compact plant.

Propagation: Normally from stem tip cuttings taken in the spring for early flowering or in the autumn for flowering later. They need a temperature of 61°F (16°C). When the cuttings are rooted after 3 to 4 weeks, pot them up 3 or 4 in a pot to make a bushy plant and insert a hoop or cane for them to climb.

Life expectancy: If you have no greenhouse or conservatory then they are best discarded after flowering. With a greenhouse they will go on indefinitely. However, it is advisable to propagate new stock from time to time as old plants get woody.

Plant companions: Jasmines are best grown on their own.

Ease/difficulty: With a greenhouse and a little experience they are quite easy to keep going from year to year. Without a greenhouse they are difficult.

Repotting

1 Repot in spring after flowering when plant does not grow and roots show through pot base. Carefully remove any hoop or cane and water plant well.

2 Prepare pot 1 size larger with drainage layer and layer of damp, loam-based No. 2 compost.

3 Hold old pot with one hand covering compost, fingers either side of stems. Tap edge of pot. Plant and compost will come out.

4 Carefully remove stale soil from roots, using stick or pencil. Do not damage roots.

5 Place plant in centre of new pot, root-ball on compost.

6 Add new compost to fill pot. Make sure that all roots are covered. Press down well. Leave in the shade without water for 2 days to encourage roots to grow into compost. Replace hoop.

What goes wrong

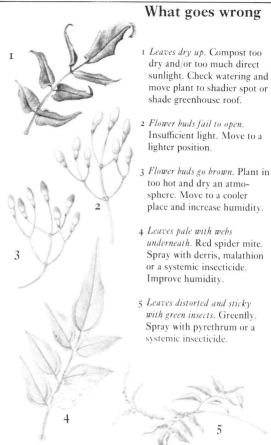

1 *Leaves dry up.* Compost too dry and/or too much direct sunlight. Check watering and move plant to shadier spot or shade greenhouse roof.

2 *Flower buds fail to open.* Insufficient light. Move to a lighter position.

3 *Flower buds go brown.* Plant in too hot and dry an atmosphere. Move to a cooler place and increase humidity.

4 *Leaves pale with webs underneath.* Red spider mite. Spray with derris, malathion or a systemic insecticide. Improve humidity.

5 *Leaves distorted and sticky with green insects.* Greenfly. Spray with pyrethrum or a systemic insecticide.

Stem tip cuttings

1 Take cuttings in spring after the flowers have died. Prepare pot with drainage and compost of ½ peat, ½ sand.

2 Choose shoot or stem tip with at least 2 pairs of healthy leaves and a growing point. Cut off below second pair of leaves, close to main stem. Cuttings should be 3–4in (8–10cm) long.

3 Prepare cuttings by trimming off stem just below a leaf.

4 Remove the lowest pair of leaves.

5 Dip the cut surface in hormone rooting powder. Shake off the surplus.

6 Make small holes in compost around edge with stick or pencil.

7 Insert cutting so that end of stem is at bottom of hole and leaves are level with compost.

8 Water well and cover with polythene supported by wire. Remove cover for 5 minutes a day and never let compost dry out. Keep at 61 F (16 C). Remove cover after 21 days and when cuttings are growing well, repot in normal compost.

Training round a hoop

1 Push one end of flexible cane or wire hoop into compost at side of pot, stopping when end of cane is ⅔ down pot.

2 Bend hoop to other side of pot and push into compost.

3 Gently twine plant stem around hoop, taking care not to damage stem or leaves.

4 If necessary, tie some twine to lower part of hoop. Thread it along hoop, looping it around the stem as you go. The plant will continue to grow along the hoop and can be trained to circle the hoop again or to retrace its steps.

Spraying

Spray with water twice a week in summer, once a week in winter. Hold the spray about 6in (15cm) from the leaves. Do not spray the flowers.

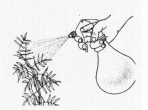

KALANCHOE

The *Kalanchoe* is a winter flowering plant that is easy to keep in flower all through the season. They have brilliant colours at a time of the year when everything is beginning to get grey and humdrum. They are succulents and are members of the Crassulaceae. Their name has a Chinese derivation but the plant is found in many parts of the world besides China, including Africa, Arabia, India and Malaysia. Most people treat kalanchoes as annuals and discard them after flowering. It is possible to keep them going from year to year, although after one entire year they get a bit untidy. It is not difficult to propagate them and so produce a continuous succession of vigorous plants.

Care should be taken with watering these plants, especially in winter for if the temperature drops the plant can soon start to rot and mildew will develop. As soon as any is noticed the affected portions of the plant should always be cut away and discarded.

Kalanchoes have had quite a lot of attention from plant breeders, who have developed attractive dwarf varieties in bright red, orange and pink. They are all hybrids of *K. blossfeldiana* which originally came from Madagascar. By sowing seed at different times of the year, growers can now produce them in flower all the year round.

Look carefully at the flowers of the plant you are purchasing. Only half should be fully coloured. If any of the flowers are faded, beware, for the first and most attractive flush of flowers is over. Look also for patches of mildew on the leaves. This is the first sign of rot.

Hybrids of *Kalanchoe blossfeldiana* are now produced in flower throughout the year and in various colours. They are excellent plants for hot, sunny windowsills. The leaves are succulent and the plants should never be overwatered.

Size: Normally grown in $3\frac{1}{2}$ in (9 cm) pots, a good specimen is about 5 in (12 cm) across and the same in height.

Growth: Seed sown in March and cuttings taken in May will be in flower in November and December of the same year.

Flowering season: Through the winter, from November to March, depending on when seeds were sown or cuttings struck.

Scent: None.

Light: During the winter this plant should be in the maximum light, preferably on a south-facing windowsill. In the summer it should be placed where it does not catch the midday sun.

Temperature: They grow better if they are not too hot in the winter, 50–60°F (10–15°C) is about the best, but keep them away from fires and radiators if your room is hotter. Maximum summer temperature is 80°F (27°C).

Water: Great care must be taken with watering otherwise the plant can rot. Water only when the soil is really dry, which can be every 10–14 days in winter and every 5–6 in summer. If the leaves droop withhold water – it already has too much.

Feeding: Add liquid food to the water once a month when the plant is growing and flowering.

Humidity: Do not spray overhead. If the atmosphere is very dry, place the pot in another pot packed with wet peat. They are more tolerant of dry air than most house plants.

Cleaning: Wipe the leaves with a damp cloth every 14 days. Do not use leaf shine.

Atmosphere: Keep well away from gas fires and radiators.

Soil: Loam-based No. 1.

Repotting: In the spring immediately after the plant has flowered.

Pruning: Remove the dead flower stems and any diseased leaves.

Propagation: Most plants are reared from seed sown in March and April at about 70°F (21°C). It is also possible to take stem tip cuttings in May and June, inserting them into sand and loam using rooting hormone. Young growth for cuttings is produced after the dead flower stems have been removed. Keep cuttings at 70°F (21°C).

Life expectancy: Most people regard them as annuals and discard them after flowering. It is not difficult to keep them going at least for one more flowering season. After that they lose their vigour and become rather untidy. It is then best to start again with young plants or seeds.

Plant companions: They make good visitors in bowls of mixed house plants. Remove them after the flowers have all finished.

Ease/difficulty: Easy.

Repotting

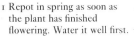

1 Repot in spring as soon as the plant has finished flowering. Water it well first.

2 Prepare pot 1 size larger with drainage layer and layer of damp, loam-based No. 1 compost.

4 Carefully remove stale soil from roots, using stick or pencil. Do not damage roots.

5 Place plant in centre of new pot, root-ball on compost.

3 Hold old pot with one hand covering compost, fingers either side of stems. Tap edge of pot. Plant and compost will come out.

6 Add new compost to fill pot. Make sure that all roots are covered. Press down well. Leave in the shade without water for 2 days to encourage roots to grow into compost.

1 Mildewed and blackened areas on leaves. Mildew. Dust with flowers of sulphur and improve ventilation. Do not let water remain on the leaves.

2 Leaves droop, especially in winter. Overwatering. Allow to dry out and then water less often.

3 Only small new leaves produced after flowering. Plant needs repotting.

Stem tip cuttings

1 In spring plant produces new shoots which can be used for cuttings. Prepare small pot with drainage layer and mixture of sharp sand and loam-based compost.

2 Choose shoot or stem tip with at least 2 pairs of healthy leaves and a growing point. Cut off below second pair of leaves. Cuttings should be 3–4in (8–10cm) long.

3 Prepare cuttings by trimming off stem just below a leaf.

4 Remove the lowest pair of leaves.

5 Dip the cut surface in hormone rooting powder. Shake off the surplus.

6 Make small holes in compost around edge with stick or pencil.

7 Insert cutting so that end of stem is at bottom of hole and leaves are level with compost.

8 Water well and keep in a warm place at 70°F (21°C). When cuttings are growing well, repot in normal compost.

Stopping for bushiness

A plant will grow more bushily if the growing tips are pinched from the end of the main stems.

Removing dead flowers

When flower has died, cut off flower stem just above the top pair of leaves.

Watering

1 Kalanchoes must never be overwatered. Wait until the compost feels really dry before adding water. Don't water if the leaves are drooping—it shows it is already too wet.

2 Add water at top of pot, using rainwater if possible. Empty excess from saucer after 15 minutes.

PARADISE PALM

The *Kentia* is perhaps the most popular of all the palms grown in the house. It is the plant of the palm courts of large hotels and transatlantic liners and associates well with all Victoriana. They are easy to grow with the minimum of care, and are extremely elegant with their long leaves bending gracefully outwards from the centre of the plant. Normally they are grown several plants to one pot so as to make a bushy, well furnished plant with palm fronds at all levels.

They have only one native habitat, the Lord Howe Islands in the Pacific, which gives them their alternative genus name of *Howea*.

There are two species cultivated. *K. forsteriana* is the most popular and more widely grown. The other is *K. belmoreana*. This is not quite so hardy, requires higher temperatures and will grow larger. It also has finer leaves. Both species are very slow growing and therefore very expensive to buy.

Kentias can be purchased as single plants from 1 ft (30 cm) to 4 ft (over 1 m) high and this is the least expensive way to acquire them. Several plants potted together are expensive, even when small and a large clump 8 ft (2½ m) tall may cost into three figures.

Choose kentias for the elegance and balance of their shape. They should be showing new growth without browning of the older leaves. For preference select plants without brown tips to the leaflets. Beware being offered palms with a yellowish appearance and thinner fronds. This is the yellow palm, *Areca lutescens*. It is often half the price of the true *Kentia* and looks similar when young. Although graceful in their own right and quicker growing they begin to look different from kentias as they mature.

Kentias are elegant palms, much in demand but expensive.

Right: *Kentia forsteriana*, the species most commonly available. Here several plants have been potted together.

Left and below: *Kentia belmoreana*.

Size: Mature specimens will grow to 10 or 12 ft (3–4 m) in the house. In the tropics *K. belmoreana* will grow to 35 ft (11 m) and *K. forsteriana* is only slightly smaller.

Growth: Very slow, one or perhaps two leaves per year in the house, slightly quicker in a greenhouse.

Flowering season: None.

Scent: None.

Light: Although they will grow more quickly in a light position, they will tolerate dark and shady places.

Temperature: *K. forsteriana* will tolerate a temperature as low as 50°F (10°C) in winter, although is happier at 60°F (16°C). *K. belmoreana* requires 60° to 65°F (16–18°C) as a minimum. Maximum summer temperatures are 75°F (24°C).

Water: In winter keep just moist, watering every 10 to 14 days or so. In summer water at least twice a week.

Feeding: Add liquid food to the water every 14 days in the summer.

Humidity: They like to be sprayed with a fine mist twice a week in summer and once in winter. Stand them out in the rain occasionally in summer.

Cleaning: Spraying should keep the leaves clean, however a good wipe with a damp cloth every couple of months is beneficial. Do not use leaf shine as this causes the fronds to turn brown.

Atmosphere: Will tolerate most man-made conditions, but does not like to be in a small unventilated room for too long. Keep out of draughts.

Soil: Loam-based No 2 with ¼ measure by volume of extra peat.

Repotting: Once a year in the spring when young. Mature plants in large pots or tubs should have the topsoil changed in spring. Deep pots are best for palms. Never use shallow pans.

Pruning: Remove dead leaves that develop occasionally at the base of the plant. If the tips of the leaves go brown this indicates too dry an atmosphere. Cut off the dead areas and re-point the ends but do not cut into living tissue.

Propagation: From fresh imported seeds. This is best left to the experts as a temperature of at least 80°F (27°C) is required.

Life expectancy: They should last a very long time provided they are not over-watered in winter. This causes sudden rot and death.

Plant companions: They make good backing plants in mixed tub and trough displays but look at their best alone.

Ease/difficulty: Very easy.

Repotting

1 Repot young plants in spring when roots grow from pot base and no new fronds appear. Water plant well.

2 Prepare deep pot 1 size larger with drainage and layer of compost made up of 3 parts damp, loam-based No. 2 and 1 part peat.

3 Hold old pot with one hand covering compost, fingers either side of stems. Tap edge of pot. Plant and compost will come out. Carefully remove stale soil from roots, using stick or pencil. Do not damage roots.

4 Place plant in centre of new pot, root-ball on compost.

5 Add new compost to fill pot. Make sure that all roots are covered.

6 Press down well. Leave in the shade without water for 2 days to encourage roots to grow into new compost.

What goes wrong

1 *Tips of leaves turn brown.* Atmosphere too dry, especially in central heating. Spray plant frequently or place on a tray of wet pebbles. Check that the plant is not in a draught.

2 *Entire leaves turn brown.* Plant dried out or has been kept in a very hot and dry atmosphere. Cut off brown leaves, check watering and move to a cooler place. Improve humidity.

3 *Plant goes black and rots at base.* Too wet from over-watering. Usually fatal but if you allow it to dry out it may just recover.

4 *Plant fails to produce new growth in spring.* Needs repotting or feeding as the soil is exhausted.

5 *White or brown scaly insects under the fronds and on stems.* Scale insect. Remove them individually with a swab dipped in methylated spirits or spray with a systemic insecticide.

6 *Fronds seem yellowed and have webs underneath.* Red spider mite. Spray with derris, malathion or a systemic insecticide. Improve the humidity.

7 *Leaves show silvery, scarred areas with black/grey flying insects.* Thrips. Spray with a systemic insecticide.

Replacing topsoil

1 Plants in large tubs should have the top inch (2½cm) compost changed in spring. Use a stick or trowel and be careful not to damage roots.

2 Add new compost to fill pot.

3 Press down firmly all round, making sure roots are all well covered.
Leave in shade without water for 2 days to encourage roots to grow into new compost.

Growing from seed

Growing from seed is difficult but if you use a propagator or can keep the seed tray warm and humid, you may be successful.

1 Prepare a seed tray or propa-gator with a drainage layer and sterilized, seed-growing compost.

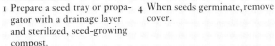

2 Scatter the seeds very evenly and add thin layer of com-post, no thicker than depth of seed. Water well.

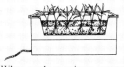

3 Cover propagator. Remove cover for 5 minutes a day to prevent rot and make sure the compost does not dry out. Keep at 80°F (27°C).

4 When seeds germinate, remove cover.

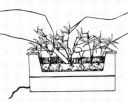

5 When seedlings are large enough to handle, thin out the weaker ones, leaving about 1in (2½cm) between each one.

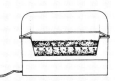

6 When remaining ones are growing well, repot in separate small pots.

Cleaning

Wipe dust off leaves with soft cloth and sponge with tepid water. Support leaf with other hand.
Do not use leaf shine.

Spraying

Spray with water twice a week in summer, once a week in winter.

Trimming the fronds and leaves

Cut out dead lower fronds. Cut as close to main stem as possible.

If the tips of the leaves are brown and dry, trim them off with sharp scissors, cutting just above healthy leaf tissue.

PRAYER PLANT

The marantas and their close relatives the calatheas are among the most spectacular and attractive of all foliage house plants. Each leaf appears to be hand painted with markings that are distinctive to each variety. Calatheas and marantas are both members of the Marantaceae family but although there are botanical differences between them, there is much confusion between the two genera. Marantas are generally low and squat and calatheas are more upright, but both names are often used indiscriminately.

The marantas are named after Bartolomeo Maranti, a Venetian botanist who was famous in the mid-sixteenth century. There are some fourteen species, coming from tropical Central and South America. Calatheas (from the Greek word *kalathos*, a basket) are more numerous with about a hundred species, also from tropical Central and South America and the West Indies.

The two best known marantas are *Maranta leuconeura* 'Kerchoveana' with green and black markings which give it the common name of rabbit's tracks; and *M. leuconeura* 'Erythrophylla' or 'Tricolor' with two shades of green and red vein markings. This is commonly known as the red herring bone plant. Both of these varieties are also known as prayer plants because their leaves curl up at night and remind people of praying hands.

Calatheas commonly available include *C. mackoyana*, the peacock plant with beautiful upright leaves of an oval shape, delicately painted in various shades of green with brown stems. *Calathea* (or *Maranta*) *insignis* has more pointed leaves, also beautifully marked.

Make sure that members of the Marantaceae family are bright and healthy and that none of the leaves is dried or withered.

Marantas have spectacular leaf markings which are different in each variety.

Left: *Maranta leuconeura* 'Kerchoveana'.

Right: *Calathea* (or *Maranta*) *mackoyana*.

Below: *Maranta leuconeura* 'Erythrophylla'.

Size: Marantas will grow to about 18in (46cm) across, and the same height upwards if trained up a trellis. Calatheas will grow up to 3ft (1m) at their best.

Growth: In the home they will put on 5 or 6 new leaves a year.

Flowering season: An insignificant single white flower is produced on a stem in the summer. They are grown mainly for their beautiful leaf markings.

Scent: None.

Light: They do not like too much light, certainly not a south or west facing window, and are good plants to have in a shady position. However, they like more light in the winter.

Temperature: Whilst they will survive at temperatures down to 50°F (10°C) if given only a little water, they prefer to be at about 60°F (16°C). They can stand much higher temperatures, up to 80-85°F (27-29°C), if the humidity is increased.

Water: The compost must be open and porous and should be kept well damp at all times. Water 2 to 3 times a week in summer and once a week in winter. If the temperature is as low as 50°F (10°C) water only about every 10 days.

Feeding: Add half the recommended dose of liquid food to the water every 14 days during the growing period.

Humidity: High humidity is an essential element in the successful cultivation of marantas and calatheas. Spray daily in the summer and stand the pot on damp pebbles. In winter spray once or twice a week.

Cleaning: Spraying should keep the plants clean. If not, wipe leaves gently with a damp cloth. Never use leaf shine.

Atmosphere: Keep them out of draughts and away from open gas fires.

Soil: They like an open compost, so the peat-based composts are best.

Repotting: Normally once a year in the spring. Make sure the plant has good drainage. Do not firm the compost down too hard.

Pruning: Cut out straggly shoots and dried up or damaged leaves.

Propagation: By gently dividing the roots and stems in the spring when repotting.

Life expectancy: Not the easiest of plants, but if you understand their needs they will go on for many years. However it is better to divide your plant every third year to maintain the vigour of the stock.

Plant companions: They enjoy the company of other plants and the humidity they create. Any of the green foliage plants, such as *Ficus*, philodendrons, dracaenas etc. are good trough companions.

Ease/difficulty: Not for the novice, but anyone with a good working knowledge of indoor plants who is willing to take a little trouble to provide the right care has a good chance of success.

Repotting

1 Repot in spring when plant looks top-heavy but does not grow. Water plant well.

2 Prepare pot 1 size larger with drainage layer and layer of damp, peat-based compost.

3 Hold old pot with one hand covering compost, fingers either side of stems. Tap edge of pot. Plant and compost will come out.

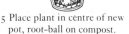

4 Carefully remove stale soil from roots, using stick or pencil. Do not damage roots.

5 Place plant in centre of new pot, root-ball on compost.

6 Add new compost to fill pot. Make sure that all the roots are covered but do not press it down too hard. Leave the plant in the shade without water for 2 days to encourage roots to grow into compost.

What goes wrong

1 *Leaves curl and wither.* Plant too dry and cold. Raise temperature and gradually increase watering as it gets warmer. Keep plant out of draughts.

2 *Leaves become pale.* Too much direct sunlight. Move to slightly shaded position. If paleness continues, feed weekly during the growing season.

3 *Leaves fade and have webs underneath.* Red spider mite. Spray with derris, malathion or a systemic insecticide. Improve the humidity.

Root division

Divide large, old plants in early spring.

1 Prepare 2 pots with drainage layer and compost.

3 Gently pull roots and stems apart with your hands.

2 Remove plant from pot and gently prise away compost.

4 Repot both sections in the usual way.

Pruning for shape

Remove any straggly growths that appear at any time, to encourage strong growth from the centre.

Removing dead leaves

When dead leaf is quite dry cut it off with sharp scissors where leaf stem joins plant.

Cleaning the leaves

Wipe dust off leaves with soft cloth and sponge with tepid water. Support leaf with other hand.

Do not use leaf shine.

Humidity

Stand pot in saucer with water, pebbles or gravel. Make sure pot base is clear of water.

Marantas and calatheas both need high humidity. Spray every day in summer and once or twice a week in winter.

Put pot in outer container packed with damp peat.

Watering

1 Test compost with fingers. If it is light and crumbly, the plant needs water.

2 Add water at top of pot, using rainwater if possible. Empty excess from saucer after 15 minutes.

SWISS CHEESE PLANT

The *Monstera* is a most handsome plant when well grown. It will easily, although slowly, grow to 8 ft (230 cm) in the home. A member of the Araceae or Arum family, it is closely related to the philodendrons and is a genus of some thirty species of evergreen tropical plants from the West Indies and Central America. One of its common names, the Mexican bread fruit plant, comes from the seed pod, which contains an edible pulp around the seeds.

The leaves can be very large, at up to 2 ft (60 cm) across. They are deeply cut and holed, a feature which gives the plant its second attractive name of the Swiss cheese plant and also indicates that it comes from a region where there are strong winds. In the wild, the holes allow wind to pass unhindered, preserving the large leaves from damage.

The plant grows naturally as a horizontal creeper and a strong pole or stake must be provided if it is to be made to climb vertically. When growing healthily it will produce a number of aerial roots which in its natural habitat anchor the plant. These should not be removed as they add to the plant's appearance, and will often grip the stake or moss pole.

Monsteras are one of the easier house plants to keep but they can be demanding in the amount of room they require. They should not be confused with *Philodendron pertusum* which has smaller but similarly shaped leaves and grows much more quickly.

When purchasing a plant choose one with undamaged leaves of a deep rich green. You can tell damaged from naturally split and holed leaves because the damaged ones will be dry and brown around the tear. Young leaves are a fresh, pale green.

Size: Although normally bought in a 5 in (12 cm) pot some 18–24 in (46–60 cm) tall, this plant will slowly grow into a big specimen with leaves some 2 ft (46 cm) across. It can reach 8 ft (230 cm) after many years.

Growth: Slow. It produces one or two leaves a year at the most.

Flowering season: A yellowish flower resembling an arum will appear on a mature plant in the summer time. This is quickly followed by the fruit, which is edible when it is fully ripe.

Scent: None.

Light: This plant is tolerant of shady corners, hence its popularity as a good house plant. It should at all times be kept out of direct sunlight, especially during summer.

Temperature: A minimum temperature of 55°F (13°C) in the winter but it will tolerate 50°F (10°C) if water is reduced. In the summer it will flourish at a higher temperature, up to 75°F (24°C).

Water: This plant does not like to be over-watered and it is best to let it dry out between watering. Watch the soil condition and judge by its feel when to water. About once a week in summer unless the weather is very hot, and about every 14 days in the winter should be enough.

Feeding: Add liquid food to the water every 21 days in the summer when the plant is growing.

Humidity: Like all jungle plants it enjoys plenty of moisture. Spray regularly with soft water and stand the pot on wet pebbles or pack it in an outer pot with wet peat.

Cleaning: Clean the leaves by hand with a damp cloth, carefully supporting them from underneath. Leaf shine may also be used every 2 months. This gives the plant a good glossy appearance but should not be used too frequently.

Atmosphere: Very tolerant. It is a good plant for offices and show-rooms.

Soil: It prefers peat-based composts which are open and allow good drainage.

Repotting: Once a year in the spring. When it has reached the maximum desired size, just change the top of the compost. Support the plant with a stake or moss pole.

Pruning: Not really necessary. If the plant gets too big the top can be cut off and rooted and the plant will reshoot.

Propagation: In early summer, by stem tip cuttings in a propagator at 75–80°F (24–27°C). Joint cuttings can also be used but are slower to grow and require a high temperature of 90°F (34°C). Tip cuttings can be rooted in water.

Life expectancy: With minimal care this plant will go on for many years.

Plant companions: As young plants monsteras will go well with any number of green and coloured foliage plants. As they grow into mature plants it is probably best to grow them on their own.

Ease/difficulty: A good plant for beginners.

The *Monstera* is one of the most popular of all house plants. Its spectacular leaves (below) are naturally split and holed, giving it the common name Swiss cheese plant.

Right: This specimen of *Monstera deliciosa* has leaves of different ages. The young, lower ones are heart shaped, and the intermediate leaves are cut at their edges. Only the topmost leaf has its full complement of holes.

Humidity

Stand pot in saucer with water, pebbles or gravel. Make sure pot base is clear of water.

or Put pot in outer container packed with damp peat.

Spraying

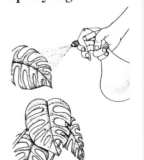

Spray with water twice a week in summer, once a week in winter. Hold the spray about 6 in (15 cm) from the leaves.

Cleaning

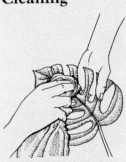

Wipe dust off leaves with soft cloth and sponge with tepid water. Support leaf with other hand.
Use leaf shine but not more than once every 2 months.

1 *Black patches on the leaves.* Too cold. Move to a warmer position.

2 *Lower leaves go yellow and then brown, especially in winter.* Overwatering. Allow plant to dry out until recovered, then water less often.

3 *Leaves pale and scorched with round holes among the scorch marks.* Too much direct sun. Move to a semi-shaded position.

4 *Leaves pale.* Lack of food. Feed weekly in the growing season.

5 *Leaves pale with webs underneath.* Red spider mite. Spray with derris, malathion or a systemic insecticide. Improve the humidity.

Replacing the topsoil

1 When plant is over 3ft (1m) tall, do not repot. Water, then remove top inch (2½cm) of old compost. Do not damage roots.

2 Add new compost to fill pot.

3 Press down firmly all round, making sure roots are all well covered.
Leave in shade without water for 2 days to encourage roots to grow into new compost.

Adding a moss pole

1 Prepare new pot with drainage and layer of damp, peat-based compost.

2 Position moss pole and add a little compost around it to hold it firm.

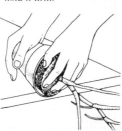

3 Remove plant from pot.

4 Place plant in pot beside moss pole.

5 Add new compost to fill pot. Make sure that all roots are covered. Press down well.

6 Tie plant stem to moss pole with raffia or twine at intervals.

Propagation in water

Take cuttings in early summer.

1 Put 3 or 4 small pieces of charcoal in shallow jar and fill ⅔ with water.

2 Cover with kitchen foil held in place with a rubber band or string.
Pierce a hole in the foil.

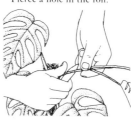

3 Remove stem tip (the young tip leaf with the leaf below it). Make cut just above the third leaf and trim the cutting itself to just below the second leaf.

4 Push the stem through foil into the water. Keep warm (75–80 F, 24–27 C).

5 When new roots form, remove the cutting from water and repot it.

6 Water well and cover with polythene cover for a few days to give extra humidity.

Musa cavendishii

DWARF BANANA

This plant has been cultivated for a very long time and, incidentally, shows how widely spread the Roman empire was for it was first brought back from the tropics by legionnaires returning home. It was named after Antonius Musa, physician to Octavius Augustus, first emperor of Rome (62-14 BC). It is from the family Musaceae which contains some forty species spread across the tropics. In the wild some are full sized trees, with gigantic leaves and fruit which is an important crop. The smaller varieties were much favoured by the Victorians for growing in their tropical plant houses.

Musa is really a fairly tolerant plant for it does not mind how hot it is as long as there is plenty of moisture at its roots and in the air around it. It will also grow at normal room temperatures as long as these are not below about 60°F (15°C). However, the leaves, which grow up to 3 ft (1 m) long and 1 ft (30 cm) across are very delicate. Great care must be taken not to knock them for they split very easily along the veins.

Only one species is commonly grown today in the house, *Musa cavendishii*, the dwarf Canary banana which came originally from China in 1829. Its fruit is edible and it is much grown commercially in the Canary Isles and Florida. This miniature variety can be grown in the house in a good light position. It can also be grown as a hydroculture plant but it is better to convert a mature plant from soil than to propagate straight in water.

As the fruit of *M. cavendishii* is seedless, this variety must be propagated from rooted suckers. Plants capable of existing on their own roots will therefore be at least 2 ft (60 cm) high and are quite expensive. Smaller seed raised plants are likely to be of other varieties. Choose a plant with new growth, no browning on the edges of the leaves and preferably untorn leaves. Take it home with care.

Left: The leaves of all *Musa* species are delicate and easily torn.

Right: *Musa cavendishii*. This species will grow to 6 ft (200 cm) and will then fruit.

Below: *Musa ensete* 'Rubra' can be raised from seed. It rarely fruits indoors.

Size: Will grow to 5-6 ft (150-200 cm). Leaves can be up to 3 ft (1 m) long and 1 ft (30 cm) wide.
Growth: Fairly quickly, at 2-3 ft (60-100 cm) a year.
Flowering season: June and July. The flowers are quite small. A large plant will produce fruit.
Scent: None.
Light: They need plenty of light and do not mind direct sunshine as long as moisture does not remain on the leaves to cause burning and marking.
Temperature: They will grow in normal room temperature. A minimum of 60°F (15°C) in winter is needed.
Water: Water freely during summer – 2 or 3 times a week. In winter keep drier, watering about every 10 days.
Feeding: Provide rich potting compost and add liquid food to the water every 14 days.
Humidity: Place on wet pebbles and spray the leaves once or twice a week. If in direct sunlight, gently shake off the surplus water after spraying.
Cleaning: By spraying or careful dusting. Take great care, for the leaves are thin and split easily. Do not use leaf shine.
Atmosphere: They like an airy position and will not do well in a stuffy room.

Soil: A good rich compost such as loam-based No. 3.
Repotting: Every spring. Once the plant is too large to repot, remove and replace the topsoil in spring.
Pruning: Not necessary, except to remove dead leaves at the bottom of the plant and old stems which have fruited and died down.
Propagation: *M. cavendishii* is seedless and can only be propagated from suckers split from the mother plant in spring and potted up in a high temperature and humidity (65-70°F, 18-21°C). There are some varieties that can be grown from seeds in spring at a temperature of 70-80°F (21-27°C). Soak the seeds for 72 hours in water before planting them.
Life expectancy: 4-5 years. If a plant produces fruit the fruited stem will normally then die, having first thrown out 2 or 3 suckers to replace itself.
Plant companions: Its large, droopy leaves look best by themselves, unless the plant is in a large conservatory where any tropical plant combination will do well.
Ease/difficulty: With the minimum attention this plant will grow well in the home. It is not difficult but does need some space.

Humidity

Musa can stand quite high temperatures but must always have plenty of humidity.

Put pot in outer container packed with damp peat.

or Stand pot in saucer with water, pebbles or gravel. Make sure pot base is clear of water.

Cleaning the leaves

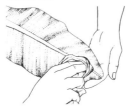

Wipe dust off leaves with soft cloth and sponge with tepid water. Support leaf with other hand.
Take care, the leaves are very delicate.

Do not use leaf shine.

Spraying

Spray once or twice a week. Do not allow the water to stay on the leaves in direct sunlight. Gently shake the surplus off.

What goes wrong

1 *Leaf edges turn brown and dry.* Compost and atmosphere too dry. Increase watering and improve humidity.

2 *Slimy rot on stems or trunk.* Too much water and/or spraying while temperature is low. Dust with sulphur and raise temperature.

3 *No new growth appears in spring.* Compost exhausted. Repot or feed regularly.

4 *Leaves torn and ragged.* Damage by humans or heavy overhead watering. Check plant is not in a position where it can be knocked. Cut off old, tattered leaves as new ones appear.

5 *White woolly patches, especially in the axils of older leaves.* Mealy bug. Remove them individually with a swab dipped in methylated spirits or spray with malathion or a systemic insecticide.

Replacing the topsoil

1 Young plants need repotting every spring. When they are large, just remove the top inch (2½cm) of soil. Water well first.

2 Add new compost to fill pot. Use damp, loam-based No. 3.

3 Press down firmly all round, making sure roots are all well covered.

4 Leave in shade without water for 2 days to encourage roots to grow into new compost.

Growing from seed

1 Some *Musa* species can be grown from seed. Soak the seeds for 72 hours before planting.
Prepare a seed tray or propagator with a drainage layer and sterilized, seed-growing compost.

2 Scatter the seeds very evenly and add thin layer of compost, no thicker than depth of seed. Water well.

3 Cover propagator. Remove cover for 5 minutes a day to prevent rot and make sure the compost does not dry out. Keep at 70–80 F (21–27°C).

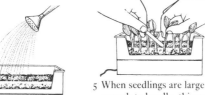

4 When seeds germinate, remove cover.

5 When seedlings are large enough to handle, thin out the weaker ones, leaving about 1in (2½cm) between each one.

6 When remaining ones are growing well, repot in separate small pots.

Propagation: Offsets

When *Musa cavendishii* has reached about 6ft (2m) tall, it may produce offsets at its base.

1 Prepare new pot with drainage and loam-based No. 3.

2 Loosen compost with knife around top edge of pot. Remove plant, holding it firmly by base of stem and supporting the upper part.

3 Gently pull roots and stems apart with your hands. The offset will have roots.

4 Pot offset in new pot, firming compost around base. Water and cover with polythene to give extra humidity.

CARTWHEEL PLANT

Unlike most bromeliads, neoregelias flower deep within their central urn.

Right: *Nidularium (Neoregelia) carolinae* 'Marechalli'.

Left: A young plant of *Neoregelia carolinae tricolor*. Below: A more mature plant of the same species producing its violet flowers.

What a pity that the botanists could not really agree on the correct name for one of the most spectacular of all the bromeliads. Originally there were two genera, *Nidularium*, meaning 'like a bird's nest' and *Aregalia*, named after a famous Russian botanist, E. A. von Regal, who lived in St Petersburg during the nineteenth century. Although there are slight botanical differences, particularly in the flowers, the genera have now been combined and named *Neoregelia* – but both names are still to be found on plants in the shops.

All neoregelias make good house plants and are particularly suitable for mixed plantings in tubs and troughs. They are nearly all natives of the jungles of Brazil and were introduced as indoor plants in the mid-nineteenth century. All are distinguished by stiff, strap-like leaves which radiate from the central funnel in which small, usually purple flowers appear. This funnel has to be kept filled with water for it is from water that the plants draw most of their nourishment, not from the compost. The flowers themselves are not very spectacular but as they appear the leaves around the centre of the plant turn a brilliant red colour which lasts a long time.

Neoregelia carolinae tricolor is perhaps the most striking, for in addition to its red centre, the radiating green leaves are striped in yellow. A new variety has recently been introduced, *N.c. tricolor* 'Perfecta', which has even more brilliant colouring. *N.c.* 'Marechalli' has plain green leaves and a bright red centre which can spread over nearly half the plant. Less well known is *N. spectabilis,* where the red colour is at the tips of the leaves.

When purchasing your plant, make sure that the leaves are fresh and bright. There should be no evidence of old flowers in the funnel.

Size: *N. carolinae tricolor* is the biggest of the neoregelias and can easily have a span of 2 ft (60 cm). Normally plants have a span of about 15–18 in (38–46 cm).

Growth: They grow fairly slowly in the house, from plantlets to flowering size in 2–3 years.

Flowering season: Flowering can take place at any time but is normally in the summer months. The red colour lasts much longer than the actual flowers.

Scent: None.

Light: They like plenty of light and colour up better when exposed to some sunshine. Avoid the hot midday summer sunshine.

Temperature: A constant all-the-year-round temperature of 60°F (15°C) is best, but this can drop to 55°F (13°C) in winter and should not rise above 70°F (21°C) in summer.

Water: The funnel should be kept filled with water at all times. Change it about once a week if possible. During the winter this water will be sufficient: the compost can be left dry. In summer keep the compost wet as well, watering about once a week unless very hot, then increase to twice a week.

Feeding: Add half the recommended dose of liquid food to the water you put in the funnel every 14 days in the summer.

Humidity: Spray overhead weekly.

Cleaning: The leaves can be wiped with a damp cloth. Be careful, for the leaves are serrated and can easily tear flesh. Do not use leaf shine.

Atmosphere: They are tolerant of most conditions, but keep them away from gas or open fires.

Soil: They like a light open compost, so mix equal quantities by bulk of a peat-based compost and loam-based No. 2.

Repotting: This is best done in May. Their roots are small, so they are unlikely to be pot bound, but the leaves may spread widely and unbalance the pot if it is not changed.

Pruning: Cut back damaged or decayed leaves.

Propagation: From seed which can be purchased and sown in a propagator at about 75°F (24°C) or by the young plantlets produced around the mother plant after flowering. Wait for the plantlets to grow to about half the size of the mother before separating them. Pot into a very sandy compost in a humid atmosphere and put into a 5 in (12 cm) pot after about 3 months.

Life expectancy: The life cycle of a *Neoregelia* is approximately 2–3 years.

Plant companions: Whilst they can be grown on their own as specimens they look particularly well when planted in troughs or tubs with other plants such as *Ficus,* philodendrons and dracaenas.

Ease/difficulty: A good plant for the novice to progress to after simpler plants.

Repotting

1 Repot in late spring when plant looks unbalanced in its pot. Water well first.

2 Prepare pot 1 size larger with drainage layer and layer of peat and loam compost.

3 Hold old pot with one hand covering compost, fingers either side of leaves. Tap edge of pot. Plant and compost will come out.

4 Carefully remove stale soil from roots, using stick or pencil. Do not damage roots.

5 Place plant in centre of new pot, root-ball on compost.

6 Add new compost to fill pot. Make sure that all roots are covered. Press down well. Leave in the shade without water for 2 days to encourage roots to grow into compost.

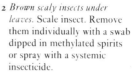

1 *Plant shrivels*. Too dry. Water at roots and add water to the central funnel.

2 *Brown scaly insects under leaves*. Scale insect. Remove them individually with a swab dipped in methylated spirits or spray with a systemic insecticide.

3 *Leaves become pale*. Lack of light. Move plant to a position with some direct sunlight.

4 *The base of the rosette rots*. Soil too wet while in too low a temperature. Usually fatal. Allow to dry out and if it recovers, keep it warmer in future.

Fixing a bromeliad to bark

Neoregelias have shallow roots and obtain nourishment from water in their central well. They look good on a piece of bark or wood.

1 Choose suitable piece of cork bark, a branch or some well shaped driftwood.

2 If there is no natural hollow, chisel a shallow well where plant will rest.

4 Wrap roots in damp sphagnum moss and tie with plastic-coated wire.

5 Hold moss and root-ball firmly against wood or bark and bind in place with wire.

Offsets

1 Wait until flowers and leaves of plant have died before removing offset. Offset should be about $\frac{1}{2}$ size of parent.

2 Prepare small pot with drainage layer and damp peat and sand.

3 Knock plant from pot and remove offset and roots from parent plant with sharp knife.

4 The offset must have its own small roots. If it has not, it will not grow.

5 Pot offset in new pot, firming compost around base. Water well and cover with polythene cover for a few days to give extra humidity.

6 The young offset will grow to flowering size in 2–3 years.

Watering

Keep about 1in (2½cm) of water in central funnel. Empty and refill every week . Rainwater is best.

Spraying

Spray once a week overhead with a fine mist spray. Hold spray about 6in (15cm) from leaves.
Use rainwater if possible.

3 Remove plant from pot, keeping compost round the root ball.

6 Fix bark to wall or prop it up, making sure the plant is growing upright. Keep central funnel filled with water and spray regularly. Keep root ball damp.

LADDER FERN

Ferns are good plants to grow in the house for they will tolerate quite dark places. However, they need high humidity at all times so do not always do well in centrally heated homes unless a special effort is made to keep the air around them moist. The species of *Nephrolepis* are no exception to this but are otherwise fairly tough and attractive plants. Members of the Polypodiaceae family, their name comes from the Greek words *nephros*, a kidney and *lepis*, a scale – presumably from the shape of the leaflets. As a group they are commonly known as ladder ferns, after the symmetrical way the foliage grows out from the central stem of the fronds.

There are some thirty-five known species and they are found throughout the tropics. *Nephrolepis* was a genus of ferns much loved by the Victorians for its soft, drooping fronds and it is equally popular with modern decorators. The ferns' flowing lines and lush growth mix well with both modern and traditional styles of decor. They do equally well in pots or in hanging baskets, provided that they are kept well watered at all times and given high humidity.

Several species are grown, all requiring the same care and conditions. *Nephrolepis exaltata* is perhaps the best known, its varieties such as 'Rooseveltii', 'Plumosa' and 'Bostoniensis' (the Boston fern) being the most popular. *N. cordifolia*, which has more upright fronds, is also a popular plant.

Specimens in the shop should be bright green, without any bent fronds or dropping foliage and with no dried up fronds in the centre of the plant, where new growth first appears.

There are many different varieties of *Nephrolepis*. Some are tougher than others but all prefer some humidity.

Above: *Nephrolepis* 'Rooseveltii'.

Above left: A frond of *Nephrolepis gloriosa*.

Left: The foliage of *Nephrolepis exaltata*.

Right: *Nephrolepis exaltata*.

Size: Normally planted in 5 in (12 cm) pots with fronds 18–20 in (46–50 cm) long. They will grow into large plants with fronds up to 30 in (76 cm) long.

Growth: They will double their size in a year.

Flowering season: Being ferns, they do not produce flowers. Tiny reproductive spores appear on the backs of the fronds, usually in spring or summer.

Scent: None.

Light: They will tolerate quite shady places. They do not like direct sunshine in the summer.

Temperature: A winter temperature of 57–60°F (14–15°C) is ideal. They can stand 5°F (3°C) lower, but if they are at a low temperature, keep them on the dry side, watering only about once a week. In summer keep at 65–70°F (18–21°C). They do not enjoy temperatures above 75°F (24°C) unless the humidity is high.

Water: Unless they are at a low temperature, keep them very moist at all times, watering 2–3 times a week in summer and at least once a week in winter. Use rainwater for preference.

Feeding: Add liquid food to the water every 14 days in the summer. This helps to keep the plant growing vigorously.

Humidity: A fine spray of lime-free water every day is desirable, though not always possible if you live in an area where the water is hard. If the plant is in a pot, stand it on damp pebbles. If in a hanging basket, a daily spray is really essential.

Cleaning: The spraying should keep the plant clean. Never use leaf shine.

Atmosphere: They do not like it too dry or too hot. Keep them away from gas fires and draughts. Any of these conditions may kill the plant.

Soil: A peat-based compost is ideal.

Repotting: It is as well to repot the plant every spring. Use plastic pots as these retain moisture better than clay ones.

Pruning: Not necessary, apart from removing fronds that have died.

Propagation: In spring, pot up the little plantlets that form on runners or stolons out of the crown of the plant. These will normally have rooted at the side of the pot. A propagator is not needed.

Life expectancy: They will normally go on from year to year but will occasionally suddenly deteriorate and die for no obvious reason. They are likely to be short lived in a dry atmosphere.

Plant companions: Small and medium sized plants go well in tubs and troughs of mixed plants. Large plants make good specimens.

Ease/difficulty: A fairly easy plant, but it flourishes better with good care and attention.

Making a fern garden

Nephrolepis ferns grow well when planted together or with other ferns in a larger container. Water plants well.

1 Prepare container with a layer of drainage and layer of damp, peat-based compost. If there is no drainage hole, add some charcoal and sphagnum moss. The moss will soak up excess moisture and the charcoal will prevent water from becoming stagnant.

2 Knock plants from pots and remove stale soil from roots.

3 Place first fern in container and add compost to cover roots.

4 Arrange other plants around it, leaving space for growth.

5 Add compost to cover roots and hold them upright but do not press it down too firmly.

6 Leave in the shade without water for 2 days, then water normally.

1 *Leaves become brittle and drop.* Plant has been allowed to dry out and/or atmosphere too

dry. Soak in a bucket of water allow to drain and place in an outer pot of damp peat. Spray daily. If the foliage does not recover, cut it back to 2in (5cm) and spray the stubble daily until new fronds appear.

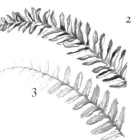

2 *Foliage withers but plant has not dried out.* Plant may have been sprayed with leaf shine. Cut it back. Check that it is not in a draught or suffering from gas fumes.

3 *Plant is poor colour and produces no new growth.* Needs repotting or feeding.

Repotting

1 Repot in spring when plant looks top-heavy, fronds turn pale and few new ones grow. Water plant well.

2 Prepare pot 1 size larger with drainage layer and layer of damp, peat-based compost. Plastic pots are best: they retain moisture.

3 Hold old pot with one hand covering compost, fingers either side of stems. Tap edge of pot. Plant and compost will come out.

4 Carefully remove stale soil from roots, using stick or pencil. Do not damage roots.

5 Place plant in centre of new pot, root-ball on compost.

6 Add new compost to fill pot. Make sure that all the roots are covered but do not press it down too hard. Leave the plant in the shade without water for 2 days to encourage roots to grow into compost.

Propagation: plantlets

1 In spring, plantlets grow on runners.

2 Remove plant from pot and separate plantlets with a sharp knife. The plantlets will already have roots.

3 Pot plantlets separately, water them and cover them with polythene for a few days. Keep them at a temperature of 55°F (13°C). Make sure they stay moist.

Watering

1 Test compost with fingers. If it is light and crumbly water at once. It must not dry out.

2 Add water at top of pot, using rainwater if possible. Empty excess from saucer after 15 minutes.

Humidity

Stand pot in saucer with water, pebbles or gravel. Make sure pot base is clear of water.

or Put pot in outer container packed with damp peat.

Spraying

Nephrolepis ferns in hanging baskets must have a daily spray of water. Even plants kept in pots do better if they are sprayed regularly. Use lime-free water if possible.

OLEANDER

This is a sun-loving, subtropical plant often seen growing wild along the Mediterranean coast and is much favoured for sun-rooms and plant-rooms. It is also found in subtropical Asia and Japan. The name is an ancient Greek one used by Dioscorides although it is more commonly known by its second name of *Oleander*. It is a member of the Apocynaceae and was first introduced in 1596.

Oleanders are attractive plants with beautiful, soft coloured flowers of white, pink, purple and orange. There are both single and double forms. The willow-like foliage can be either plain green or pleasantly variegated. Each leaf is long, narrow and paired down the stem. However the plant is highly poisonous and eating of the leaves can be fatal for animals. The flowers can be fatal if eaten by humans. Nevertheless, oleanders are popular because there are not many indoor plants requiring a bright, warm and airy position. Plants are sold in flower from June onwards. Then it is possible to choose the required flower colour, individual strains being unnamed. The variegated types, with yellow edges to the leaves and pink flowers, are called *Nerium oleander* 'Variegata'.

Like geraniums (also Mediterranean plants) neriums can be put outside in the summer. In frost-free temperate areas they can be planted out permanently against a south-facing wall. Protect them in winter with straw or polythene in case the temperature drops too low.

Always choose a plant with plenty of buds still to open because each flower is over fairly quickly. Check that the plants are free from pests as oleanders are susceptible to mealy bug and other pests.

Nerium oleander is a Mediterranean plant which needs full sun in summer and a cool season in winter. In the wild it grows along creeks on sunny hillsides, showing that it likes moisture at its roots.

Right: A young plant of the common pink form.

Below: A flower and buds.

Size: Will grow into a large shrub some 7–15 ft (2–5 m) tall and up to 20 ft (6 m) across. However in a pot they are normally about 18 in (46 cm) tall.

Growth: They grow fairly quickly at 10–12 in (25–30 cm) per year.

Flowering season: All through the summer. The flowers need a lot of light and warmth to open, so buds formed in autumn often fail to open unless they are very warm.

Scent: None.

Light: Plenty of light is essential at all times. In the summer months it will flourish out-of-doors. In the winter it also requires a light position. It is better in a conservatory than a house and is happy in full sun.

Temperature: Not too warm as it is a temperate plant. It does not enjoy temperatures above 60°F (16°C) unless the ventilation is excellent. In winter all is well as long as the temperature does not fall below 40°F (5°C). It dislikes central heating.

Water: Water frequently, almost daily in the summer. In the winter once every 10 days. At all times rainwater is best. It is most important that the water is warm or the flowers may not open.

Feeding: Add liquid food to the water every 14 days in summer when growing.

Humidity: Appreciates a spray once a month but this is not essential.

Cleaning: Leaves do not get very dirty as they are long and narrow. They can be wiped but it is probably easier to spray with tepid water. Do not use leaf shine, the leaves have a naturally matt, rather leathery texture.

Atmosphere: They like plenty of air and some air movement.

Soil: Loam-based No. 3 or similar rich compost.

Repotting: They like to be in large pots or tubs, but do not move them too often. Once every 2–3 years at the most. Do this in March.

Pruning: Cut back hard after flowering to maintain a good bushy shape. Side shoots can also be removed below flowering buds to help the latter form.

Propagation: By stem tip cuttings taken in the spring. Can be rooted in either soil or warm water. They grow more quickly in the warm and if taken in early spring will flower the same year. However, cuttings will also root in July and August. Root them at 61–64°F (16–18°C). Seed can be sown in April at 64–70°F (18–21°C).

Life expectancy: Very long if watered, fed and protected from frost in winter.

Plant companions: This one is a loner, prefering movement of air around it.

Ease/difficulty: If you keep it as a sun-room or patio plant it is very easy. In central heating or poor light it will fail to flower.

Repotting

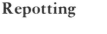

1 Repot in spring every 2–3 years when plant looks top-heavy but does not grow any more and roots show through pot base. Water well first.

2 Prepare pot 1 size larger with drainage layer and layer of damp, loam-based No. 3 compost.

3 Hold old pot with one hand covering compost, fingers either side of stems. Tap edge of pot. Plant and compost will come out.

4 Carefully remove stale soil from roots, using stick or pencil. Do not damage roots.

5 Place plant in centre of new pot, root-ball on compost.

6 Add new compost to fill pot. Make sure that all roots are covered. Press down well. Leave in the shade without water for 2 days to encourage roots to grow into compost.

What goes wrong

1 *Flower buds do not open.* Too cold. Raise temperature and always use tepid water to water the plant.

2 *Plant fails to produce flowers or buds but is otherwise healthy and strong.* Lack of sunlight. Move into direct light or outside into a sunny position for the summer.

3 *Plant fails to flower and growth is lanky.* The effect of central heating: too hot with poor ventilation. Move to an airier room.

4 *White, woolly patches on leaves.* Mealy bug. Remove them individually with a swab dipped in methylated spirits or spray with malathion or a systemic insecticide.

5 *Brown scaly insects under leaves and on stems.* Scale insects. Remove them individually with a swab of cotton wool dipped in methylated spirits or spray with a systemic insecticide.

Propagation in water

Cuttings taken in early spring will flower the same year.

1 Put 3 or 4 small pieces of charcoal in shallow jar and fill ⅔ with tepid water.

2 Cover with kitchen foil held in place with a rubber band or string.
Pierce several small holes in foil with a pencil or stick.

3 Remove a shoot of about 3in (7cm) from plant.
Wear gloves. The plant is poisonous.

4 Push the stem through foil into the water. Repeat with other shoots.
Keep warm (61–64°F, 16–18°C).

5 When new roots form, remove the shoots from water and repot them in small pots. Be careful not to damage the delicate roots.

6 Water well and cover with polythene cover for a few days to give extra humidity.

Pruning for shape

1 After flowering, cut main stems back by half and side shoots to 4in (10cm).

2 Make cuts with secateurs just above a bud or side shoot, cutting at an angle.

Wear gloves. The plant is poisonous.

3 When the plant is in bud, cut off side shoots below flowers. This will encourage the buds to open. Use the side shoots as cuttings.

Removing dead flowers

When complete flower head has died cut it off with secateurs, close to the leaf immediately below it.

Spraying

Spray once a month with tepid water to keep the leaves clean.

Watering

Add water at top of pot, using rainwater if possible. Empty excess from saucer after 15 minutes.
Always use warm water.

LOLLIPOP PLANT

This is a plant that has recently been rediscovered. It comes from central tropical America and is a member of the Acanthaceae family. Having been familiar to plant collectors in the nineteenth century it fell from favour at the turn of the century and was reintroduced in the late 1960s and early 1970s. It is closely related to the genus *Beloperone* and to *Jacobinia*. Indeed it is often confused with the latter, but is easier to grow. Its similarity to *Beloperone* has given it one of its common names, the golden shrimp plant.

The leaves are dark green, oval, pointed and slightly indented along the veins. Bracts appear at the end of the growing tips and are coloured bright yellow. They provide an attractive contrast to the leaves, and one that is unusual in house plants. The true flowers are white tongues which emerge as the bract develops.

Pachystachys is often regarded as a flowering plant to be discarded when the flowers have passed. However it is quite possible to keep a plant for many years, particularly if it is pruned back in the spring.

When buying a plant look for good crisp foliage that goes all the way down the stem as this plant has a tendency to drop its lower leaves. Also the bracts on the flowers should be tight with no signs of white tongues showing.

Pachystachys lutea produces spikes of yellow bracts which closely resemble those of *Beloperone*, although in this species they do not droop.

Below: The true flowers are white and emerge in succession from the bracts.

Right: A compact plant. *Pachystachys* needs pruning for bushiness if it is to be kept a second year.

Size: They are best grown as small plants some 5–6in (13–15cm) tall and 4–5in (10–13cm) wide. If allowed to grow too tall they look untidy.

Growth: They are slow growers, producing about 3–4in (8–10cm) a year. They need to be kept short to flower well.

Flowering season: All through the summer. The bracts are long lasting.

Scent: None.

Light: They will take plenty of light including full sun in summer. In winter, place away from window.

Temperature: Normal room temperature in summer with a maximum of 70°F (21°C). They are better kept cooler in winter when resting, and the temperature can drop to 45°F (7°C) in which case the plant will temporarily drop its leaves.

Water: They like to be kept very moist during the summer but it is essential that the plants drain well so that the compost does not become waterlogged. In the winter keep compost just moist, watering once every 14 days. Never allow the compost to dry out.

Feeding: Add liquid food to the water every 21 days in summer but not at all in winter.

Humidity: They enjoy standing on damp pebbles or having the pot packed around with peat. Do not spray overhead when in flower, as this will damage the bracts.

Cleaning: Remove dust with a soft brush when necessary. Do not use leaf shine.

Atmosphere: Will stand most atmospheres and is fairly tolerant. Keep out of draughts.

Soil: Loam-based compost No. 2.

Repotting: Adult plants require repotting every spring, to replace the spent soil. Always make sure that the drainage is good.

Pruning: Clip back into neat shape in spring, or if very straggly cut right down to about 2in (5cm) and allow the plant to start again.

Propagation: Take young stem tip cuttings in spring about 3–4in (8–10cm) long and place in a propagator or cover the pot with a polythene bag. The temperature should be 65–70°F (18–21°C). Use sharp sand with peat added.

Life expectancy: Will go on for a long time but as with many small shrubby plants it is better to re-propagate young plants every other year.

Plant companions: They enjoy the company of other plants and do well in mixed bowls. However if the bowl is for a shady position the bracts may turn a little pale.

Ease/difficulty: A good plant for the person who has mastered the first principles of indoor gardening. Not really challenging but demands a little skill to keep in tip-top condition.

Repotting

1 Repot in spring when leaves look pale and no new ones appear. Water plant well.

2 Prepare pot 1 size larger with drainage layer and layer of damp, loam-based No. 2 compost.

3 Hold old pot with one hand covering compost, fingers either side of stems. Tap edge of pot. Plant and compost will come out.

4 Carefully remove stale soil from roots, using stick or pencil. Do not damage roots.

5 Place plant in centre of new pot, root-ball on compost.

6 Add new compost to fill pot. Make sure that all roots are covered. Press down well. Leave in the shade without water for 2 days to encourage roots to grow into compost.

1 *Flowers rot and drop off.* Lack of ventilation and/or over-head spraying. Provide humidity by tray of wet pebbles or peat pack instead of by spraying. Make sure there is some movement of air around plant.

2 *Leaves pale green and lack gloss.* Needs feeding as soil exhausted. Check if it also needs repotting.

3 *Leaves flop and then drop.* Plant dried out. Soak pot and allow it to drain. Then water more often.

4 *Leaves lack gloss and droop. Lower ones drop.* Too cold and/or waterlogging. Move to a warmer place and water less often.

Humidity

Stand pot in saucer with water, pebbles or gravel. Make sure pot base is clear of water.

Pruning

Pachystachys can be cut back by half in spring to prevent them becoming straggly.

Watering

1 Test compost with fingers. If it is light and crumbly, the plant needs water.

2 Add water at top of pot, using rainwater if possible. Empty excess from saucer after 15 minutes.

Stem tip cuttings

1 Prepare pot with layer of drainage and mixture of ½ peat, ½ sharp sand.

2 Choose shoot or stem tip with at least 2 pairs of healthy leaves and a growing point. Cut off below second pair of leaves. Cuttings should be 3–4in (8–10cm) long.

3 Prepare cuttings by trimming off stem just below a leaf.

4 Remove the lowest pair of leaves.

5 Dip the cut surface in hormone rooting powder. Shake off the surplus.

6 Make small holes in compost around edge with stick or pencil.

7 Insert cutting so that end of stem is at bottom of hole and leaves are level with compost.

8 Water well and cover with polythene supported by wire. Remove cover for 5 minutes a day and never let compost dry out. Keep at 65–70°F (18–21°C). Remove cover after 21 days and when cuttings are growing well, repot in normal compost.

137

PASSION FLOWER

It is not strictly accurate to classify *Passiflora caerulea*, the passion flower, as a house plant for its life would be limited if it were grown permanently in normal room conditions. It is really a plant for a conservatory, greenhouse or garden room where the humidity it needs can easily be provided. It is a rapid grower and needs a trellis or lattice of canes to grow up. In the right conditions it will flower freely and may even fruit.

Its common name was first given by missionaries who discovered it in tropical South America in the early eighteenth century. They thought that the strange flower portrayed the crucifixion. The five anthers represent the five wounds Christ received on the cross, the triple style represents the three nails and the central receptacle the main pillar of the cross. The fringing corona is the crown of thorns and the five sepals and petals together represent the ten apostles (excluding Peter and Judas).

There are many species of passion flower, all coming from South America and belonging to the Passifloraceae family. *Passiflora caerulea* is the only species normally grown indoors. Its flowers are blueish purple. Pink or red species are occasionally seen. It is best to grow *P. caerulea* in a pot, even if it is buried in the ground in a greenhouse bed for this restricts the root growth and helps to produce more flowers. The flowers are short-lived, each one surviving for only about twenty-four hours.

Plants are normally bought trained round a wire hoop. Make sure that there are plenty of buds to come out, and that these are not just the husks of spent flowers. Avoid spindly plants with foliage of a poor colour and lush plants with no flower buds.

Left: *Passiflora coccinea* is best grown in a conservatory.

Right: *Passiflora caerulea* is a climber often trained on a hoop.

Below: The highly complex flower of *Passiflora caerulea*. It has been seen by some to symbolize the crucifixion and this has led to the plant's common name.

Size: They will easily grow to 10ft (3m) tall and about 6ft (2m) wide if trained across a trellis.

Growth: They will produce many shoots each year and these can easily be 6–8ft (2–2½m) long.

Flowering season: All through the summer. Each flower lasts only 24 hours at the most. Mature plants will produce small yellow fruits in mid-summer.

Scent: None.

Light: They must have a good light and because of this are not really suitable as permanent house plants. They should be grown in a conservatory or sun room.

Temperature: They can be grown out-of-doors on a protected wall in sunny, frost-free climates. If grown indoors keep at a temperature of 40°F (50°C) during the winter so that they can rest. They do not like a hot and dry atmosphere. If grown indoors in summer at normal room temperature, ventilate the room well. They do not enjoy temperatures much above 70°F (21°C).

Water: Give water profusely, at least every other day in summer. Keep on the dry side in the winter when the plant is resting. Watering every 7 to 10 days in winter should be enough.

Feeding: Add half the recommended dose of liquid food to the water every 7 days when the plant is growing.

Humidity: They appreciate a spraying with tepid water 2 or 3 times a week in the summer, but not when the direct sun is on them.

Cleaning: The spraying should be enough to keep it clean. Do not use leaf shine.

Atmosphere: They need the humid atmosphere of a conservatory or garden room and do not like the dryness of a house. They appreciate good ventilation.

Soil: Loam-based No. 3.

Repotting: They will flower best if their roots are restricted. Repot annually in spring for the first year or two and thereafter just change the top layer of compost in spring.

Pruning: Cut back the leading shoots in the spring by about a third of their length.

Propagation: Make cuttings of young stem tips about 6in (15cm). Pot into small pots of ½ sand with ½ compost at a temperature of 70°F (21°C) and keep well sprayed until they being to grow.

Life expectancy: They will go on for many years if kept in the right conditions.

Plant companions: In view of the rampant nature of the growth they are better grown by themselves. In a mixed bed they will quickly smother other plants.

Ease/difficulty: A very easy plant to grow provided a conservatory or garden room is available to house it.

Replacing the topsoil

1 Repot in spring for the first two years, then remove the top inch (2½cm) of soil, taking care not to damage any roots. Water plant first.

2 Add new compost to fill pot. Use damp, loam-based No. 3.

3 Press down firmly all round, making sure roots are all well covered.

4 Leave in shade without water for 2 days to encourage roots to grow into new compost.

Pruning

Prune in spring. Cut back any very weedy shoots and cut side shoots to 6in (15cm). Make cuts just above a leaf stem or bud.

Spraying

Spray 2 or 3 times a week with tepid water. Do not let direct sun shine on the wet leaves.

What goes wrong

1 *Leaves seem dried up in summer.* Too dry. Water more often.

2 *Plant produces no flowers.* Insufficient light. Move to a lighter place.

3 *Plant produces no flowers but has lush leaf growth.* Overfeeding. Stop feeding until plant flowers. Do not repot: it will flower better if potbound.

4 *Leaves distorted and sticky with green insects.* Greenfly. Spray with pyrethrum or a systemic insecticide.

Stem tip cuttings

1 In spring plant produces new shoots which can be used for cuttings. Prepare small pot with drainage layer and mixture of sharp sand and loam-based compost.

4 Remove the lowest pair of leaves.

7 Insert cutting so that end of stem is at bottom of hole and leaves are level with compost.

2 Choose shoot or stem tip with at least 2 pairs of healthy leaves and a growing point. Cut off below second pair of leaves.

5 Dip the cut surface in hormone rooting powder. Shake off the surplus.

8 Water well and cover with polythene supported by wire. Remove cover for 5 minutes a day and never let compost dry out. Keep at 70°F (21°C). Remove cover after 21 days and when cuttings are growing well, repot in normal compost.

3 Prepare cuttings by trimming off stem just below a leaf.

6 Make small holes in compost around edge with stick or pencil.

Training round a hoop

1 Push one end of flexible cane or wire hoop into compost at side of pot, stopping when end of cane is ⅔ down pot.

3 Gently twine plant stem around hoop, taking care not to damage stem or leaves.

2 Bend hoop to other side of pot and push into compost.

4 If necessary, tie some twine to lower part of hoop. Thread it along hoop, looping it around the stem as you go.

5 The plant will continue to grow along the hoop and can be trained to circle the hoop again or to retrace its steps.

Watering

1 Test compost with fingers. If it is light and crumbly, the plant needs water.

2 Add water at top of pot, using rainwater if possible. Empty excess from saucer after 15 minutes.

139

GERANIUM

The name *Pelargonium* means nothing to a novice gardener for these plants are generally known as geraniums. True geraniums belong to the same family, the Geraniaceae, but are hardy, outdoor plants grown in garden borders. The genus *Pelargonium* includes some 230 species and gets its name from the Greek word *pelargos*, a stork. This refers to the fruit which can resemble a stork's bill.

The collecting and showing of pelargoniums was very popular in the nineteenth century and many hybrids came and went. There are many cultivars grown today and provided they are given a lot of light (they are real sun lovers) they make good house plants. We cultivate four main groups, nearly all of which are hybrids developed over the years. Perhaps the most popular of the indoor grown varieties are the fancy or regal pelargoniums. The original parentage is obscure but was probably *P. grandiflorum*.

The common or garden 'geranium' used for bedding is the zonal *pelargonium*. It is probably a cross between *P. zonale* and *P. inquinans* and gets its name from the brown zone markings on the leaves. Many colours are available and recently some double varieties have been introduced that are particularly attractive as indoor plants.

Trailing geraniums or, more properly, ivy-leaved pelargoniums, are very popular for window-boxes and hanging baskets. They can also be grown up a stick or a small trellis to stand on a windowsill. Their original parent was *P. peltatum*.

Gaining greatly in popularity nowadays are the scented-leaved pelargoniums. These plants have insignificant flowers but the attractive lace-like leaves give off a beautiful perfume.

Pelargoniums should be bought as compact plants with short distances between the leaf joints. Avoid leggy plants and those with yellowed leaves.

Above and below: The showy flowers of hybrids of the regal *Pelargonium* group.

Right: The common or garden geraniums are really zonal pelargoniums. They are all Mediterranean plants thriving in full sun and rather poor soil. Once raised entirely from cuttings they are now also grown from seed. Although available later in the spring, such plants are less expensive and freer from disease. The picture shows the seed raised hybrid 'Sprinter'.

Size: The average plant is about 18 in (46 cm) tall. They will grow bigger, but tend to get leggy and flower less often so it is best to repropagate and keep young plants.
Growth: 9–12 in (23–30 cm) per year is average.
Flowering season: All summer.
Scent: The flowers have none, but all the leaves give off a pungent smell typical of pelargoniums. The scented varieties give a particularly strong smell when the leaves are crushed.
Light: They must be in full light.
Temperature: Ordinary room temperature in summer with a maximum of 75 F (24 C) but not too hot in winter. 55–60 F (13–16 C) is the maximum.
Water: Water generously 2–3 times a week in the summer. In the winter they can be kept almost dry. Only give water if the temperature is up to or over 60 F (16 C).
Feeding: Add liquid food to the water every 14 days in the summer.
Humidity: They do not like to be sprayed overhead, as this can cause them to rot. They like a dry atmosphere.
Cleaning: If they get too dusty use a feather duster. Do not use leaf shine.
Atmosphere: They like plenty of air, particularly in the summer.

Soil: Either loam-based No. 1 or a peat-based compost.
Repotting: They flower better if pot bound. Repot as they grow from young cuttings but once they reach about 10 in (25 cm) tall leave them in the same pot.
Pruning: Cut back in spring. Snap off dead flowers or leaves by hand where they join the main stem.
Propagation: Either by stem tip cuttings taken in late summer or early spring, or by seed. A propagator is not required. With the high cost of fuel for overwintering the stock plants, propagation by seed is now popular with nurserymen. Seeds germinate easily when sown in the spring in a sandy compost at between 60–65 F (16–18 C).
Life expectancy: They will survive for a long time but it is better not to keep them longer than two years as they get very woody and either flower less or produce only small blooms.
Plant companions: They can be used as temporary visitors to mixed bowls but really are better on their own as they need plenty of light and ventilation.
Ease/difficulty: Easy, especially when placed in a window.

Repotting

1 Repot in spring and summer when water goes straight through pot, and there are many flowers but hardly any new leaves. Water plant well.

2 Prepare pot 1 size larger with drainage layer and layer of damp, loam-based No. 1 compost.

4 Carefully remove stale soil from roots, using stick or pencil. Do not damage roots.

5 Place plant in centre of new pot, root-ball on compost.

3 Hold old pot with one hand covering compost, fingers either side of stems. Tap edge of pot. Plant and compost will come out.

6 Add new compost to fill pot. Make sure that all roots are covered. Press down well. Leave in the shade without water for 2 days to encourage roots to grow into compost.

What goes wrong

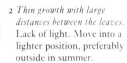

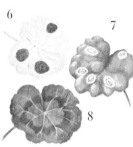

1 *Abundance of healthy, leafy growth and few flowers.* Overfeeding. Stop feeding. In future use a compost which is less rich, particularly less rich in nitrogen.

2 *Thin growth with large distances between the leaves.* Lack of light. Move into a lighter position, preferably outside in summer.

3 *Stem bases go black and rot.* Black leg: a fungal disease caused by overwatering and low temperatures. Usually fatal.

4 *A mass of leafy, distorted shoots appear at ground level.* Leafy gall. No cure, a bacterial disease. Destroy the plant. Do not use it for cuttings.

5 *White insects fly away from the plant when touched.* Whitefly. Spray with a resmethrin-based insecticide.

6 *Lower leaves go yellow and develop brown blotches.* Soil too dry. Increase watering. Improve ventilation.

7 *Pale yellow concentric rings appear on leaves. Leaves become distorted.* Virus disease. No cure. Destroy plant and do not use it for cuttings.

8 *Foliage and stems develop a red tinge.* Temperature too low at night. Move to a warmer position.

Stem tip cuttings

1 Prepare pot or propagator with drainage layer and mixture of $\frac{1}{2}$ sand, $\frac{1}{2}$ peat.

4 Remove the lowest pair of leaves.

2 Choose shoot or stem tip with at least 2 pairs of healthy leaves and a growing point. Cut off below second pair of leaves, close to main stem. Cuttings should be 3–4in (8–10cm) long.

5 Dip the cut surface in hormone rooting powder. Shake off the surplus.

7 Insert cutting so that end of stem is at bottom of hole and leaves are level with compost.

3 Prepare cuttings by trimming off stem just below a leaf.

6 Make small holes in compost around edge with stick or pencil.

8 Water well and cover with polythene supported by wire. Remove cover for 5 minutes a day and never let compost dry out. Keep at 55–60 F (13–16 C).
Remove cover after 21 days and when cuttings are growing well, repot in normal compost.

Pruning

Cut plants back by $\frac{1}{3}$ to $\frac{1}{2}$ in spring. Dust cuts with sulphur to prevent fungal disease.

Watering

1 Test compost with fingers. If it is light and crumbly, the plant needs water.

2 Add water at top of pot. Empty excess from saucer after 15 minutes.

DESERT PRIVET

The peperomias are a group of small plants which never grow above 8 in (20 cm). They are popular as house plants although they are not among the easiest to keep going from year to year in healthy condition. Originally stove house plants they are now grown in much cooler conditions. They are members of the Piperaceae or peppers, the name meaning 'related to pepper'. Some four hundred are known, mostly from Central and South America. They are shade-loving plants and in the wild are often found growing at the base of trees or as epiphytes.

All the varieties we grow have very distinctly marked leaves which are fleshy in texture and are on the whole easily distinguished one from another. *P. magnoliaefolia* 'Variegata' sometimes known as desert privet, has green leaves sharply marked with cream and is a very compact plant. *P. hederifolia* has pale grey leaves which are slightly indented. *P. caperata*, has dark green leaves that appear to be corrugated in texture. *P. scandens* 'Variegata' has smallish green and cream leaves. This plant has a trailing habit and can be used in hanging baskets. *P. obtusifolia* has slightly bigger leaves than the others and is the most like a succulent with fleshy smooth leaves. Lastly, *P. sandersii* or, as it is now sometimes called, *P. argyreia*, is perhaps the most spectacular of them all with smooth green leaves marked with silver stripes. With its red stems it makes a very pretty plant.

None of these is the easiest of plants to keep going for a long time, but it is very worthwhile making an effort.

Choose bushy, compact plants with good colour markings. Make sure the brittle leaves and stems are not damaged and that there is no rot at the base of the stems.

Most peperomias have quilted or succulent leaves. Some of them also flower.

Right: *Peperomia magnoliaefolia* 'Variegata'.

Left: *Peperomia hederifolia*. Below left: *Peperomia caperata*. Both these varieties need propagating by leaf and stem cuttings in a similar manner to *Saintpaulia*.

Below: A recent introduction, *Peperomia* 'Aztec Gold'.

Size: These are small plants, never growing above 8 in (20 cm) tall and some 10 in (25 cm) wide.

Growth: They grow fairly quickly when young, about 4–5 in (10–13 cm) a year, and as much in spread.

Flowering season: Summer. The flowers are in the form of long vertical spikes, rather like mouse tails. They are white in colour and contrast well with the leaf form.

Scent: None.

Light: They do not like direct light as this can make the leaves go dull and lifeless. However, avoid really dark corners. In bowls they benefit from the shade of their neighbours.

Temperature: About 60–65°F (15–18°C) is best in winter, although this can drop to about 50°F (10°C) if water is reduced. Maximum summer temperature is 75°F (24°C).

Water: Water sparingly, perhaps every 10 days in summer and every 14 to 18 days in winter. Use lime-free water. The plants store water in their leaves and will rot if overwatered.

Feeding: Add half the recommended dose of liquid food to the water every 14 days in summer.

Humidity: They like a humid atmosphere, particularly in higher temperatures. Stand on damp stones or in an outer pot of moist peat. They like the steamy atmosphere of a well used kitchen.

Cleaning: As the leaves are rather brittle it is as well not to wipe them. Spray with tepid water. Do not use leaf shine.

Atmosphere: Fairly tolerant of most conditions except wintery draughts.

Soil: Loam-based No. 1.

Repotting: The spring is the best time to repot. However they are best kept in small pots or shallow pans as they do not develop a large root system.

Pruning: Only to remove damaged or diseased leaves.

Propagation: By stem tip cuttings about 1 in (2.5 cm) long in the spring. Use a sand and leaf mould compost, dust the stem with hormone rooting powder, cover the pot with polythene and keep at a temperature of 64°F (18°C). until rooted. A propagator can also be used.

Life expectancy: After a year or two they get a bit straggly and untidy so it is probably better to start again with newly propagated plants.

Plant companions: They enjoy the humidity provided by other plants and do well in mixed plantings with hederas, dracaenas, philodendrons, *Ficus* etc.

Ease/difficulty: Not the easiest of plants but with a little knowledge can be kept flourishing for several years.

Stem tip cuttings

P. magnoliaefolia can be propagated from stem tip cuttings in spring.

1 Choose shoot or stem tip with at least 2 pairs of healthy leaves and a growing point. Cut off below second pair of leaves,

2 Prepare cuttings by trimming off stem just below a leaf.

3 Remove the lowest pair of leaves.

4 Dip the cut end in hormone rooting powder and insert it in a pot of ½ sand, ½ leaf mould. Base of stem should rest on bottom of hole, lowest leaf level with the compost.

5 Water well and cover with polythene supported by wire. Remove cover for 5 minutes a day and never let compost dry out. Keep at 64 F (18 C). Remove cover after 21 days and when cuttings are growing well, repot in normal compost.

Humidity

All peperomias like humidity, especially if the temperature is high.

Stand pot in saucer with water, pebbles or gravel. Make sure pot base is clear of water.

What goes wrong

1 *Leaves go dull and pale.* Too much direct sun. Move to a place in indirect light.

2 *Leaves drop.* Too cold. Move to a warmer place.

3 *Base of stems and parts of leaves go black and rot.* Over-watering. Allow plant to dry out until recovered. Remove rotted stems and dust with sulphur. In future, allow plant to dry out between waterings.

4 *Leaves appear blistered.* Waterlogging. Check plant is not standing in water. Check drainage in pot. Allow to dry out until recovered, then water less often.

5 *Leaves yellowed with webs underneath.* Red spider mite. Spray with derris, malathion or a systemic insecticide. Improve the humidity.

Leaf and stem cuttings

1 *P. caperata* and *hederifolia* are propagated by leaf and stem cuttings in spring. Prepare pot with drainage and compost of $\frac{1}{2}$ sand, $\frac{1}{2}$ leaf mould.

2 Choose plant with several healthy stems and leaves and cut one with sharp knife just above compost.

3 Dip the cut surface in hormone rooting powder. Shake off surplus.

4 Make small holes in compost around edge with stick or pencil.

5 Insert stem as far as base of leaf. End of stem must rest on bottom of hole. Firm compost around cutting. Add other cuttings in the same way.

6 Water well and cover with polythene supported by wire. Make sure compost never dries out and remove cover for 5 minutes a day to prevent rot. Keep at 64 F (18 C).

7 New plants will form at base of old leaves. When growing well, prepare small pots.

8 Pull new plant gently from old leaf. Do not damage delicate roots.

9 Repot new plants. Water and leave in the shade for 2 days.

Repotting

1 Repot in spring when plant looks very top-heavy. Water well first.

2 Prepare pot 1 size larger with drainage layer and layer of damp, loam-based No. 1 compost.

3 Hold old pot with one hand covering compost, fingers either side of plant. Tap edge of pot. Plant and compost will come out easily.

4 Carefully remove stale soil from roots, using stick or pencil. Do not damage roots.

5 Place plant in centre of new pot, root-ball on compost.

6 Add new compost, firming it until the pot is filled. Make sure all roots are covered. Leave in the shade without water for 2 days to encourage roots to grow into compost.

UPRIGHT PHILODENDRONS

The philodendrons as a genus are probably the easiest group of plants to cultivate in the home. They are more tolerant of abuse and neglect even than the rubber plant and are more versatile and useful decoratively. There are a very large number of varieties in cultivation and they are divided here into two groups, the bush and the climbing types. The plants described here are the smaller ones, the bush group, and are cared for in the same way.

Philodendrons are members of the Arum family (Araceae). There are about 120 known species and many hybrids have now been developed commercially. Their name comes from the Greek words *phileo*, to love, and *dendron*, a tree. They come mainly from central America.

Philodendron bipinnatifidum is a good, low growing plant from Brazil. The name '*bipinnatifidum*' is derived from the latin word for a feather and refers to the way the leaves are slit around the edges. These leaves may be as much as 2 ft (60 cm) long and 1½ ft (40 cm) wide, but normal plants are smaller, about half this size.

Philodendron callinofolium is a much more compact plant with slender, bright green leaves whose stems look as if they are swollen. *Philodendron* 'Black Prince' is another most attractive plant, a new variety with very dark, compact leaves which contrasts well with greener plants. *Philodendron wendlandii* is less common. Its simple, lance-shaped leaves can be as long as 14 in (35 cm) and grow almost in a circle from the centre of the plant.

When choosing a *Philodendron*, look for one with strong, undamaged, well coloured leaves, showing signs of new growth.

Left: *Philodendron* 'Black Prince' has handsome, dark leaves.

Right: The most common of the bush philodendrons is *Philodendron bipinnatifidum*. It produces aerial roots which are best tucked back into the pot.

Below: *Philodendron callinofolium*.

Size: When well grown, they may reach up to 3 ft (1 m) high. Large leaved varieties may be up to 3 ft (1 m) wide.

Growth: They grow quite quickly during the spring and summer and may double the number of leaves in a year.

Flowering season: The flowers are not very attractive and are usually only produced on very old, mature plants.

Scent: None.

Light: They thrive best in good light (not direct sunlight) but will tolerate quite dark places.

Temperature: 55–65°F (12–18°C). In summer 75°F (24°C) but humidity must be high.

Water: Water regularly from the top of the pot, twice a week during the growing season, once a week or less during the winter.

Feeding: Add liquid food to the water every 14 days during the growing season.

Humidity: Spray overhead with tepid water twice a week.

Cleaning: Clean by hand with tepid water. Use leaf shine but not more than once every 2 months.

Atmosphere: They grow best when planted with a group of other plants in a trough or container, where the plants create their own miniature climate. They are tolerant of bad conditions such as gas fumes, smoke and draughts.

Soil: A good, peaty house plant compost is best but loam-based No. 2 is also suitable.

Repotting: This should be done when the plant becomes top-heavy for its pot. When the plant is mature, it is best to leave it in a large pot (7 in, 18 cm) and just to change the topsoil annually.

Pruning: Cut away damaged or ungainly leaves as they occur.

Propagation: They are normally propagated from seed grown and ripened in the tropics. Keep them at 75–80°F (24–27°C). Basal shoot cuttings can be taken, but they are not easy. Early summer is the best time to try, with leaves that have just reached maturity. Root them at a temperature of 75°F (24°C).

Life expectancy: 4–5 years. The only trouble is that a plant can get rather untidy or unwieldy in the house after a time.

Plant companions: They grow well with most other green plants – fatshederas, *Ficus*, dieffenbachias all go well together.

Ease/difficulty: An easy group of plants for the beginner.

Growing from seed

If you have a propagator and can obtain seeds, you may be able to grow several plants.

1 Prepare a seed tray or propagator with a drainage layer and sterilized, seed-growing compost.

2 Scatter the seeds evenly and add thin layer of compost, no thicker than depth of seed. Water well.

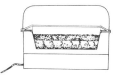

3 Cover propagator. Remove cover for 5 minutes a day to prevent rot and make sure the compost does not dry out. Keep at 75–80°F (24–27°C)

4 When seeds germinate, remove the cover.

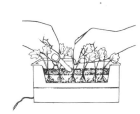

5 When seedlings are large enough to handle, thin out the weaker ones, leaving about 1 in (2½ cm) between each one.

6 When remaining ones are growing well, repot in separate small pots.

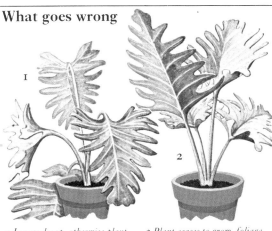

1 *Leaves droop, otherwise plant is healthy.* Too dry. Soak plant in a bucket and allow it to drain.

2 *Plant ceases to grow, foliage appears dull.* Temperature too low. Move to a warmer position.

3 *Lower leaves turn yellow and then drop.* Overwatering. Allow to dry out until recovered and then water less often, particularly in winter.

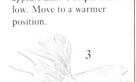

4 *Leaves are a poor colour and no new growth appears in spring.* Soil exhaustion. Repot the plant or feed it regularly.

5 *Brown or black rings on leaf or at leaf edge.* Scorch. Check that leaf is not touching a window in winter. Do not allow water to stay on the leaf in direct sun. Do not place a light bulb near the plant unless it is of the fluorescent type.

Replacing the topsoil

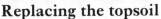

1 When plants are too large to repot easily, remove the top layer of compost in spring. Water plant well.

2 Add new compost to fill pot. Use damp, loam-based No. 2.

3 Press down firmly all round, making sure roots are all well covered.

4 Leave in shade without water for 2 days to encourage roots to grow into new compost.

Cleaning the leaves

Wipe dust off leaves with soft cloth and sponge with tepid water. Support leaf with other hand.

Use leaf shine but not more than once every 2 months.

Propagation

1 You can grow new plants from shoots that grow at the base of a leaf. The cuttings must have a good growing point—a small, new leaf emerging from its sheath. Cut the leaf stem below the new growth. Prepare pot with mixture of ½ peat, ½ sand.

2 Dip the cut surface in hormone rooting powder. Shake off the surplus.

3 Make small hole in compost and insert cutting.

4 Water well and cover with polythene supported by wire. Remove cover for 5 minutes a day and never let compost dry out. Keep at 75°F (24°C). Remove cover after 21 days and when cutting is growing well, repot in normal compost.

Tying to a cane

Leaf stems of large plants may need supporting if they lean too far over the pot edge.

 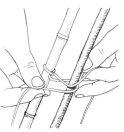

3 Loop string around stem as shown.

 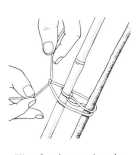

1 Push cane gently into compost a few inches away from the leaning stem stopping when cane is ⅔ down the pot.

2 Cut a 9in (23cm) length of string and tie firmly around cane on stem side.

4 Tie a firm knot against the cane.

CLIMBING PHILODENDRONS

Climbing philodendrons are much more numerous than the bushy types and are more popular as house plants. They come mostly from central America and in their native habitat grow very quickly. They are more likely to flower indoors than the bushy group, producing typical aroid flowers with a spathe and spadix, rather like wild cuckoo pint.

As climbers they need supporting at all times, with either thick bamboo poles or moss sticks. Moss sticks are preferable as these give the aerial roots thrown out by many philodendrons something to cling on to.

The best known of all the philodendrons is *P. scandens*, sometimes called the sweetheart plant because of its smallish, heartshaped leaves. It is a strong grower and will soon fill a bamboo or plastic trellis placed at the back of its pot. It can also be grown as a trailing plant and looks well in a hanging basket, sending out long trailing stems.

The second most popular types are the various *Philodendron* hybrids. They include *P. erubescens*, *P.* 'Emerald Queen', *P.* 'Red Emerald', *P. tuxla* and a new variety, *P.* 'Emerald Prince'. They have much larger leaves than *P. scandens*, some brilliant green, others reddish brown. Normally fairly quick growers, they are ideal for offices and bank decorations. Another *Philodendron*, *P. pertusum*, is like a miniature version of *Monstera deliciosa*.

There are many more philodendrons, nearly all of which are suitable for the home. *P. melanochrysum* looks like *P. scandens* but has greenish black, velvety leaves. *P. ilsemanii* is a real collector's plant but is unfortunately a slow grower. Its leaves are like the leaves of *P. erubescens* but are slightly variegated. *P. elegans*, another slow grower, has deeply cut leaves.

Choose climbing philodendrons with vigorous growth and leaves of a good, deep colour. Undernourished, spindly plants will never recover to make good specimens. Plants should have a good support provided, usually a moss pole. Avoid plants with yellowed lower leaves.

Size: Most climbing philodendrons will grow into big, sometimes straggly plants. The growing points can be made carefully to retrace their steps – to grow down a stake as well as up it. If bending a stem, do it carefully and slowly, perhaps taking 2 or 3 days, by hanging a small weight on the part to be bent down.

Growth: Individual stems may grow as much as 2–3 ft (60 cm–1 m) a year.

Flowering season: Flowers do not often appear on plants grown indoors. Spring and summer are the most likely times.

Scent: None.

Light: They thrive better in good light (but not direct sunlight) but will tolerate quite dark places.

Temperature: 55°–65°F (12°–18°C). Maximum summer temperature 75°F (24°C).

Water: Water regularly on the top of the pot, twice a week when growing, once a week or less during the winter.

Feeding: Add liquid food to the water every 14 days when the plant is growing.

Humidity: They appreciate a twice weekly spray of tepid water overhead.

Cleaning: Clean by hand with tepid water. Leaf shine can be used every 2 months.

Atmosphere: They are tolerant of bad conditions.

Soil: A good, peaty house plant compost is best but loam-based No. 2 is also suitable.

Repotting: Young plants should be repotted at least once a year. However, when they get mature this can be difficult because of their size. The best thing to do then is to replace the top soil and increase feeding.

Pruning: If a plant gets too straggly and untidy, prune hard with a sharp knife, cutting just above a leaf joint. Pinching out growing tips will make the plant more bushy.

Propagation: Either from seed grown and ripened in the tropics or, more usually, from stem cuttings. These must have a growing point if they are to get a good start and require a temperature of 70–75°F (21–24°C).

Life expectancy: They should last for at least 4–5 years but may become too large after a time for some rooms.

Plant companions: They grow well with most green plants – Fatshederas, *Ficus*, Dieffenbachias can all be planted with Philodendrons in mixed containers.

Ease/difficulty: An easy group for the beginner.

Tying to a cane

1 Push cane gently into compost a few inches away from the main stem, stopping when cane is ⅔ down the pot.

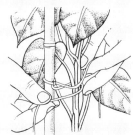

3 Loop string around stem as shown.

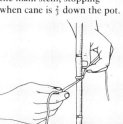

2 Cut a 9in (23cm) length of string and tie firmly around cane on stem side.

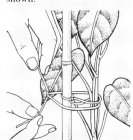

4 Tie a firm knot against the cane. Repeat at intervals up the stem.

Cleaning and Spraying

Wipe dust off leaves with soft cloth and sponge with tepid water. Support leaf with other hand.

Spray with water twice a week with a fine mist spray.

Climbing philodendrons are amongst the easiest and most vigorous of house plants. They all need staking.

Far left: *Philodendron pertusum* is similar to *Monstera deliciosa*.

Left: *Philodendron* 'Emerald Queen'.

Left: *Philodendron tuxla*. The common name of this species is elephant's ears.

Right: *Philodendron scandens*, the sweetheart vine. This plant is also excellent in a hanging basket.

What goes wrong

1 *Leaves droop, otherwise plant is healthy.* Too dry. Soak plant in a bucket and allow it to drain.

2 *Plant ceases to grow, foliage appears dull.* Temperatures too low. Move to a warmer position.

3 *Leaves are a poor colour and no new growth appears in spring.* Soil exhaustion. Repot the plant or feed it regularly.

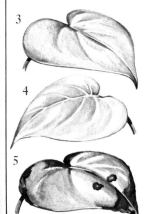

4 *Lower leaves turn yellow and then drop.* Overwatering. Allow to dry out until recovered and then water less often, particularly in winter.

5 *Brown or black rings on leaf or at leaf edge.* Scorch. Check that leaf is not touching a window in winter. Do not allow water to stay on the leaf in direct sun. Do not place a light bulb near the plant unless it is of the fluorescent type.

Repotting

1 Repot in spring when roots grow through pot base and leaves are pale. Water well first and remove cane support.

2 Add layer of drainage and layer of damp, peaty compost to new pot. If you use the same pot again, wash it out.

3 Loosen compost with knife around top edge of pot.

4 Remove plant, holding it firmly by base of stem and supporting the upper part.

5 Carefully remove stale soil from roots, using stick or pencil. Do not damage roots.

6 Place plant in centre of new pot, root-ball on compost.

7 Add new compost to fill pot.

8 Press down firmly all round, making sure roots are all well covered.

9 Replace cane, being careful not to damage the roots as you push it in. Tie plant to cane as before.

10 Leave in the shade without water for 2 days to encourage roots to grow into compost.

Stem tip cuttings

Take cuttings in early summer.

1 Prepare pot or propagator with drainage layer and mixture of sharp sand and loam-based compost.

2 Choose shoot or stem tip with at least 2 healthy leaves and a growing point. Cut off below second leaf.

3 Prepare cuttings by trimming off end of stem below leaf.

4 Remove the lowest leaf.

5 Make small holes in compost with stick or pencil. Dip cut end of stem in hormone rooting powder and insert in compost. Lowest leaf should be level with compost, end of stem resting on bottom of hole.

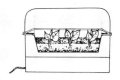

6 Water well and cover. Remove cover for 5 minutes a day and never let compost dry out. Keep at 70–75 F (21–24 C).

7 Remove cover after 21 days and when cuttings are growing well, repot in normal compost.

147

CANARY DATE PALM

Phoenix was the ancient Greek word for date palm. The dates are members of the Palmaceae family and are a genus of about ten species coming from tropical Africa and Asia.

P. canariensis comes from the Canary Islands and was introduced in 1888. It can grow to 20ft (6m) and its spiked leaves are very strong and can be rather dangerous. It is therefore a plant for somebody with a large house. It is a very handsome plant when well grown and makes a centrepiece in any sun-room or conservatory or on a warm terrace in the summer months. It is similar to *P. dactylifera,* the true, commercial date palm. This is an even larger plant but with fewer leaflets on each frond.

There is a miniature date palm, *P. roebelinii* the pygmy date palm. It has a more bushy habit, softer fronds and does not normally grow more than 4 to 5ft (1½m) tall.

Except for the small *P. roebelinii,* these palms are only suitable as house plants while they are still young. *P. canariensis* and *P. dactylifera* are both full sized trees and develop trunks when mature. However, being slow growers, they last a long time before becoming too large. They do not live very happily in central heating because they need a cool period in winter and good ventilation in summer. In average centrally heated homes they produce new growth all the year round, with the lower leaves dying off. This is likely to weaken them and make them more susceptible to insects such as scale and mealy bug.

Choose date palms which are showing new growth and are of a good shape. The lower leaves should not be browned and dry.

Date palms are dramatic plants which are easy to keep provided that they have a cool period in winter.

Phoenix roebelinii, the pygmy date palm (above) is a clump forming plant suckering from the base (left). It can be divided to produce more plants.

Right: *Phoenix canariensis.*

Size: *P. canariensis* grows up to 20ft (6m) tall with a spread of 9ft (2.8m). *P. roebelinii* grows to a maximum of 6ft (2m) tall and 2-3ft (60cm-1m) across.

Growth: Slow, a matter of 6-10in (15-25cm) a year.

Flowering season: Will not flower as a house plant.

Scent: None.

Light: Keep out of direct sunlight when young. Will tolerate quite dark places although they grow more quickly in indirect light.

Temperature: 50°F (10°C) in winter when it does not appreciate strong central heating. All species should be stood outside in a warm position during the summer months. If this is not possible keep at a maximum of 70°F (21°C) and in good ventilation.

Water: Water freely 2-3 times a week in the summer, once a week in spring and autumn and about once every 14 days in the winter season of semi-dormancy. Use tepid water.

Feeding: Add liquid food to the water every 14 days in the summer.

Humidity: The leaves will appreciate a weekly syringe except during the semi-dormant season.

Cleaning: Either by syringing or with a feather duster. Do not use leaf shine.

Atmosphere: Tolerant of most man-made conditions. They appreciate good ventilation.

Soil: Use a rich loam-based compost such as No. 3. Do not use peat-based compost except for *P. roebelinii.*

Repotting: Once a year in the spring. When large, the plant does well in a tub. It is then not feasible to repot, just change the topsoil in spring. All palms appreciate growing in deep, slightly narrow pots. Take care when handling the spiky fronds.

Pruning: Cut off bottom leaves that dry up and die.

Propagation: From seed in the spring. It may be 2 months before seedlings appear. A warm moist atmosphere of about 75°F (24°C) is essential. *P. dactylifera* can be grown from the stones of edible dates. *P. roebelinii* may be propagated from suckers.

Life expectancy: At least 8 or 9 years. Will go on until the plant gets too big for your room.

Plant companions: Not an easy plant to mix with others and best on its own.

Ease/difficulty: Easy.

Growing from seed

1 *Phoenix canariensis* can be grown from seeds (stones) in a propagator. It takes 2 months for the seeds to germinate. If you sandpaper the stones lightly before planting them they will absorb moisture more easily. You can experiment with stones from fresh dates (*P. dactylifera*). If you have no propagator, keep them warm and humid under a polythene cover.

2 Prepare a seed tray or propagator with a drainage layer and sterilized, seed-growing compost. Water well.

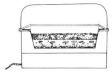

3 Cover propagator. Remove cover for 5 minutes a day to prevent rot and make sure the compost does not dry out. Keep at 75 F (24 C).

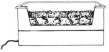

4 When seeds germinate, bring them into light and remove the cover.

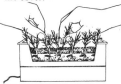

5 When seedlings are large enough to handle, thin out the weaker ones, leaving about 1in (2½cm) between each one.

6 When remaining ones are growing well, repot in separate small pots.

What goes wrong

1 *Lower leaves go brown and dry.* Atmosphere too dry and hot. In winter, move to an unheated room. In summer, improve the ventilation.

2 *Young leaves go brown and scorched.* Direct midday sun in summer has scorched the plant. Move out of direct sun and do not spray in sunlight.

3 *Plant fails to grow in spring.* Compost exhausted. Repot or feed weekly.

4 *White, woolly patches on leaves.* Mealy bug. Remove them individually with a swab dipped in methylated spirits or spray with malathion or a systemic insecticide.

5 *Leaves shrivel and go brown.* Leaflets close up. Plant has dried out. Water well and increase watering in future.

Repotting

1 Repot in spring when water goes straight through pot and plant does not grow. Water well first.

2 Add layer of drainage and layer of damp, loam-based No. 3 compost to new pot. If you use the same pot again, wash it out.

3 Loosen compost with knife around top edge of pot.

4 Remove plant, holding it firmly by base of stem and supporting the upper part.

5 Carefully remove stale soil from roots, using stick or pencil. Do not damage roots.

6 Place plant in centre of new pot, root-ball on compost.

7 Add new compost to fill pot. Make sure that all roots are covered.

8 Press down well. Leave in the shade without water for 2 days to encourage roots to grow into new compost.

Propagation

1 *P. roebelinii* produces suckers beside the parent plant. These can be separated and will grow into new plants.

2 Remove plant from pot.

3 Remove sucker from parent plant with a sharp knife.

4 Pot the sucker in loam-based No. 3 compost, making sure all its roots are well covered. Water well.

Trimming the leaves

If the tips of the leaves are brown and dry, trim them off with sharp scissors, cutting just above healthy leaf tissue.

Spraying

Spray once a week overhead with a fine mist spray. Hold spray about 6in (15cm) from leaves.

Do not spray in the resting season.

ALUMINIUM PLANT

Above: *Pilea mollis* 'Moon Valley'.
Below: The young tips of *Pilea cadierii* should be pinched out to encourage bushy growth.

Above: *Pilea muscosa* releases pollen explosively when its yellow flower heads are touched.

Right: *Pilea cadierii*.

The pileas are plants of the Nettle or Urticaceae family whose most famous cultivated member is the hop. There are some two hundred species, most of which are found throughout the tropics but not in Australia. They make good house plants if well cared for, but are best re-propagated every other year as they are most attractive when they are still young and compact.

The most popular variety grown is *Pilea cadierii*, often known as the aluminium plant because of the distinct aluminium grey markings on the oval green leaves. It comes from Indo-China and was introduced in 1938. As with all pileas it is best to keep the growing shoots pinched out to make a compact plant. There is also a naturally dwarf variety called *P. cadierii* 'Nana'.

P. involucrata or *P. spruceana* has attractive silver markings on its dark bronze and green leaves. It is a small and compact plant, ideal for display in mixed bowls. It comes from Peru and Venezuela and was found there in 1895. Its common name is the friendship plant. Another new introduction is *Pilea mollis* 'Moon Valley'. This is a little more difficult to grow, but has attractive leaves that slightly resemble those of the coleus.

P. muscosa with its fern-like leaves is the easiest of all to grow but is not so attractive and is now often difficult to obtain. It is known as the artillery or gunpowder plant for if it is shaken when in flower the flower heads explode and give off a cloud of pollen. It was introduced from tropical America as long ago as 1793.

When selecting pileas always look for clean, compact plants which have not grown too leggy.

Size: They are all best if kept small. *P. cadierii* is the biggest. It can be as much as 15 in (38 cm) tall and 12 in (30 cm) across. The other varieties are not more than half that size.

Growth: Cuttings struck in the spring will reach full size the same summer.

Flowering season: The flowers are rather insignificant and are often hidden in the leaves. They appear all through the summer and resemble the flowers of nettles.

Scent: None.

Light: They like a sunny windowsill out of the direct midday sun. This will bring out the leaf markings. Be careful that the leaves do not touch the glass in the winter for they can easily catch cold and turn black.

Temperature: Fairly tolerant; the temperature can be as low as 50°F (10°C) in the winter. If they are to continue growing, they will be better at 60°F (15°C). Summer maximum should be 70°F (21°C).

Water: Keep well watered in the summer, watering 2 or 3 times a week. Never let the compost dry out. In the winter once a week will be sufficient.

Feeding: Add liquid food to the water every 14 days in the summer when the plant is growing.

Humidity: In the summer particularly they enjoy an overhead spray with soft water. Be careful not to spray in direct sunshine or the leaves will scorch.

Cleaning: If the spraying has not kept the leaves clean, wipe the flat leaved varieties with a damp cloth. Dust crinkly leaves with a soft paintbrush. Do not use leaf shine.

Atmosphere: They do not like the fumes from gas fires, high central heating or draughts but they need some ventilation.

Soil: Mix compost of 3 parts loam-based No. 2 and 1 part extra peat.

Repotting: Repot in the spring after the plant has rested and been pruned.

Pruning: Pileas will become leggy very easily, so cut them right back in the spring to about 3 or 4 in (8–10 cm). It helps to keep pruning out the growing points every 2 or 3 weeks when the plant is growing. This encourages side shoots to appear and keeps the plants bushy and well furnished.

Propagation: Take stem tip cuttings in the spring when the plant is pruned. Insert them in sand and peat, having dipped the bases in a rooting hormone. Cover with glass or polythene and keep them at about 65°F (18°C). When rooted after 2 to 3 weeks, pot them 2 or 3 cuttings per pot.

Life expectancy: Although they will survive for years pileas get very untidy, so it is best to restock by propagating every other year to keep them healthy and tidy.

Plant companions: They all do well in mixed bowls with hederas, begonias, *Chamaedorea* and other small house plants.

Ease/difficulty: They are quite easy plants.

Repotting

1 Repot in spring when plant looks top-heavy but does not grow. Leaves may be pale with roots through pot base. Water plant well.

2 Prepare pot 1 size larger with drainage layer and layer of compost made of 3 parts loam-based No. 2 and 1 part peat.

3 Hold old pot with one hand covering compost, fingers either side of stems. Tap edge of pot. Plant and compost will come out.

4 Carefully remove stale soil from roots, using stick or pencil. Do not damage roots.

5 Place plant in centre of new pot, root-ball on compost.

6 Add new compost to fill pot. Make sure that all roots are covered. Press down well. Leave in the shade without water for 2 days to encourage roots to grow into compost.

What goes wrong

1 *Leaves go black and drop, especially in winter.* Too cold. Move to a warmer place.

2 *Leaves droop.* Too dry. Water more often.

3 *Distance between leaves increases and plant looks leggy.* Insufficient light. Move to a lighter place and pinch out tips of new growth to encourage bushiness.

4 *Leaves distorted and sticky with green insects.* Greenfly. Spray with pyrethrum or a systemic insecticide.

Watering

1 Test compost with fingers. If it is light and crumbly, the plant needs water.

2 Add water at top of pot, using rainwater if possible. Empty excess from saucer after 15 minutes.

Stem tip cuttings

1 In spring plant produces new shoots which can be used for cuttings. Prepare small pot with drainage layer and mixture of sharp sand and peat.

2 Choose shoot or stem tip with at least 2 pairs of healthy leaves and a growing point. Cut off below second pair of leaves, close to main stem. Cuttings should be 3–4in (8–10cm) long.

3 Prepare cuttings by trimming off stem just below a leaf.

4 Remove the lowest pair of leaves.

5 Dip the cut surface in hormone rooting powder. Shake off the surplus.

6 Make small holes in compost around edge with stick or pencil.

7 Insert cutting so that end of stem is at bottom of hole and leaves are level with compost.

8 Water well and cover with polythene supported by wire. Remove cover for 5 minutes a day and never let compost dry out. Keep at 65 F (18 C).

9 Remove cover after 21 days and when cuttings are growing well, repot in normal compost.

Spraying

Spray daily overhead with a fine mist spray, using rainwater if possible. Hold spray about 6in (15cm) from leaves.

Cleaning

Clean crinkly leaved plants with a soft, dry paintbrush.

Wipe flat-leaved plants with soft, damp cloth, supporting leaf with your hand.

Pruning

1 A plant will grow more bushily if the growing tips are pinched from the end of the stems.

2 Pinch out tips with fingers. Further shoots will grow from the side shoots.

An overgrown, untidy plant needs pruning to shape. Cut it back by half its height in spring.

151

STAGHORN FERN

The *Platycerium* is perhaps one of the grandest, most beautiful and most extraordinary of all the ferns. Its scientific name comes from two Greek words: *platys*, meaning broad and *keras*, a horn. Like its common name, this aptly describes its unusual appearance.

A member of the Polypodiaceae family, there are some seven known species, all of which come from South-east Asia or Australia. Only two are cultivated to any extent and both are epiphytic plants which do well as house plants. The first and by far the most popular is *Platycerium alcicorne* (or *bifurcatum*) which is native to Australia and was first brought to Europe in 1808. It is an ideal plant for a hanging basket, on a log or piece of cork bark or in a pot. As in all platyceriums, it has sterile back leaves which grow upright to support the plant and overlap each other. The other fronds are long and furled and these produce spores. These fronds grow out at all angles to give the plant its most spectacular effect. They are very tolerant and unlike most epiphytes do not mind dry air.

The other species grown indoors is *P. grande* 'Queen Wilhelmina'. This is slightly more difficult to grow, requiring higher temperatures and it is normally smaller and therefore less impressive. In this species the back leaf completely envelops the whole of the side of the pot as it grows and appears to swallow it up.

Look for undamaged leaves covered with soft down when you are buying a *Platycerium*. Do not worry if some of the back leaves are brown and papery: this is natural.

Like *Nephrolepis*, *Platycerium* is an excellent plant to display in a hanging basket. However it is far more tolerant of dry air than any other fern and will happily survive central heating.

Below: *Platycerium grande* 'Queen Wilhelmina'.

Right: *Platycerium alcicorne*, clearly showing the fertile green fronds and the brown sterile leaves from which they appear.

Size: Normally a single plant will be about 10 in (25 cm) tall with long furled leaves up to 20 or 24 in (50–60 cm) long.
Growth: Slow, 2 or 3 furled leaves a year.
Flowering season: Being a fern it produces no flowers.
Scent: None.
Light: They prefer plenty of light and sunshine. However, they will tolerate partial shade.
Temperature: A minimum of 60°F (15°C) in winter. *P. grande* likes to be a little warmer, around 65°F (18°C). Keep them at 65–70°F (18–21°C) in summer. Maximum summer temperature should be 75°F (24°C).
Water: It is as well to let them dry out between watering. Water about every 7 days in summer and 10 in winter. The best way to water a *Platycerium* is to soak the whole plant in a bucket or a sink for about 15 minutes then drain well before returning it to its normal place.
Feeding: Add liquid food to the water about once a month.
Humidity: An overhead spraying once or twice a week is beneficial.
Cleaning: Do not wipe the leaves or you will remove the downy hairs which enable the plant to tolerate dry air. The spraying or soaking should keep the leaves clean. Never use leaf shine.
Atmosphere: They are tolerant of most conditions.

Soil: If grown in a pot or basket, a peat-based compost is ideal; if on bark or a piece of wood, mix an equal quantity by volume of finely chopped sphagnum moss into the compost. It is very important for the plant to have good drainage.
Repotting: Do not repot adult plants unless you are changing the type of container, i.e. from pot to basket or bark.
Pruning: None really necessary. Do not remove the old back leaves unless they are so old they are ready to drop off.
Propagation: By spores, but this is best left to the professional. Occasionally the plant will produce small offsets which can be potted up separately. These should have roots before they are removed from the parent plant.
Life expectancy: They are very long lasting plants.
Plant companions: They are best grown on their own.
Ease/difficulty: An easy plant.

Propagation: Offsets

1 Platyceriums produce offsets at the base which can be separated and grown on their own.

3 Remove offset and roots from parent plant with sharp knife.

2 Prepare pot with drainage and all peat compost. Knock plant from pot.

4 The offset must have its own small roots. If it has not, it will not grow.

5 Water well and cover with polythene cover for a few days to give extra humidity.

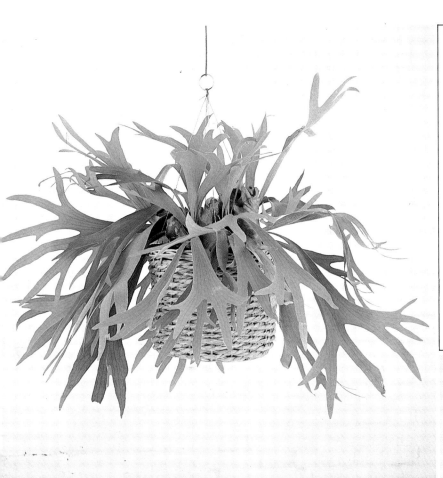

What goes wrong

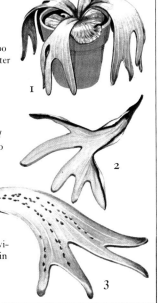

1 *Leaves become limp.* Plant too dry. Soak in a bucket of water and then water more frequently.

2 *The green fronds rot and fall off.* Plant too wet and/or too cold. Water less often and raise temperature.

3 *Brown scaly insects.* Scale insects. Remove them individually with a swab dipped in methylated spirits. Do not spray with an insecticide.

Removing dead fronds

Cut off old, yellowed fronds at the base. Do not remove the back leaves unless they look ready to drop off naturally.

Watering

Allow platyceriums to dry out between watering, then give them a thorough soaking. Remove after 15 minutes and allow to drain.

Spraying

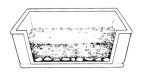

Spray once or twice a week, especially if the plant is fixed to bark or in a hanging basket.

Making a fern garden

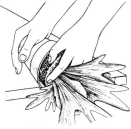

1 Platyceriums look spectacular if 2 or 3 are planted together in a large hanging container. Prepare container with drainage and peat-based compost. If you are using a container with no drainage, add some charcoal to stop the water becoming stagnant.

2 Knock plants from their pots.

3 Position first plant and add a little compost mixture to hold it in place.

4 Place the other plants around it so that their fronds hang over the edge of the container. Leave space between for the roots to grow. Add compost.

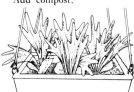

5 Hang the container very securely: it will be heavy.

Fixing to bark

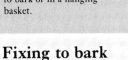

1 Choose suitable piece of cork bark, a branch or some well shaped driftwood.

2 If there is no natural hollow, chisel a shallow well where plant will rest.

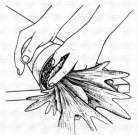

3 Remove plant from pot, keeping compost round the root ball.

4 Wrap roots in damp sphagnum moss and tie with wire.

5 Hold moss and root-ball firmly against wood or bark and bind in place with wire. Keep root ball damp. Spray regularly.

Pteris tremula

RIBBON FERN

The *Pteris* ferns are one of the largest groups in the Polypodiaceae family, with some two hundred and fifty known species distributed across the temperate and subtropical world. A number of the varieties that are now grown indoors come from Australia and New Zealand.

Whilst they are among the biggest ferns, they are perhaps the easiest to grow and are the most resistant to the dry air of modern living rooms – though they do better in a more humid atmosphere. There is just one cardinal rule: never let the pot dry out. Most varieties like being in shady positions but are alright in the light provided they do not get direct sunlight.

Three main varieties are grown. *Pteris tremula* is the biggest, with large, bracken-like leaves. These tend to be rather brittle and the stems snap over if you are not very careful. *P. multifida* 'Major' is a favourite with interior decorators. It is a tough fern which will stand a lot of ill treatment and has a good, bushy shape. *P. cretica* has very many varieties, some of which are variegated. It is not quite as robust as *P. multifida* but is nevertheless well worth growing and is very commonly available. Some of its varieties have crested fronds and were originally cultivated for use by florists as cut foliage. These are known under the collective name of *P. cretica* 'Wimsettii'. Another species, *P. ensiformis*, has varieties with white variegations. They are known as the silver ferns. The most common is *P. ensiformis* 'Victoriae'.

When buying ferns, look for good healthy foliage, unbroken stems and no brown, deadened leaves in the middle of the plant.

Most *Pteris* species are tough ferns which tolerate dry air.

Right: *Pteris tremula*, the largest species normally grown indoors.

Left: *Pteris multifida* 'Major' is smaller and bushier than *Pteris cretica*, below.

Size: When in a 5in (12cm) pot, the plant will be about 10in (25cm) across and 15in (38cm) tall, depending on the variety. *P. tremula* will be between 18 and 20in (41–51cm) tall although it can grow to 4ft (1–2m).

Growth: They will double their size in one growing season.

Flowering season: As they are ferns, they do not flower.

Scent: None.

Light: They dislike direct sunlight which will quickly scorch the fronds. Keep them in a shady position.

Temperature: A minimum temperature of 50–55°F (10–13°C) in winter. Normal room temperature in summer. They do not like temperatures above 70°F (21°C) unless the humidity is high.

Water: They should be kept well watered, which may mean up to once a day in summer if the temperature is high. Water 2 or 3 times a week in winter. It is essential never to allow the compost to dry out at any time of the year. Lime-free water is to be preferred.

Feeding: Add half the recommended dose of liquid food to the water once every 14 days in the summer and once a month in the winter.

Humidity: All year they like a high degree of humidity. Spray them daily with tepid water, and stand the pot on damp pebbles or in a peat-lined pot.

Cleaning: The spraying should keep the plants clean. Never use leaf shine.

Atmosphere: They are fairly tolerant of most conditions but dislike very hot and dry atmospheres, which may kill them.

Soil: The peat-based composts are best.

Repotting: It is as well to repot every spring.

Pruning: Remove fronds that have dried up. If the plant has been allowed to dry out, cut off all the fronds, and spray the stubble daily with tepid water. New fronds should soon appear.

Propagation: Nurserymen propagate by sowing the spores produced in the autumn. The plants can easily be divided in the spring when repotting and a large plant will make several small ones. If you wish to sow spores, do so in March. They need a temperature of only 55°F (13°C). The plant often self sows indoors and young ferns may appear among mixed plantings or in the pots of other plants.

Life expectancy: With care they will go on for many years.

Plant companions: Most ferns do well in mixed plantings provided they are not in direct sunlight. They benefit from the humidity created by plants being close together.

Ease/difficulty: Generally easy, provided they are kept well watered.

Watering

1 Test compost with fingers. Compost must be moist. If it is light and crumbly, the plant needs water.

2 Add water at top of pot, using rainwater if possible. Empty excess from saucer after 15 minutes.

Humidity

Pteris needs high humidity all the year round.
Stand pot in saucer with water, pebbles or gravel. Make sure pot base is clear of water.

or Put pot in outer container packed with damp peat.

154

What goes wrong

1 Fronds become pale and some shrivel at tips. Too much light. Move to a shady spot.

2 Fronds dry, turn papery and brown. Plant too dry. Soak it in a bucket of water and then water and spray more frequently. If fronds do not recover, cut them down and spray the stubble daily.

3 Brown scaly insects on stems and under leaves. Scale insects. Remove them individually with a swab dipped in methylated spirits and then spray with a nicotine-based spray. If any other insects attack, spray with nicotine. Never use malathion.

Making a fern garden

1 Water plants well. Prepare container with a layer of drainage and layer of damp, peat-based compost. If there is no drainage hole, add some charcoal and sphagnum moss.

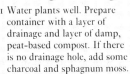

2 Knock plants from pots and remove stale soil from roots.

3 Place first fern in container.

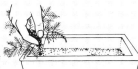

4 Add compost to cover roots.

5 Arrange other plants around it, leaving space for growth. Leave in the shade without water for 2 days.

Repotting

4 Carefully remove stale soil from roots, using stick or pencil. Do not damage roots.

5 Place plant in centre of new pot, root-ball on compost.

1 Repot in spring when plant looks top-heavy and does not grow. Water well first.

2 Prepare pot 1 size larger with drainage layer and layer of damp, peat-based compost.

3 Hold old pot with one hand covering compost, fingers either side of stems. Tap edge of pot. Plant and compost will come out.

6 Add new compost to fill pot. Make sure that all the roots are covered but do not press it down too hard. Leave the plant in the shade without water for 2 days to encourage roots to grow into compost.

Spraying

Spray daily overhead with a fine mist spray, using rain-water if possible. Hold spray about 6in (15cm) from leaves. Use tepid water.

Pruning

Cut out broken fronds and any old ones that have turned brown. Cut as close to compost as possible.

Root division

Divide large, old plants in early spring.

1 Prepare 2 pots with drainage layer and compost.

3 Gently pull roots and stems apart. Very large plants may be divided into 5–6 parts.

2 Remove plant from pot and gently prise away compost.

4 Repot both sections in the usual way.

Rhoicissus rhomboidea

GRAPE IVY

This member of the Vine family makes a good indoor climbing plant. The name in Greek means pomegranate ivy, but it is commonly known today as the grape ivy from its vine-like leaves. It comes from Natal, South Africa and was not imported as a house plant until 1947. Since then it has made great strides in popularity and along with ivies, rubber plants and monsteras it must be among the best selling of all indoor plants. It is related to the *Cissus* family.

The *Rhoicissus* does well in most situations and particularly in indirect light. It climbs well, and makes a good room divider. The leaves are dark green, toothed and about 2 in (5 cm) long, on a stem. They are arranged in threes and are often bronze when young. The plants should be well watered in summer but kept on the dry side in winter. Like most climbers they also do well in hanging baskets, particularly if the young shoots are nipped out to make the plant grow into a dense mass around the basket. Always use young plants in hanging baskets. Older plants are likely to develop woody stems which may break and which make the basket look sparse. A trellis or pyramid of bamboo canes also helps to display *Rhoicissus* at its best.

R. rhomboidea is the variety usually grown. However, a new variety has been introduced recently. Named *R. rhomboidea* 'Ellen Danica', it has longer, more divided leaves and is a most attractive innovation. It is not as easy, particularly if overwatered in winter.

Another *Rhoicissus*, *R. capensis*, is sometimes available. This also comes from South Africa and has foliage very like that of the true grapevine. It needs slightly cooler, more humid conditions than *R. rhomboidea* but in other ways its care is the same.

Always buy bushy plants showing plenty of new growth. The leaves should be neither limp nor brittle.

Rhoicissus is a very popular, vigorous climber.

Right: A good plant of *Rhoicissus rhomboidea* will produce young growth at many points.

Left: *Rhoicissus* climbs by means of tendrils.

Below: The comparatively new variety, *Rhoicissus rhomboidea* 'Ellen Danica'.

Size: They will grow into large plants, up to 9-10 ft (3-3½ m) tall.

Growth: 2-3 ft (60-100 cm) a year.

Flowering season: They do not normally flower in the house.

Scent: None.

Light: They enjoy a position facing north or east, preferring not to be in direct sunlight.

Temperature: Maintain 55°-60°F (13-15°C) in winter. Normal room temperatures in summer, 60-70°F (15-21°C). They will not enjoy temperatures above 75°F (24°C).

Water: Twice a week in summer but check soil conditions at each watering. Overwatering, even in summer, can cause the leaves to droop and rot. In winter water about every 14 days, again checking soil.

Feeding: Add liquid food to the water about every 14 days in summer.

Humidity: They like a weekly spray in summer. Stand the pot on damp pebbles.

Cleaning: Mist the plant with rainwater weekly. A leaf shine spray can be used occasionally but not more than once every 2 months.

Atmosphere: Tolerant of most conditions including gas and oil fumes.

Soil: Loam-based No. 2.

Repotting: Once or twice a year depending on the strength of the growth, until the plant has reached its required size. Then rely on feeding and changing the topsoil to maintain vigour.

Pruning: Pinch out the leading growths from time to time in the growing season to keep the plant dense and bushy. If it gets straggly, cut down to within 9 in (23 cm) of the pot and let it shoot again.

Propagation: Use young tip shoots with a growing point and two leaves. Insert them in a mixture of half compost and half sharp sand in spring and early summer at a temperature of 65°F (18°C).

Life expectancy: At least 5 or 6 years, but can suddenly collapse and die in old age.

Plant companions: Most other green plants. They do well in mixed plantings if care is taken with watering. They make good background plants.

Ease/difficulty: A comparatively tolerant and easy plant.

Tying to a cane

1 Push cane gently into compost a few inches away from the main stem, stopping when cane is ⅔ down the pot.

3 Loop string around stem as shown.

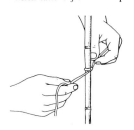

2 Cut a 9 in (23 cm) length of string and tie firmly around cane on stem side.

4 Tie a firm knot against the cane. Repeat at intervals up the stem.

Stopping for bushiness

Young plants should be 'stopped' to encourage bushy growth.

Pinch out the growing tip at the end of the stem.

What goes wrong

1 *Leaves lack lustre, droop and drop.* Overwatering. Allow to dry out until recovered, then water less often. Check that temperature is not too low.

2 *Leaves curl and dry up, becoming papery, then drop.* A few lower leaves doing this is normal. Remove them. Otherwise plant has dried out or is in a hot and dry atmosphere. Water and improve humidity.

3 *Young leaves dwarfed, all leaves turn pale.* Plant needs repotting or feeding.

4 *Leaves yellowed with webs underneath.* Red spider mite. Spray with derris, malathion or a systemic insecticide.

5 *Young leaves distorted and sticky with green insects.* Greenfly. Spray with pyrethrum or a systemic insecticide.

Stem tip cuttings

1 In spring plant produces new shoots which can be used for cuttings. Prepare small pot with drainage layer and mixture of sharp sand and loam-based compost.

4 Remove the lowest leaf.

7 Insert cutting so that end of stem is at bottom of hole and lowest leaf level with the compost.

2 Choose shoot or stem tip with at least 2 healthy leaves and a growing point. Cut off below a leaf stem .

5 Dip the cut surface in hormone rooting powder. Shake off surplus.

8 Water well and cover with polythene supported by wire. Remove cover for 5 minutes a day and never let compost dry out. Keep at 65°F (18°C).

3 Prepare cuttings by trimming off end of stem below leaf.

6 Make small holes in compost around edge with stick or pencil.

9 Remove cover after 21 days and when cuttings are growing well, repot in normal compost.

Repotting

1 Repot in spring when leaves look pale or yellowed and plant does not grow well. Water well and prepare pot with drainage and layer of damp, loam-based No. 2 compost.

4 Lay plant on table and remove old compost from roots with stick or pencil. Do not damage roots.

2 Loosen compost with knife around top edge of pot.

5 Place plant in centre of new pot, root-ball on compost.

3 Remove plant, holding it firmly by base of stem and supporting the upper part.

6 Add new compost, firming it until the pot is filled. Make sure all roots are covered. Leave in the shade without water for 2 days to encourage roots to grow into compost.

AFRICAN VIOLET

Saintpaulia belongs to the family Gesneriaceae and is related to the gloxinia. In spite of its common name, it has nothing to do with the European violet. It was named after Baron Walter von Saint Paul St Claire, who discovered it in the late nineteenth century in the Usambara mountains in Cape Province, South Africa. Like many other house plants, it was first grown successfully indoors in America. It is now the most popular of all indoor flowering plants and is available all the year round.

The original species is the deep blue *Saintpaulia ionantha* but breeders have worked hard to produce varieties with flowers that do not drop, in a number of different colours. Known as the Rhapsodie strain, they are protected by plant patents which control their commercial cultivation strictly. The deep blue remains a firm favourite but there are now mauve, red, white, pink and lilac varieties, as well as some with double flowers. Many produce a succession of delicate flowers all the year round. More and larger flowers can be encouraged if the plants are rested for six weeks at a lower temperature than usual (about 55–60°F, 12–15°C) and kept drier than before, being watered only about once a week. This treatment encourages a lot of flower buds to form and can be given at any time of the year.

Choose plants with plenty of buds still to open. Check that there are no signs of rot anywhere on the plant and that the leaves are of a dark green with a good gloss. Avoid plants with speckled or deformed leaves for these are likely to come from virus-ridden stock. Do not expect the rarely available white flowered plants to remain true to colour: they are likely to start colouring at the edges of the petals. In winter make sure the plants are well wrapped before taking them home. They are very susceptible to cold.

Size: Normally about 4in (10cm) tall, spreading to 5–6in (12–15cm) across. If several plants are put together in a 6in (15cm) pot they appear like one large plant, the size of a dinner plate, with a mass of blooms in the centre.

Growth rate: Fairly fast. Cuttings taken in early summer flower by autumn.

Flowering season: All the year round with more flowers appearing in summer.

Scent: None.

Light: Keep in a good, light position. Grows well on a windowsill. Keep out of direct sun except in winter.

Temperature: Minimum of 55°F (12°C) in winter but will grow better if 60°F (15°C) can be maintained.

Water: Water from the bottom of the pot to make sure the leaves and crown do not get wet, empty out the excess. Water twice a week all the year round, but do not let the compost get waterlogged. If water gets on the leaves they may become mouldy or, in sunlight, may develop scorch marks.

Feeding: Add liquid food to the water every 3–4 weeks in summer.

Humidity: Needs a humid atmosphere, but never spray. Either stand the pot on damp pebbles or put it in an outer pot, packed with damp peat or moss.

Cleaning: Clean with a soft, dry paintbrush, never with liquid or leaf shine.

Atmosphere: Does well in kitchens or bathrooms where there is steam. They do not like gas fumes or draughts.

Soil: They grow best in peat-based compost.

Repotting: Repot when leaves become smaller and crowded, probably every other year. Use pot only one size larger: they will flower better if slightly pot-bound. As they have a shallow root system use wide shallow pots instead of the normal deep ones.

Pruning: Not necessary. Remove broken or damaged leaves if they become brown and pick off dead, discoloured flowers.

Propagation: From leaf cuttings with stem attached in compost or water. Take them in late spring and keep at a temperature of 70°F (21°C). They will reach flowering size in 6 months and will be true to their parent's characteristics. Plants can be raised from seed in spring but the seedlings will vary in quality. 65–70°F (18–21°C) is required for germination.

Life expectancy: Although they will live almost indefinitely it is better to propagate new plants every 12–18 months to ensure a good quantity of flowers and healthy stock.

Plant companions: Any small plant such as little ferns or tradescantias grow well with them but saintpaulias are at their most effective grown in masses of their own kind.

Ease/difficulty: A good and popular room plant. Not demanding but responds well to the correct care.

Saintpaulia ionantha, the African violet, is now available in many colours and flower forms. The white variety (above) is rare but other colours come in double (below, left) and single forms (below, right).

Some hybrids have attractive frilled petals.

Right: The original species of *Saintpaulia* is deep blue. The leaves of this specimen are healthy and undamaged.

Watering

1 Test compost. If it feels light and crumbly, add water.

2 Put pot in container and fill container with water to just below the rim of the pot. Leave it there for 15 minutes, then allow it to drain. Never allow water to touch the leaves.

Humidity

Saintpaulia needs humidity but must not be sprayed. Stand pot in saucer with water, pebbles or gravel. Make sure pot base is clear of water.

Cleaning the leaves

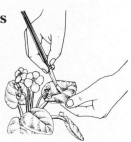

Brush leaves gently with soft, dry paintbrush. Never add water or leaf shine.

What goes wrong

1 *Leaves and flowers rotting.* Too much water or plant watered overhead. Allow to dry out until recovered and then water less often, always from below.

2 *Leaves turn pale.* Needs feeding or is receiving too much direct sunlight. Feed or move to a shadier spot.

3 *Leaves curl or look limp and dehydrated.* Needs watering.

4 *Leaves small and close together.* Needs repotting.

5 *Plant healthy and growing well but without flowers.* Add a little super phosphate to the water. Often necessary for year old plants.

6 *Flowers very weedy and sparse.* Often occurs after heavy growth of flowers. Remove every flower stem and bud and feed well.

Repotting

1 Repot in spring every second year when foliage is crowded and young leaves are small and pale. Water plant well.

2 Prepare pot 1 size larger with drainage layer and layer of damp, peat-based compost.

3 Hold old pot with one hand covering compost, fingers either side of stems. Tap edge of pot. Plant and compost will come out.

4 Carefully remove stale soil from roots, using stick or pencil. Do not damage roots.

5 Place plant in centre of new pot, root-ball on compost.

6 Add new compost to fill pot. Make sure that all roots are covered. Press down well. Leave in the shade without water for 2 days to encourage roots to grow into compost.

Leaf and stem cuttings

1 Prepare container with layer of drainage, layer of compost and 1in (2½cm) layer of sharp sand.

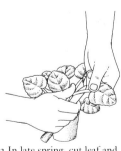

2 In late spring, cut leaf and stem from plant. Cut near compost so stem is a good length.

3 Dip the cut surface in hormone rooting powder. Shake off surplus.

4 Make small holes in sand around edge with stick or pencil.

5 Insert stem as far as base of leaf. End of stem must rest on bottom of hole. Firm sand around cutting. Add other cuttings in the same way.

6 Water well and cover with polythene supported by wire. Remove cover for 5 minutes a day and never let compost dry out. Keep at 70°F (21°C). New plants will form at base of old leaves. When growing well, prepare small pots.

7 Pull new plant gently from old leaf. Do not damage delicate roots.

8 Repot new plants. Water and leave in the shade for 2 days.

MOTHER-IN-LAW'S TONGUE

Affectionately known as mother-in-law's tongue, the *Sansevieria* is a member of the lily family. They were named after an eighteenth century prince, Raimondo di Sangro of San Severo in Italy, and come from West Africa. They have been cultivated as ornamental plants for several centuries. Whilst there are some fifty known species, only about five or six are grown commercially as house plants.

Sansevierias are good house plants which will thrive and grow in almost any conditions, provided they are not overwatered. The best known variety is *Sansevieria trifasciata* 'Variegata', sometimes also called 'Laurentii'. It has a yellow stripe down the edges of tall, sword-like leaves. When grown well the leaves can be as much as 3 ft (1 m) tall. The all green variety, though not so striking, has a charm of its own. A recent addition is *S. futura* which has chubbier leaves, still pointed, and seems a little less susceptible to overwatering. Lastly, *S. hahnii* and *S. hahnii* 'Variegata' are two varieties with squat rosettes of leaves like those of an aloe.

Sansevierias produce a tall, yellow flower spike with tiny star-like flowers. The spike emerges straight out of the compost beside the leaves.

Despite their dislike of overwatering when grown in soil, all these sansevierias do well in hydroculture.

When you buy one, always make sure that the leaves are unmarked by dead patches and that the leaf edges are undamaged. Try and check that the plant is well rooted. They tend to be top-heavy and can easily fall over and get damaged if they are not well anchored by a good strong root system.

Size: The individual leaves will grow to 3 ft (1 m) tall. However, a more usual size for the plant in the home is between 12 and 18 in (30–46 cm) tall with 5 to 12 leaves in a pot.

Growth: Two or three leaves a year will be produced on an average sized plant.

Flowering season: Sansevierias can produce a flower stem at any time, but it is probably more likely to happen in the summer. The stem is normally about half the height of the leaves and has tiny star-like flowers. Cut it off after flowering.

Scent: The flowers have a delicate perfume.

Light: Whilst they flourish best in full sunlight, they will tolerate quite dark positions.

Temperature: They will tolerate 50°F (10°C) in winter, but will only continue to grow if the temperature can be kept at 60°F (16°C) or above. Normal room temperature in summer, not above 75°F (24°C).

Water: Do not overwater. Giving too much water is the best way to kill the plant. Water only once every 7–10 days in the summer, every 21 days in winter.

Feeding: Add liquid food to the water about every 21 days in the summer.

Humidity: They like a dry atmosphere.

Cleaning: Wipe the leaves with a damp cloth whenever they seem dusty. Do not use leaf shine.

Atmosphere: They will tolerate most conditions. However, do not grow them on a mantelpiece above an open or gas fire.

Soil: Loam-based No. 2 is best. Make sure that the drainage is good and that the plant is well anchored in the pot for it tends to be top-heavy and can easily fall over.

Repotting: Do not repot too often as they flourish better if pot-bound. Re-pot not more than once every 2 years.

Pruning: Cut out diseased or damaged leaves.

Propagation: To maintain the colour of the variegated varieties propagate by dividing the plant in the spring. New plants can also be produced by leaf cuttings taken in summer. Cut a leaf into 3 in (8 cm) sections, allow them to dry and then insert into sharp sand. They will root in about a month at 70°F (21°C), but will produce only green not variegated plants.

Life expectancy: Very long indeed provided they are not overwatered.

Plant companions: Because they need so little water it is difficult to include them in mixed plantings. However, their leaf shape and colour contrasts well with other plants and it is possible to include them in mixed tubs and larger containers. Leave the *Sansevieria* in its pot and put this in an outer pot packed with dry sand. The double pot can then be planted in the tub and surrounded by normal compost. The *Sansevieria* will be isolated from the moisture in the surrounding soil and can be watered separately when necessary.

Ease/difficulty: Very easy, provided it is not overwatered.

Repotting

1 Repot in spring every 2 years when the suckers are growing vigorously and roots show through pot base. Water well first.

2 Prepare pot 1 size larger with drainage layer and layer of damp, loam-based No. 2 compost.

3 Hold old pot with one hand covering compost, fingers either side of stems. Tap edge of pot. Plant and compost will come out.

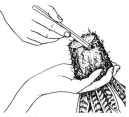

4 Carefully remove stale soil from roots, using stick or pencil. Do not damage roots.

5 Place plant in centre of new pot, root-ball on compost.

6 Add new compost to fill pot. Make sure that all roots are covered. Press down well. Leave in the shade without water for 2 days to encourage roots to grow into compost.

Far left: *Sansevieria* 'Laurentii', green form.

Left: Some sansevierias occasionally flower.

Below left: *Sansevieria hahnii* is one of the less common rosette species.

Right: The commonest species, *Sansevieria trifasciata* 'Laurentii'.

Below: The sculpturesque shape of *Sansevieria futura*.

What goes wrong

1 *Bases of leaves rot*. Too much water, especially in winter. Reduce watering and never let water rest in the crown of the plant.

2 *Edges of leaves damaged*. Plant unstable in pot and has fallen. Stabilize pot in larger outer container. Plant may have rested against window and been scorched by the cold. Move further into room.

3 *Brown patches on the leaves*. Overwatering. Do not let plant dry out completely but water less often.

4 *Leaves pale*. Lack of light. Move into direct light.

5 *White woolly patches on leaves*. Mealy bug. Wipe them off individually with a swab dipped in methylated spirits or spray with malathion or a systemic insecticide.

Leaf cuttings

1 Prepare seed tray or propagator with layer of drainage, layer of compost and ½in (1cm) of sharp sand.

2 Choose healthy leaf and cut off at base.

3 Lay leaf on hard surface and cut it into 1in (2½cm) pieces across its width. Make a small slit in the cut edges that were nearest the base of the original leaf.

4 Push half of each cut section into the sand, making sure that the part covered is the part nearest the base of the original leaf.

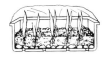

5 Water well and cover. Remove cover for 5 minutes a day to prevent rot and make sure the compost does not dry out. Keep at 70 F (21 C). New roots and leaves will grow from cut sections.

6 When the new plants have 2 or 3 new leaves, lift them from compost and pull them gently away from the old leaf. Pot separately.

Cleaning

Wipe dust off leaves with soft cloth and sponge with tepid water. Support leaf with other hand. Do not use leaf shine.

Root division

S. laurentii loses its variegation if propagated by leaf cuttings. However, it produces suckers which can be divided in spring.

1 Prepare 2 pots with drainage layer and compost.

2 Remove plant from pot and gently prise away compost.

Watering

Sansevierias must never be overwatered or they will rot at the base. Wait until the compost feels dry. Empty excess after 15 minutes.

3 Gently pull roots and stems apart with your hands.

4 Repot both sections in the usual way.

Planting a mixed bowl

1 Sansevierias can be used in mixed plantings but because they need less water than most plants they should be kept separated from the compost in the container.

2 Put pot in outer container packed with dry sand.

3 Place pot and outer container in the mixed trough. Disguise the rim with compost.

4 The plant is isolated from the main group and can be watered when necessary.

Saxifraga sarmentosa

MOTHER OF THOUSANDS

We always associate the genus Saxifraga with alpine and rock gardens but there is one species that is a very good and easy house plant. This is *Saxifraga stolonifera* or, as it is more usually called, *S. sarmentosa*. Its common names of mother of thousands and strawberry geranium both come from the fact that it produces lots of runners with young plantlets in the same way that a strawberry plant does. *Saxifraga sarmentosa* comes from China and was introduced in 1815. It is almost hardy and will stand temperatures as low as 45°F (7°C) quite happily.

The runners are produced in great profusion during the summer months when they make the plant look most attractive. The young plantlets hang down rather like a lace frill and can best be seen when the plant is grown in a hanging basket. The leaves are round, attractively marbled and formed into a neat rosette. It flowers profusely, with white flowers rather like one of the garden saxifrages, 'London pride'. It is an excellent 'ground cover' plant and can be used effectively to fill any bare areas in a large container.

There is also a most attractive variegated variety known as *S. stolonifera* 'Tricolor' with green, cream and red leaves. This variety is a little more tender. It requires a higher winter temperature of 50°F (10°C) and does not throw out so many runners. It is also rather more difficult to obtain.

When buying a *Saxifraga* look out for well formed rosettes beginning to throw runners and plantlets.

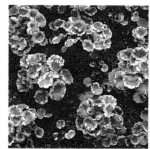

Left: The leaves of *Saxifraga stolonifera* 'Tricolor' are tinged with pink.

Right: *Saxifraga sarmentosa* is a good plant for a hanging basket or macramé hanger. This plant is just beginning to produce plantlets.

Below: The dainty flowers of *Saxifraga sarmentosa*.

Size: Rosettes are about 4 or 5 in (10–12 cm) across. Several can be planted together in a pot if a larger plant is required.

Growth: They will grow from plantlets to flowering size in one growing season.

Flowering season: Lacy, small white flowers with yellow centres will normally appear in June.

Scent: None.

Light: They enjoy a windowsill position, shielded from the direct midday sun in high summer.

Temperature: They prefer it cool, and are unsuitable for extreme central heating. The temperature can drop as low as 45°F (7°C) in winter. In summer 55–60°F (13–16°C) is ideal. They do not enjoy temperatures much above 65°F (18°C).

Water: Provided the drainage is good, water at least 3 times a week in summer. In winter the plant should dry out between watering. Judge by the feel of the soil – it will probably not need water more than once a week.

Feeding: Add half the recommended dose of liquid food to the water once a month in summer.

Humidity: Humidity is not as important as with most other house plants. An occasional overhead spray in summer to remove the dust is beneficial.

Cleaning: Rely on the spraying to keep it clean. The leaves are slightly hairy so never use leaf shine on them.

Atmosphere: Very tolerant but they dislike a very hot, dry atmosphere. They appreciate good ventilation.

Soil: Loam-based No. 2.

Repotting: Repot once a year in the spring.

Pruning: None necessary except to remove dead leaves.

Propagation: Pot up young plantlets from the runners in the spring. Room temperature is sufficient.

Life expectancy: This plant is more vigorous and looks better when it is young. It is best to propagate on a 2 year cycle and throw away the old plants. Otherwise they will go on virtually for ever, though tending to get untidy and less vigorous as they grow old.

Plant companions: They can be grown on their own as hanging plants, but can be planted in the front of mixed bowls of any larger plants.

Ease/difficulty: Definitely an easy plant for a beginner, provided the winter room temperature is not too high.

Propagation: plantlets

1 Prepare small pot with mixture of ½ sand, ½ loam-based No. 2 compost.

Saxifraga sarmentosa produces small plantlets on runners – long stems which creep along the ground or, if the plant is in a hanging container, trail down attractively. The plantlets at the ends of the runners develop small roots and once established in compost of their own, can be separated from the parent plant.

2 Place pot next to parent plant and position plantlet in centre. Firm compost around it. Water well and keep moist.

3 When plant is growing, sever from parent.

What goes wrong

1 *Leaves distorted and sticky with green insects.* Greenfly. This plant is very susceptible. Spray monthly with pyrethrum or a systemic insecticide.

2 *Ragged, dead leaves at the base of the rosette.* Plant getting old. Propagate new ones from the runners and discard old plant.

3 *Plant not producing runners.* Needs feeding. Check roots to see if it needs repotting.

4 *Growth lanky and rosette loose rather than compact.* Too hot. Move to cooler, airier place.

Cleaning

Spray once a fortnight in summer to keep the leaves clean.

Do not use leaf shine.

Repotting

1 Repot in spring when old leaves look ragged, no new leaves appear and roots show through base of pot. Water plant well first.

2 Prepare pot 1 size larger with drainage layer and layer of damp, loam-based No. 2 compost.

3 Hold old pot with one hand covering compost, fingers either side of stems. Tap edge of pot. Plant and compost will come out.

4 Carefully remove stale soil from roots, using stick or pencil. Do not damage roots.

5 Place plant in centre of new pot, root-ball on compost.

6 Add new compost to fill pot. Make sure that all roots are covered. Press down well. Leave in the shade without water for 2 days to encourage roots to grow into compost.

Watering

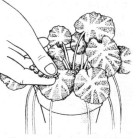

1 Test compost with fingers. If it is light and crumbly, the plant needs water.

2 Add water at top of pot, using rainwater if possible. Empty excess from saucer after 15 minutes.
In winter allow the plant to dry out between waterings. Make sure that plants in hanging baskets are kept watered.

A hanging basket

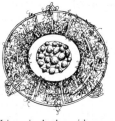

1 Line wire basket with moss and place saucer of charcoal in centre to prevent smell.

2 Stand basket on a bucket and add layer of damp compost.

3 Place plants around edge of basket so that runners will trail over.

4 Fill up with compost and firm around roots.

5 Water well, and hang in position. Make sure it is secure. Plants in wire baskets dry out easily if they are hanging outside. If you are planting directly into pottery or other solid hanging container make sure there is a drainage hole in the bottom.

UMBRELLA TREE

A native of Australia and New Zealand, this plant has only recently found favour with commercial growers. It is an excellent house plant which will tolerate poor light and some cold, but when grown in good conditions it soon becomes a most handsome specimen plant. It will grow to a considerable size, up to 8 ft (2–4 m) tall and 4 to 5 ft (120–140 cm) across. It is commonly called the umbrella tree because of the way its leaves spread and hang. It is a member of the *Aralia* family and was named after J. C. Scheffler, a botanist from Danzig. It is also sometimes known as *Heptapleurum* or *Brassaia*.

Schefflera actinophylla is the most common species grown. It is a bit like an 'ugly duckling' when small for the size of the leaves is out of proportion to the stem. However, when it exceeds 2 ft (60 cm) it becomes a much better balanced plant. When young, its leaves have only three leaflets; only when the plant is adult does it produce leaves divided into five sections. Recently a small species named *Schefflera arboricola* has been introduced. It has two varieties, *S. arboricola* 'Hong Kong' and *S. arboricola* 'Geisha Girl'. They are both very similar, with compact clusters of leaves growing on upright stems. Both *S. actinophylla* and *S. arboricola* grow well in hydroculture.

Look for good green leaves when buying. They should look like highly polished green leather. If buying *S. actinophylla* make sure you obtain a well shaped plant.

Scheffleras are plants which will tolerate shady corners. *Schefflera arboricola* produces leaves of nine leaflets (left). This species grows tall and narrow. It is often potted three per pot (below) to make a bushier display.

Right: A young plant of *Schefflera actinophylla*.

Size: *S. actinophylla* is a big plant, up to 8 ft (2½ m) tall and 4–5 ft (120–140 cm) across. *S. arboricola* grows up to 4 ft (120 cm) tall and about 2 ft (60 cm) across.

Growth: Both are fairly vigorous and will easily put on a foot or more (30 cm) in one summer growing season.

Flowering season: Although they both have small green flowers these do not often appear on pot grown specimens.

Scent: None.

Light: Like most plants they prefer a light position but not direct sun in summer. They will often adapt themselves to fill a shady corner.

Temperature: They like a moderate temperature in winter, not falling below 55°F (12°C) and not rising above 65°F (18°C). Keep at normal room temperatures in summer or they can be placed outside. Maximum summer temperature 70°F (21°C).

Water: They must be kept well watered which will probably mean 2 or 3 times a week in summer and once a week in winter.

Feeding: Add half the recommended dose of liquid food to the water every 14 days in the summer.

Humidity: They benefit from a spray of rainwater two or three times a week.

Cleaning: If the spraying does not keep the leaves clean, wipe them with a damp cloth or use leaf shine – but not more than once every 2 months.

Atmosphere: They are very tolerant of draughts and fumes. However, give some flow of air.

Soil: Loam-based No. 2.

Repotting: Do not repot more than every other year. It is better just to change the top layer of compost. Large plants will need this treatment annually in spring.

Pruning: *S. actinophylla* is a single stemmed plant so needs no pruning. *S. arboricola* should only need pruning if it gets too large and unwieldy. Then cut back the tips and it will branch.

Propagation: Generally from seed sown at 70–75°F (21–24°C). It is possible to root pruned cuttings in water for growing in hydroculture.

Life expectancy: With reasonable treatment they will be very long lived.

Plant companions: When small they mix well with most other green plants. When big they make superb specimen plants. *S. actinophylla* is wide so needs plenty of space around it.

Ease/difficulty: A nice easy plant that can be seen to grow well.

Repotting

1 Repot every second spring when roots show through pot base, leaves are pale and plant fails to grow. Prepare pot 1 size larger with drainage and layer of damp, loam-based No. 2 compost. Water plant well.

2 Loosen compost with knife around top edge of pot.

3 Remove plant, holding it firmly by base of stem and supporting the upper part.

4 Lay plant on table and remove old compost from roots with stick or pencil. Do not damage roots.

5 Place plant in centre of new pot, root-ball on compost.

6 Add new compost, firming it until the pot is filled. Make sure all roots are covered. Leave in the shade without water for 2 days to encourage roots to grow into compost.

What goes wrong

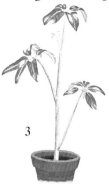

1 *Brown scaly insects on stems and leaf stalks and under leaves.* Scale insect. Remove them individually with a swab dipped in methylated spirits or spray with a systemic insecticide.

2 *White woolly patches on leaves.* Mealy bug. Remove them individually with a swab dipped in methylated spirits or spray with malathion or a systemic insecticide.

3 *Plant becomes lanky with long spaces between leaves.* Too hot. Move to a cooler place. Improve light conditions.

4 *Leaves turn pale green to yellow.* Needs feeding.

5 *Leaves yellowed with webs underneath.* Red spider mite. Spray with derris, malathion or a systemic insecticide. Improve the humidity.

6 *Leaves have only a few leaflets.* These are juvenile leaves and are normal on a young plant.

7 *Leaves distorted and sticky with green insects.* Greenfly. Spray with pyrethrum or a systemic insecticide.

Growing from seed

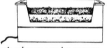

Both plants can be grown from seed in a propagator.

1 Prepare propagator with sterilized, seed-growing compost.

2 Scatter seeds very evenly and add thin layer of compost, no thicker than depth of seed. Water well.

3 Cover propagator. Remove propagator cover for 5 minutes a day to prevent rot and make sure the compost does not dry out. Keep at 70–75°F (21–24°C).

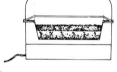

4 When seeds germinate, bring them into light and remove the cover.

5 When seedlings are large enough to handle, thin out the weaker ones, leaving about 1in (2½cm) between each one.

6 When remaining ones are growing well, repot in separate small pots.

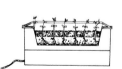

Tying to a cane

1 Push cane gently into compost a few inches away from the main stem, stopping when cane is ⅔ down the pot.

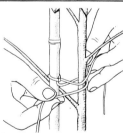

3 Loop string around stem as shown.

2 Cut a 9in (23cm) length of string and tie firmly around cane on stem side.

4 Tie a firm knot against the cane. Repeat at intervals up the stem.

Spraying

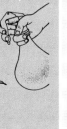

Spray the leaves with rainwater 2 or 3 times a week.

Cleaning the leaves

Wipe dust off leaves with soft cloth and sponge with tepid water. Support leaf with other hand.

Use leaf shine but not more than once every 2 months.

DEVIL'S IVY

The *Scindapsus* is a member of the Araceae or Arum family. Its scientific name is derived from an ancient Greek word meaning 'like ivy' and its common name of devil's ivy also stresses the similarity. There are some twenty known species, all climbing plants which throw out aerial roots that quickly attach themselves to any pole or cane used to support them. They look very like the smaller leaved philodendrons, to which they are in fact related.

The most popular variety grown as a house plant is *Scindapsus aureus* which comes from the Solomon Islands. It has heart-shaped leaves that grow bigger as the plant matures and may become more than twice the size of the juvenile leaves. They are prettily marked with streaks of yellow on pale green and will easily keep this variegation if they are given a minimum of light. They do not like to be too wet, otherwise brown patches appear on the leaves; but they grow well in hydroculture.

Another variety, *S. aureus* 'Marble Queen' is also available. It has almost white leaves with green markings. It grows much more slowly and is a more delicate plant than *S. aureus*, requiring higher temperatures and more care. Like all climbers, both varieties can be grown as trailers and look very attractive in hanging baskets.

When buying a *Scindapsus*, look for well variegated leaves. Make sure the leaves are growing fairly close together, making a well furnished plant. Some growers list this plant under the name of *Pothos* or *Rhaphidophora*.

Size: The plant is usually bought in a 5 or 7 in (12-18 cm) pot with a height up a cane or pole of between 2 and 4 ft (60-120 cm). Being a climber it will eventually grow 15 ft (4½ m) tall at least.

Growth: In the home each leading growth will extend between 12 to 18 in (30-46 cm) a year.

Flowering season: They will not flower in the house.

Scent: None.

Light: Whilst they will tolerate a semi-shaded position, the variegation is more pronounced if they are kept in a good light position, out of the midday sun.

Temperature: A minimum temperature of 55°F (13°C) is necessary to keep the plant healthy in the winter. Keep at 65-70°F (18-21°C) in summer. Maximum summer temperature 75°F (24°C).

Water: They do not like to be overwatered. Allow them to dry out between watering, giving it every 4-5 days in summer and 7-8 days in winter. Before watering check the soil to find out how dry it is.

Feeding: Add half the recommended dose of liquid food to the water once a month all the year round.

Humidity: In the summer spray the leaves with tepid water 2 or 3 times a week. In winter wipe the leaves with a damp cloth every 14 days.

Cleaning: Wipe over the leaves with a damp cloth. This will keep the plant clean and also improve the humidity. Do not use leaf shine. They react badly to it.

Atmosphere: Keep out of draughts, and if possible away from gas or oil fumes.

Soil: Loam-based No. 2.

Repotting: They do not like to be repotted too often. Repot every other year at the very most. Make sure the drainage is good.

Pruning: They can be cut back in spring if they get too large. If you require a bushier plant, prune back the leading growths to half their length in April or May.

Propagation: Stem tip cuttings can be rooted in the spring either in water or in soil. A temperature of about 65-70°F (18-21°C) is required.

Life expectancy: Given a little care, this plant will go on for many years.

Plant companions: Provided the drainage is good, *Scindapsus* mixes well with other green plants in tubs and troughs. It will, of course, need a cane to support it.

Ease/difficulty: A medium to easy plant that will thrive in the hands of those with a little experience.

Repotting

1 Repot in spring but not more than once every other year. Roots showing through pot base and little new growth show when soil is exhausted. Water well first.

2 Prepare pot 1 size larger with drainage layer and layer of damp, loam-based No. 2 compost.

3 Hold old pot with one hand covering compost, fingers either side of stems. Tap edge of pot. Plant and compost will come out.

4 Carefully remove stale soil from roots, using stick or pencil. Do not damage roots.

5 Place plant in centre of new pot, root-ball on compost.

6 Add new compost to fill pot. Make sure that all roots are covered. Press down well. Leave in the shade without water for 2 days to encourage roots to grow into compost.

Scindapsus looks rather like an ivy but is more tender than true ivy and requires more warmth, more light and less water.

Left: The leaves of *Scindapsus* are heart shaped. They become much larger as the plant matures.

Left: *Scindapsus aureus* 'Marble Queen' is highly variegated. Some leaves can be pure white.

Right: *Scindapsus aureus*. Here several cuttings have been trained together onto a moss pole. The plant can also be grown in a hanging basket in which case the trailing stems may extend to the floor.

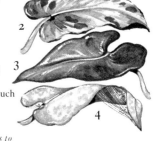

What goes wrong

1 *Leaves become pale*. Too much direct sunlight. Move to a semi-shaded place.

2 *Brown spots and black edges to the leaves*. Plant too cold and/or too wet. Move to a warmer position and reduce watering.

3 *Leaves revert to green*. Insufficient light. Move to a lighter place.

4 *Leaves yellowed with webs underneath*. Red spider mite. Spray with derris, malathion or a systemic insecticide. Improve the humidity.

Pruning

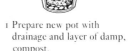

Prune leggy plants to half their height in late spring.

Watering

Scindapsus must never be overwatered. Let the plant dry out between waterings and always test compost. Empty any excess from saucer after 15 minutes.

Stem tip cuttings

Take cuttings in spring. A propagator is best to make sure they are humid but you can experiment with a polythene cover if you have no propagator.

1 Prepare pot or propagator with drainage layer and mixture of sharp sand and loam-based compost.

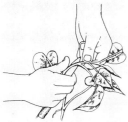

2 Cut off shoot or stem tip with at least 2 healthy leaves and a growing point.

3 Prepare cuttings by trimming off end of stem below leaf.

4 Remove the lowest leaf.

5 Dip the cut surface in hormone rooting powder. Shake off the surplus.

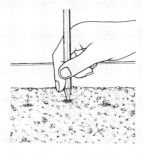

6 Make small holes in compost with stick or pencil.

7 Insert cutting so that end of stem is at bottom of hole and lowest leaf level with the compost.

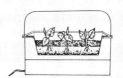

8 Water well and cover. Remove cover for 5 minutes a day and never let compost dry out. Keep at 65–70 F (18–21 C).

9 Remove cover after 21 days and when cuttings are growing well, repot in normal compost.

Adding a moss pole

1 Prepare new pot with drainage and layer of damp, compost.

2 Position moss pole and add a little compost around it to hold it firm.

3 Remove plant from pot.

4 Place plant in pot beside moss pole.

5 Tie plant stem to moss pole with raffia or twine at intervals.

6 Add new compost to fill pot. Make sure that all roots are covered. Press down well.

GLOXINIA

Everybody knows this plant as *Gloxinia* but in fact this is only its common name. Botanically it is *Sinningia speciosa hybrida*. It comes from Brazil and is a member of the Gesneriaceae family which includes some twenty species.

The name Gloxinia was given in honour of Benjamin Peter Gloxin a French botanical writer working at the end of the eighteenth century. The genus name honours Wilhelm Sinning, head gardener at the University of Bonn in the mid nineteenth century. He was associated with the hydridization and selection work which has given us today one of the most beautiful of summer flowering indoor plants.

The original plant had drooping, purple flowers, resembling a foxglove in shape. The modern hybrids have flowers which are upright, borne on short stems, bell shaped and in bright colours of red, pink, mauve and white. Some of the varieties have frilled edges, touched with white. The leaves are large, flat and velvety.

Gloxinias can be grown from seed or tubers in early spring. If bought in flower, ensure that the plant has plenty of buds still to open. The leaves should not be torn or damaged and should be deep green. Pale plants will have been underfed. Check that there is no rot anywhere on the plant. Great care should be taken in transporting this plant for the fleshy leaves are delicate in structure and can easily crack.

Gloxinias should produce many blooms. The heart of the plant should be full of buds as the first flowers open (left).

Right: A healthy gloxinia will have foliage of a deep green.

Below: The flowers, like the leaves, have a velvety texture. Avoid spraying the flowers with water.

Size: Normally about 12 in (30 cm) high when in flower with a 15 in (38 cm) span across the leaves.

Growth: Seeds sown early in the year will flower the same summer. Tubers will sprout to flowering size in about 5 months.

Flowering season: By staggering the sowing of seeds or the planting of old tubers it is possible to get a succession from May to September. The plants tend to produce their flowers all at once.

Scent: None.

Light: They require a very light position but need to be protected from the midday sun in the summer.

Temperature: Room temperature in summer, 60–70°F (15–21°C). In winter the dormant tubers should be kept dry and frost free. They require a high temperature of 70°F (21°C) to start them growing in the early spring. Maximum summer temperature is 75°F (24°C).

Water: Give plenty of water, 2–3 times a week in summer. Water from below to keep water off the leaves and flowers. Gradually reduce watering in the autumn as the leaves die and the plant becomes dormant. When it has died down, leave completely dry.

Feeding: Add liquid food to the water every week while the plant is in flower.

Humidity: Young plants appreciate an early morning spray with tepid water but avoid spraying the flowers and do not let excessive water remain on the plant. Stand the pot on damp peat.

Cleaning: The spraying will be enough. Never use leaf shine.

Atmosphere: Keep away from draughts.

Soil: One of the peat-based composts.

Repotting: Young plants from seed or cuttings should be potted twice or three times during the growing season. Old tubers should be potted once when started into growth in February/March. The top of the tubers should be level with the surface of the compost.

Pruning: Not necessary, except to remove damaged leaves and dead flowers.

Propagation: From seed sown in early spring at a temperature of about 70°F (21°C). Be careful that the young plants do not rot through overwatering and poor ventilation. Stem tip cuttings 2–3 inches (5–7 cm) long can be taken from old tubers started into growth in spring. These tubers can also be cut into pieces each with a growing point. Leaf cuttings can be taken when the leaves are mature in summer. Cuttings of whichever type will root at 70°F (21°C).

Life expectancy: The tubers will survive from year to year but they should not be kept longer than 2 or 3 years as old plants tend to lose their vigour.

Plant companions: Best grown on their own.

Ease/difficulty: With a little care and attention these are really quite easy plants to keep, at least through one season.

Repotting

1 Repot dormant tubers in early spring as they start to bud. Repot young plants 2 or 3 times in the growing season as soon as the pot fills with roots. Water well first.

2 Prepare pot with drainage layer and layer of damp, peat-based compost.

3 Hold old pot with one hand covering compost, fingers either side of stems. Tap edge of pot. Plant and compost will come out.

4 Carefully remove stale soil from roots, using stick or pencil. Do not damage roots.

5 Place plant in centre of new pot, root-ball on compost.

6 Add new compost to fill pot. The top of the tubers should be level with the surface of the compost.
Leave in the shade without water for 2 days to encourage roots to grow into compost.

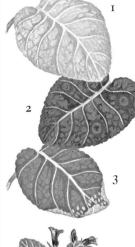

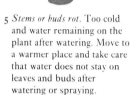

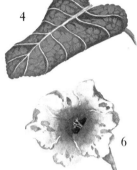

1 *Pale green leaves.* Needs feeding.

2 *Brown rings on leaves.* Tomato spotted wilt virus. No cure: destroy plant.

3 *Leaves distorted and sticky with green insects.* Greenfly. Spray with pyrethrum or a systemic insecticide.

4 *Leaves curl.* Too sunny. Move to a partially shaded place.

5 *Stems or buds rot.* Too cold and water remaining on the plant after watering. Move to a warmer place and take care that water does not stay on leaves and buds after watering or spraying.

6 *Stained flowers.* Marked by water. Avoid spraying flowers.

Division

1 Tubers can be divided in spring as they start to bud. Prepare 2 pots with drainage, compost and an inch (2½cm) sharp sand.

2 Remove plant from pot.

3 Carefully remove stale soil.

4 Lay tuber on hard, flat surface and cut cleanly in half with a sharp knife. Each section must include a shoot.

5 Dust cut ends with sulphur to prevent fungal infection.

6 Pot each section separately with the top of the tuber level with the compost.

Leaf cuttings

1 Prepare a seed tray or shallow pot with layer of drainage, compost and ½in (1cm) sharp sand. Cut several 1in (2½cm) lengths of plastic coated wire.

2 Choose good healthy leaf and cut off at base. Cut off stem.

3 Lay leaf upside down on hard surface and cut the thick veins below vein junctions.

4 Lift leaf carefully and lay face upwards on the sand. Peg it down in several places with wire. Make sure veins touch sand closely.

5 Water well and keep at 70°F (21°C). Cover with glass or polythene and never let the compost dry out. New plants will grow from cut veins.

6 When new plants have 2 or 3 new leaves lift them from the sand, pull them gently away from old leaf and pot them separately in small pots.

Humidity

Humidity is essential for Sinningias.

Spray every day with tepid water but do not spray the flowers.

Stand pot in saucer with water, pebbles or gravel. Make sure pot base is clear of water.

or Put pot in outer container packed with damp peat.

WINTER CHERRY

Solanums form a large genus with some nine hundred species in the family Solanaceae. They come from many countries throughout the tropical and temperate regions of the world. The most famous member of the family is the ordinary domestic potato, *Solanum tuberosum*.

There are only two members of the family grown as house plants. These are the capsicums (p. 52) and *Solanum capsicastrum*, commonly known as the winter or Jerusalem cherry. This was introduced from Brazil in the seventeenth century. It is a popular indoor plant usually bought in fruit at Christmas time. It lasts quite well indoors, but does require a lot of humidity, so spray it regularly overhead when in the home. Like the *Capsicum* it is a useful plant to display in window-boxes in the autumn. Provided the winter is not too severe it will last well on towards Christmas.

The hybridizers have made great improvements in the strains available. Now there are varieties that are more compact, produce more fruit and do not drop their fruit as much as the older strains did. Their berries should not be eaten. Whilst they are not deadly poisonous they can cause temporary stomach upsets, particularly in young children.

Buy plants with good green leaves and berries just beginning to colour yellow and orange.

Winter cherries produce fruit which ripens from green, through yellow to orange. Always choose a plant with deep green foliage.

Below: The berries last many weeks on the plant. Do not eat them: they are poisonous.

Right: A well-berried plant of *Solanum capsicastrum*.

Size: Normally sold between 12–15 in (30–38 cm) tall. The smaller size will be in a 3½ in (9 cm) pot and the larger in a 5 in (13 cm). They will be a little bigger if grown on for a second year.

Growth: They will grow from seed to 15 in (38 cm) in one season.

Flowering season: They flower in June and July but the colourful orange berries are the main feature of this plant. They are in colour from October onwards.

Scent: The flowers have no scent but the foliage has a pungent smell.

Light: To survive long in the home they require plenty of light.

Temperature: They do not like it too warm in winter. 55 F (13 C) is an ideal temperature. In summer it is best to place them out-of-doors. Indoors, the maximum temperature should be 65 F (18 C).

Water: Water profusely (every other day) when growing, and indeed never let them dry out in the winter. Two or three times a week should be enough. If plants are being left for a second season keep them on the dry side when resting and after pruning, watering only about once every two weeks.

Feeding: Add liquid food to the water every 14 days in the summer as the plant is growing.

Humidity: They love a damp atmosphere and should be sprayed daily with soft water when the plant is in the house.

Cleaning: The spraying should suffice. Do not use leaf shine.

Atmosphere: They are fairly tolerant provided the atmosphere is not too dry and there is a good flow of air.

Soil: Loam-based No. 2.

Repotting: Plants will require potting on when grown from seed, perhaps twice depending on how quickly they grow. Also, if plants are kept for a second year it is advisable to repot when the plants are pruned in the spring.

Pruning: Only necessary if plants are kept for a second year. They should then be cut back to half their size in April/May and stood in the open until the middle of the summer. It is also best to restrict growth in September by pinching out the non-flowering tips to make a compact growing plant.

Propagation: They germinate easily from seed sown in March at about 60 F (16 C).

Life expectancy: They are normally treated as annual plants and thrown away after one season. However they are not difficult if you have space to keep them for a second season. After that they get very woody and are less likely to flower and fruit.

Plant companions: They are normally grown on their own, but can go as visitors into bowls or tubs of mixed green plants.

Ease/difficulty: Quite easy provided they are given plenty of light and humidity.

Repotting

1 Repot plants grown from seed throughout summer as and when roots fill the pot. Repot older plants kept for a second year in spring after pruning. Water well first.

2 Prepare pot 1 size larger with drainage layer and layer of damp, loam-based No. 2 compost.

3 Hold old pot with one hand covering compost, fingers either side of stems. Tap edge of pot. Plant and compost will come out.

4 Carefully remove stale soil from roots, using stick or pencil. Do not damage roots.

5 Place plant in centre of new pot, root-ball on compost.

6 Add new compost to fill pot. Make sure that all roots are covered. Press down well. Leave in the shade without water for 2 days to encourage roots to grow into compost.

What goes wrong

1 *Foliage limp, berries begin to drop.* Too dry. Soak in a bucket immediately and allow to drain.

2 *Growth is weak; long distances between leaves.* Lack of light. Move to a lighter position.

3 *Young shoots covered with a grey fungal growth.* Grey mould. Move to a warmer position and improve ventilation. Spray with a systemic fungicide.

4 *Foliage a poor colour and lower leaves go yellow with brown spots.* Magnesium deficiency. Feed regularly with a liquid fertilizer containing magnesium e.g. one formulated for feeding tomatoes.

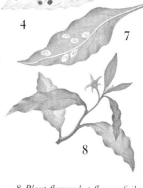

5 *Foliage a poor colour.* Plant needs food. Repot it or feed weekly.

6 *Leaves become yellowed and are webbed underneath.* Red spider mite. Spray with derris or a systemic insecticide. Improve the humidity.

7 *Plant is stunted with yellow concentric rings on leaves.* Tomato spotted wilt virus. No cure. Destroy plant.

8 *Plant flowers but flowers fail to set fruits.* In future spray the open flowers with warm water.

Growing from seed

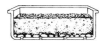

1 Solanum can be grown from seeds sown in spring. Prepare seed tray with drainage and seed-growing compost.

4 When seeds germinate, bring them into light and remove the glass cover.

2 Scatter seeds very evenly and add thin layer of compost, no thicker than depth of seed. Water well.

5 When seedlings are large enough to handle, thin out the weaker ones, leaving about 1in (2½cm) between each one.

3 Cover with glass and put in dark place or cover with dark cloth. Make sure the compost never dries out and turn glass over daily. Keep warm (60 F, 16 C).

6 When remaining ones are growing well, repot in separate small pots.

Stopping for bushiness

Pinch out the growing tips of young plants to keep them bushy.

Pruning

If you are keeping the plant for a second year, prune it to half its size in late spring.

Spraying

Spray daily with soft **tepid** water when indoors. Spray daily while it is in flower to encourage the berries to set.

Watering

1 Test compost with fingers. If it is light and crumbly, the plant needs water.

2 Add water at top of pot, using rainwater if possible. Empty excess from saucer after 15 minutes.

171

Sparmannia africana

AFRICAN HEMP

The *Sparmannia* is a very beautiful room plant that deserves to be more widely grown. It is already well loved in parts of Europe, particularly in Germany, but in other countries is sometimes difficult to obtain.

A member of the Tiliaceae or Lime family, there are some four known species. They are all natives of South Africa where they grow into sizeable trees about 12 ft (4 m) high. The plant was named after Dr Ardens Sparmann, a Swede who lived from 1748–1820 and accompanied Captain Cook on his second voyage. Its common names are African hemp and room or house lime. Only one variety is normally available, *Sparmannia africana*.

The plant grows rapidly even in the home, but requires a good light position. The leaves, which resemble those of the outdoor lime in shape, are covered with soft hairs which make them a little difficult to clean. Very dusty plants can be cleaned in summer by standing them out in light rain. They seem to like this very much. When the plant is a fair size (3 ft (1 m) or more) it will carry a cluster of white single flowers with purple stamens which are sensitive to the touch, opening even if they are blown by a breeze. Large plants are a bushy shape and are best grown alone so that air can circulate freely around them.

When buying in the spring or early summer look for a bright colour in the lime-green leaves and no yellowing of lower leaves. Make sure no branches are broken for the new growth is very soft and can easily be damaged on its journey from the nursery to the shop.

Sparmannias are members of the lime family and the foliage (left) resembles the lime although it is hairy and soft to the touch.

Right: The elegance of *Sparmannia africana* is best brought out when it is in dappled sunlight.

Below: When kept in good light the plants will flower.

Size: When planted in a greenhouse or conservatory bed they will easily reach 12 ft (4 m) or more. They can be kept under control by pruning and restricted to 6 ft (2 m) in a pot or tub.

Growth: They are very fast growers and can easily put on 18–24 in (46–60 cm) growth in one year.

Flowering season: Flowers will only appear on a mature plant in excess of 3 ft (1 m) tall. Flowers appear in May and June.

Scent: The flowers have a faint limey smell which is not very distinct.

Light: They must have plenty of light otherwise the leaves go yellow. However try to avoid strong sunlight for this can burn the delicate leaves.

Temperature: They will stand and benefit from a fairly low temperature in winter, 45°F (7°C) being the minimum. At this temperature the plant must be left on the dry side, watering about once every 10 days. Maximum summer temperature should be 70°F (21°C).

Water: Water profusely in the summer, at least every other day. Give less in the winter depending on the temperature. About once a week should be sufficient in normal room temperatures.

Feeding: Add liquid food to the water every 14 days during the summer.

Humidity: Spraying in the summer is beneficial. Do this 2 or 3 times a week.

Cleaning: This is difficult as the leaves are hairy and the young stems weak and so liable to snap off. A feather duster lightly flicked over will remove dust, or you can use a soft paint brush very gently. In summer stand out in light rain. Never use leaf shine.

Atmosphere: They are fairly tolerant but do not like draughts. They appreciate some ventilation in summer.

Soil: They like a rich soil, so use loam-based No. 3.

Repotting: During the first year they will probably require repotting 2 or 3 times. After this, once a year in the spring should be enough. If left pot-bound the plant will flower at a younger age.

Pruning: Prune in the spring to keep the plant a neat shape. If the plant is too leggy it can be cut back quite drastically after flowering.

Propagation: Young stem tip cuttings root easily in peat and sand in spring. Use a rooting hormone powder and keep at 61°F (16°C). Cuttings will also root in water.

Life expectancy: With a minimum of care the plant will go on for many years.

Plant companions: They look well in mixed plant combinations, the lime green of their leaves contrasting very well with the darker green of *Ficus* and philodendrons. A mixed planting like this would, of course, require a very large container. Large plants are best on their own.

Ease/difficulty: Quite an easy plant, but a little knowledge and experience will make it grow even better.

Cleaning the leaves

Brush leaves gently with soft, dry paintbrush. Never add water or leaf shine.

In summer stand the plant outside in light rain to wash the dust off its leaves.

Pruning

Prune in spring to keep the plant a manageable size.

Make cuts with secateurs just above a leaf or side shoot, cutting at an angle.

Spraying

Spray 2 or 3 times a week in summer to provide humidity.

1 *All leaves droop.* Too dry. Soak plant in bucket of water and never let it dry out.

2 *Leaves turn yellow, lanky growth.* Too dark. Move to the lightest possible position without direct sunlight.

3 *Leaves turn brown in patches and seem scorched.* Direct sun on the leaves. Move out of the midday sun.

4 *White woolly patches on leaves.* Mealy bug. Remove them individually with a swab dipped in methylated spirits or spray with a systemic insecticide.

Stem tip cuttings

1 Take cuttings in spring. They will root in compost or water. Prepare a pot with drainage layer and compost of ½ peat, ½ sand.

2 Cut off shoot or stem tip with at least 2 healthy leaves and a growing point.

3 Prepare cuttings by trimming off end of stem below leaf.

4 Remove the lowest leaf.

5 Dip the cut surface in hormone rooting powder. Shake off the surplus.

6 Make small hole in centre of pot.

7 Insert as far as base of lowest leaf stem. End of stem must rest on bottom of hole.

8 Water well and cover with polythene supported by wire. Remove cover for 5 minutes a day and never let compost dry out. Keep at 61°F (16°C).

9 Remove cover after 21 days and when cutting is growing well, repot in normal compost.

Repotting

1 Repot in spring when plant does not grow and leaves begin to look slightly yellow. Water well first.

2 Prepare new pot 1 size larger with drainage and layer of damp, loam-based No. 3 compost. If using the same pot again, wash it out well.

3 Loosen compost with knife around top edge of pot.

4 Remove plant, holding it firmly by base of stem and supporting the upper part.

5 Lay plant on table and remove old compost from roots with stick or pencil. Do not damage roots.

6 Place plant in centre of new pot, root-ball on compost.

7 Add new compost, firming it until the pot is filled. Make sure all roots are covered. Leave in the shade without water for 2 days to encourage roots to grow into compost.

SAIL PLANT

Spathiphyllum is one of the few house plants that has beautiful leaves and the extra attraction of delicate flowers all through the summer. A member of the Arum family, there are some twenty-seven species, mostly to be found in tropical America although at least one comes from Malaysia. The name refers to the flower spathe which, when it first appears, looks like a leaf. They are moderate to easy plants to keep in the house but are satisfying to grow and particularly to bring into flower. They do well grown in hydro-culture.

Spathiphyllum wallisii, from Colombia, is the most popular species grown. The leaves are bright green, lance shaped and they lean out gracefully from the centre of the plant. The flowers are white and grow on a long stem. Their sail-like spathe and central spadix make them rather like those of an *Anthurium* in shape. They last a long time, slowly turning green before dying. There is a larger hybrid, *S.* 'Mauna Loa', which can grow to nearly 3 ft (1 m) tall.

Spathiphyllums are related to anthuriums but are much easier to grow. As with anthuriums their flowers can be cut for decoration and will last some time. If you have a humid greenhouse they are excellent plants to grow under the staging where they will flower well.

Make sure the plant you buy has either a flower or bud and that the leaves are a bright, glossy green.

Spathiphyllums like plenty of water and some warmth. With these conditions they should flower almost continually. The flower (left) consists of a wide spathe and a narrow central spadix.

Right: *Spathiphyllum wallisii*.

Below: *Spathiphyllum* 'Mauna Loa', a large hybrid.

Size: *S. wallisii* grows to about 1 ft (30cm) tall but can spread to 3 ft (1 m) across. *S.* 'Mauna Loa' is bigger in leaf and flower and can achieve 3 ft (1 m) in height.

Growth: They will double their size in one growing season.

Flowering season: They produce a constant succession of flowers all through the summer. The larger the plant, the more flowers it produces. Occasionally flowers will appear in the winter if a high degree of humidity is achieved.

Scent: None.

Light: In the winter keep them in as light a position as possible. In the summer they require a semi-shaded position away from direct sunshine. *S.* 'Mauna Loa' needs more light than *S. wallisii*.

Temperature: They prefer a winter temperature of 60–65°F (16–18°C) but will survive at 55°F (13°C) for short periods. Keep at least at 65–70°F (18–21°C) in summer. Maximum summer temperature is 80°F (27°C) when humidity must be kept high.

Water: They like plenty of moisture at all times. Water 2 or 3 times a week in summer and once a week in winter. They do very well in hydroculture.

Feeding: Add liquid food to the water every 14 days when they are growing and flowering in the summer.

Humidity: They benefit from a high degree of humidity all the year round. Spray overhead, stand their pot on damp pebbles or place in an outer pot surrounded by damp peat.

Cleaning: Wipe the leaves with a damp cloth to keep them nice and glossy. Do not use leaf shine.

Atmosphere: They do not like gas fumes or draughts.

Soil: They like the richness of loam-based No. 3 with extra peat added (about $\frac{1}{4}$ more by volume).

Repotting: This is best carried out annually in the spring. Make sure that there is a good drainage layer in the bottom of the pot.

Pruning: Not really necessary except to remove dead leaves and flowers.

Propagation: They can be grown from seed in high humidity at about 70°F (21°C) in a propagator, but are more easily propagated by division of the root stock in the spring. Keep the divided sections warm (70°F, 21°C) and well shaded until they start to grow again.

Life expectancy: They will go on for a long time, although it is best to divide the plants every 3 to 4 years to keep them vigorous in growth.

Plant companions: They enjoy the humidity provided by mixed plantings. Use any combination of green foliage plants.

Ease/difficulty: An easy plant for anybody with a little basic knowledge.

Repotting

1 Repot in spring when plant rides up in its pot with roots showing at top and through base. Water well.

2 Prepare pot 1 size larger with drainage layer and layer of damp compost made up of 3 parts loam-based No. 3 and 1 part peat.

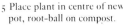

4 Carefully remove stale soil from roots, using stick or pencil. Do not damage roots.

5 Place plant in centre of new pot, root-ball on compost.

3 Hold old pot with one hand covering compost, fingers either side of stems. Tap edge of pot. Plant and compost will come out.

6 Add new compost to fill pot. Make sure that all roots are covered. Press down well. Leave in the shade without water for 2 days to encourage roots to grow into compost.

What goes wrong

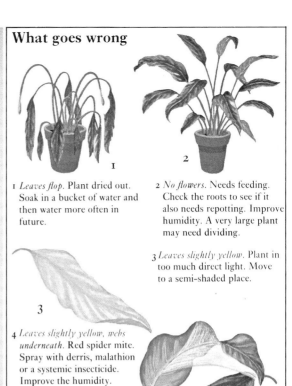

1 *Leaves flop*. Plant dried out. Soak in a bucket of water and then water more often in future.

2 *No flowers*. Needs feeding. Check the roots to see if it also needs repotting. Improve humidity. A very large plant may need dividing.

3 *Leaves slightly yellow*. Plant in too much direct light. Move to a semi-shaded place.

4 *Leaves slightly yellow, webs underneath*. Red spider mite. Spray with derris, malathion or a systemic insecticide. Improve the humidity.

5 *Leaves distorted and sticky with green insects*. Greenfly. Spray with pyrethrum or a systemic insecticide.

Root division

Divide large plants in spring.

1 Prepare 2 pots with drainage layer and compost.

3 Gently pull roots and stems apart with your hands.

2 Remove plant from pot and gently prise away compost.

4 Repot both sections in the usual way.

Removing the flower stem

When flowers have withered, cut stem at base with sharp scissors or secateurs.

Humidity

Three ways to provide the humidity spathiphyllums love.

Spray daily overhead with a fine mist spray, using rainwater if possible. Hold spray about 6in (15cm) from leaves.

Put pot in outer container packed with damp peat.

or Stand pot in saucer with water, pebbles or gravel. Make sure pot base is clear of water.

Removing dead leaves

When dead leaf is quite dry cut it off with sharp scissors where leaf stem joins plant.

Cleaning the leaves

Wipe dust off leaves with soft cloth and sponge with tepid water. Support leaf with other hand.
Do not use leaf shine.

Watering

Test compost with fingers. If it is light and crumbly, the plant needs water.
Add water at top of pot, using rainwater if possible. Empty excess from saucer after 15 minutes.

MADAGASCAR JASMINE

The name *Stephanotis* comes from the Greek words *stephanos*, a crown and *otis* an ear, probably referring to the way the flowers are formed in bunches. A member of the Asclepiadaceae family there are some fifteen known species of this evergreen climber which comes from Madagascar, Peru, Malaysia and southern China. Only one variety is grown indoors to any extent. This is *Stephanotis floribunda* which was introduced from Madagascar in 1839. Its common name of Madagascar jasmine shows its origin.

It is not the easiest of plants to grow in the house as it requires so much light. It is really better suited to a conservatory or greenhouse. There it looks its best when trailing along a rafter so that the clusters of lovely white flowers can hang down delicately. However, it can be grown quite successfully in a pot, up a cane or around a wire hoop and if kept in a window where it can receive good light, it will flower well.

The strongly scented waxy flowers, much used by summer brides for their bouquets, are the plant's strong point. Without its flowers it looks rather ordinary.

When buying, look for good, healthy, green foliage. The plant should have two or three clusters of flower buds, preferably with one or two flowers just opening. Look out for and reject plants that have dropped some of their flower buds.

Size: If the plant is grown in a pot it should be kept compact by training the leading growths up and down a cane or round a wire hoop. Individual shoots can grow as long as 20 ft or more (over 6m).

Growth: Shoots can easily put on 2 ft (60 cm) in one growing season.

Flowering season: All through the summer, although there is normally a main flowering period in May or June. If it is in a pot, do not move it about or the buds may drop.

Scent: A most beautiful lily-like perfume.

Light: They must have plenty of light, preferably in a greenhouse or a conservatory. Otherwise place them in a window, but shade them from direct midday sun in summer.

Temperature: In summer a minimum of 60°F (15°C) is necessary and 65°F (18°C) is preferable. In winter keep them slightly cooler at 55°F (13°C). Maximum summer temperature 75°F (24°C).

Water: Water 2 or 3 times a week in summer and once a week in winter. Use lime-free and tepid water when possible.

Feeding: Add half the recommended dose of liquid food to the water once every 14 days in the spring and summer when the plant is growing and flowering.

Humidity: They should be sprayed every day in summer with lime-free, tepid water but do not spray the flowers. Stand the pot on damp pebbles to provide constant humidity.

Cleaning: The spraying should keep the leaves clean, but they can also be wiped with a damp cloth. Do not use leaf shine.

Atmosphere: The plant dislikes draughts and gas fumes. It appreciates some ventilation.

Soil: Loam-based No. 2.

Repotting: When young, repot about twice a year. After the first 2 years repot every spring. If the plant gets too old or difficult to move just replace the top soil in the pot or tub.

Pruning: Cut back any leading growths that get too straggly or lose their leaves. This is best done in the spring. Side shoots can be shortened to 3 in (8cm) at the same time. Cut out all weak shoots.

Propagation: Take lateral stem tip cuttings from last year's wood in the spring and plant them in a propagator or in a polythene-covered pot at a temperature of 70°F (21°C). They may take 6 weeks to root.

Life expectancy: With care they will go on for many years.

Plant companions: Because they need a lot of light and are vigorous climbers, they are best grown on their own.

Ease/difficulty: Not a plant for the novice.

Stephanotis floribunda is a heavily perfumed climber that grows best in a conservatory.

Below: The flowers are waxen and appear in groups or 'pips' along the stems.

Right: *Stephanotis* is supplied trained around a hoop or canes. If you unwind it for planting in a conservatory the stem may well be already 4ft (over 1m) long.

Training round a hoop

1 Push one end of flexible cane or wire hoop into compost at side of pot, stopping when end of cane is ⅔ down pot.

4 If necessary, tie some twine to lower part of hoop. Thread it along hoop, looping it around the stem as you go.

2 Bend hoop to other side of pot and push into compost.

3 Gently twine plant stem around hoop, taking care not to damage stem or leaves.

5 The plant will continue to grow along the hoop and can be trained to circle the hoop again or to retrace its steps.

What goes wrong

3 *Flower buds drop.* Plant has been moved about or the pot turned. Leave it alone.

4 *Leaves turn yellow.* Too dark. Move plant to lighter place.

1 *Young leaves turn yellow.* Chlorosis from lime in the water. Water once with a solution of sequestered iron and then water only with lime-free water.

2 *Flower buds shrivel.* Too dry. Water more often.

Stephanotis is susceptible to insect attack.

5 *Brown scaly insects on stems and under leaves.* Scale insects.

6 *Leaves turn slightly yellow and have webs underneath.* Red spider mite.

7 *White, woolly patches on stems and leaves.* Mealy bug.

To prevent all these, spray monthly with malathion. Scale and mealy bug can also be removed individually with a swab dipped in methylated spirits. The plant will be more resistant to insect attack if it rests in winter at 55°F (13°C).

Stem tip cuttings

1 Take cuttings in spring using stems that grew the year before. Prepare pot or propagator with drainage and compost of ½ peat, ½ sand.

2 Choose shoot or stem tip with at least 2 pairs of healthy leaves and a growing point. Cut off below second pair of leaves. Cuttings should be 3–4in (8–10cm) long.

3 Prepare cuttings by trimming off stem just below a leaf.

4 Remove the lowest pair of leaves.

5 Dip the cut surface in hormone rooting powder. Shake off the surplus.

6 Make small holes in compost around edge with stick or pencil.

7 Insert cutting so that end of stem is at bottom of hole and leaves are level with compost.

8 Water well and cover with polythene supported by wire. Remove cover for 5 minutes a day and never let compost dry out. Keep at 70°F (21°C). Remove cover after 21 days and when cuttings are growing well, repot in normal compost.

Repotting

1 Repot in spring when roots show through pot base and plant does not grow. Water well first and remove hoop or cane.

2 Prepare pot 1 size larger with drainage layer and layer of damp, loam-based No. 2 compost.

3 Hold old pot with one hand covering compost, fingers either side of stems. Tap edge of pot. Plant and compost will come out.

4 Carefully remove stale soil from roots, using stick or pencil. Do not damage roots.

5 Place plant in centre of new pot, root-ball on compost.

6 Add new compost to fill pot. Make sure that all roots are covered. Press down well. Replace hoop.
Leave in the shade without water for 2 days to encourage roots to grow into compost.

177

CAPE PRIMROSE

A few years ago the *Streptocarpus* or Cape primrose was only seen with small, delicate mauve flowers. Now at last plant breeders have taken notice of this delightful but rather neglected plant and a range of pretty pastel colours are available with larger flowers. The breeders have also turned their attention to producing more compact leaves for the broad, strap-like leaves break easily, particularly when the plant is being transported from grower to customer.

A member of the Gesneriaceae family, there are some eighty species found in tropical and southern Africa, Madagascar, Burma and Thailand. The modern hybrid *Streptocarpus* sold as house plants originate from South Africa – the source of their common name Cape primrose. They were mainly imported during the second half of the nineteenth century although some species were discovered as recently as 1940.

The flowers appear in succession all through the late spring and early summer and the plants themselves live for two or three years before looking rather 'tired' and untidy. It is possible to propagate them from seed and leaf cuttings root easily so that new plants can be raised to replace the older ones as they pass their best.

Streptocarpus hybrids are closely related to both saint-paulias and gloxinias. The commonest hybrid is the mauve one (above left) although the pink is some-

times available. Recently introduced new hybrids include the Wiesmoor hybrids (below). Right: *Streptocarpus* 'Meissen's White'.

Size: A single plant will have leaves 6–7 in (15–18 cm) or more long, normally coming out at opposite sides of the plant. Flower stems rise up to 8 in (20 cm) above the crown of the plant.

Growth: They will grow to flowering size from a seedling or rooted cutting in one growing season.

Flowering season: Each plant will produce a succession of flowering spikes all through the late spring and summer.

Scent: None. The flower relies on its colour to attract pollinating insects.

Light: They require good light to flourish. A north or east facing window is ideal, but they should be shaded from the midday sun in summer.

Temperature: A minimum of 60°F (15°C) in winter is ideal. If the temperature drops below this, the plant must be kept drier as it will become almost dormant. 65–70°F (18–21°C) in summer is ideal. Maximum summer temperature is 75°F (24°C).

Water: Water 2 or 3 times a week during the summer, but never let the pot stand in water, otherwise the plant will rot. In winter water only once a week or even less often if the temperature is below 60°F (15°C). Use softened, tepid water whenever possible.

Feeding: The plant does not need much feeding. Add half the recommended dose of liquid food to the water once a month.

Humidity: They enjoy a humid atmosphere provided drainage is good. It is best to stand their pots on damp pebbles or in an outer pot packed with damp peat to give a constant humid atmosphere.

Cleaning: This is difficult for the leaves are very brittle. A gentle flick with a feather duster or a soft paintbrush is best. Never use leaf shine.

Atmosphere: They enjoy a well ventilated position but not draughts. They dislike gas fumes and tobacco smoke.

Soil: The peat-based composts are best as these allow good drainage.

Repotting: They should be repotted each spring even if they are returned to the same size of pot.

Pruning: Remove broken, torn or diseased leaves and old flowering spikes as soon as the flowers have dropped.

Propagation: They can be grown from seed sown at a temperature of 64°F (18°C). Leaf cuttings taken in summer and inserted into sharp sand will also produce good plants. Cut a leaf lengthwise all along the central vein, dust the cut with rooting hormone and insert the cut surface into sharp sand. Cover it with glass or a polythene bag and keep at 60°F (15°C). Plantlets should appear along the leaf after about 4 weeks.

Life expectancy: It is possible to keep plants going for years but they get a bit tired after 2–3 seasons. It is better to propagate then and replace them with young plants.

Plant companions: They can be used in bowls of mixed plants but really look best on their own or with other *Streptocarpus* plants with differently coloured flowers.

Ease/difficulty: Quite an easy plant provided a little care is taken with watering in winter.

Repotting

1 Repot in spring to renew soil, when new leaves are small. You can use the same size pot. Water plant well.

4 Carefully remove stale soil from roots, using stick or pencil. Do not damage roots.

2 Prepare pot 1 size larger with drainage layer and layer of damp, peat-based compost.

5 Place plant in centre of new pot, root-ball on compost.

3 Hold old pot with one hand covering compost, fingers either side of stems. Tap edge of pot. Plant and compost will come out.

6 Add new compost to fill pot. Make sure that all roots are covered. Press down well. Leave in the shade without water for 2 days to encourage roots to grow into compost.

What goes wrong

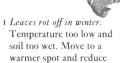

1 *Leaves rot off in winter.* Temperature too low and soil too wet. Move to a warmer spot and reduce watering. Dust plant with sulphur.

2 *Leaves shrivel.* Too dry. Water more frequently.

3 *Green, sticky insects on flower stems.* Greenfly. Spray with pyrethrum or a systemic insecticide.

Leaf cuttings

1 Prepare seed tray or propagator with layer of drainage, compost and 1in (2½cm) of sharp sand.

2 Choose healthy leaf and cut off at base.

3 Lay leaf upside down on hard surface and cut along its length, down the middle of the central vein.

4 Dip the cut surface in hormone rooting powder. Shake off surplus.

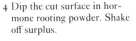

5 Make a shallow trench in sand and push in leaf, vein edge downwards. Firm sand around it.

6 Cover with glass or polythene, keep warm 60 F (15 C) and do not let the compost dry out. New plants will grow along length of vein, where side veins join the main vein.

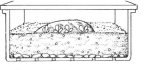

7 When new plants have 2 or 3 new leaves, lift them from sand and gently pull them from old leaf. Pot them separately in small pots.

Removing the flowers

Cut out dead leaves when they are yellow and shrivelled. Cut off dead flower stalks at the base.

Growing from seed

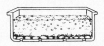

1 Prepare a seed tray or propagator with a drainage layer and sterilized, seed-growing compost.

2 Scatter seeds very evenly and add thin layer of compost, no thicker than depth of seed. Water well.

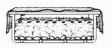

3 Cover with glass and put in dark place or cover with dark cloth. Make sure the compost never dries out and turn glass over daily. Keep warm, 64 F (18 C).

4 When seeds germinate, bring them into light and remove the glass cover.

5 When seedlings are large enough to handle, thin out the weaker ones, leaving about 1in (2½cm) between each one.

6 When remaining ones are growing well, repot in separate small pots.

Humidity

Stand pot in saucer with water, pebbles or gravel. Make sure pot base is clear of water.

Cleaning the leaves

Brush leaves gently with soft, dry paintbrush. Never add water or leafshine.

GOOSE FOOT PLANT

We owe a great debt to the Araceae or Arum family for, as you will have noticed in this book, they have provided so many interesting house plants. The *Syngonium* is yet another member of the family, with approximately fourteen species coming from tropical Central and South America.

Syngoniums are very closely related to philodendrons and their treatment is very similar although the *Syngonium* is perhaps slightly more difficult to care for. They are essentially climbers and flourish better when given a moss pole or a bamboo cane to climb. Some varieties are variegated but the plain green ones are easier to grow and also grow more quickly.

Two species are generally cultivated. *Syngonium podophyllum* is probably the more compact of the two. Its variegated forms *S. podophyllum* 'Albolineatum' and 'Emerald green' are the ones usually available in the shops. The second species, *S. vellozianum*, is also a climber and has more attractive, glossier leaves than the other varieties. They all do well in hydroculture but feeding has to be watched carefully as the leaves soon deteriorate if the feed in the water is used up.

When buying a *Syngonium* see that the plant has bright, unmarked leaves. Plants with pale leaves are likely to have been underfed in the nursery. Make sure that the plant is well tied to its stake. Check that it is not pot-bound. They grow so quickly that they often need repotting immediately. They are sometimes labelled *Nepthytis*.

Size: They are normally bought in a 5 or 6 in (12 or 15 cm) pot. In a larger container the plant will grow to about 5 ft (150 cm) after which it will be rather too large to keep in a pot indoors unless you have room for a very large container.

Growth: They will produce perhaps 12 in (30 cm) a year, or about 6 or 7 new leaves.

Flowering season: They do not flower when grown in a pot.

Scent: None.

Light: They like a reasonably light position, but not strong sun in the summer. The dark leaved varieties will tolerate more shade.

Temperature: A minimum of 60°F (15°C) in winter is required for this plant to survive successfully. Keep at 65–70°F (18–21°C) in the summer. Maximum summer temperature should be 75°F (24°C).

Water: Water freely in the summer, 2 or 3 times a week. Keep on the drier side in winter, watering once a week or slightly less often (depending on temperature). Test the compost to find out how dry it is. Use tepid water if possible.

Feeding: Add half the recommended dose of liquid food to the water every 21 days during the growing season in summer.

Humidity: They enjoy and require a humid atmosphere. Spray daily if possible in the summer, and at all times stand the pot on wet pebbles or in an outer pot of peat.

Cleaning: The spraying should keep the leaves clean. If not, wipe them gently with a damp cloth. Do not use leaf shine.

Atmosphere: They are fairly tolerant but like many plants do not like cold draughts in winter, or a very dry atmosphere.

Soil: Loam-based No. 2 with $\frac{1}{4}$ by volume of extra peat is the best mixture to use.

Repotting: They usually require to be repotted every year in the spring, twice a year if growing very fast.

Pruning: If the plant gets too straggly it can safely be cut back to 6–9 in (15–23 cm) above the pot, and it will soon start shooting again. This is best done in the spring.

Propagation: Stem tips about 5–6 in (13–15 cm) long should be used as cuttings. Dust the base of each with hormone rooting powder and place in a humid propagator or in a polythene-covered pot at 65°F (18°C).

Life expectancy: With a little care they will go for quite a few years.

Plant companions: They enjoy the humid atmosphere created by mixed planting and go well with philodendrons, aralias, hederas etc.

Ease/difficulty: A moderately easy plant, but best grown by somebody with a little experience of easier plants.

Repotting

1 Repot in spring when plant looks top-heavy and roots grow through pot base. Water well first.

2 Prepare pot 1 size larger with drainage layer and layer of damp, loam-based No. 2 compost mixed with $\frac{1}{4}$ by volume of peat.

4 Carefully remove stale soil from roots, using stick or pencil. Do not damage roots.

5 Place plant in centre of new pot, root-ball on compost.

3 Hold old pot with one hand covering compost, fingers either side of stems. Tap edge of pot. Plant and compost will come out.

6 Add new compost to fill pot. Make sure that all roots are covered. Press down well. Leave in the shade without water for 2 days to encourage roots to grow into compost.

Syngoniums are very vigorous climbers.

Left: The characteristic shape of *Syngonium* leaves.

Below left: *Syngonium podophyllum* 'Emerald Green'.

Right: Syngoniums need frequent repotting and staking.

Below: *Syngonium podophyllum* 'Albolineatum'.

What goes wrong

1 *Stems grow long and straggly with long spaces between leaves.* Too dark. Move to a lighter place.

2 *Leaves become pale.* Needs feeding. Check roots to see if plant also needs repotting.

3 *Leaves pale yellow with webs underneath.* Red spider mite. This plant is very susceptible. Spray monthly with derris or a malathion-based insecticide and keep the humidity high.

Humidity

Syngoniums need humidity at all times. Spray daily.

Stand pot in saucer with water, pebbles or gravel. Make sure pot base is clear of water.

Watering

1 Test compost with fingers. If it is light and crumbly, the plant needs water. Use tepid water.

2 Add water at top of pot, using rainwater if possible. Empty excess from saucer after 15 minutes.

Adding a moss pole

1 Prepare new pot with drainage and layer of damp, peat and loam compost.

2 Position moss pole and add a little compost around it to hold it firm.

3 Place plant in pot beside moss pole.

4 Add new compost, firming it until the pot is filled.

5 Tie plant stem to moss pole with raffia or twine at intervals.

Stem tip cuttings

1 Take cuttings 5–6in (13–15cm) long in spring. Prepare propagator or pot with drainage and mixture of ½ peat, ½ sand.

2 Choose shoot or stem tip with at least 2 healthy leaves and a growing point. Cut off below second leaf, close to main stem.

3 Prepare cuttings by trimming off stem just below a leaf.

4 Remove the lowest leaf.

5 Dip the cut surface in hormone rooting powder. Shake off the surplus.

6 Make small holes in compost around edge with stick or pencil.

7 Insert stem as far as base of leaf. End of stem must rest on bottom of hole.

8 Water well and cover with polythene supported by wire. Remove cover for 5 minutes a day and never let compost dry out. Keep at 65 F (18 C).

9 Remove cover after 21 days and when cuttings are growing well, repot in normal compost.

181

WANDERING JEW

Tradescantia is one of the plants that every beginner starts with for it is both easy and rewarding. Named after the famous gardener to Charles I, John Tradescant, the plant belongs to the Commelinaceae family. There are some hundred known species, from North and South America. Some of these belong to the garden, but the creeping and trailing varieties are a must for any indoor collection. They are commonly known as wandering Jew or wandering sailor, presumably because they grow and spread easily. Because of this they are best replaced by young rooted cuttings every year otherwise the plants get very leggy and untidy. They are good plants for growing in hanging baskets.

The most popular species grown indoors is *Tradescantia fluminensis* 'Variegata' and it comes in several forms, all with stripes of yellow, silver or grey on a green background. Some varieties have a pink tinge to the leaves which is most attractive. Sometimes all green leaves appear. These should be immediately removed or the plant will revert to green.

T. blossfeldiana is a smaller species with slightly hairy, mauve leaves. It is a more tender plant and grows more slowly. For those who like silver foliaged plants there is a hairy species, *T. sillamontana*. This has upright, fluffy stems and carmine flowers throughout the summer.

Zebrina pendula can also be grouped with *Tradescantia* as there are only slight botanical differences. Like *Tradescantia* it produces flowers but these are small and not of great significance. It prefers slightly higher temperatures.

Plants should be compact when purchased and the pot well filled with variegated foliage. Look out for diseased or rotten leaves. Plants with leaves reverting to plain green should be rejected.

Zebrina pendula (above and above right) is closely related to *Tradescantia*. This plant will take on rose purple colourations in good light conditions.

Right: *Tradescantia blossfeldiana* 'Variegata'.

Below: *Tradescantia fluminensis* 'Quicksilver'.

Size: They are normally grown in 3 in (8 cm) pots, in which they will produce trails up to 12 in (30 cm) long. They can also be planted in hanging containers.

Growth: They will easily make 10-12 in (25-30 cm) of growth in a season.

Flowering season: They produce little white flowers in the summer. However, this is usually a sign that the plants require to be repotted or replaced by young rooted cuttings.

Scent: None.

Light: Whilst they will tolerate fairly dark positions, lack of light tends to make them leggy. Their variegation is also better if they are kept in good light.

Temperature: A minimum of 50°F (10°C) in winter is sufficient. *Zebrina pendula* needs at least 55°F (13°C). Keep them in normal room temperatures in summer – or they can be placed outside. Maximum summer temperature should be 65°F (18°C).

Water: Whilst they like to be kept fairly moist they will not die if watering is missed. Water about twice a week in summer and once a week in winter.

Feeding: Add liquid food to the water every 14 days in the summer.

Humidity: They like to stand on moist pebbles, although this is not essential.

Cleaning: Give them an occasional spray with tepid water to remove the dust. Do not use leaf shine.

Atmosphere: They are tolerant of most conditions.

Soil: Use loam based No. 2 compost.

Repotting: 4 or 5 rooted cuttings should be potted into 3 in (8 cm) pots, and unless large show plants are required, you will not need to repot them again. It is better to replace old, straggly plants with young cuttings than to keep repotting them. Old plants tend to get bare of leaves at the base of their stems.

Pruning: If plants get too leggy cut them off 1 in (2½ cm) above the pot and allow them to produce young shoots which can be used as cuttings.

Propagation: Propagate stock every spring and discard old plants. Take stem tip cuttings about 3 in (8 cm) long and root them in a mixture of sand and potting compost at room temperature. They also root easily in water. When they are rooted, put 4 or 5 cuttings into a pot.

Life expectancy: One or two years at the most. Then replace by young stock.

Plant companions: They are good plants to use in bowls and small tubs. They will settle down with any plant including cacti!

Ease/difficulty: A must for the beginner. They are ideal for learning about simple propagation.

Repotting

1 If you keep the plant a second year, repot in spring. Pot young plants when their roots get crowded.

2 Prepare pot 1 size larger with drainage layer and layer of damp, loam-based No. 2 compost. Water plant well.

4 Carefully remove stale soil from roots, using stick or pencil. Do not damage roots.

5 Place plant in centre of new pot, root-ball on compost.

3 Hold old pot with one hand covering compost, fingers either side of stems. Tap edge of pot. Plant and compost will come out.

6 Add new compost to fill pot. Make sure that all roots are covered. Press down well. Leave in the shade without water for 2 days to encourage roots to grow into compost.

What goes wrong

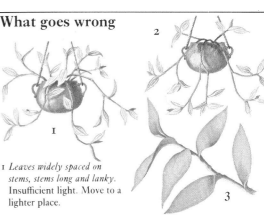

1 *Leaves widely spaced on stems, stems long and lanky.* Insufficient light. Move to a lighter place.

2 *Stems bare at base.* Plant is old. Use shoot tips as cuttings and discard old plant.

3 *Plant produces all green shoots.* Overfeeding and not enough light. Move to a lighter place, stop feeding and pinch out green leaves.

4 *Leaves turn brown.* Too dry. Water more frequently.

5 *Leaf tips turn brown.* Too much direct sun. Move into indirect light.

6 *Leaves distorted and sticky with green insects.* Greenfly. Spray with pyrethrum or a systemic insecticide.

Propagation in water

If you keep the plant for a second year, cut it back so that it will produce strong young shoots. Use these for cuttings.

1 Put 3 or 4 small pieces of charcoal in shallow jar and fill ⅔ with water.

2 Cover with kitchen foil held in place with a rubber band or string.

3 Pierce several small holes in foil with a pencil or stick.

4 Remove a shoot of about 3in (8cm) from plant.

5 Push the stem through foil into the water. Repeat with other shoots. Keep warm (61°F, 16°C).

6 When new roots form, remove the shoots from water and repot them in small pots. Be careful not to damage the delicate roots.

Stopping for bushiness

Pinch out tips of young cuttings to make them grow more bushily.

Pruning

If all green leaves appear on variegated plants cut them out. When stems become old and bare at base, cut off tips to use as cuttings.

Watering

1 Test compost with fingers. If it is light and crumbly, the plant needs water.

2 Add water at top of pot, using rainwater if possible. Empty excess from saucer after 15 minutes.

Humidity and Spraying

Plants in hanging baskets dry out easily. Keep them watered and put damp peat in outer container.

Clean the leaves by spraying them all over with tepid water from a mist sprayer. Hold the spray about 6in (15cm) from leaves.

Do not use leaf shine.

Vriesia splendens

FLAMING SWORD

The *Vriesia* is the last of the bromeliads in this book and, like the others, is striking and spectacular in its own way. Named after a nineteenth century Dutch botanist, W. H. de Vriese, this genus is a native of tropical Central and South America. There are some hundred species known.

Nearly all vriesias follow the standard bromeliad shape with a funnel which has to be kept full of clean water. From this emerges a flower spathe which in the case of *V. splendens* colours up to bright orange. The sheaf is made of bracts which overlap like tiles and often rise up very slightly to let out the small yellow flowers which are shaped rather like a lobster's claw. The entire flowering stem gives the plant its common name of flaming sword. The smooth edged leaves are tough, dark green and have bands of dark brown across them. Many species are grown mainly for their foliage but others have interesting bracts which branch, sometimes like a candelabrum. In the wild the yellow flowered varieties open their flowers during the day and the white at night.

As with all bromeliads the mother plant dies after flowering but reproduces itself with two or three tiny plantlets which can be grown into new plants. It is best to buy a plant with the flower spathe just emerging from the centre of the funnel and not yet fully coloured. Never buy a plant with the flowers showing, as it will not last long.

Vriesias are bromeliads with attractively striped and marbled foliage. Some produce flowering spikes.

Left: *Vriesia fenestralis* is grown for its foliage although it does produce fragrant flowers.

Right: The variety most commonly available, *Vriesia splendens*.

Below: *Vriesia fosteriana*.

Size: The rosette is up to 18in (46cm) across and 12in (30cm) tall. The flower stem can be up to 21in (52cm) tall. The bigger the rosette, the taller the flower spathe.

Growth: From offset to flowering size in 1–2 years.

Flowering season: Flowering will normally take place in the summer. However, depending on when the seed is sown or the baby rosette potted up, it is possible for flowering to occur at any time.

Scent: None.

Light: The leaf markings and the flower spathes colour up best if the plant is grown in direct light. However, if possible keep it in a position away from the midday sun.

Temperature: 65°–70°F (18°–21°C) in winter. In summer, normal room temperature with a maximum of 80°F (27°C).

Water: The compost should be kept damp at all times, which will probably mean watering 3 times a week in summer and once or twice a week in winter. The rosette should also be filled with water, except when the flower spathe starts to emerge. If water is left in then, it can cause rotting. If the temperature is likely to drop below the recommended level in winter, stop watering in the rosette. Always use tepid, lime-free water.

Feeding: Add half the recommended dose of liquid food to the water every 14 days when the leaves and/or the flower spike are growing.

Humidity: They enjoy a humid atmosphere so are either stood on wet pebbles or in an outer pot filled with damp peat.

Cleaning: Wipe the leaves with a damp cloth every fortnight. Do not use leaf shine.

Atmosphere: They are fairly tolerant, but dislike heat from a gas or coal fire.

Soil: The peat-based composts are best for vriesias as they like open textured soil. Always make sure that the drainage is good.

Repotting: The plant will require repotting twice from young offset stage to flowering.

Pruning: Not necessary except to cut off the tips of the leaves if they become brown through dryness. Remove the flower spathe after it has finished flowering.

Propagation: From seed, but this is really a specialist's job as the seeds have to be sown under sterile conditions in a laboratory atmosphere. They can best be grown from the young plants produced after the mother plant has flowered and died. These should be detached carefully, with roots intact, put into small pots and left moist and warm at 75°F (24°C) for at least 3 weeks. Do this in spring or summer but not before the offsets are half the size of the adult.

Life expectancy: Being a bromeliad it has a definite life cycle from separation of the offset to flowering and the production of new offsets ready for potting as independent plants. This is between 2 and 2½ years. Plants grown from seed may take 10–15 years to reach flowering size.

Plant companions: They enjoy the humidity provided by other plants, so grow and look well in mixed plantings of all types of green plants.

Ease/difficulty: Like most bromeliads it is not difficult.

Watering

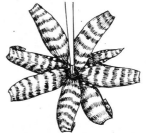

Vriesias need water on the soil as well as in their central rosette. Use tepid water.

1 Keep about 1in (2½cm) of water in central funnel. Empty and refill every 3 weeks. Rainwater is best.

2 Test compost with fingers. If it is light and crumbly, the plant needs water.

3 Add water at top of pot, using rainwater if possible. Empty excess from saucer after 15 minutes.

Removing the flower stem

When the flowers have died, cut out central stem at base with secateurs.

1 *Tips of leaves turn brown, dry and crinkled.* Too dry. Increase watering and spray daily.

2 *Leaves fade and have webs underneath.* Red spider mite. Spray with derris, malathion or a systemic insecticide. Increase the humidity.

3 *Rosette dies back.* Normal after plant has flowered. Propagate from the new offsets which will be appearing.

4 *Flower spike emerges but then rots.* Too much water in the central funnel while in too low a temperature. Usually fatal. Empty central well and if plant recovers, keep in warmer place.

Repotting

1 A plant bought in flower will not need to be repotted but those grown from young offsets should be repotted when they look top-heavy for their pot. Water plant well.

2 Prepare pot 1 size larger with drainage layer and layer of damp, peat-based compost. Make sure drainage is good.

4 Carefully remove stale soil from roots, using stick or pencil. Do not damage roots.

5 Place plant in centre of new pot, root-ball on compost.

Fixing a bromeliad to bark

1 Choose suitable piece of cork bark, a branch or some well shaped driftwood.

2 If there is no natural hollow, chisel a shallow well where plant will rest.

3 Remove plant from pot, keeping compost round the root ball.

4 Wrap roots in damp sphagnum moss and tie with plastic-coated wire.

5 Hold moss and root-ball firmly against wood or bark and bind in place with wire.

6 Fix bark to wall or prop it up, making sure the plant is growing upright. Keep central funnel filled with water. Dampen root ball and spray regularly.

Offsets

1 The leaves will begin to die off but keep the plant until its offsets are ½ the size of the parent plant.

2 Remove offset and roots from parent plant with sharp knife.

3 The offset must have its own small roots. If it has not, it will not grow.

4 Pot offset in new pot, firming compost around base. Water plant well.
Keep warm. 75°F (24°C).

3 Hold old pot with one hand covering compost, fingers either side of stem. Tap edge of pot. Plant and compost will come out.

6 Add new compost to fill pot. Make sure that all roots are covered. Press down well. Leave in the shade without water for 2 days to encourage roots to grow into compost.

SPINELESS YUCCA

There are between thirty and forty known species of *Yucca*, growing naturally in South America. Many can be grown outside in more temperate climates and some even survive severe frosts. They produce beautiful white flowers outdoors but these must be fertilized by a special species of moth only found in their native areas, so cultivated plants do not produce seeds.

Only a few species are suitable for growing indoors and even these are more suited to a garden room, conservatory or greenhouse than to the dry atmosphere of a centrally heated room. In recent years, *Yucca elephantipes*, sometimes known as *Y. guatemalensis*, has become very popular. Mature stems or 'canes' of the plants are imported from the West Indies. These are planted up in a warm greenhouse. Roots develop at the bottom, rosettes of leaves appear at the top, and sometimes at other points on the cane as well. They make attractive, unusual plants with their stark brown upright stem and a head of green at the top. It is a plant which will also do well in hydro-culture. Although the leaves are pointed and stiff they are not very dangerous to touch. *Y. aloifolia* however, is very different. It is a much bigger plant, and the leaves can only be described as vicious. Their points are very sharp, and can cause considerable damage to skin and flesh. Aptly, its common name is Spanish bayonet.

When purchasing a *Yucca* plant make sure the rosettes are fairly well developed. Do not buy the plant if they are only just breaking. If entire leaves are blackened the plant has been damaged while strapping it secure during transit. The canes of *Y. elephantipes* should be sufficiently well rooted to hold them secure in their pots.

Yuccas are easy to grow provided they are treated to a cool period in the winter.

Below: *Yucca aloifolia* is almost hardy and survives outdoors in sheltered spots. Its spiky foliage gives it the name of Spanish bayonet.

Right: The superb creamy white flowers of *Yucca aloifolia*. If you are lucky the plant may give a repeat performance every second year.

Far right: *Yucca elephantipes* is grown from canes of the mature plant imported, potted and forced by high temperature to shoot.

Size: *Y. elephantipes* is a fairly small plant, the rosettes being up to 10 in (25 cm) across. Its height depends on the height of the cane which can be from 6 in (15 cm) to 4 ft (120 cm). *Y. aloifolia* normally has a span of about 2–3 ft (60–100 cm), and height again varies from 2–10 ft (60 cm–3 m).

Growth: They are fairly slow growers, producing about 6–12 in (15–30 cm) growth per year. The truncated canes of *Y. elephantipes* will not grow themselves but the rosettes will enlarge.

Flowering season: They will normally only flower if planted out in a greenhouse bed. They have the tall spike of flowers that is typical of all yuccas.

Scent: None.

Light: They require plenty of light to flourish. They like to be placed out-of-doors in the summer and make excellent plants for a sunny patio.

Temperature: They do not like it too hot in the winter and prefer a temperature of between 45 and 55°F (7–12°C) if possible. In the summer, normal room temperature or any sunny spot outdoors are suitable.

Water: Give plenty of water in the summer, watering 2 or 3 times a week. In the winter water about every 10 days.

Feeding: Add liquid food to the water every week in the summer months. Dilute it to half the recommended dose.

Humidity: They appreciate a weekly spray in the summer, particularly if they are not out-of-doors.

Cleaning: Leaves can be wiped with a damp cloth. Be careful, especially with *Y. aloifolia* for the spiky leaves are dangerous. Do not use leaf shine.

Atmosphere: They do not like it too hot and dry particularly in the winter and do better in a greenhouse than in a hot room.

Soil: Loam-based No. 2.

Repotting: About once a year when young. After 3 or 4 years just remove the top compost and replace it with fresh. Take care when handling.

Pruning: None necessary except to remove any dead leaves at the bottom of the plant.

Propagation: By dividing the root stock, by rooting offsets, or by inserting portions of stems (canes) in a propagating bed. All best done in the spring. High temperatures of 80°F (27°C) are required to induce canes to shoot.

Life expectancy: If given plenty of air and not allowed to get too hot in winter, they will go on for many years.

Plant companions: The canes of *Y. elephantipes* go quite well in mixed plantings for tubs and troughs. *Y. aloifolia* is very much a loner.

Ease/difficulty: A moderately easy plant if given plenty of light.

Repotting

1 Repot young plants in spring when they look top-heavy in their container and roots are crowded. Water well first.

2 Prepare pot 1 size larger with drainage layer and layer of damp, loam-based No. 2 compost.

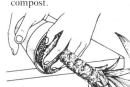

3 Hold old pot with one hand covering compost, fingers either side of stem . Tap edge of pot. Plant and compost will come out. Take care with Y. *aloifolia*. Its leaves are very sharp.

4 Carefully remove stale soil from roots, using stick or pencil. Do not damage roots.

5 Place plant in centre of new pot, root-ball on compost.

6 Add new compost to fill pot. Make sure that all roots are covered. Press down well. Leave in the shade without water for 2 days to encourage roots to grow into compost.

What goes wrong

1 *Leaves go yellow, usually starting with lower leaves.* Insufficient light. Cut off the discoloured leaves and move plant to a lighter place.

2 *Grey mould on leaves.* Botrytis. Dust the affected parts with sulphur. Improve the ventilation.

3 *Brown scaly insects under leaves and on stems.* Scale insect. Remove them individually with a swab dipped in methylated spirits or spray with a systemic insecticide.

Spraying

Spray once a week in summer, with a fine mist spray. Hold spray about 6in (15cm) from leaves.

Watering

1 Test compost with fingers. If it is light and crumbly, the plant needs water.
Take care with *Y. aloifolia.* Its leaves are very sharp.

2 Add water at top of pot, using rainwater if possible. Empty excess from saucer after 15 minutes.

Replacing the topsoil

1 After 3 or 4 years do not repot but remove top inch (2½cm) soil in spring. Water well first.

2 Add new compost to fill pot.

3 Press down firmly all round, making sure roots are all well covered.
Leave in shade without water for 2 days to encourage roots to grow into new compost.

Cleaning the leaves

Wipe dust off leaves with soft cloth and sponge with tepid water. Support leaf with other hand.
Do not use leaf shine.
Take care with *Y. aloifolia's* sharp leaves.

Stem sections

1 *Y. elephantipes* can be grown from cane sections. Canes can sometimes be purchased or an existing plant can be sawn up. You will need a propagator.

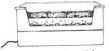

2 Prepare propagator with compost of ½ peat, ½ sand.

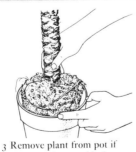

3 Remove plant from pot if you are using an old plant.

4 Lay whole stem flat on a hard surface and saw it into the lengths required.
Sections should be not less than 4in (10cm).

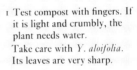
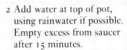

5 Dip the lower cut surface of each section in hormone rooting powder.
Shake off the surplus.

6 Push the sections into the compost until they stand upright without support. They should not touch the bottom of the propagator.

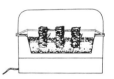

7 Put the cover over the propagator. If the sections are too long, cover the propagator with a large polythene bag supported by wire. Remove polythene for 5 minutes a day to prevent rot and make sure the compost does not dry out. Keep at 80 F (27 C).

8 Remove cover after 21 days and when cuttings are growing well, repot in normal compost.

CACTI AND SUCCULENTS

Cacti and succulents really demand a book on their own and indeed many have been written. The information here is essentially basic and those who wish to know more are recommended to more specialized works.

Most varieties make ideal house plants for they will tolerate, and even demand, the hot, dry atmosphere common to many centrally heated homes. In the summer they should be treated as normal plants and regularly watered, provided that they have good drainage. However, in the winter they are best treated to a cool, dry resting period which ensures the production of their most spectacular flowers.

Whilst all cacti are succulents, not all succulents are cacti. The difference is botanical in that all cacti have what is known as an areole. This is a small tuft of felt or hair at the base of the spines. Cacti and succulents belong mainly to two families, Cactaceae and Crassulaceae, although some are members of the Liliaceae and Amaryllidaceae. Of the principal genera of cacti, *Cereus* species are tall and upright while mammillarias are perhaps the most popular of the round, prickly types. *Echinocactus* species are some of the most spiteful of the round ball varieties. Opuntias are the prickly pears of western films. This genus is now often used as a rootstock upon which other species are grafted. *Zygocactus*, the Christmas cactus, has a mass of relatively long lasting, usually pink flowers in December. There are many other genera available including aloes, agaves and schlumbergeras. Many flower, though the flowers are generally short lived and, surprisingly, some do well in hydroculture.

Succulents have fleshy leaves, often covered with a most attractive grey 'bloom'. There are many species available, especially from the genera *Crassula, Euphorbia, Echeveria* and *Lithops*. Many of them flower. The genus *Euphorbia* also includes many other common house plants such as poinsettias and crotons. One of the most popular succulent species is *Euphorbia splendens*.

When buying cacti check that the plants are firm in their pots, otherwise the roots may be damaged. The plant should not have damage marks or signs of rot. Check that the leaves of succulents are not torn or broken.

Size: This varies with variety from the size of a marble to 6 or 7 ft (2 m) tall, even as a house plant.
Growth: They are slow growers in the main, and some varieties enlarge only very minutely every year. Others such as opuntias produce sizeable new 'ears' of top growth.
Flowering season: Spring and summer. The flowers last only a day or so.
Scent: None.
Light: They enjoy and require light. They flourish on a windowsill in full sunlight.
Temperature: In summer they will stand any amount of heat. Keep cool in winter but not below 40–45 F (5–7 C) in which case the plants should be almost completely dry.
Water: In summer water frequently, probably 2 or 3 times a week. In winter water once a month.
Feeding: Feed about every 14 days in the summer. Use a high nitrate-based feed, either diluted in the water or sprayed onto the leaves.

Humidity: They like a dry, hot atmosphere but spray or water overhead once a month in the summer to keep them clean.
Cleaning: If the spraying does not remove dust, use a soft brush. Don't touch by hand.
Atmosphere: Tolerant.
Soil: As a general rule use loam-based compost No. 1 with half as much sharp sand added.
Repotting: Do not repot more than necessary, preferably every 3 or 4 years. Always wear thick protective gloves as the spikes or hairs can be very painful and dangerous.
Pruning: Cut away any diseased parts and dust the wound with sulphur.
Propagation: By seed, cuttings, division, or plantlets that fall off the mother plant. The method depends on the variety.
Life expectancy: Practically everlasting unless they are overwatered in winter.
Plant companions: Most can be planted together to make table-top cacti gardens.
Ease/difficulty: Easy even for beginners.

Leaf cuttings

Most cacti are propagated by seed sown in spring at 70 F (21 C). The young plants are potted up as soon as they are large enough to handle. Many succulents such as *Crassula cooperi* can be propagated by leaf cuttings.

1 Prepare pot with layer of drainage, layer of growing compost and ½in (1cm) layer of sharp sand.

2 Cut a sprig from the plant and pull off each leaf.

3 Gently push each leaf into the sand, the broken end downwards.

4 Water the compost. Do not cover the pot. Place it out of direct sunshine at normal room temperature. New plantlets will grow from the base of the leaf.

Plantlets

Some succulents such as *Bryophyllum* produce plantlets at the edges of their leaves. These will root to form new plants.

1 Prepare pot with layer of drainage, layer of growing compost and ½in (1cm) layer of sharp sand.

2 Mature plantlets will show tiny roots. Pull these gently off the parent leaf.

3 Plant the tiny plantlet into the sand. Water it and place pot in a shaded place at normal room temperature. They will grow to adult size.

Above: *Echinocactus submammulosus*. This genus has fine spines. Occasionally they flower.

Above: *Zygocactus truncatus* flowers at Christmas. It will grow well in hanging baskets.

Left: *Euphorbia splendens* bears thorns and crimson bracts. It comes from Madagascar.

Right: *Mammillaria zeilmanniana* comes from Mexico. Its flowers may be followed by fruits.

What goes wrong

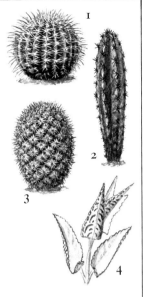

1 *Plants go black and rotten at the base.* Overwatering. Usually fatal. Plants with rot other than at the base can have it cut out and dusted with sulphur.

2 *Plants shrivel up and lose their firmness.* Too dry. Water well and increase watering in future.

3 *Plants of flowering species fail to flower.* Plants kept too hot in winter.

4 *Cacti grow very slowly and succulents lean towards the light.* Insufficient light. Move to a sunny window.

5 *Plants become covered with white, woolly patches.* Mealy bug. Spray with malathion.

6 *Plants become discoloured, wilt and die.* Insects on the roots. Root mealy bug. Drench roots with malathion diluted to the usual strength for spraying.

Stem tip cuttings

Succulents such as *Crassula argentea* can be propagated from stem cuttings.

1 In spring, prepare small pot with drainage layer and compost of ½ loam-based No. 1, ½ sharp sand.

2 Choose shoot or stem tip with at least 2 pairs of healthy leaves and a growing point. Cut off below a pair of leaves.

3 Prepare cuttings by trimming off stem just below a leaf.

4 Remove the lowest pair of leaves.

5 Dip the cut surface in hormone rooting powder. Shake off the surplus.

6 Make small hole in centre of the pot.

7 Insert the cutting. The base of the stem should rest on the bottom of the hole. Water and place in a shaded place at room temperature.

8 As succulents contain a lot of water it is not advisable to cover them with polythene to encourage rooting. They may rot if you do. If they rot even uncovered, take new cuttings and allow them to dry for 3 days before planting them.

9 Once rooted, the young plants can grow on in the same small pots and compost until they become rootbound.

Division

Cacti such as *Mammillaria zeilmanniana* can be divided when they have developed several rosettes.

1 Prepare pot with layer of drainage, layer of growing compost and ½in (1cm) layer of sharp sand.

2 Wear gloves. Turn pot upside down and tap it on a hard surface. The root-ball will come away from the pot.

3 Cut the plant into sections, each with an undamaged rosette and roots.

4 Pot up the rooted rosette. Use a pencil or similar stick to firm the soil around the plant more easily.

The spines of cacti can be painful or irritating if they puncture the skin. Always wear gloves if you are handling them. Large spines can be removed immediately by hand. Small spines and tiny irritating hairs can only be removed by washing repeatedly in very hot, soapy water.

SPRING AND SUMMER BULBS

Bulbs can be grown in pots to flower at their normal time or be 'forced' to flower early, usually during the winter. The forcing of bulbs is extremely popular for there cannot be a more cheerful sight than a beautiful bowl of flowering hyacinths at Christmas, or the bright yellow of a pot of daffodils on a miserable January day. When planned successfully it is possible to have a succession of flowers all through the cold winter months.

Forcing of bulbs in pots is not a difficult art but a few simple rules must be followed. Firstly always buy top quality bulbs. Rejects and bulbs dug up from the garden will never flourish. Secondly, never try to force the same bulbs two years running. Most spring flowering bulbs must be put in a dark place in the cold for some weeks before forcing so that they make a good root system. Use an airy, unheated cupboard or 'plunge' them outdoors in a sheltered place covered with sand or ashes. Do not try to cheat and bring them on too quickly in a warmer place. This can make the bulbs wilt or go 'blind', that is, fail to produce a flower bud.

Good drainage is also an important key to success. If planting a bowl without a drainage hole make sure that there is plenty of absorbent material such as sphagnum moss or crushed brick in the bottom to take up any surplus water and some charcoal to stop the water from going sour. Always use bulb mixture or a potting compost to which you should add half the volume again of peat. Do not overfill the pots with compost; leave space for watering.

Always water bulbs at soil level, never from overhead as water on the leaves and flowers may cause rot. Do not spray them for the same reason. The bowls or pots should never be allowed to dry out and will probably need watering about once a week. They should not dry out during the 'plunge' period either. If they are outside in a sheltered place check that they are getting enough moisture and water them if necessary. If bulbs are planted in bowls with no drainage holes at the bottom it is a good idea to tip them on one side after watering so that the excess can drain away.

The following list of spring bulbs is by no means complete—you can experiment with many other types. With all of them allow plenty of time for the bulbs to develop roots in the dark before starting to force them into bloom in the warmth. Increase the temperature gradually so as not to force flowering too quickly. All bulbs also need to be gradually accustomed to full light. Do this by shading them first of all with paper. Try to keep them in the coolest possible position when in bloom to prolong their flowering. Remember that they flower naturally when the weather is still cold.

After flowering allow them to dry out in a cool place and plant them in the garden in spring. It may be a year or more before they flower again.

Hyacinths
These are the most popular of all bulbs for growing in pots. By careful staggering of the planting times a succession can be obtained from Christmas until spring. For early flowering buy prepared bulbs in August. These have been given first hot then cold treatment to convince them that summer and part of winter have come and gone and thereby induce rapid flowering. These are followed up with ordinary 'first size' bulbs. They should be planted with their noses just peeping out of the top of the compost. They should stay in the dark for at least 2 months before being brought gradually into a light, warmer position for forcing. Remember to label and date the pots so that you remember which to bring in first.

Daffodils and Narcissi
These will not flower quite so early as hyacinths but the same growing method should be followed. To produce a pot massed with blooms plant the bulbs in two layers. Plant the first at the bottom of the pot. Cover these with compost so it is just level over them and plant the second layer right on top with their tips just showing over the top of the pot. 'Carlton' and 'Golden Harvest' daffodils and 'Geranium' and 'Cragford' narcissi are all varieties that do well.

Tulips
Tulips should be left longer in the dark. Plant them between September and October and do not bring them into warmth for forcing until about January. Choose varieties which naturally grow fairly short as tulips tend to get rather leggy indoors and flop over. The early double varieties such as 'Peach Blossom' and 'Orange Nassau' force well and also have a delightful scent.

Crocus and Iris reticulata
Both grow well in pots and can be brought into flower for January and February from a November planting. When these are plunged outside it may be necessary to put wire netting around the pots to keep away mice for they find the young shoots very tasty. Always pack plenty of bulbs into the pot so as to get a mass of flowers. After flowering, plant them out into the garden as soon as possible. After a year the bulbs will recover and flower at their natural season outdoors.

Snowdrops
Snowdrops do not force well. If you want them indoors they can be dug up from the garden in January (unless the ground is frozen) put in a pot and allowed to flower in a cool place indoors before returning them to the garden.

There are several other bulbs that can be grown in pots but these need to flower at their normal time and should not be forced. They should be potted in well-

Hyacinth 'Edelweiss'

Narcissus 'Carlton'

Crocus, Dutch striped variety

Tulip 'Compostella'

Anemone de Caen

Lilium auratum

What goes wrong

1 *Hyacinths: Flower bud flowers very short and leaves never get bigger than 2 or 3in (5-8 cm).* Plants brought into heat for forcing after too short a time in the plunge. They have inadequate roots formed. No remedy.

2 *Hyacinths: Segments of the flower turn brown and rot.* Possible damage when unearthing from plunge or water allowed to rest on the flower spikes through overhead watering. No remedy.

3 *Daffodils and narcissi, tulips and crocus: Flower buds appear and then turn brown.* This is called 'blindness' and is caused by the plants having dried out at some time. No remedy.

4 *Crocus and narcissi, iris and snowdrop: Foliage grows very tall, no flowers ever emerge.* Caused by trying to force bulbs in too high a temperature too quickly. No remedy.

5 *All bulbs: Grey fungal growth on the emerging shoots.* Grey mould caused by poor ventilation in cupboards used as 'plunges'. Dust with sulphur and improve ventilation.

6 *All bulbs: Leaf tips yellow.* Overwatering. Allow to dry out and then water less often.

7 *All bulbs: Flower bud rots.* Water from overhead spraying. Do not spray the flowers or buds.

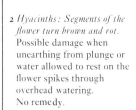

Forcing spring bulbs

1 Soak bulb fibre and squeeze out excess water.

2 Prepare bowl with sphagnum moss and charcoal at bottom and a layer of bulb fibre.

3 Plant hyacinths, daffodils and narcissi with tips of bulbs protruding; all others should be buried below, with half their depth of fibre above them.

4 Place bowl in a well-ventilated, dark cupboard, in a cool temperature. They should not be warmer than 40 F (4 C), but must be frost-free.

or

5 Prepare a plunge bed by digging a hole at the foot of a wall outdoors, placing the bowl in it and covering it with at least 6in (15 cm) of sand or ash to prevent the bulbs being frosted.

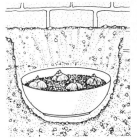

6 Bring into the house when shoots are well out of their bulbs. Shade for a few days with newspaper cone opened at the top until they are acclimatized to the light.

7 As they come towards flowering, move them gradually into a warmer position.

8 After flowering remove the flower heads and allow to dry out in a cool place before planting in the garden. Bulbs forced one year cannot be forced the next.

---

drained pots with ordinary loam-based compost. Not all need a cool period in the dark before display in the house or greenhouse but all must be kept in a light position indoors. Frequency of watering depends on temperature: never let the compost dry out while they are growing.

Amaryllis or Hippeastrum

When purchased and planted in the autumn or winter this lily can be brought into flower in the spring or early summer. The bright coloured flowers in red, pink or white are borne on the top of a thick, fleshy stem before the strap-like leaves appear. The bulbs are large and are usually grown singly. Feed them every fourteen days when the plant is flowering and later producing its leaves. Remove the dead flowers and allow the stem to dry off. After the leaves have developed the plant should be allowed to dry off and rested in a cool place for three months in late summer. Repot it every third year. Do not plant it outside.

Lilies

Most lilies can be grown in pots and can be treated like hippeastrums. *Lilium longiflorum* (the Madonna Lily), *Lilium auratum* and the mid-century hybrids such as 'Destiny' and 'Enchantment' all do well in pots in loam-based composts all year round. However if planted in autumn they appreciate a cool period before being brought into the house. All of them need staking. They can be planted outside after flowering. Allow them to dry out in a cool place first.

Anemones

Anemones can be grown in pots to flower in the spring from October planting. They are best left outdoors until the flower buds appear and then brought indoors. After flowering let them dry out in a cool place and plant them in the garden.

Pests and diseases

Bulbs may be attacked by virus diseases which produce symptoms in the flowers, leaves and stems. Daffodils, narcissi, hyacinths, iris and snowdrops sometimes develop distorted foliage, mottled and striped with yellow. Tulips may have brown spots or streaks on the stems and leaves and flowers with abnormal stripes and streaks. All these are symptoms of virus disease for which there is no cure. The bulbs should be destroyed. Tulips, hyacinths and narcissi are sometimes also attacked by stem and bulb eelworm which causes malformed stems and leaves and rots the bulbs. Again, there is no cure and the bulbs should be destroyed. The most common pest is greenfly which distorts the leaves and covers their tips with sticky secretion. Dusting with pyrethrum dust is the safest cure.

FLOWERING ANNUALS

An annual is a plant that grows from seed, flowers, sets seed, and then dies naturally all in one year. They should be distinguished from biennials, which are flowers that follow the same cycle but take two years to complete it.

Annuals are well known in the garden for summer display and for the house they also fill a need for flowering colour. They are usually cheap to raise or buy but must be regarded as expendable. Nearly all of them require to be raised and displayed in cool temperatures.

To raise from seed the varieties listed here you need a greenhouse and some propagation equipment. It can be great fun and immensely satisfying. Given patience and time a whole range of flowering plants can be grown giving a succession of plants to be taken into the house.

Alternatively, the plants can be bought from florists as they are just coming into bloom. Always look for good clean foliage. The flowers should just be showing colour and should not be too far developed. Check that there are no pests on them, particularly greenfly. The species are listed below in the order in which they flower and become available in the shops.

Primulas

The following four varieties of primulas are technically perennials but are treated as annuals for indoor display. *P. acaulis (vulgaris)* is a hybrid of the common primrose, now available in a wide range of colours. *P. malacoides* has clusters of small flowers in soft delicate shades borne on stems above the leaves. *P. obconica*, the toughest of them all, has larger flower clusters again in delicate shades. *P. sinensis* is a small, compact plant with attractive, hairy leaves. It is rather more delicate.

For all varieties seeds should be sown in cool conditions from February to June to flower in the following spring. They should be put in small pots as soon as the seedlings can be handled after germination. Pot them on as they grow and put them finally into their flowering pots in the early autumn. Keep them moist at all times. The frequency of watering depends very much on the temperature: never let the compost dry out. They should be germinated and grown on at a temperature of 50 to 55°F (10–13°C). A liquid feed should be given every 14 days as the flower buds appear. Keep them out of direct sunlight and display them in the house in a very cool position.

Cinerarias

Cinerarias are spring flowering plants which become available in the middle of the *Primula* season and continue into late spring. Their latin name is *Senecio cruentus* and they require a little more care than primulas. The temperature should again be cool. The large, attractive leaves curl up and droop if the plant is exposed to too much sun. The plant is happiest in a shaded greenhouse or a north-facing window.

Seed should be sown in July and August. It is fine and should not be covered with compost. Cover the seed box with glass or polythene. Keep the compost regularly sprayed and remove the covering as soon as the seedlings appear. Pot up individually as soon as the plants can be handled in September or October. Grow on in a cool greenhouse at not more than 45 to 50°F (7–10°C). When the buds appear in spring raise the temperature a little to 55°F (13°C) to bring the plants into flower. Shade from midday sun.

Calceolarias

Calceolarias become available shortly after cinerarias. Growing instructions are the same as for cinerarias except that calceolarias will stand just a little more sun. Also keep them on the dry side in mid-winter, otherwise mildew can set in.

Schizanthus

Schizanthus is the least well known of the annuals mentioned here and deserves much more attention from the professional growers. The plant has a mass of multicoloured flowers in late spring and early summer. Each flower is small and orchid-like. This plant is a little taller than the three already mentioned, growing to a maximum of 2ft (60cm) but the growing requirements are very similar.

Celosias

Celosias are available throughout early summer. They are compact plants with gold or red flowers resembling a feather duster.

Seed for these plants is sown at 60 to 65°F

Growing from seed

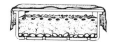

3 When seeds germinate, bring them into light and remove the glass cover.

1 Prepare a seed tray or propagator with a drainage layer and sterilized, seed-growing compost. Scatter seeds evenly and add thin layer of compost, no thicker than depth of seed. Water well.

2 Cover with glass and put in dark place or cover with dark cloth. Make sure the compost never dries out and turn glass over daily. Temperatures for annuals vary from plant to plant. Follow the instructions on the seed packet.

4 When seedlings are large enough to handle, thin out the weaker ones, leaving about 1in (2½cm) between each one.

5 When remaining ones are growing well, repot in separate small pots.

Above: *Primula obconica*.

Below: *Primula malacoides*.

Above: *Celosia* 'Golden Feather'. Plumes can be red, orange or yellow.

Above right: *Cineraria grandiflora*. Cinerarias are available in spring in many colours.

Right: Chrysanthemums are available in the shops all the year round. Buy them when the buds are just beginning to show colour.

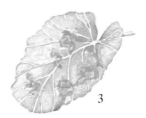

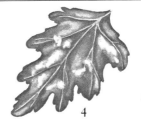

1 *All species: Crown of plant and roots go black and rot and plant collapses.* Crown and root rot due to overwatering. Usually fatal.

2 *Plant droops and soil is dry.* Too dry. Water immediately and allow to drain.

3 *Primulas and chrysanthemums especially: Grey, velvety rotting areas on the leaves.* Grey mould due to the atmosphere being too cold and damp. Move to a warmer, better ventilated position and spray with a systemic fungicide.

4 *Cinerarias and chrysanthemums especially: White, powdery areas on the leaves.* Powdery mildew. Improve the ventilation. Do not let plants dry out. Spray with a systemic fungicide.

5 *Primulas, calceolarias, schizanthus, celosia: Lower leaves elongate and go yellow.* Temperature too high. Move to a cooler, more airy spot.

Left: The unusual flowers of calceolarias.

Below: *Schizanthus* has striking orchid-like flowers.

(16–18°C) in early spring and the plants need only be repotted once before they reach flowering size. Keep moist at all times and give plenty of air and light.

Chrysanthemums

Chrysanthemums are not annual plants but are treated as such when grown as pot plants. They are purchased to provide temporary colour and are then thrown away. They are now produced all the year round by growers using artificial lighting and are treated with growth retardant to produce compact plants. They will lose this compactness if you try to keep them and plant them in the garden, so they are best discarded. They are undoubtably the best-selling of all flowering plants because they represent good value for money.

Always buy plants that have good clean foliage without any yellow or decaying leaves at the bottom. The flower heads or buds should all be approximately level, with no 'rogues' standing high. Always buy plants with buds showing colour or with some flowers out. This is particularly important in the late winter and spring when tight budded plants can fail to open

in the house. Keep the plants in a position that gets a good circulation of air. Do not let the pots stand in water. Occasionally give an overhead spray, especially in centrally heated rooms. Pick off dead flowers as they start to fade. The plants will last much longer in flower if you keep them in a cool position. The varieties principally grown are 'Princess Anne' for the doubles and 'Bonnie Lea' for the singles.

Pests and diseases

All the species mentioned may be attacked by tomato spotted wilt virus which stunts the growth and prevents flowers from forming. The leaves become mottled with yellow and the veins turn brown. There is no cure for this disease and the plants must be destroyed. Primulas, cinerarias and chrysanthemums may be infected with rust fungus. Orange raised spots appear under the leaves; the spots turn brown and finally black. Spray infected plants with a systemic fungicide.

Several pests attack annuals. Greenfly may cover young leaves with their sticky secretions, distorting their growth. Spray with pyrethrum or a systemic insecticide. Leaf miner makes white tunnel markings on the leaves of cinerarias and chrysanthemums. Pick off the affected leaves. Cinerarias and chrysanthemums may also attract thrips, small grey insects which cause the flowers and leaves to become flecked with silver. Spray the plants with malathion or a systemic insecticide. Calceolarias and chrysanthemums are susceptible to whitefly, which cover the undersides of the leaves and fly away when the plants are touched. Spray with derris or a resmethrin based insecticide. Chrysanthemums are susceptible to red spider mites which cause the leaves to become yellowed and webbed underneath. Spray with derris or a systemic insecticide and increase the humidity to prevent a new attack. In the greenhouse slugs may eat away the lower leaves of chrysanthemums and calceolarias. Place slug bait on the soil surface around the plants. Finally, all species may develop black sooty deposits on their leaves, especially after an attack by green or whitefly. Kill the pest, wipe off the mould and spray the plants with a systemic fungicide.

Glossary

Anther the uppermost part of a stamen which contains the pollen grains.

Aroid A plant belonging to the Araceae or arum family.

Biennial A plant that requires two seasons to complete its life cycle, flowering in the second year.

Bigeneric A hybrid derived from two separate genera.

Bract A modified leaf which grows near the calyx of a flower, often petal-like in appearance and sometimes highly coloured.

Bromeliad A member of the pineapple family or Bromeliaceae, many of which are epiphytes.

Bulb An underground bud, covered in scales, from which the flower stems and leaves grow, e.g. an onion or daffodil.

Corm A thickened underground stem with a bud at its tip, e.g. a crocus.

Corona The trumpet or cup in such genera as *Narcissus*.

Crown Upper part of the root, enlarged in some plants, from which the shoots appear.

Cultivar A variety bred in cultivation rather than collected from the wild.

Damping off A disease affecting seedlings. It is caused by a fungus and occurs when the seeds are overwatered.

Epiphyte A non-parasitic plant that grows on another, generally on a tree, for support and obtains nutrients from the air and decaying plants which fall upon it.

Family Group of animals or plants, subdivided into genera. For example, the family Liliaceae includes the genera *Chlorophytum*, *Dracaena* and *Sansevieria*.

Fern A large group of non-flowering plants, differing greatly in appearance. They have fronds (leaves) that are often large and divided, a stem which is often a rhizome, and roots. They reproduce by spores, usually formed on the fronds.

Genus (pl. genera) A group of plants or animals being a sub-division of a family and in turn divided into related species.

Half hardy Plants which are frost-tender and will not survive the winter outdoors.

Hardy Plants which will survive frost outdoors.

Hybrid A plant grown from a sexual cross between two different species.

Microclimate Climate in a very small area, such as inside a bottle garden, and different from the climate of the surrounding area.

Offset A young plant growing from the rootstock of its parent.

Palm A plant of the family Palmaceae. Palms are mainly unbranched shrubs or trees with large fronds in a terminal tuft. Sometimes they form a rope-like trunk with scattered leaves and stout spines.

Perennial Any plant that has an indefinite length of life, as opposed to annuals and biennials which have distinct yearly and two yearly cycles.

Pollination The transference of grains of pollen on to the stigma of a flower.

Propagate To increase plants either by seed or vegetatively (cuttings, offsets, etc).

Rhizome A stem that creeps horizontally, usually partly covered in soil. Buds grow upwards from it, roots downwards. It acts as a storage organ and is therefore swollen.

Runner An aerial stem which can form rooted young plants on contact with the soil at its tip.

To set The maturing process undergone by seeds in the ovary of the flower after it has been pollinated.

Spadix A succulent spike carrying male and female flowers.

Spathe A large bract or modified leaf surrounding a spadix. Spathes and spadixes are common in the Araceae family.

Species A distinct group of plants or animals which are mutually fertile; a subdivision of genus. Species breed true to type from seeds.

Specimen plant A plant best grown on its own for the purposes of display.

Spore A tiny single-celled body by which ferns, fungi and mosses reproduce, their counterpart of seeds.

Staging Special shelves, used in greenhouses, with drainage slats to allow for watering, spraying and ventilation.

Stamen Male organ of a flower.

Sterile The characteristic of a plant which fails to set seeds.

Stigma The tip of the female organ of a flower.

Stolon A creeping stem which roots and produces plantlets at its nodes.

Style The stalk which joins the stigma to the ovary of a female flower.

Succulents Plants, including cacti, that are specially adapted to withstand long periods of drought by having tissue capable of storing water.

Systemic The characteristic of those pesticides which are absorbed into the vein system of a plant and thus continue to poison the pests as they suck from it.

To top dress To add fresh soil to a potted plant without repotting.

Tuber A thickened underground stem, e.g. a potato.

Variegated Having patches of different colours, usually green and white and usually on the leaves.

Variety A plant that is slightly different from other members of the same species, perhaps in colour only. The difference may have been naturally occuring or have been bred. Varieties do not always breed true from seed.

Acknowledgments

Additional photographs supplied by:
A-Z Botanical Collection
Alphabet and Image
Kenneth and Gillian Beckett
The Harry Smith Horticultural Photographic Collection
Pamela Job and Sabine Loeffler kindly lent their plants.

Colour art by:
Sally Caldecott
Etchell/Ridyard
Pat Lenander
Nina Roberts
Amanda Severne
Shirley Tuckley
John Wilkinson

Edited by Susan Minter, M.A., N.C.H. She also wrote the captions.

Index by Celia F Davis
Lithos by Monographics Ltd

The publishers would like to thank Rosemary Aldridge, Rudolf Britto, Primrose Cotton, Clare Osborne and Craig Warwick for their help in preparing this book.

The names of houseplants

Because some of the botanical names of house plants are long and difficult to pronounce, many plants have been given popular names. Unfortunately these are often misleading and differ greatly from place to place. The International Committee on Horticultural Nomenclature has adopted a simple system which prevents misunderstandings. All names are in Latin and all plants are classified under four headings: botanical family, genus, species and variety. For our purposes only the genus, species and variety names are used. Plants belonging to the same genus are quite closely related; those belonging to the same species are botanically the same; a variety dffers slightly from the main species plants, possibly having a different flower colour or differently marked leaves. Varieties may either occur naturally or be cultivated (known as cultivars). As an example, Asparagus ferns belong to the genus Asparagus. Asparagus plumosos and Asparagus falcatus are both different species; Asparagus plumosus 'Nanus' is a variety of the species Asparagus plumosus, and grows in a rather denser way. The genus and species names are always written initalics but the variety or cultivar name is not. When the genus name has already been mentioned it is usual to abbreviate it to its initial letter.